I0473334

M7

LARRY WAITZ

M7

COPYRIGHT Ç 2019
ALLRIGHTS RESERVED
ISBN 987-0-692-03580-1

LARRY WAITZ

© MUTRX 2019

Propriety and Confidential

The Information contained in this drawing is the
Sole Property of Larry Waitz (MUTRX). Any repro-
ductin in part or as a whole without written
permission of Larry Waitz (MUTRX) is Prohibited

**MY OWN AMERICAN FLAG PUBLISHING
OCEANSIDE, NEW YORK**

TABLE OF CONTENTS

<u>WHY?</u>

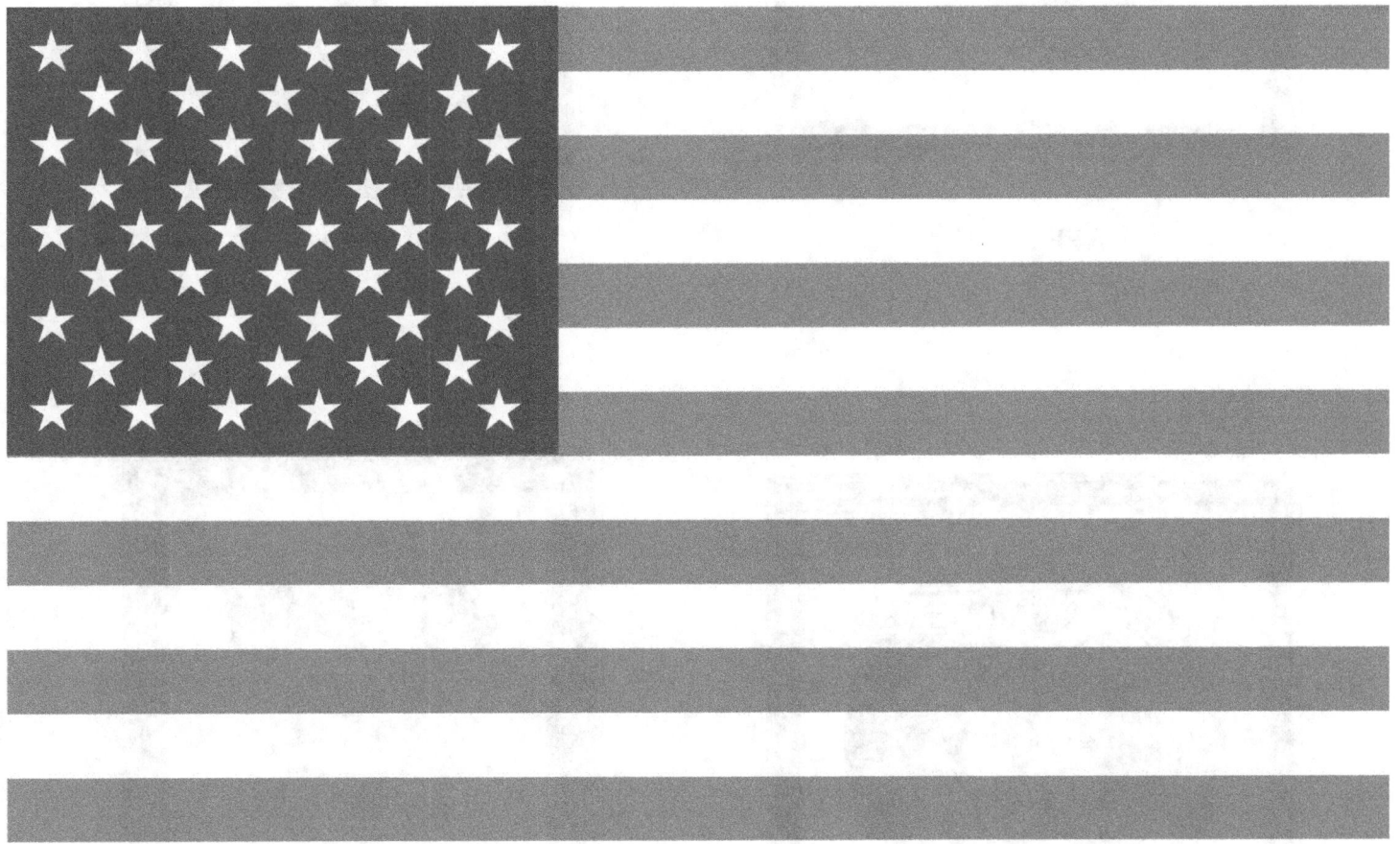

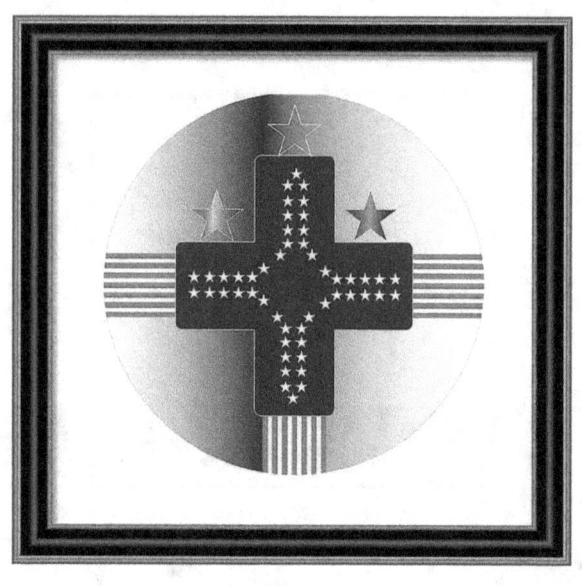

AFF-1

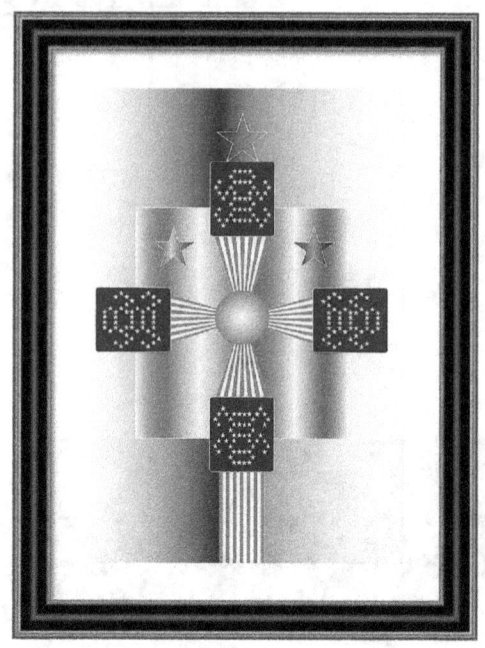

AFF-2

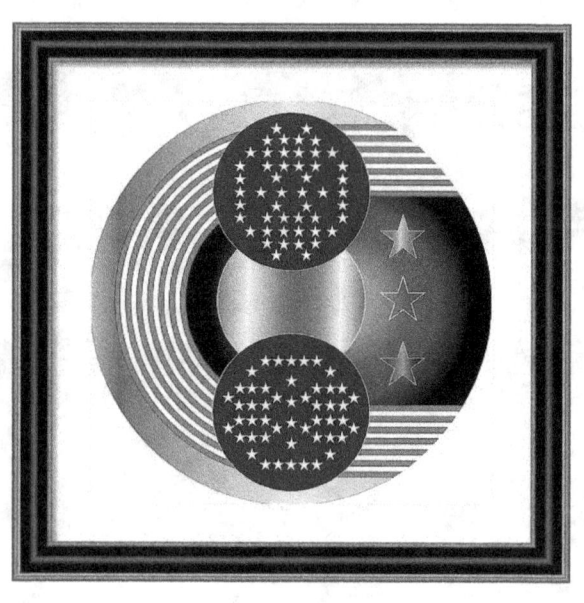

AFF-3

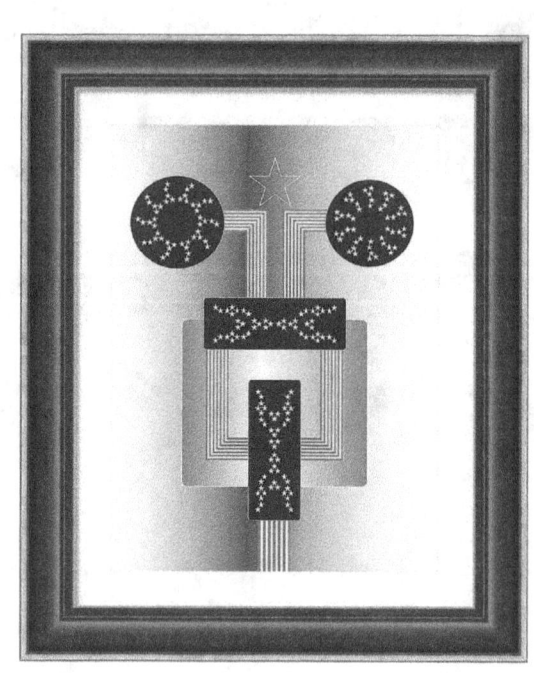

AFF-4

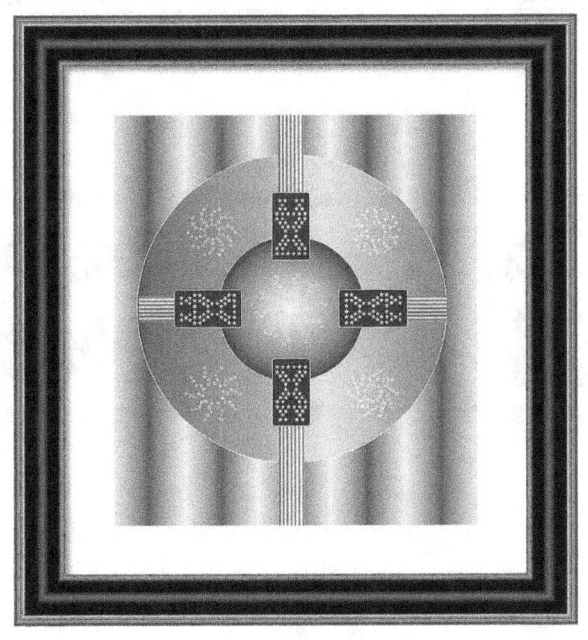

AFF-5

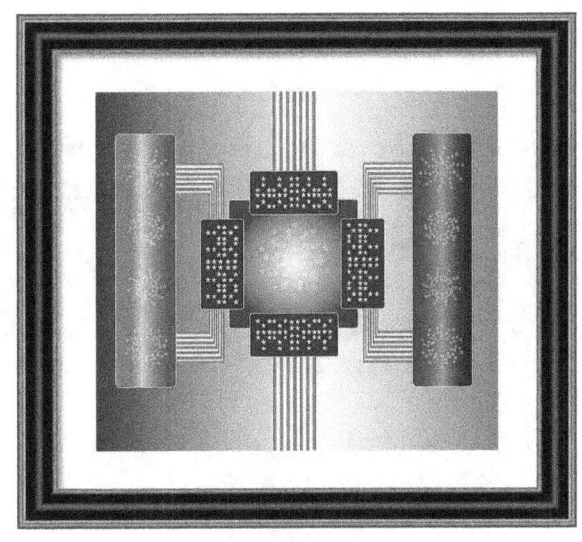

AFF-6

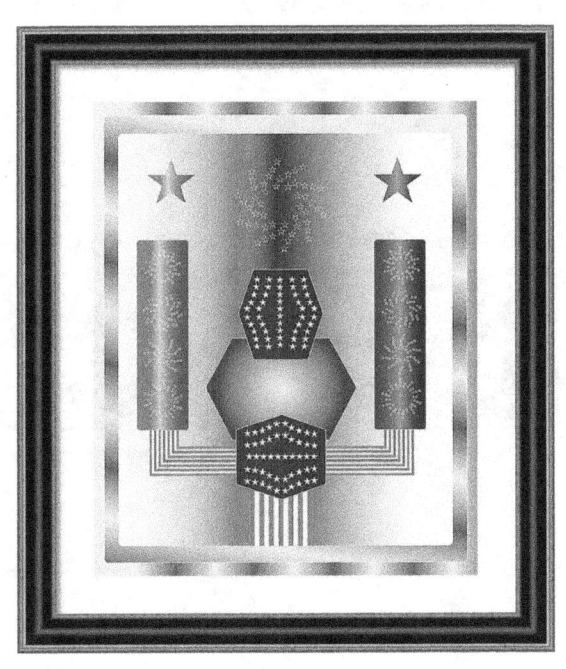

AFF-7

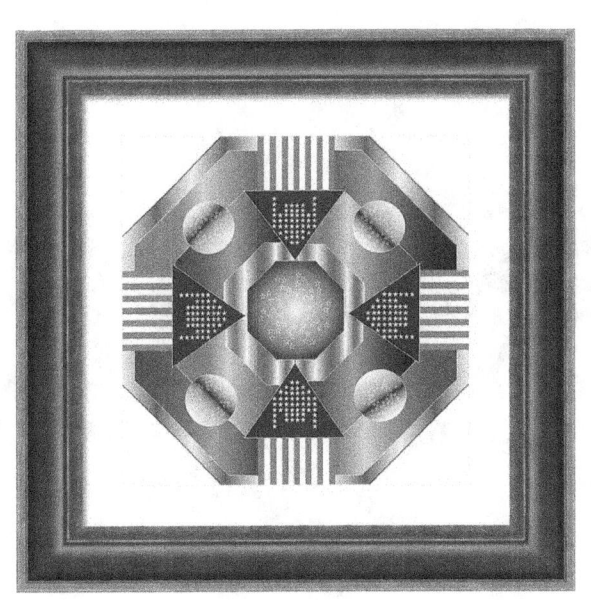

AFF-8

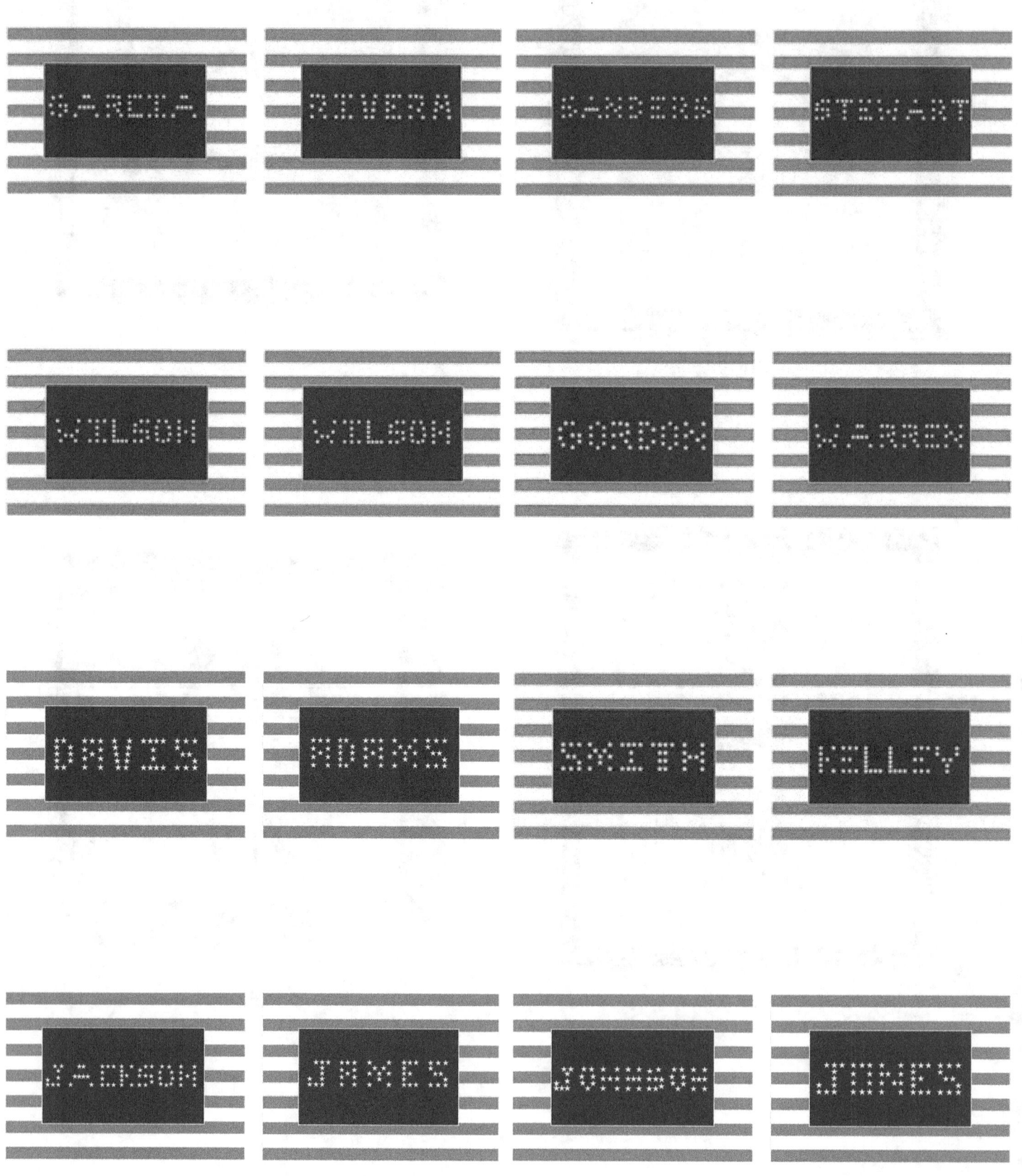

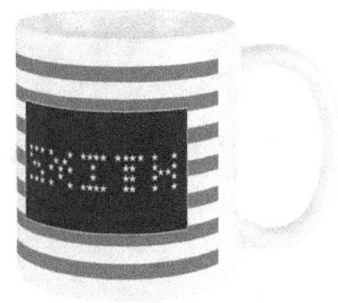 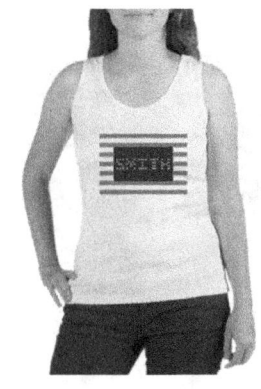 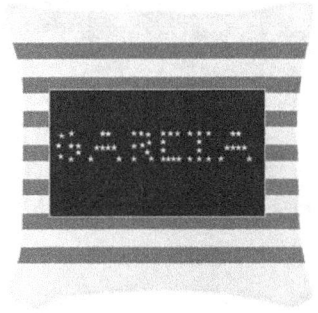

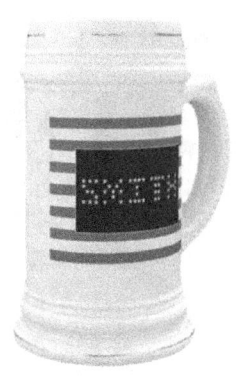 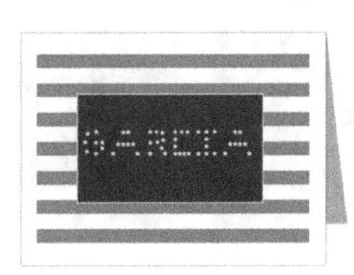 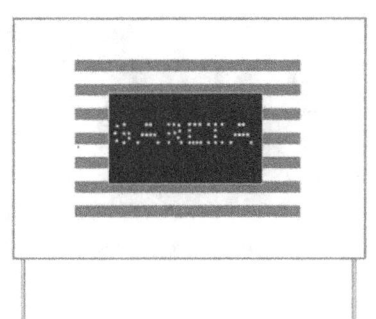

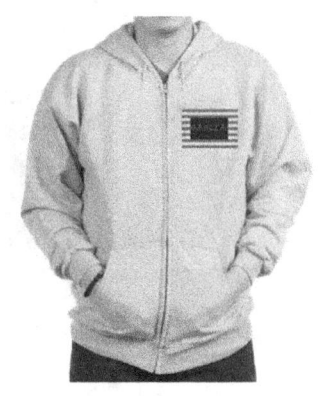 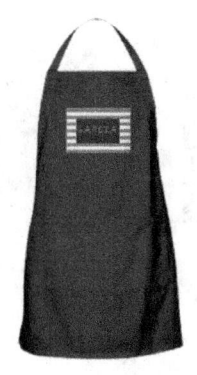 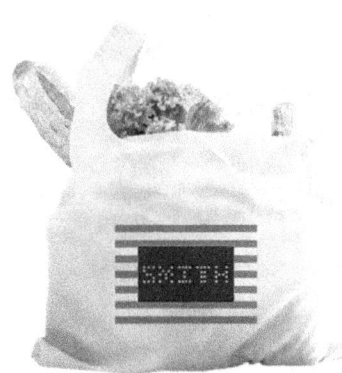

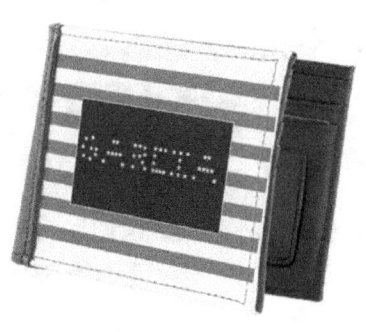 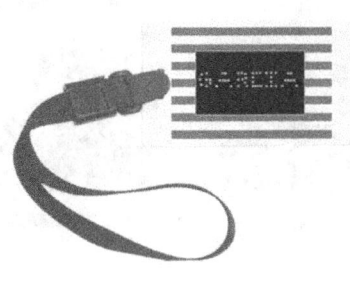

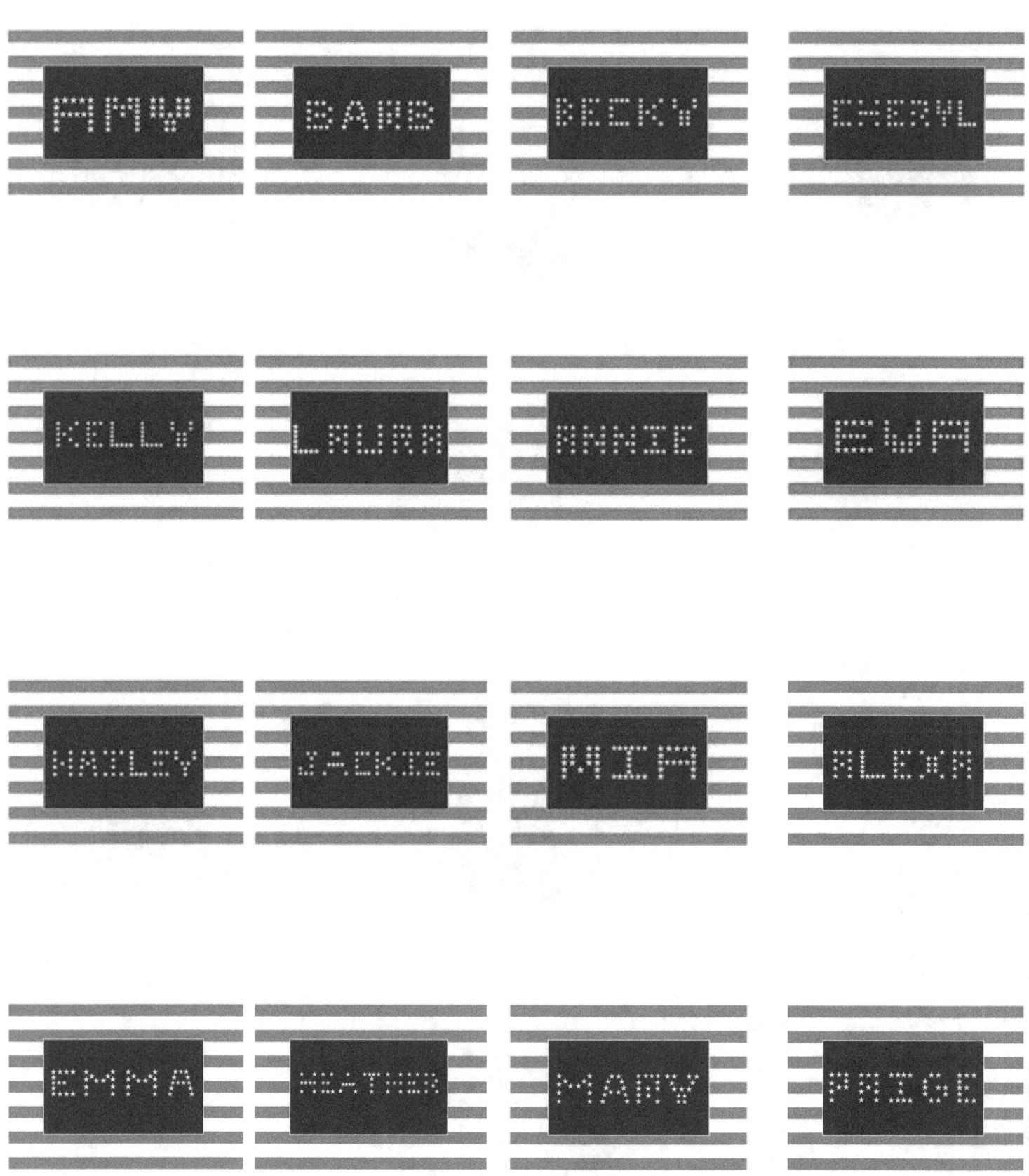

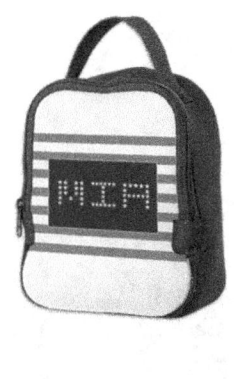
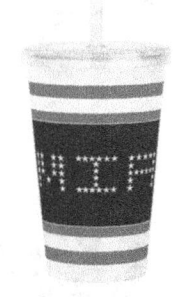
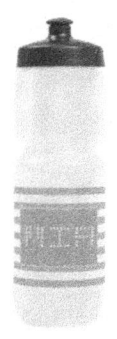
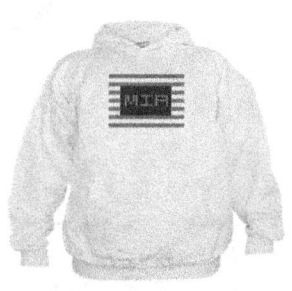
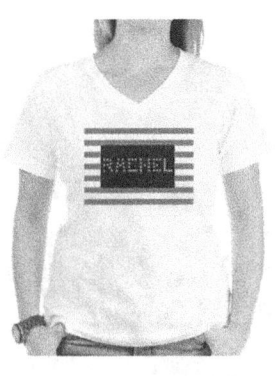
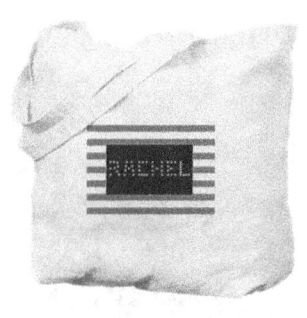
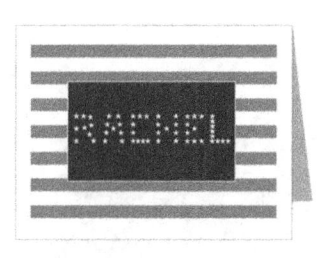
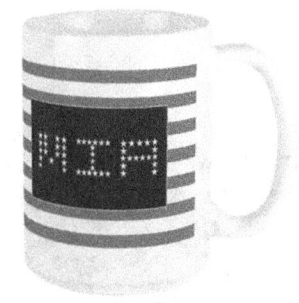
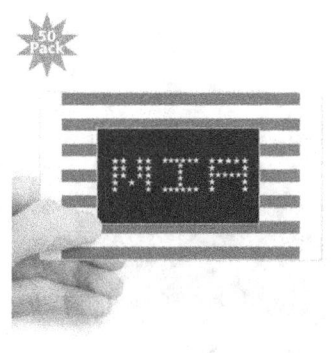
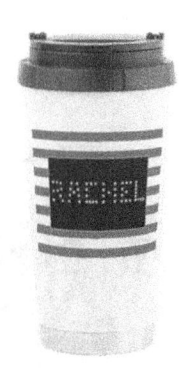
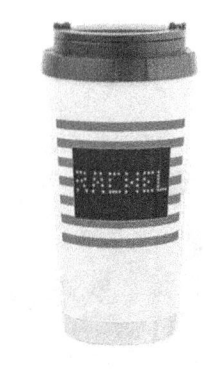
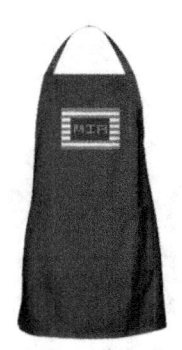
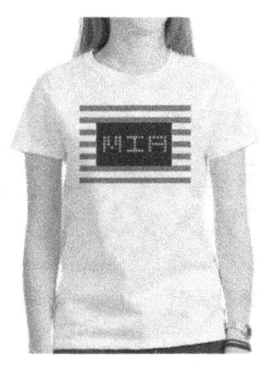
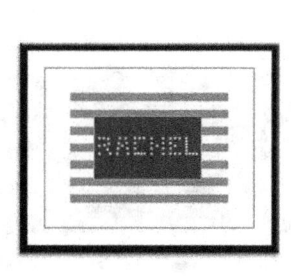
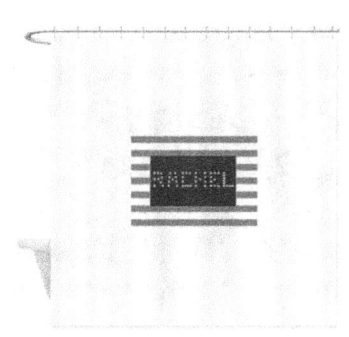
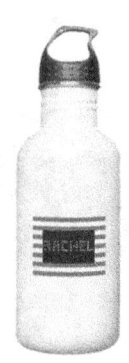

M7

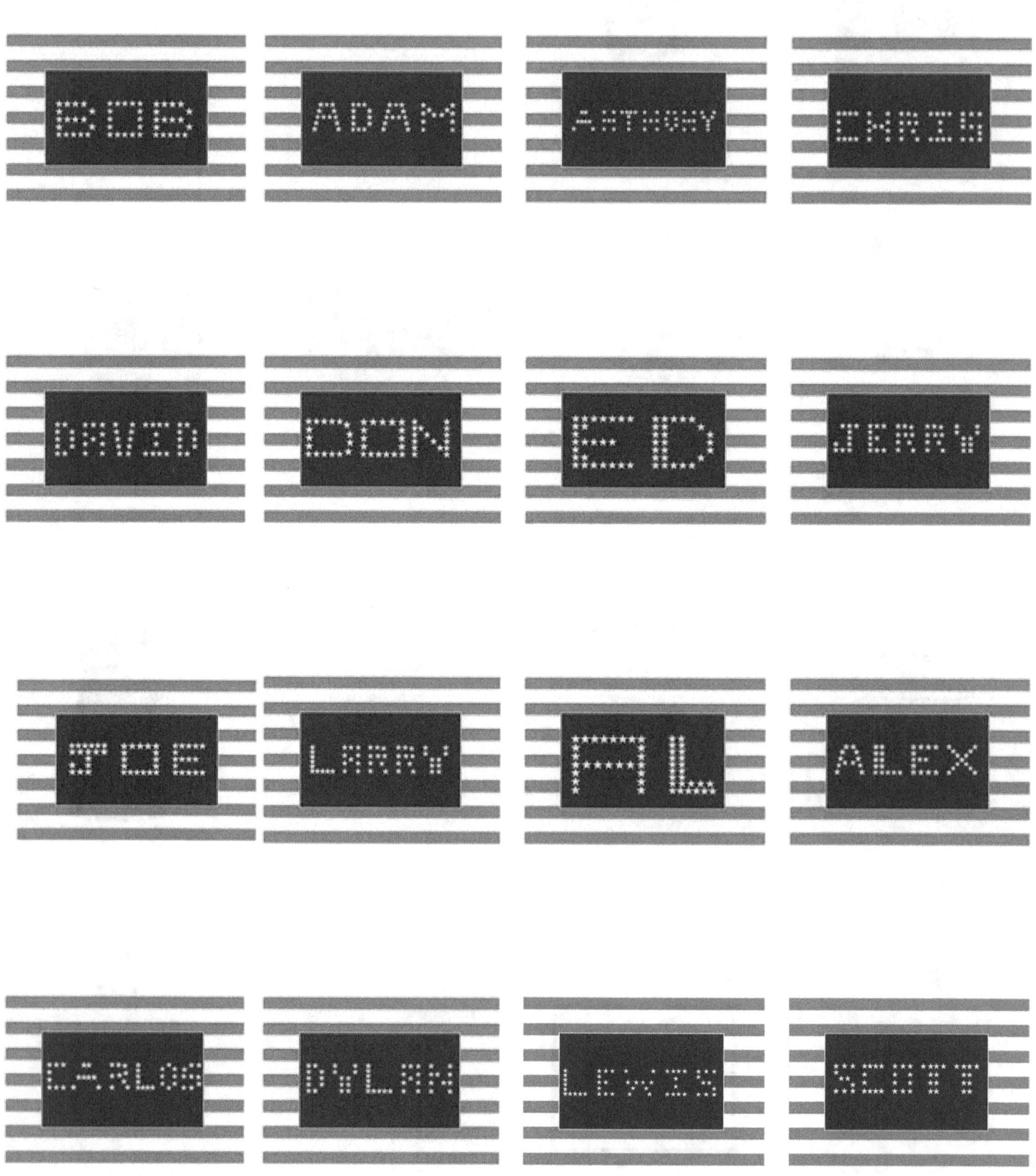

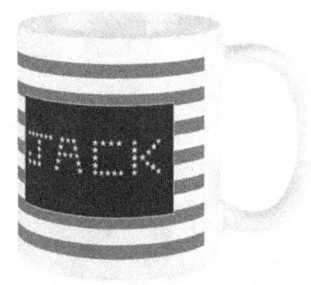 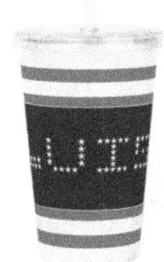 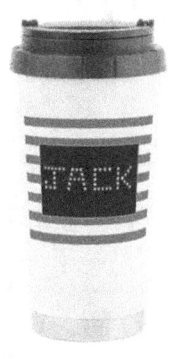 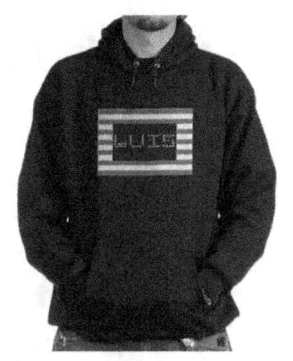

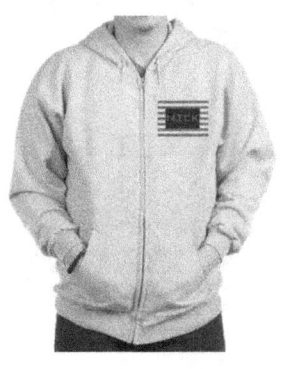 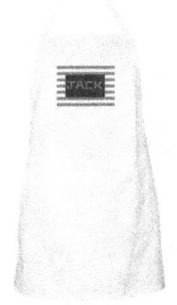 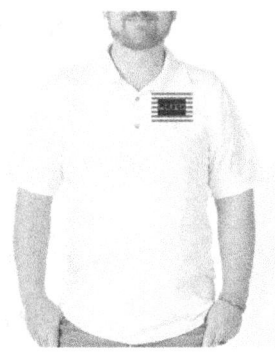 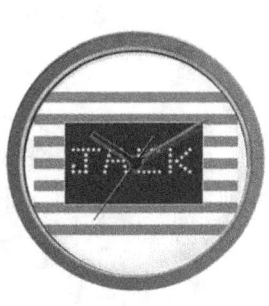

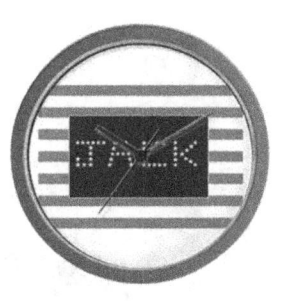 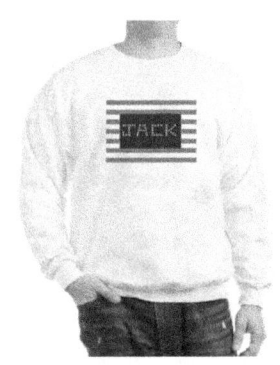 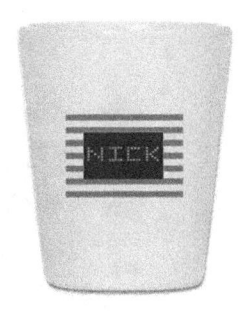 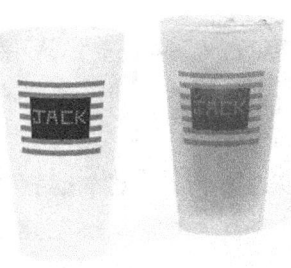

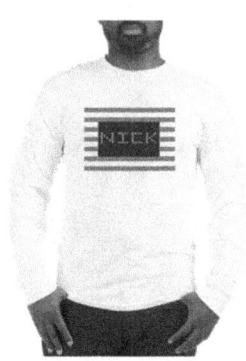 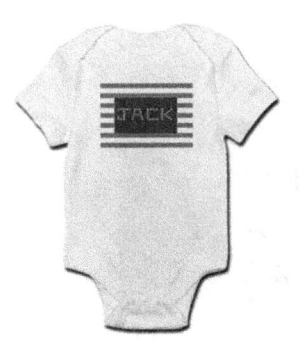

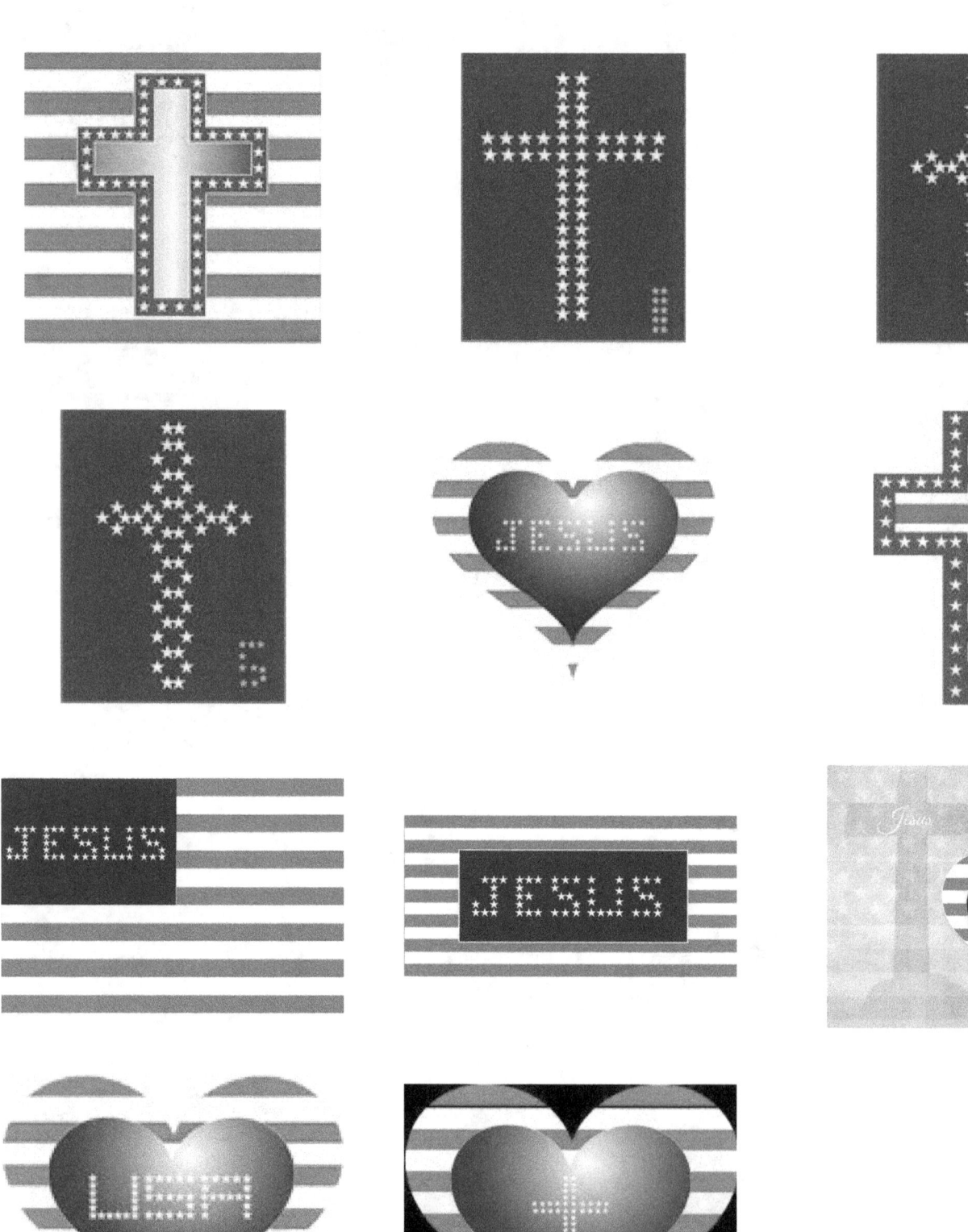

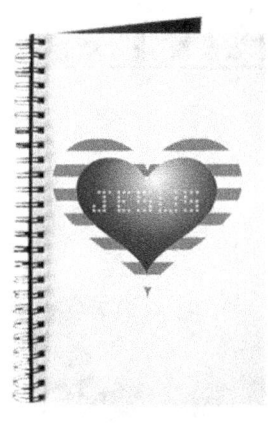
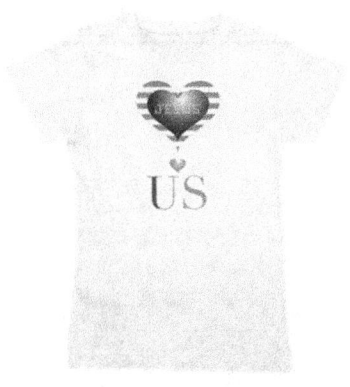
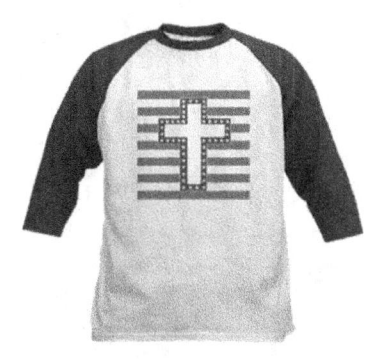
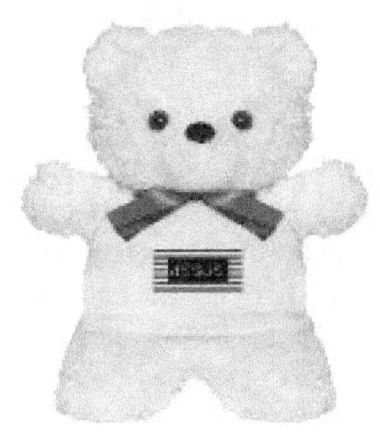
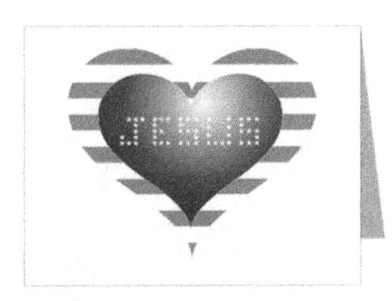
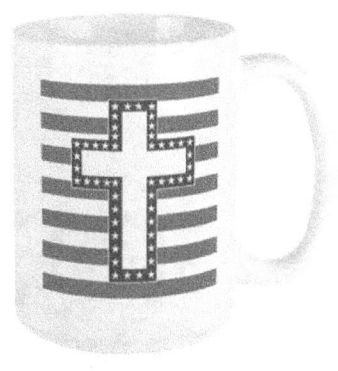
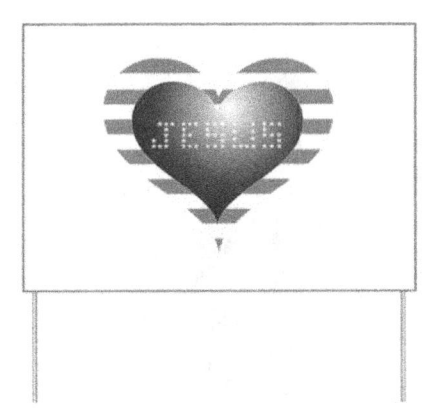
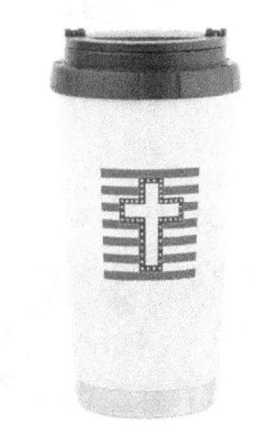
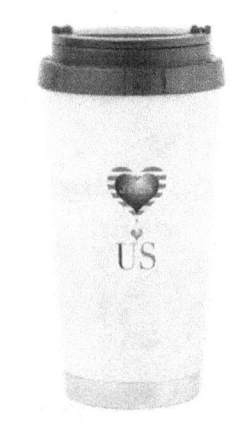
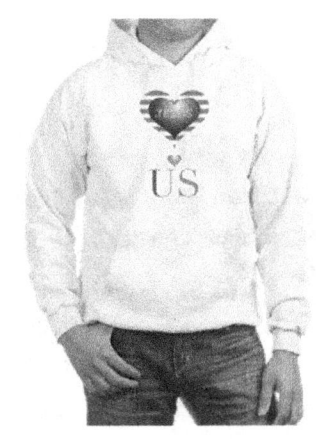
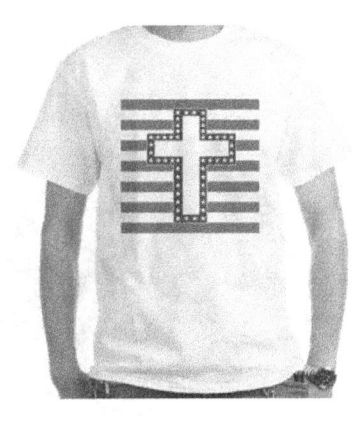
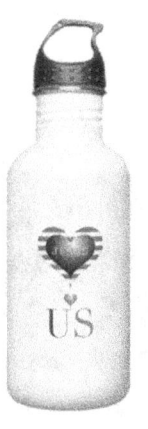

M7

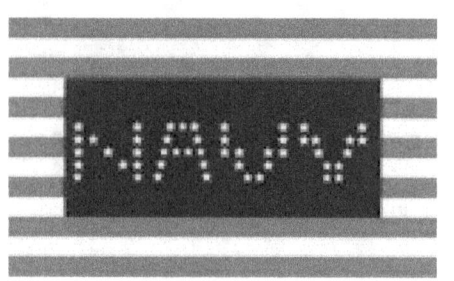
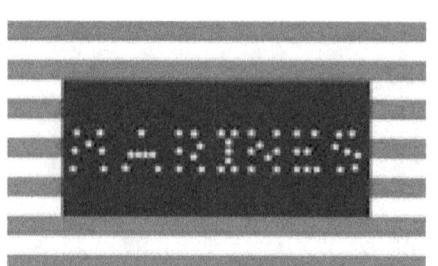
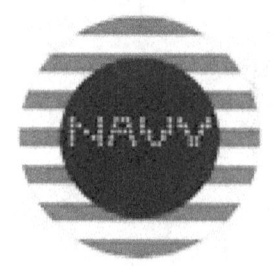
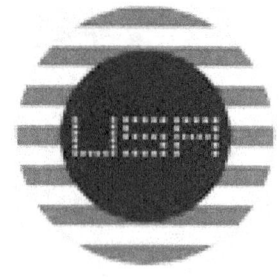
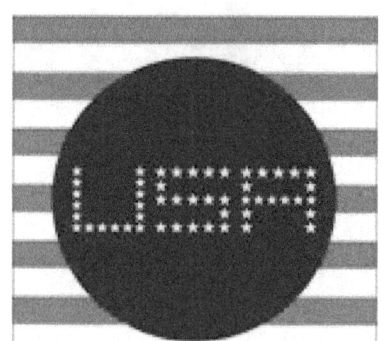

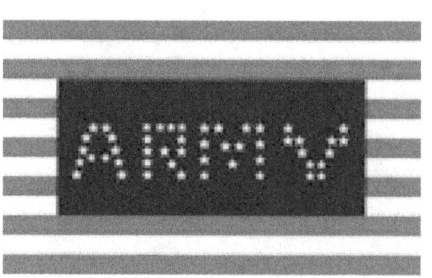
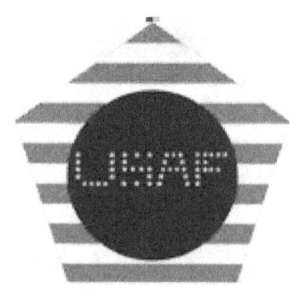

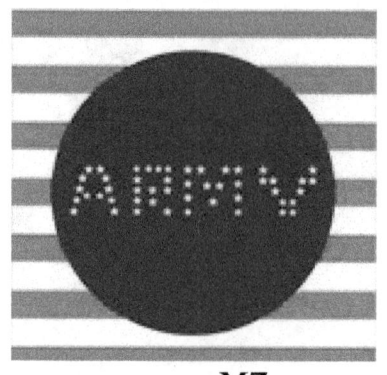

M7

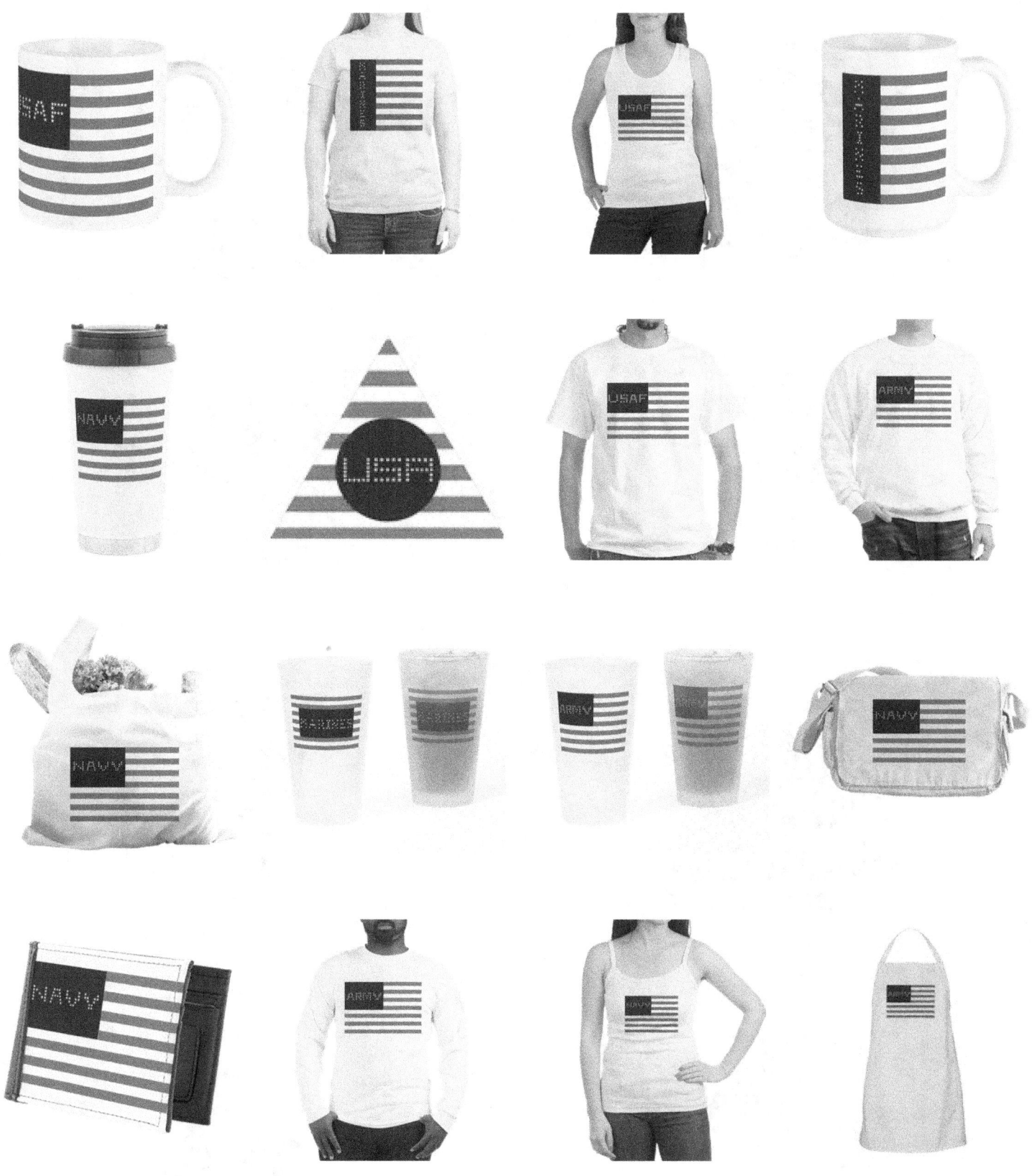

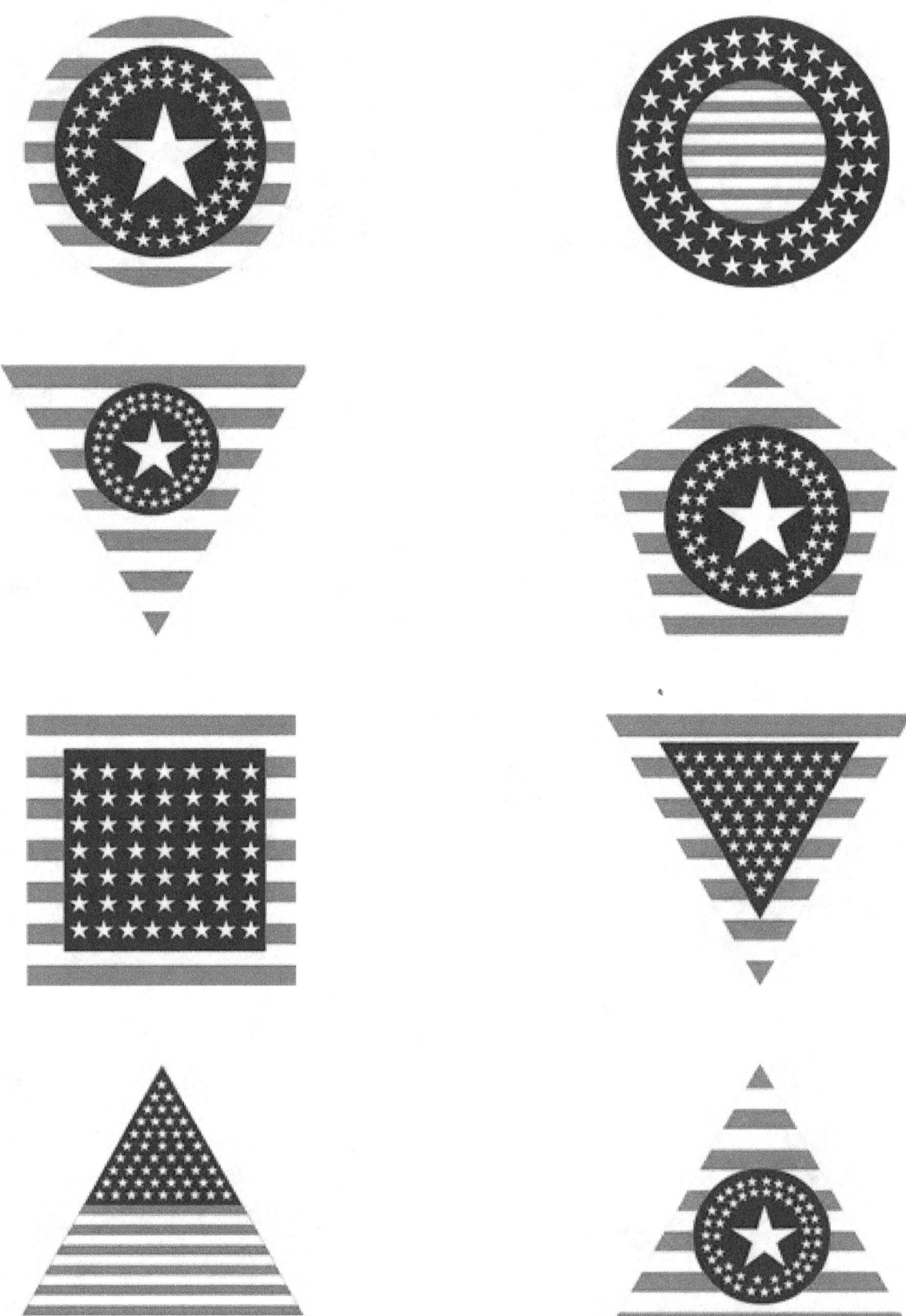

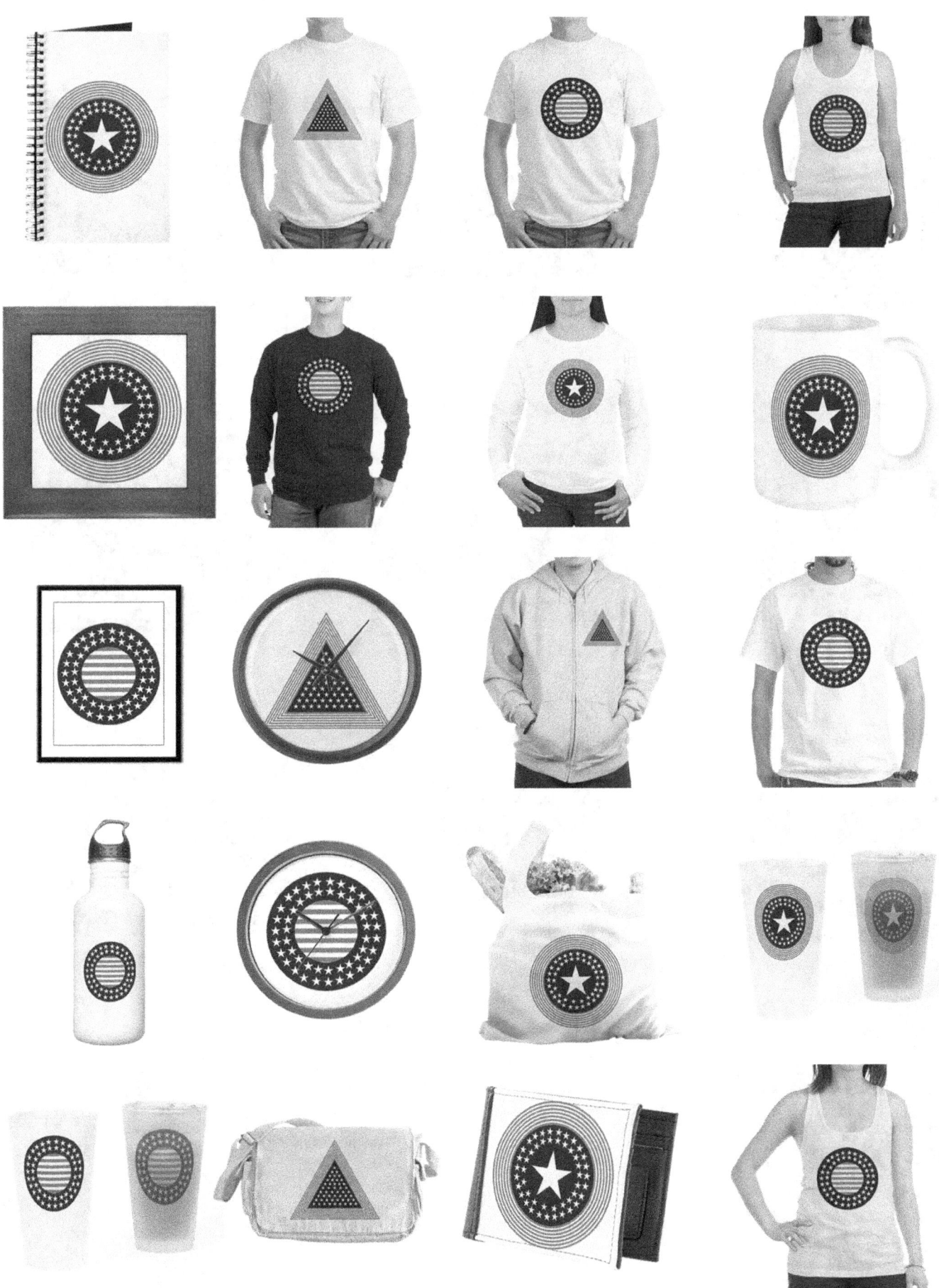

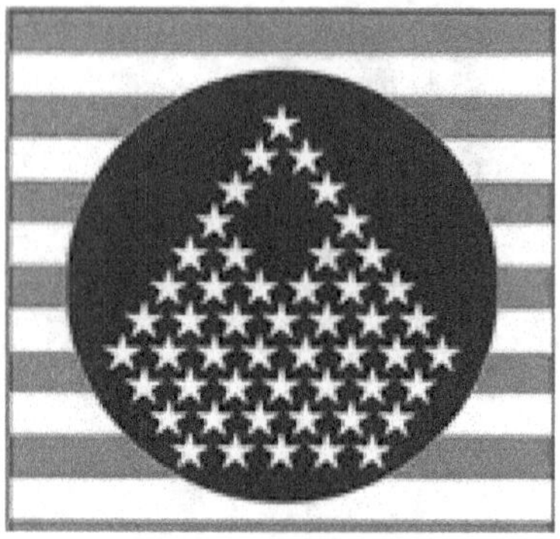

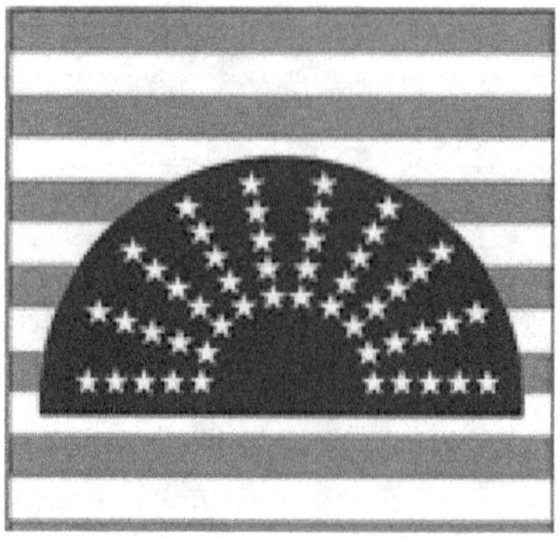

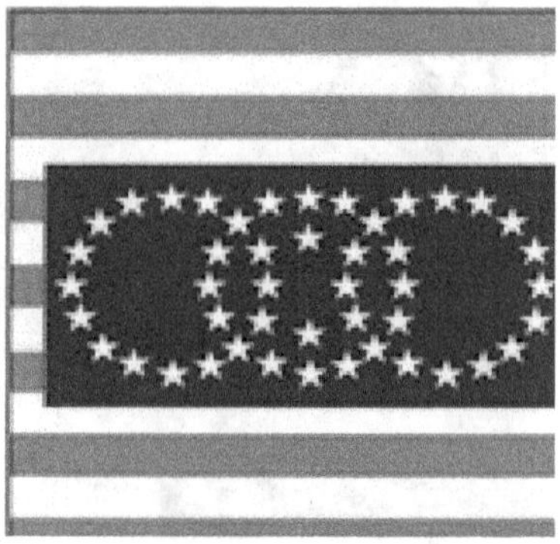

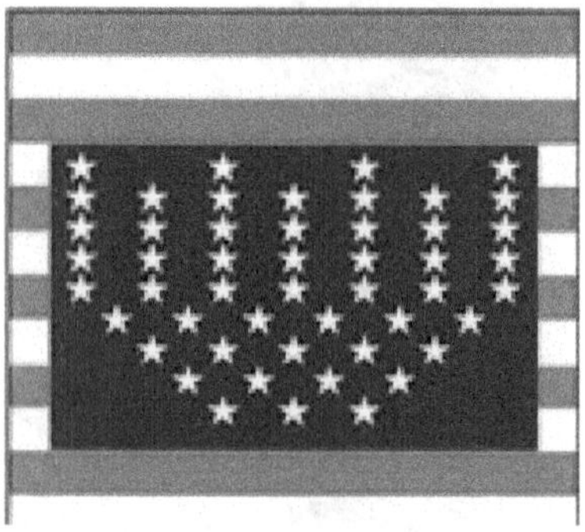

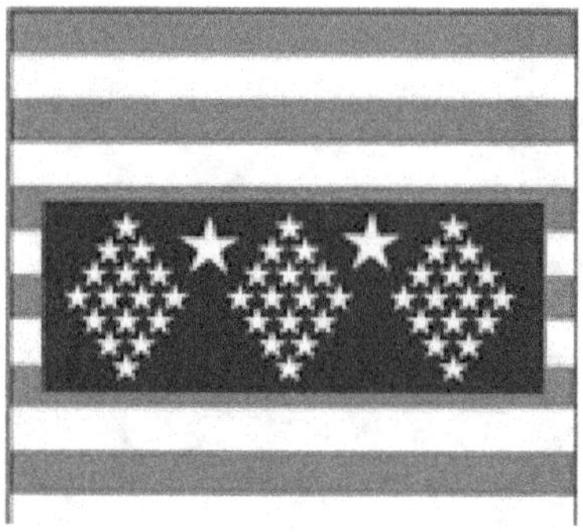

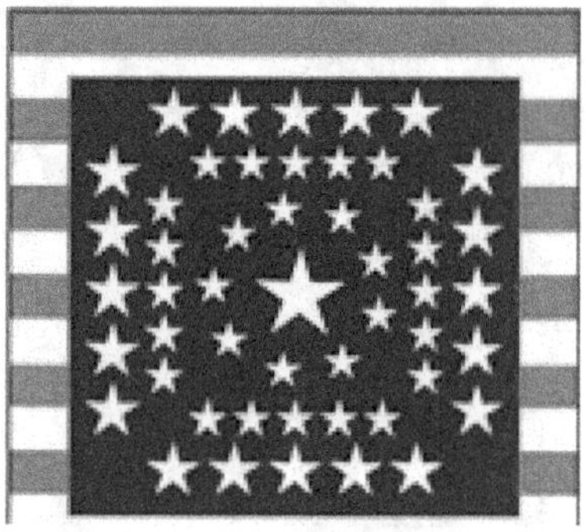

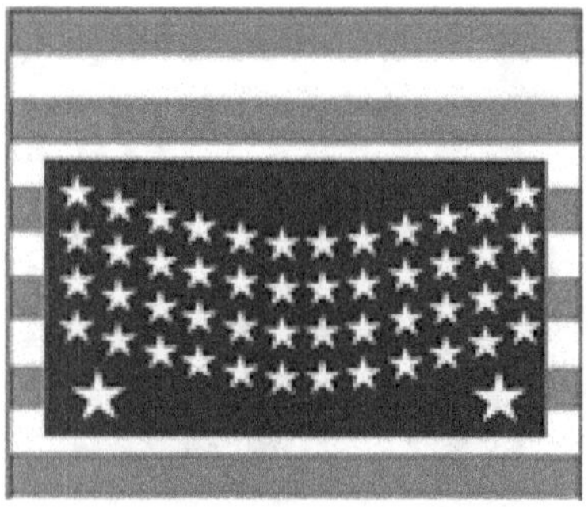

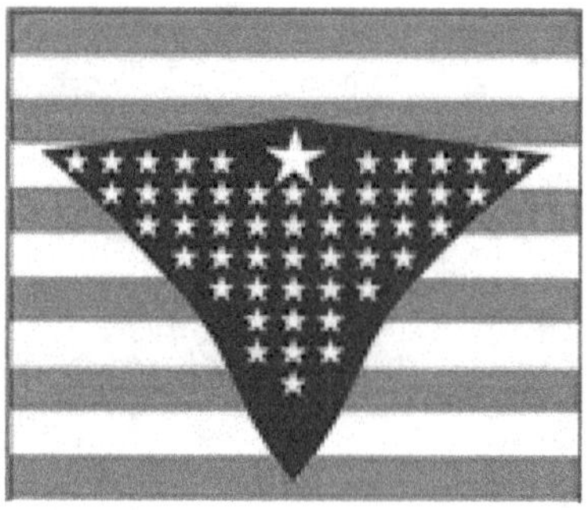

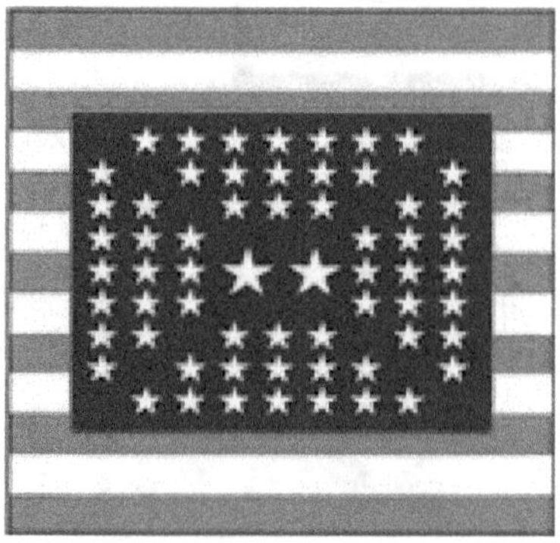

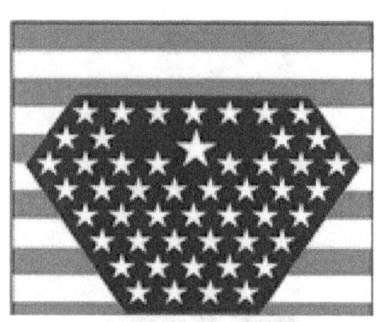

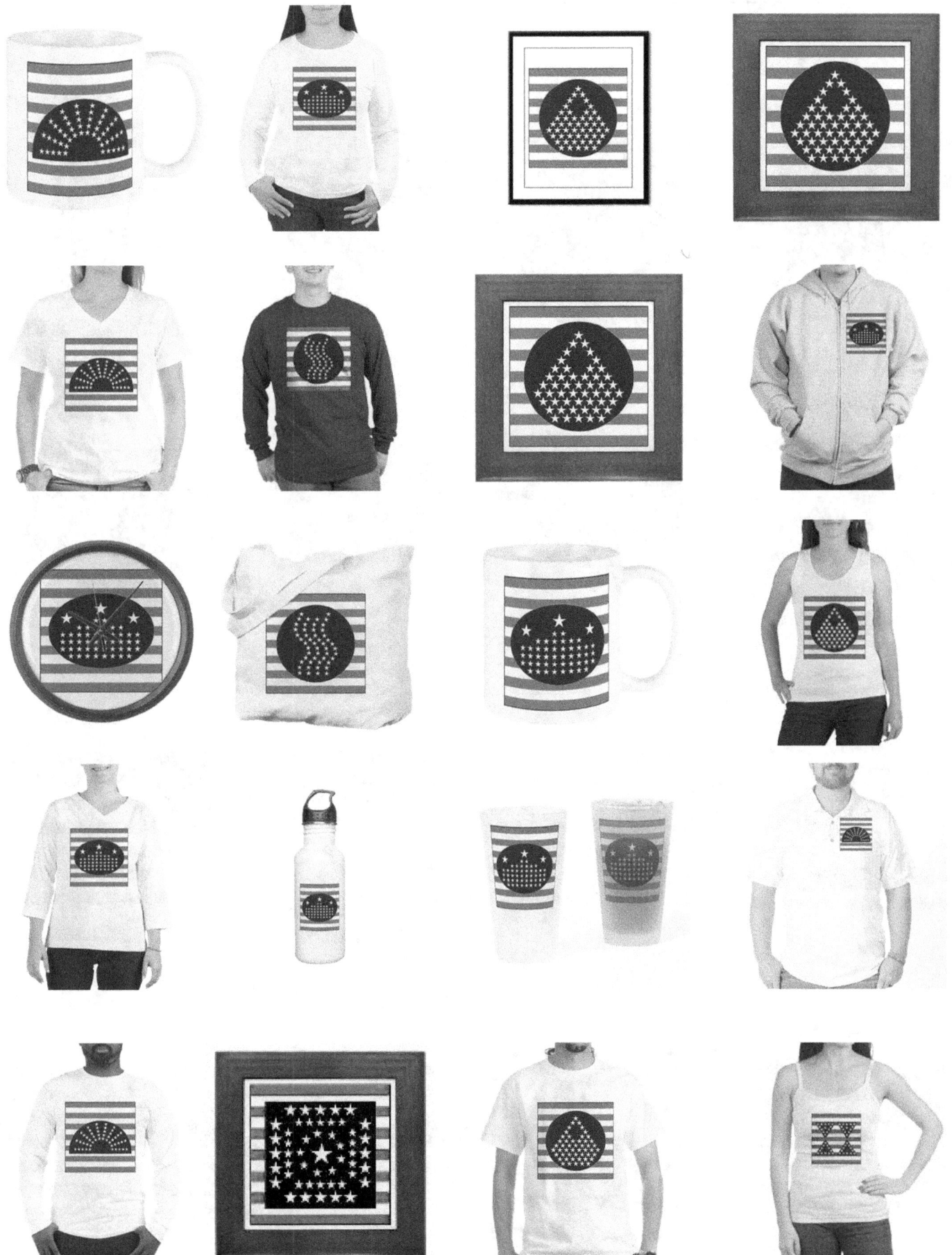

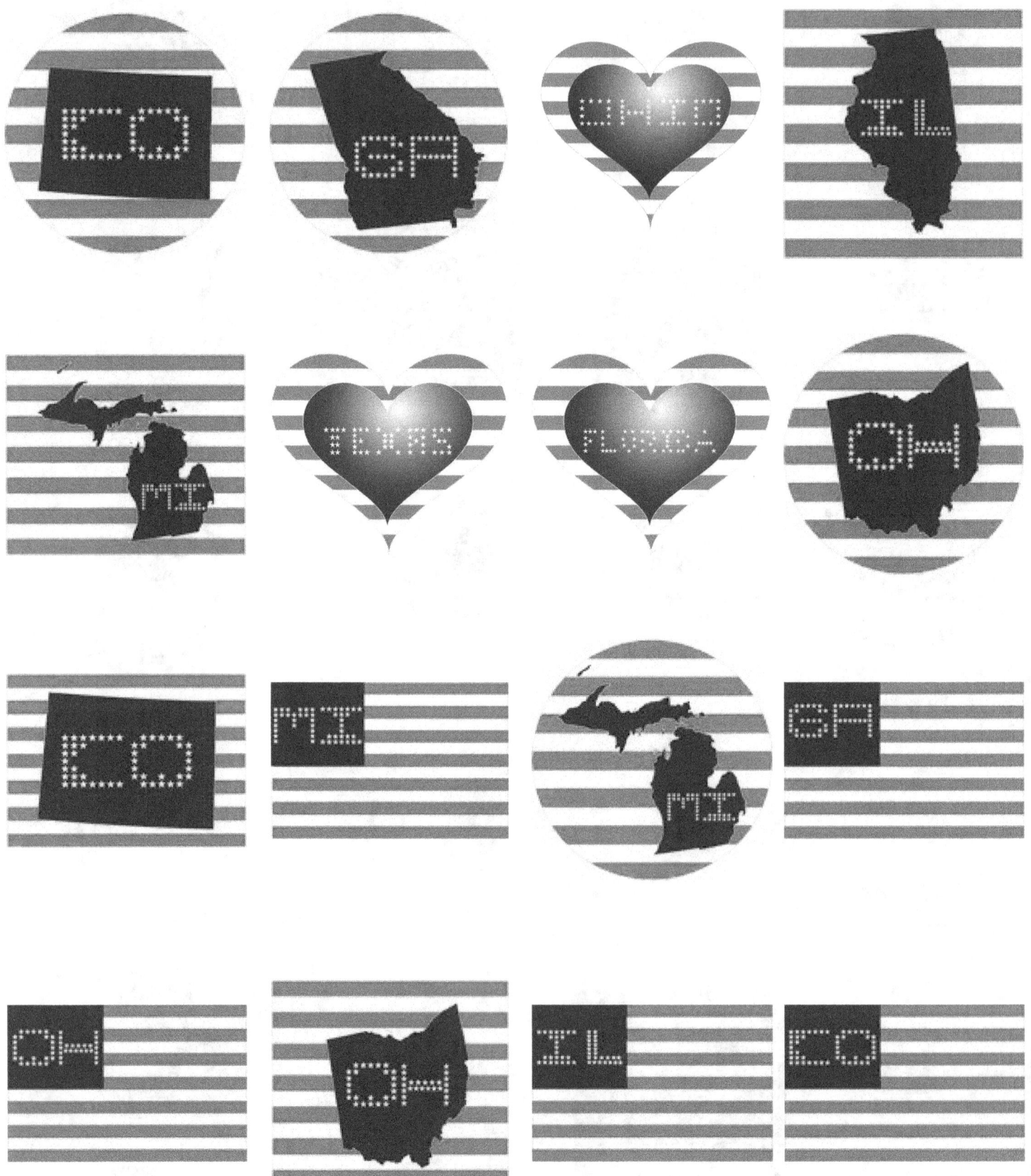

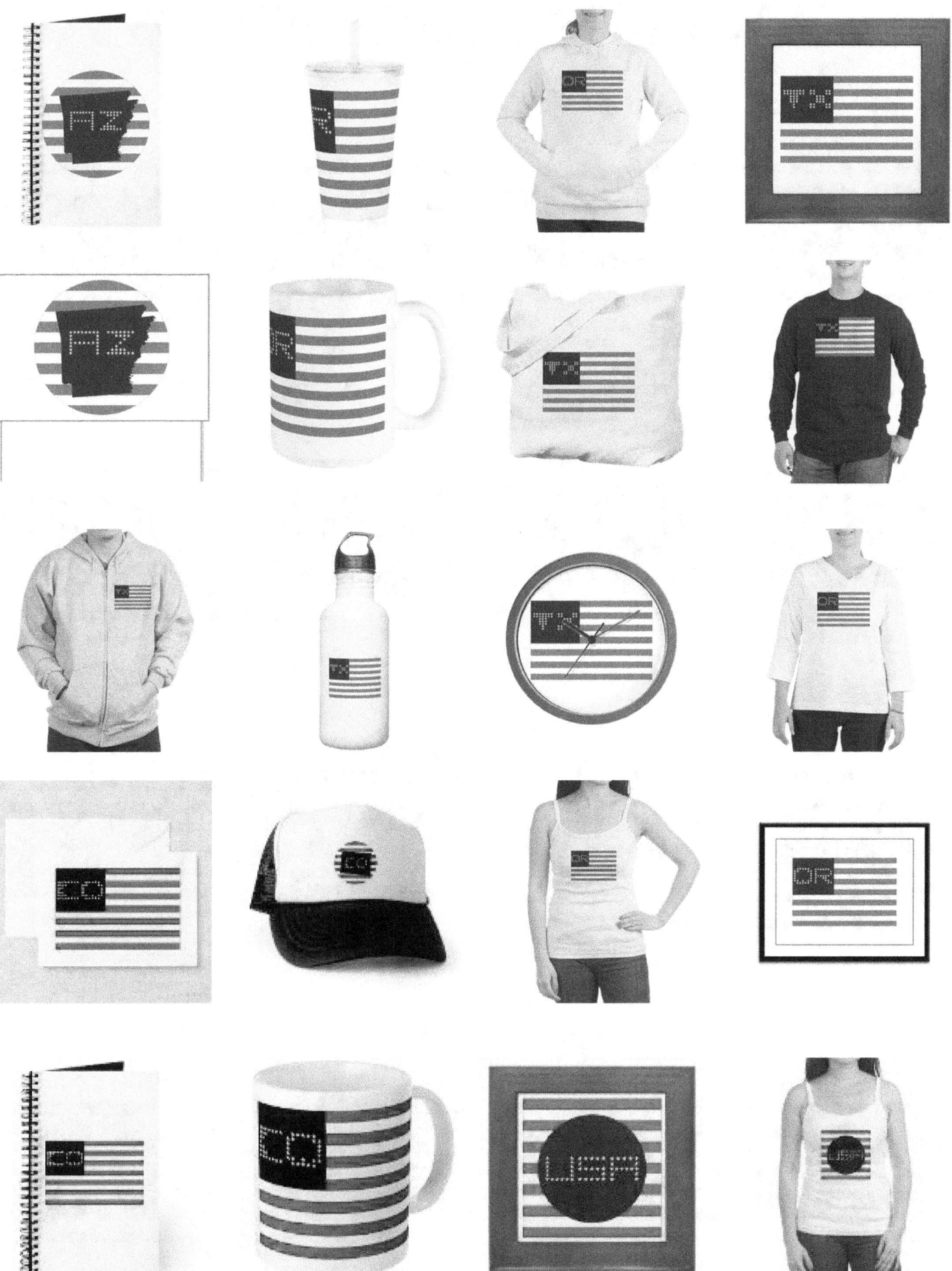

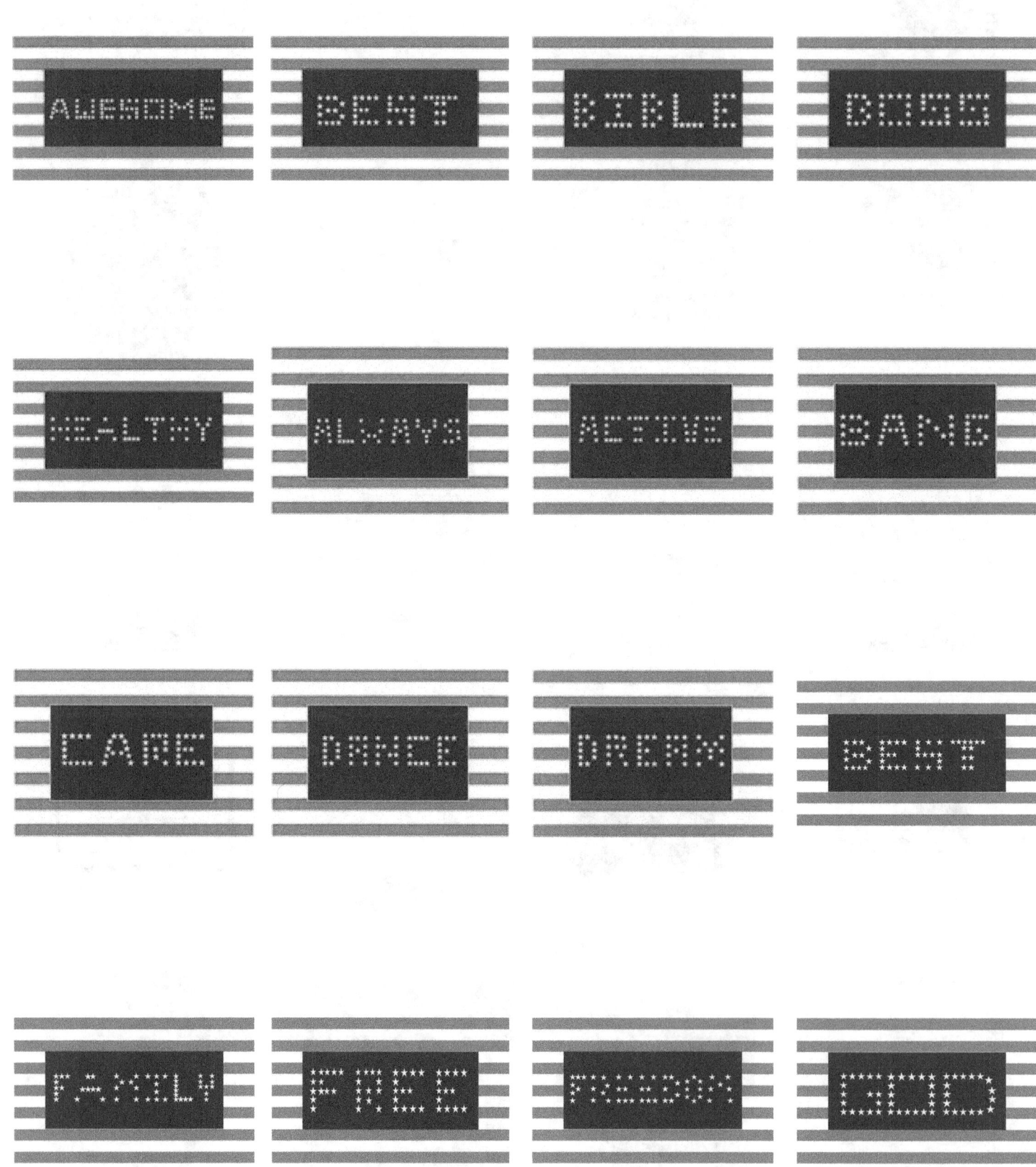

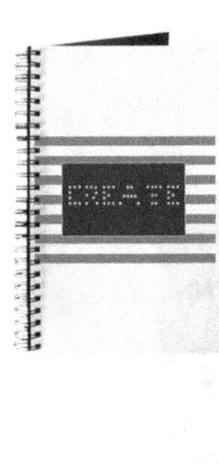
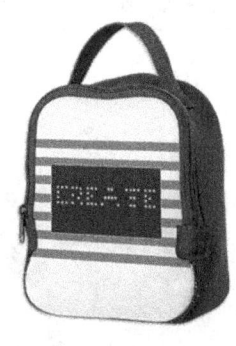
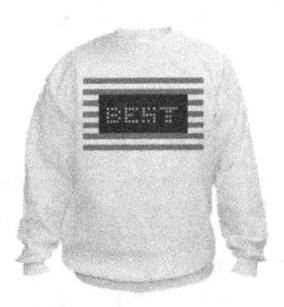
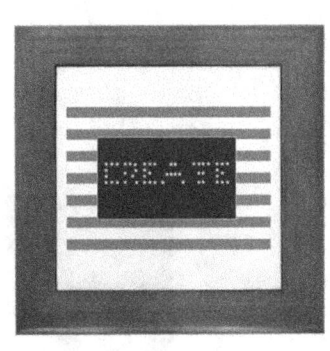

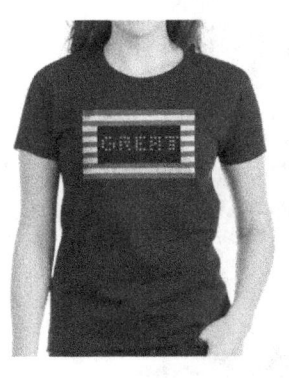
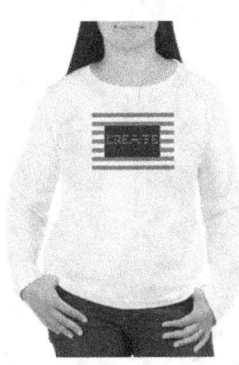
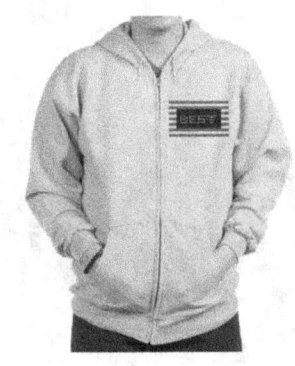
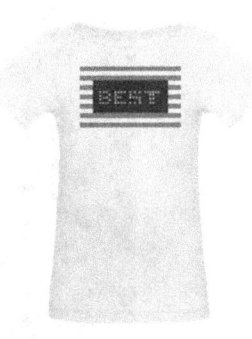

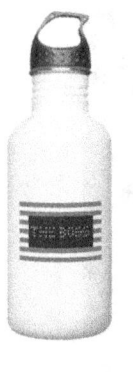
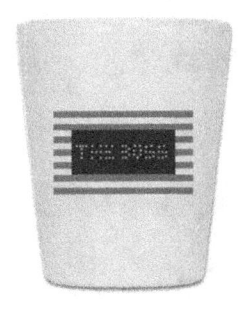
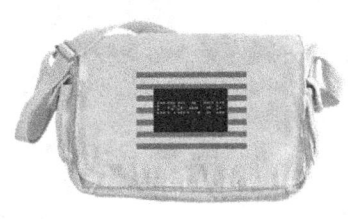
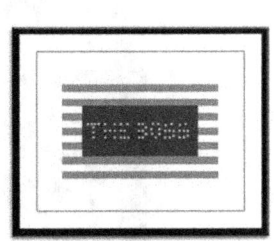

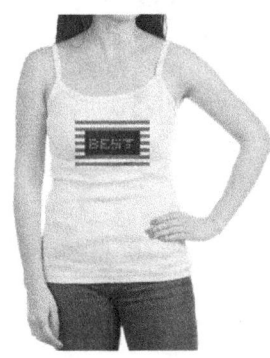
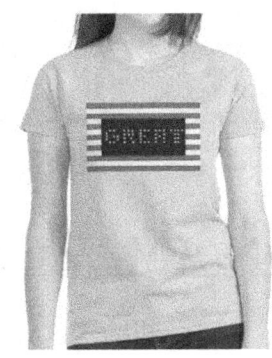
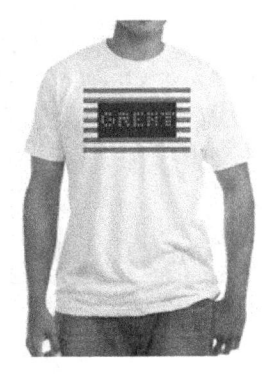

AMERICAN FLAG - BOOK

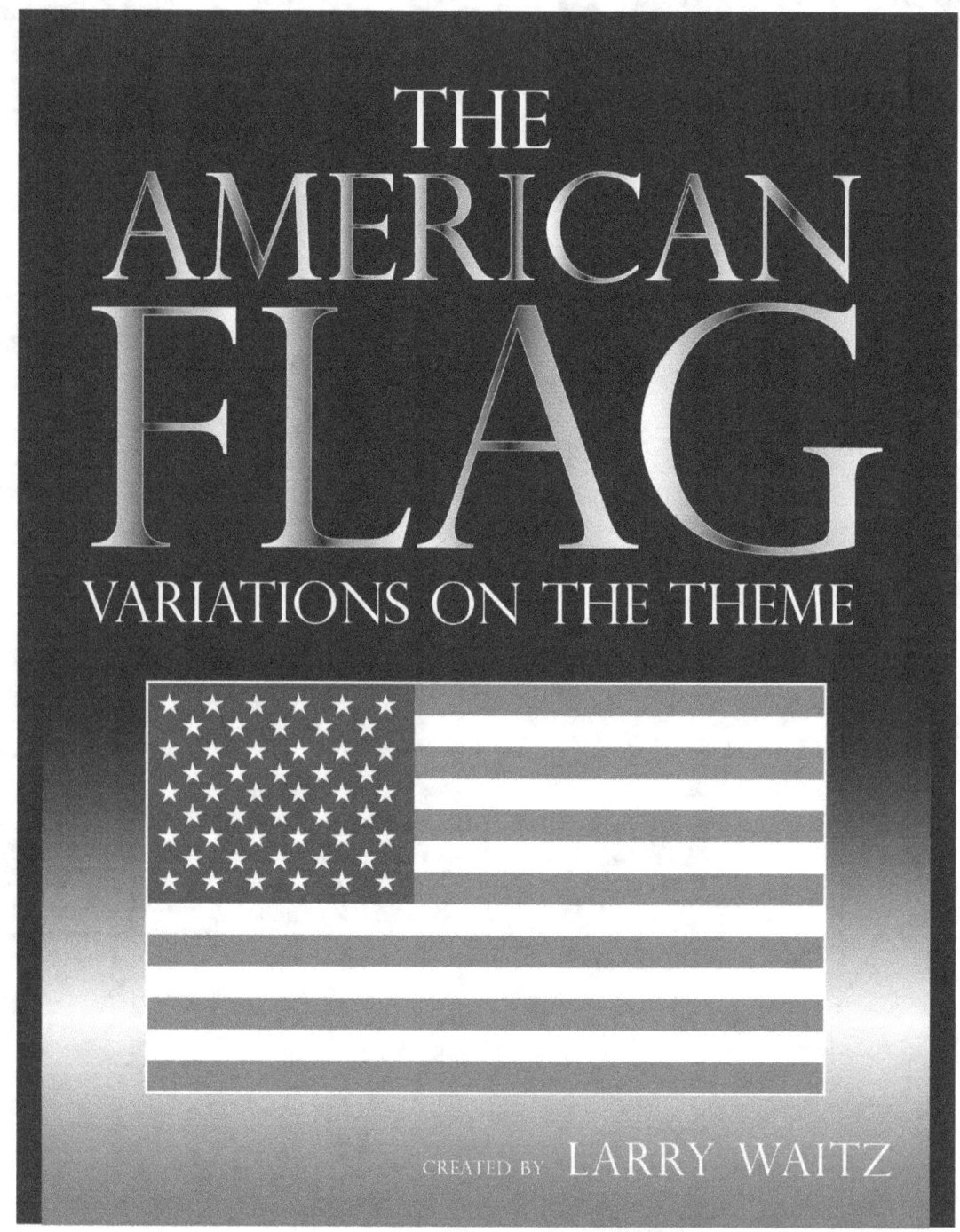

AVAILABLE ON AMAZOM

TROOP TAGS

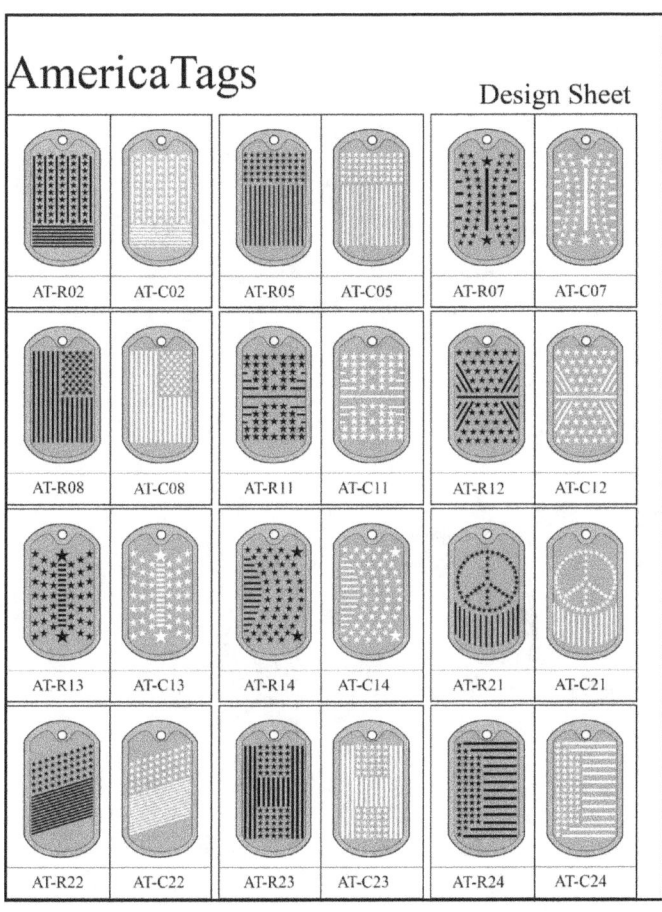

AmericaTags

Design Sheet

AT-R02	AT-C02	AT-R05	AT-C05	AT-R07	AT-C07
AT-R08	AT-C08	AT-R11	AT-C11	AT-R12	AT-C12
AT-R13	AT-C13	AT-R14	AT-C14	AT-R21	AT-C21
AT-R22	AT-C22	AT-R23	AT-C23	AT-R24	AT-C24

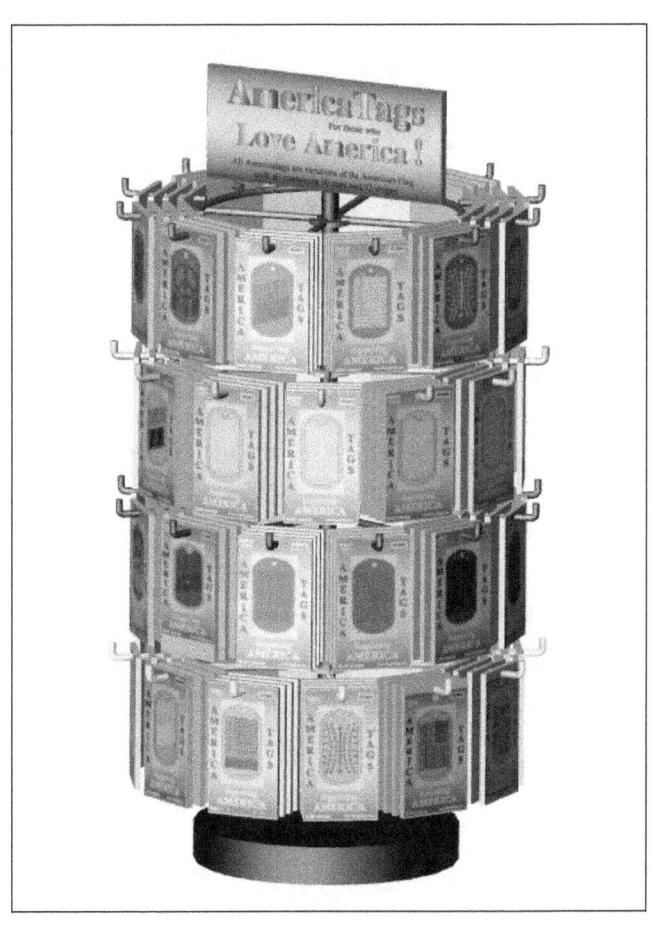

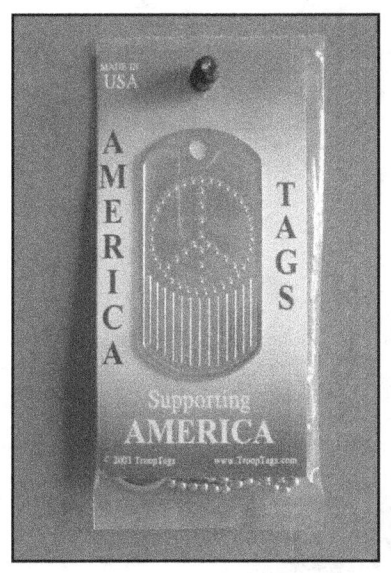

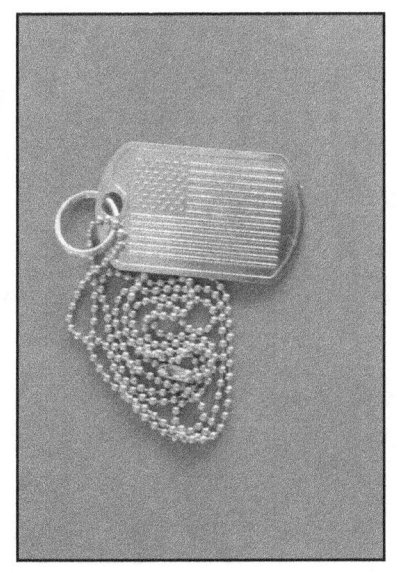

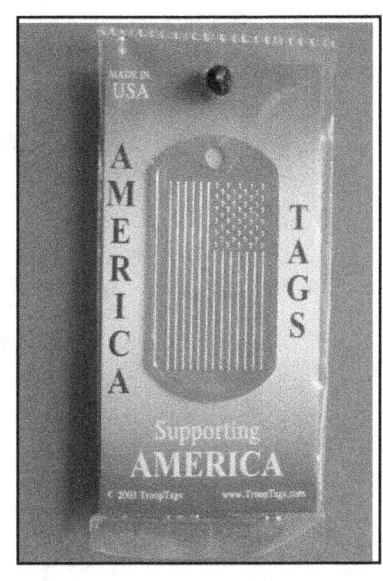

BILL BANKS

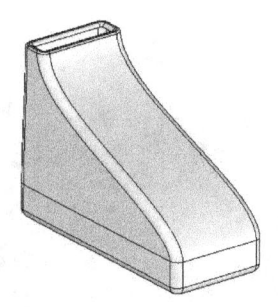

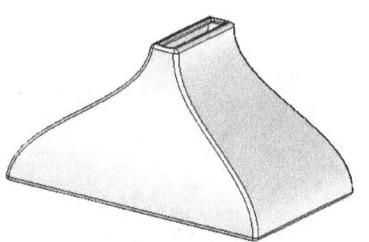

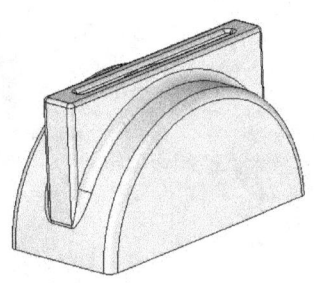

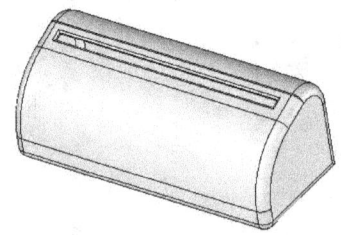

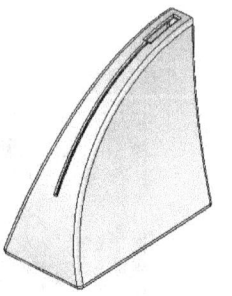

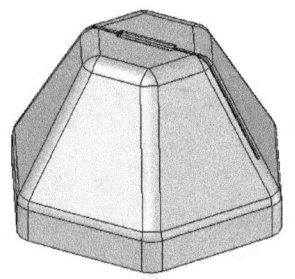

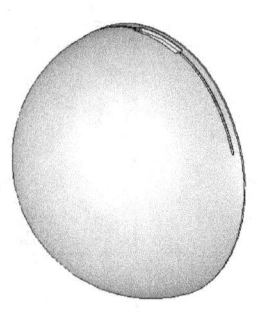

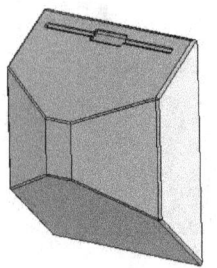

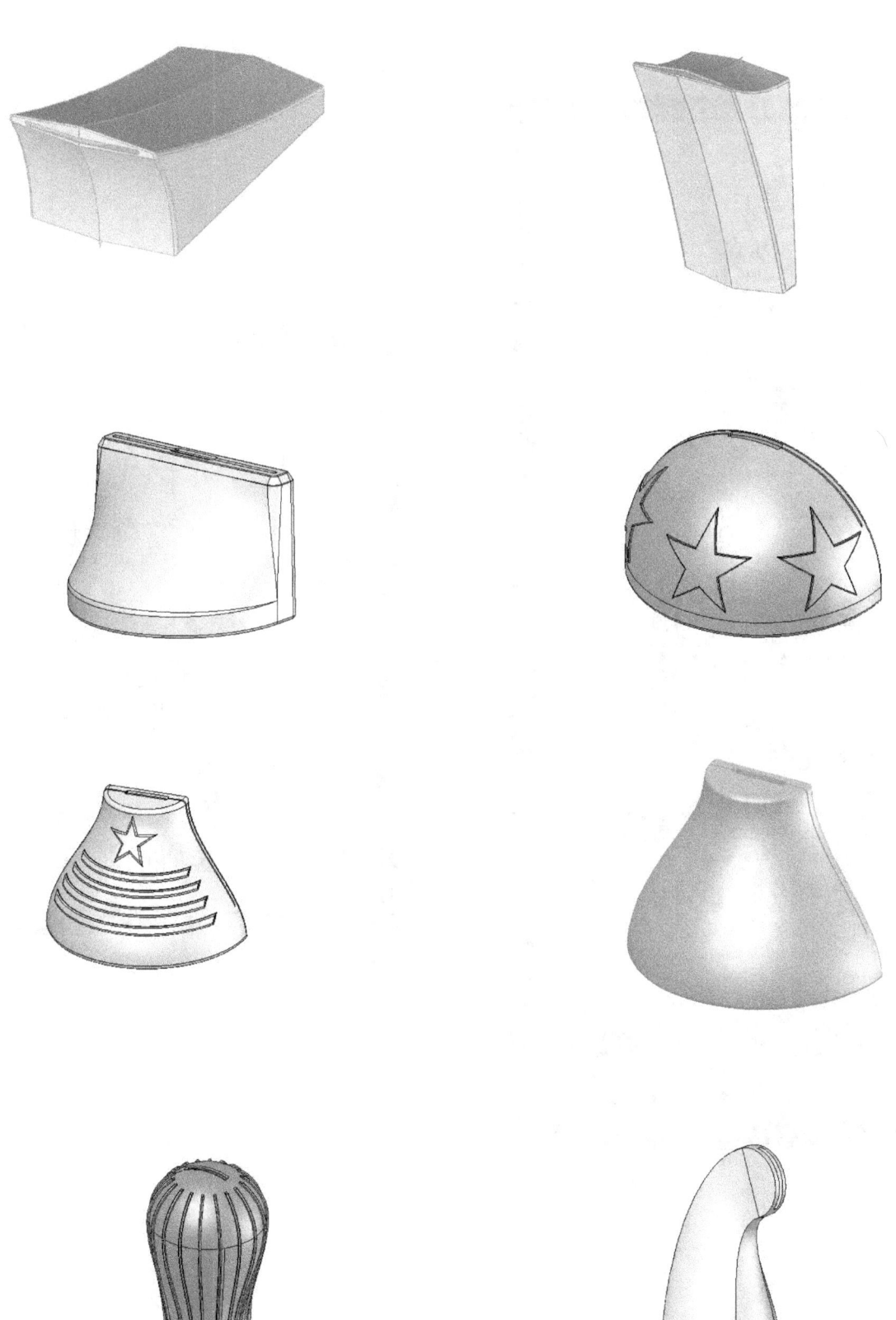

NOTABSOLUTE BOTTLES
21

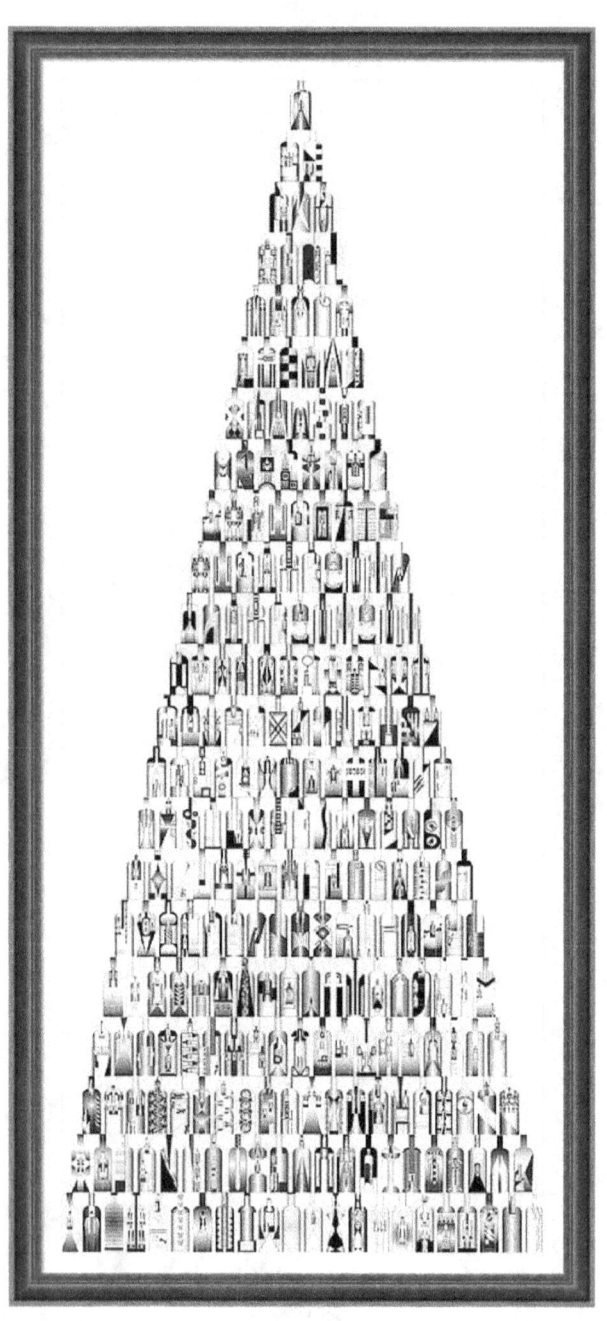

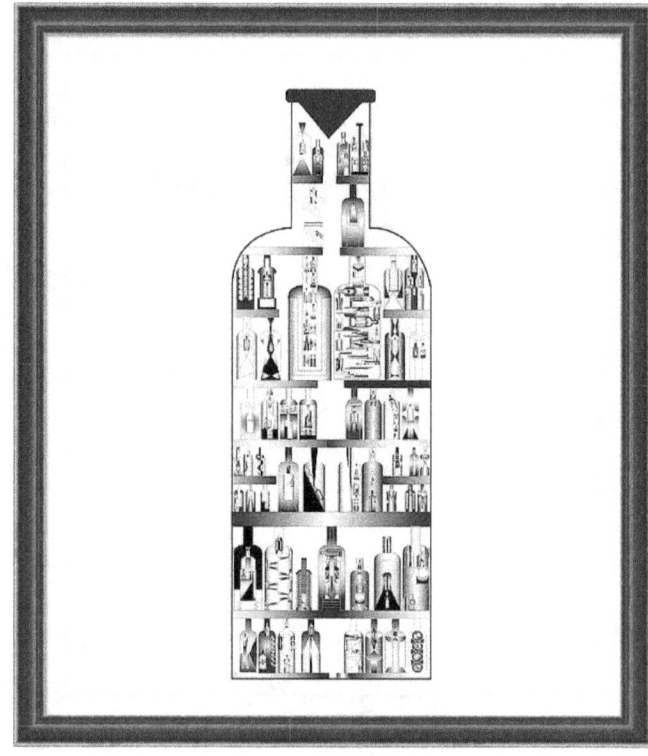

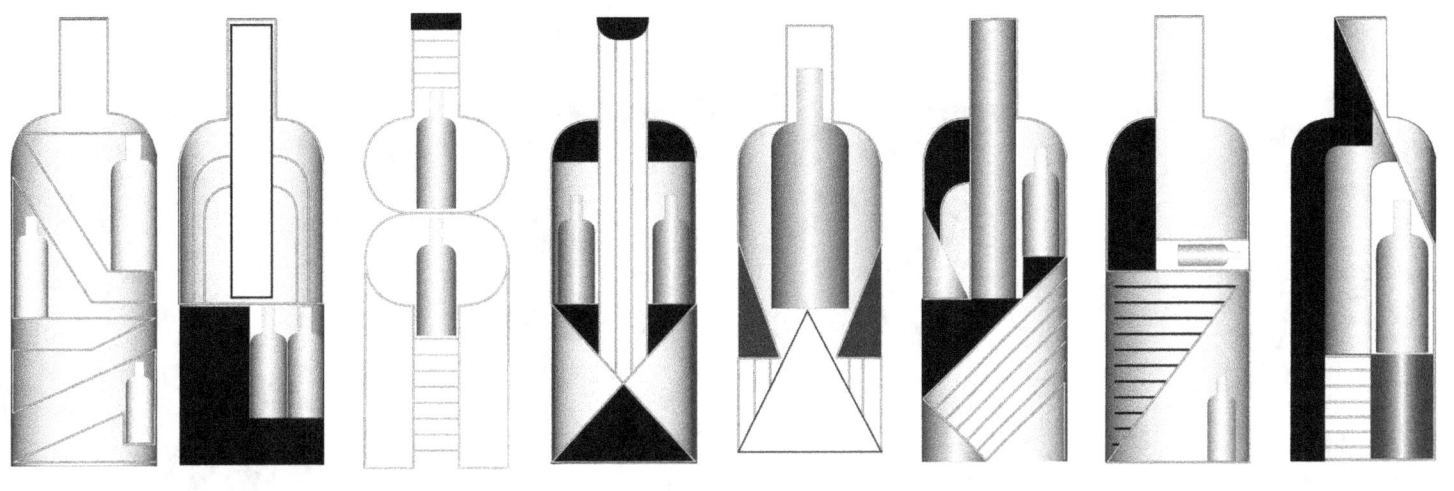

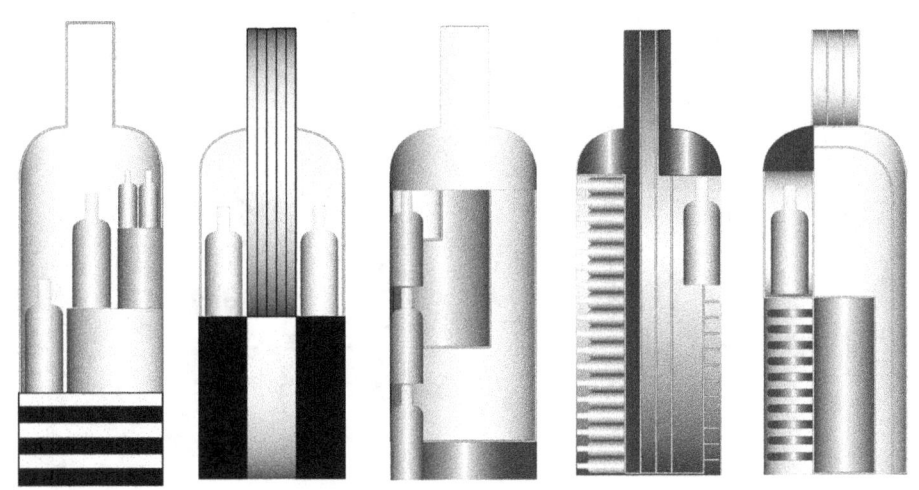

M7

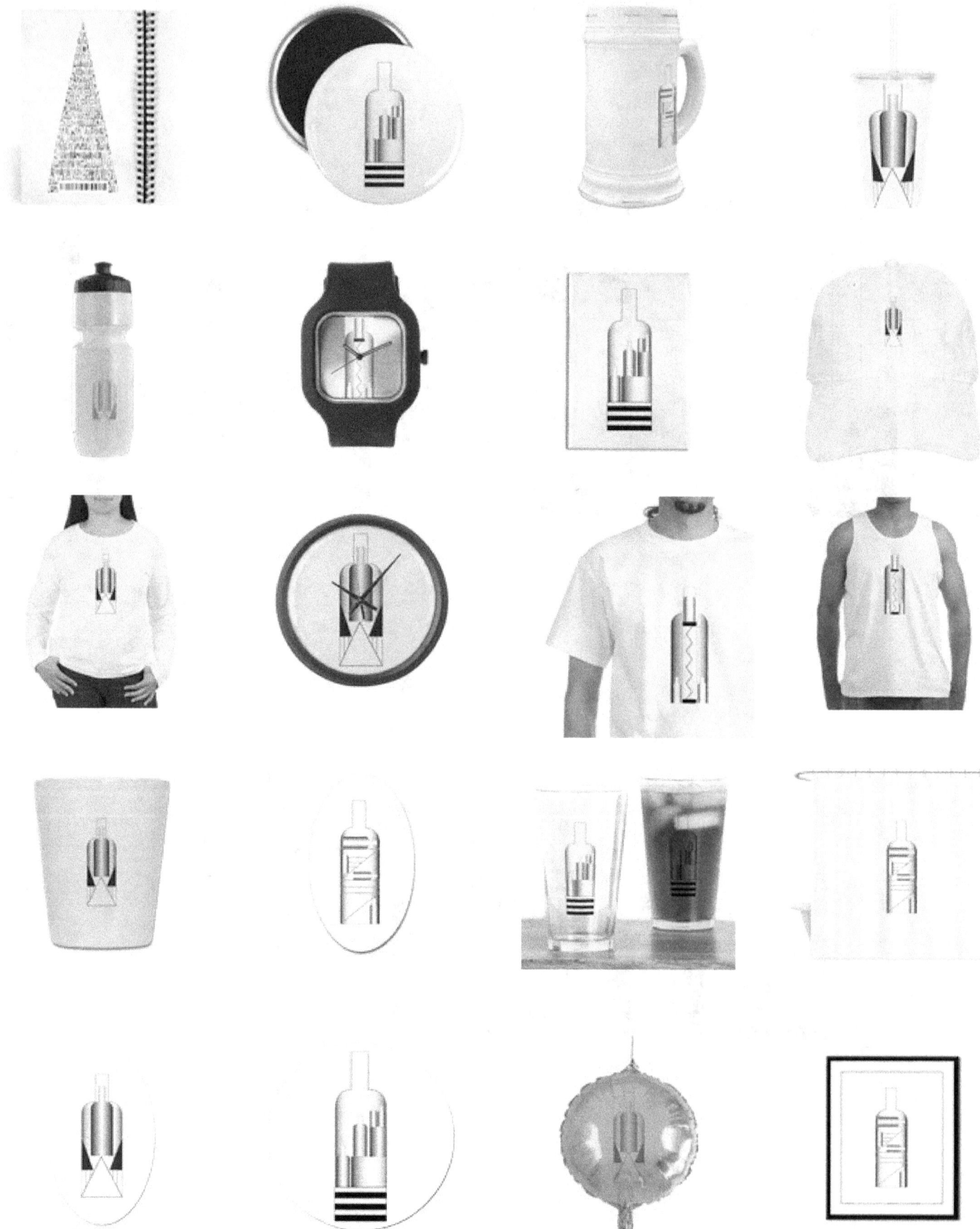

MUTRX REVOLUTION

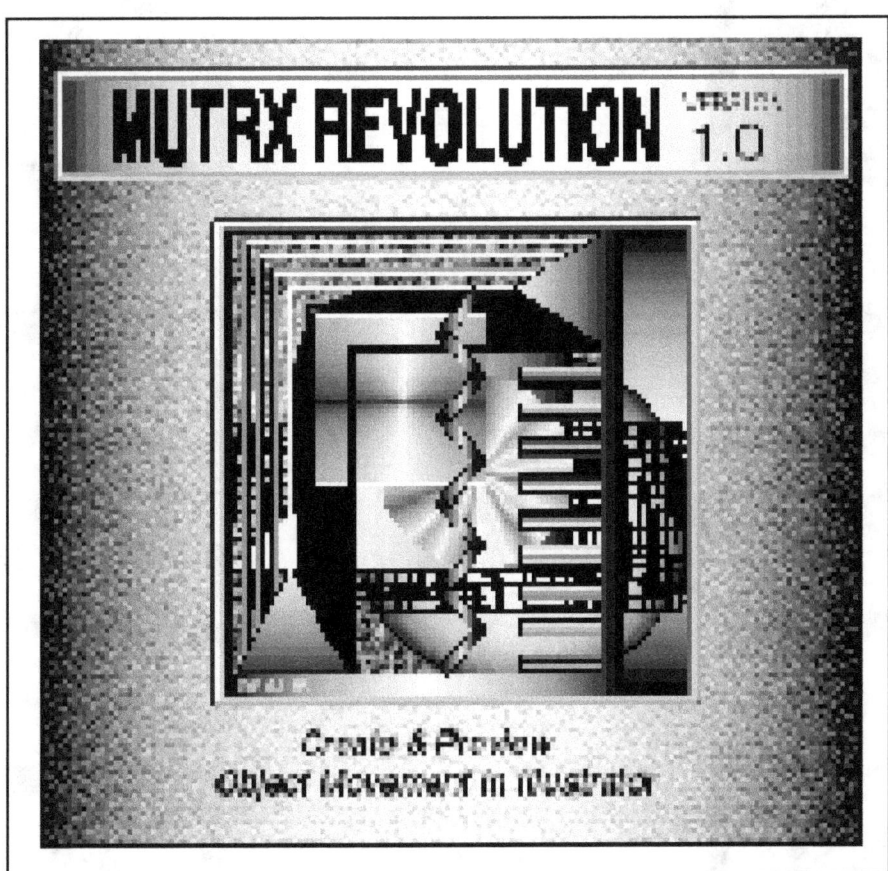

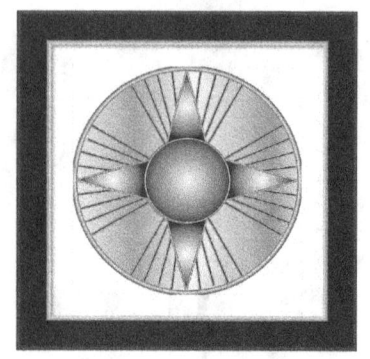

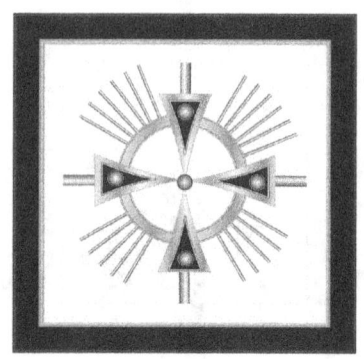

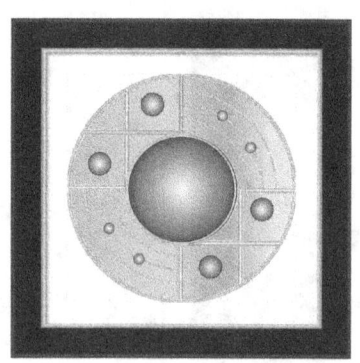

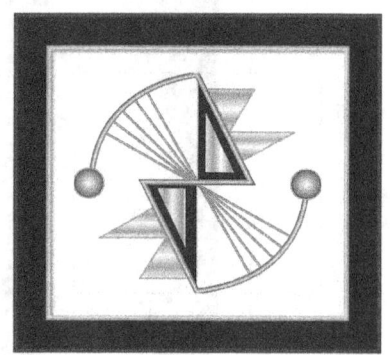

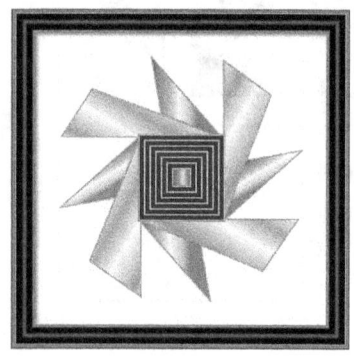

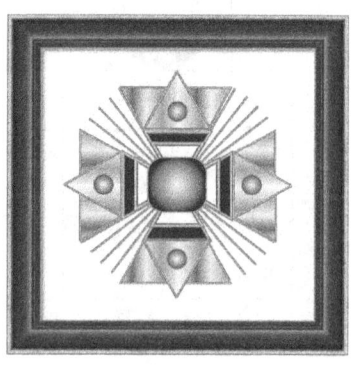

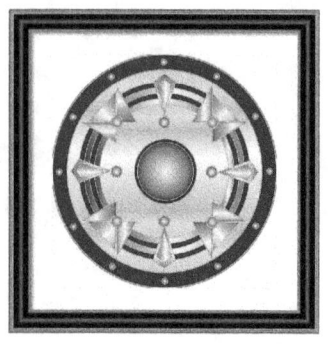

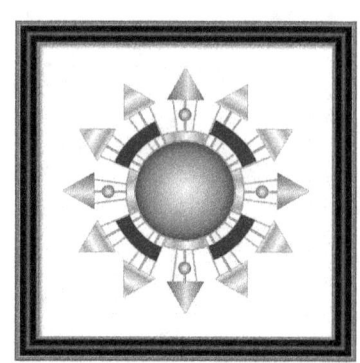

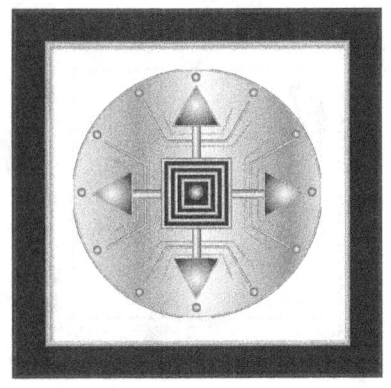

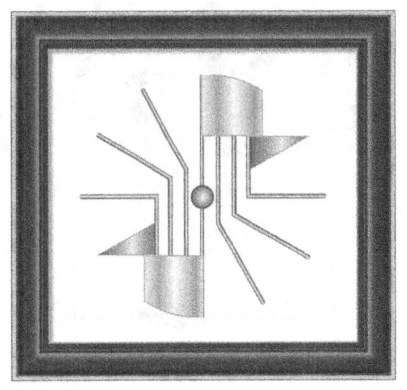

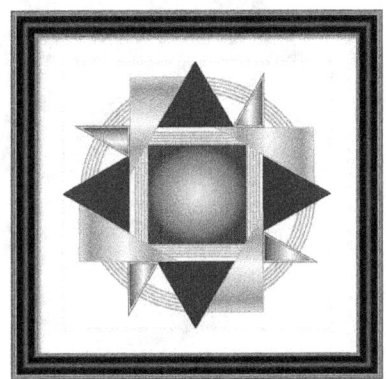

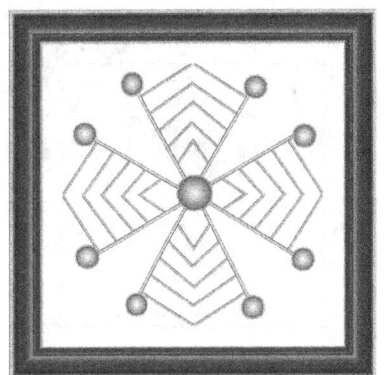

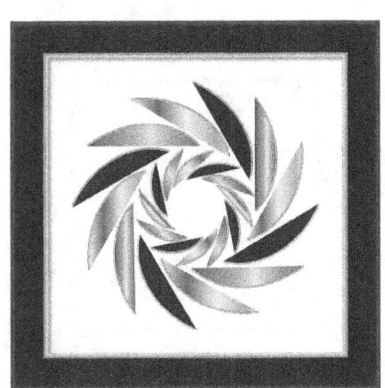

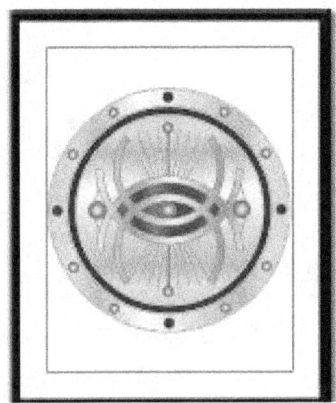

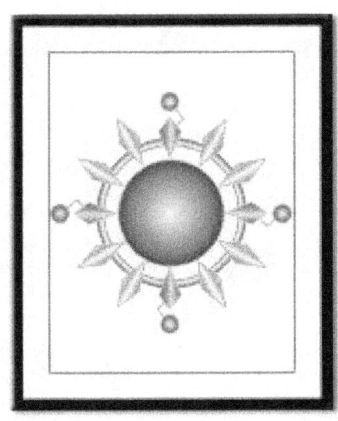

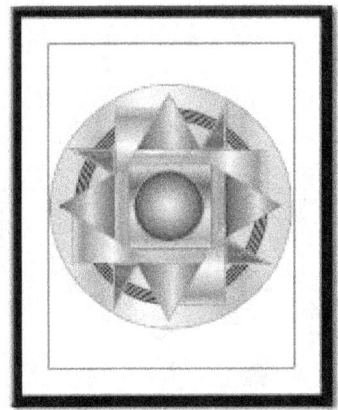

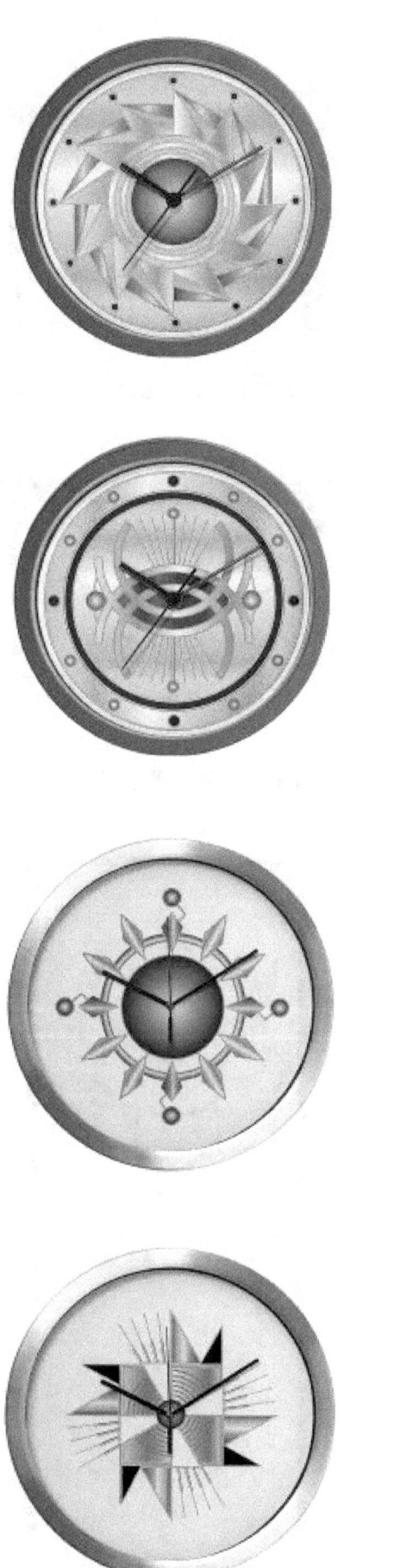
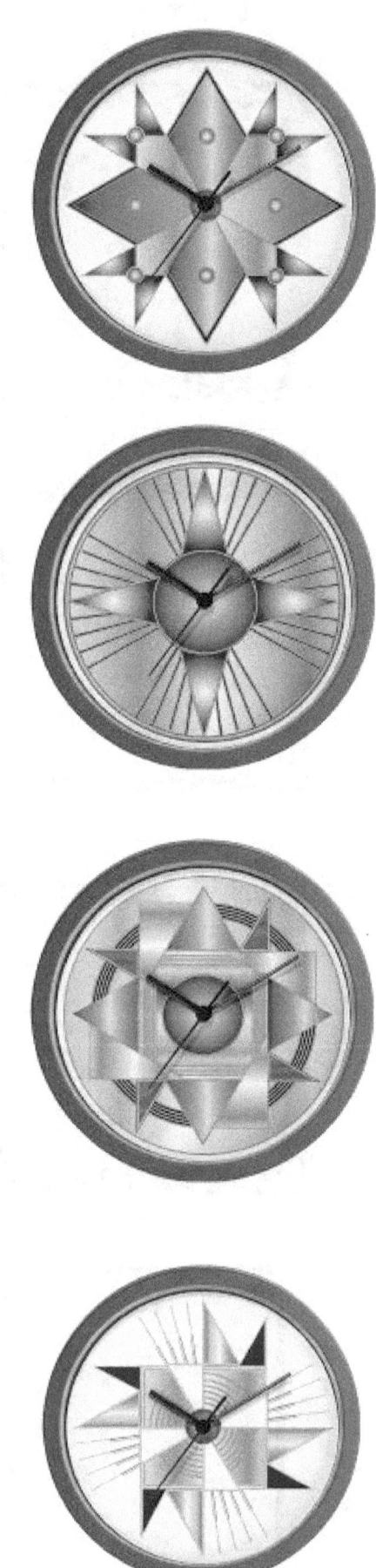

M7

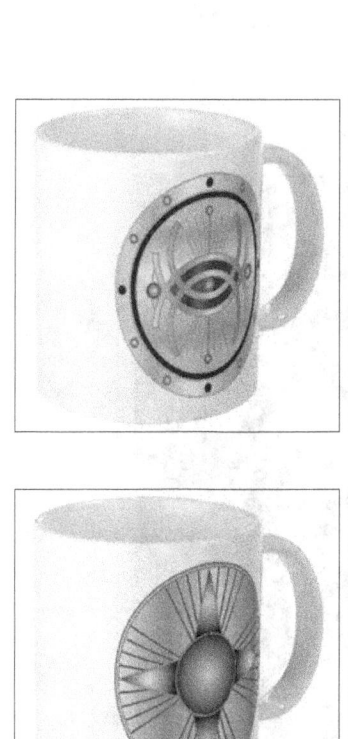
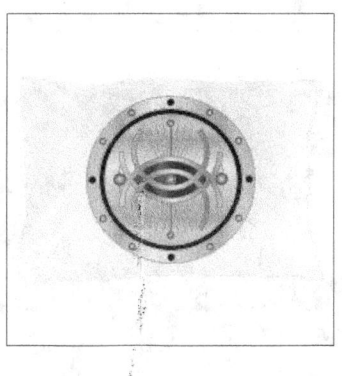
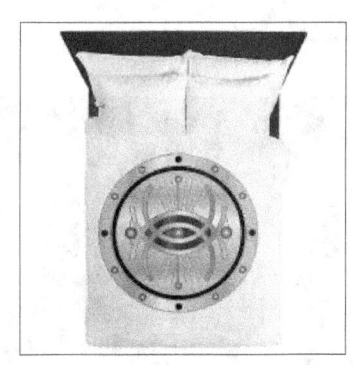
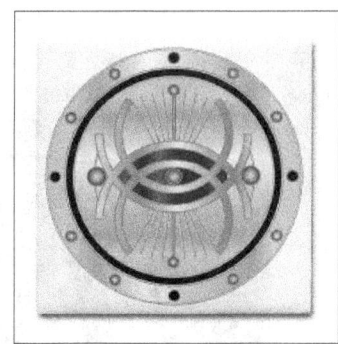
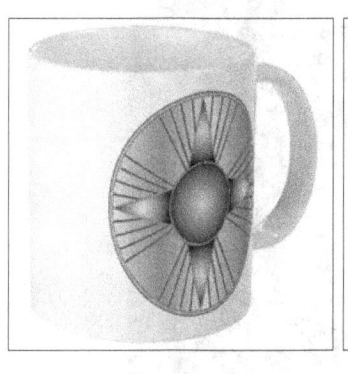
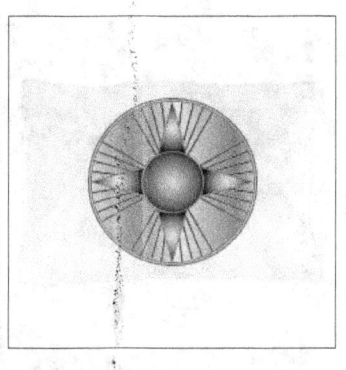
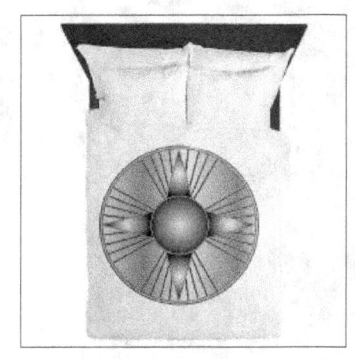
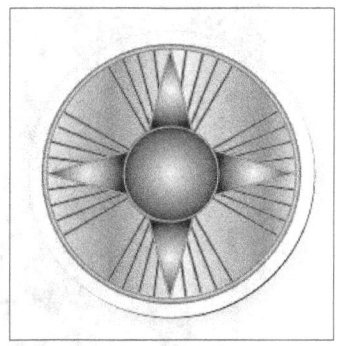
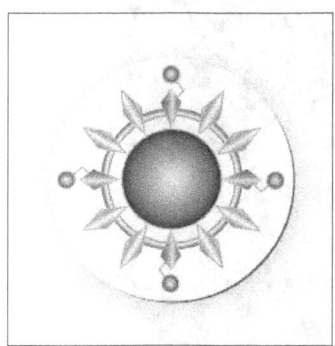
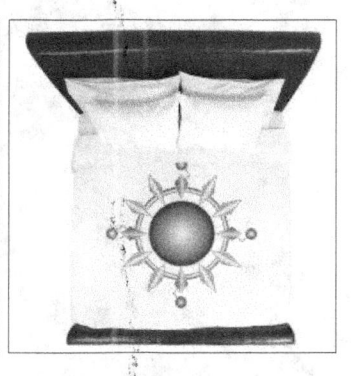
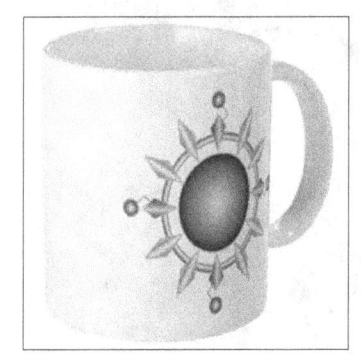
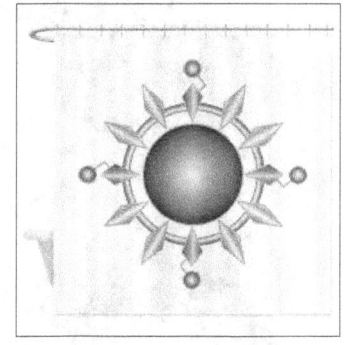
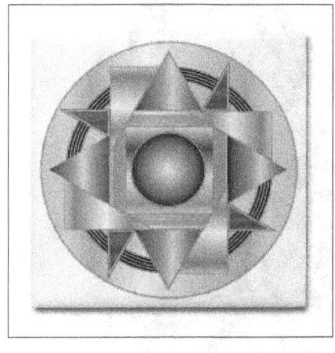
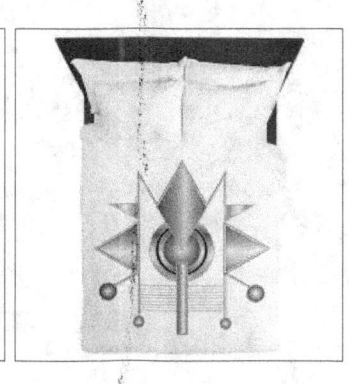
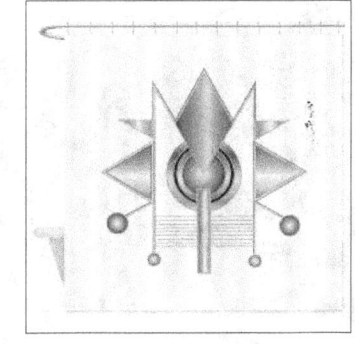
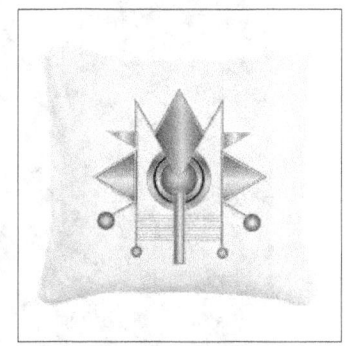
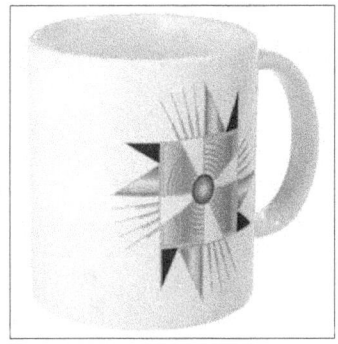
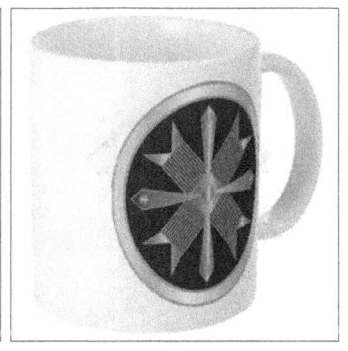
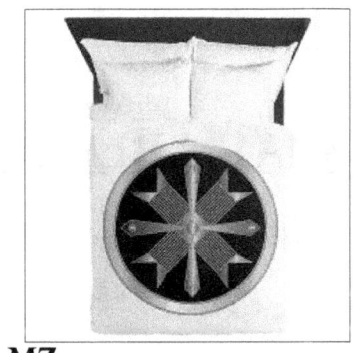
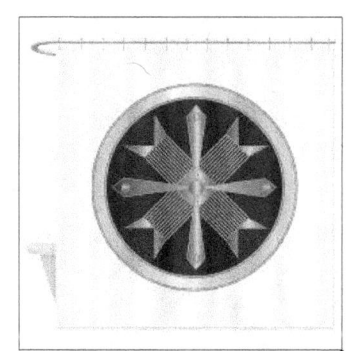

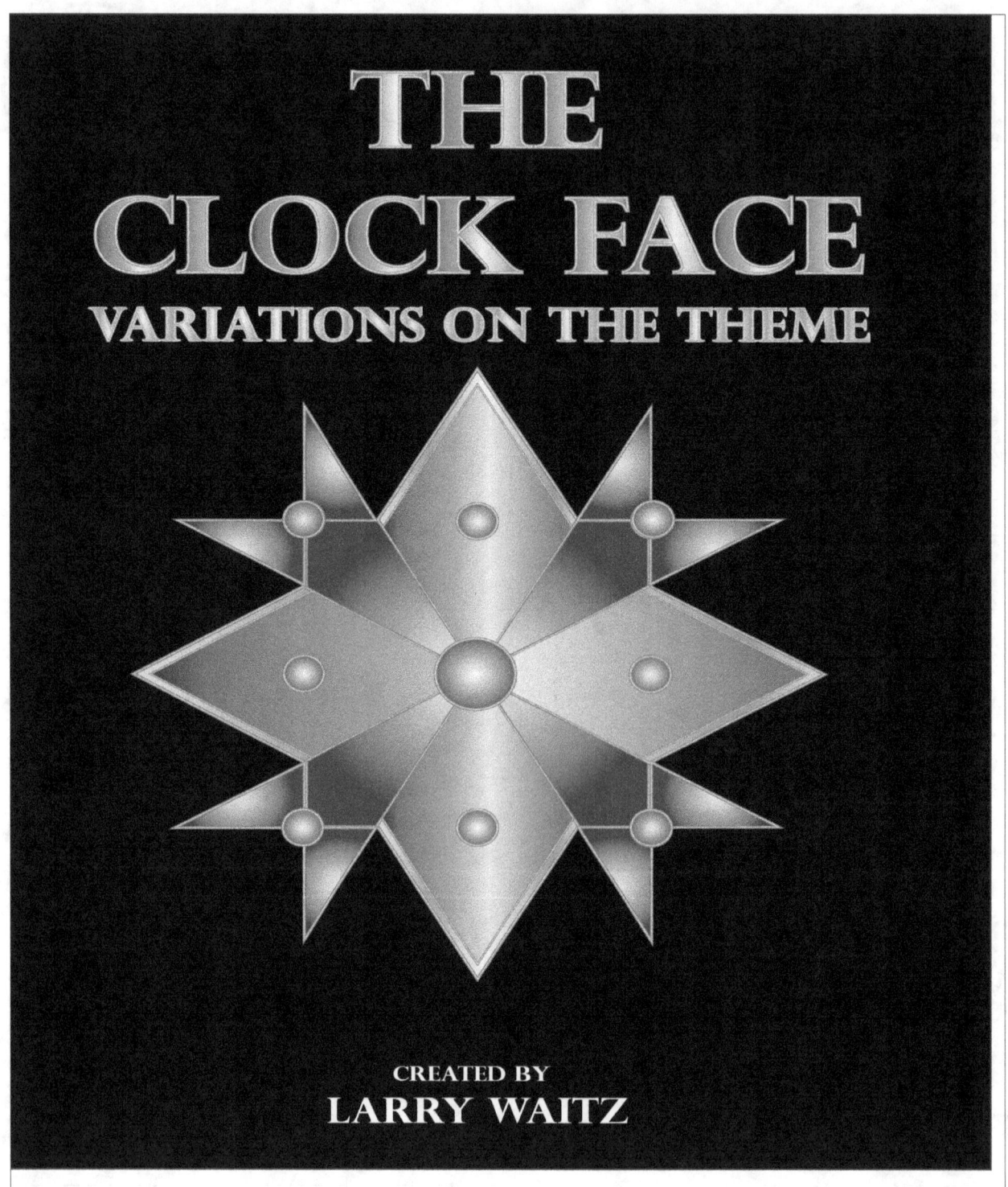

AVAILABLE ON AMAZON

SOLAR ADVOCATE

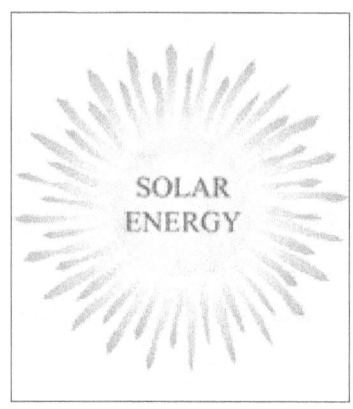

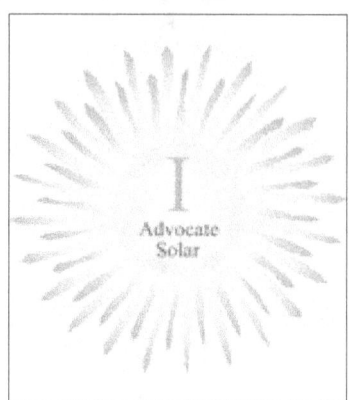

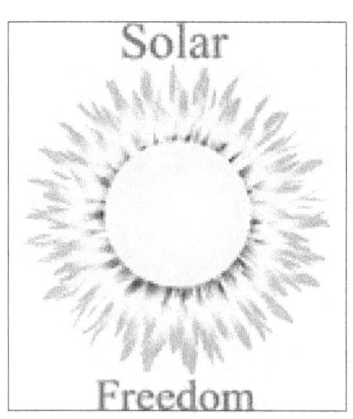

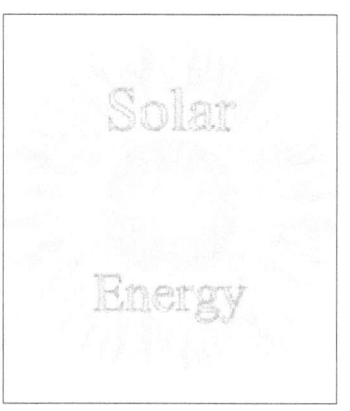

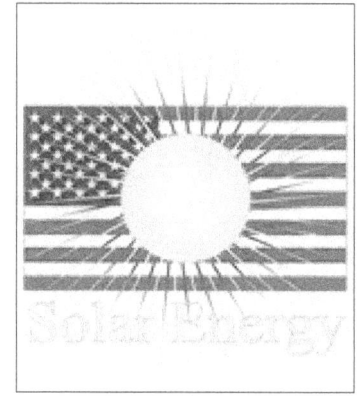

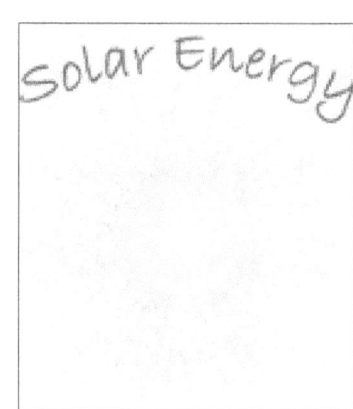

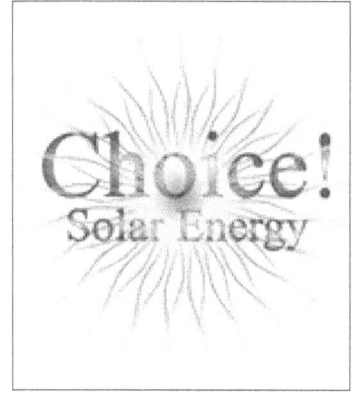

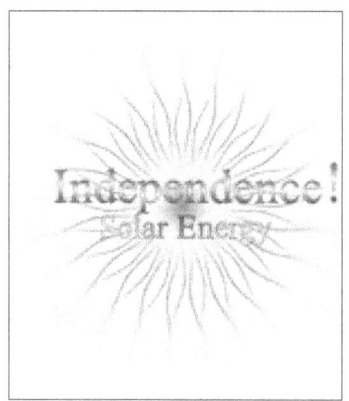

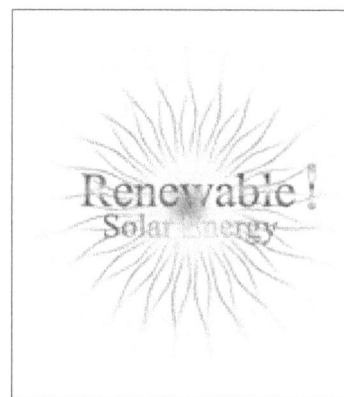

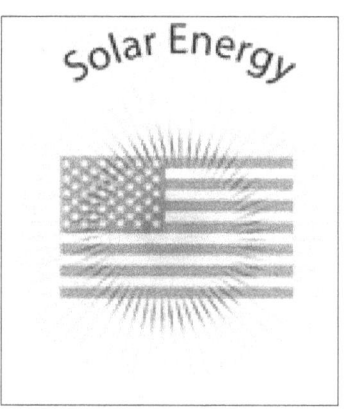

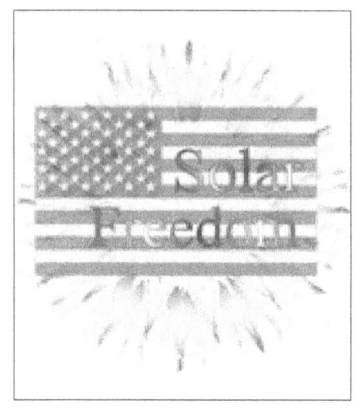

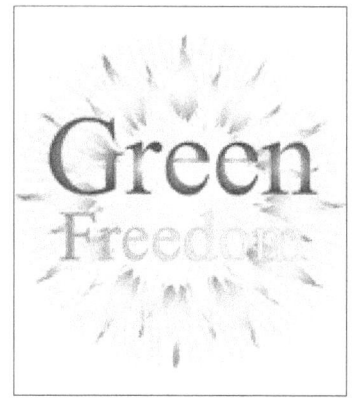

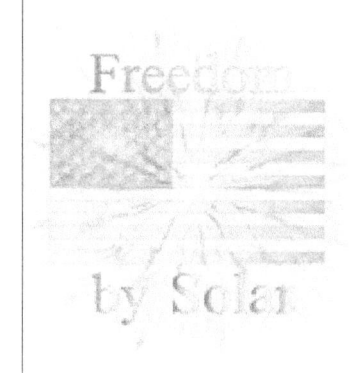

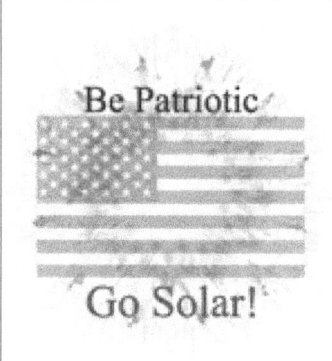

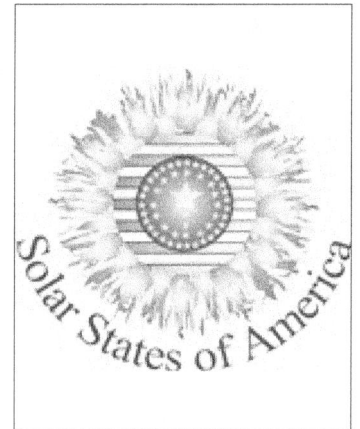

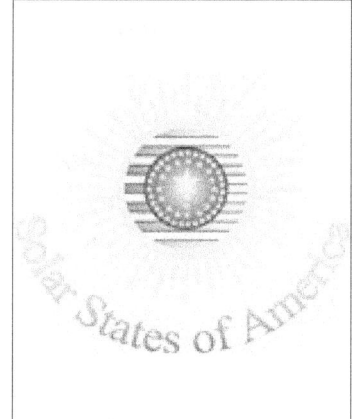

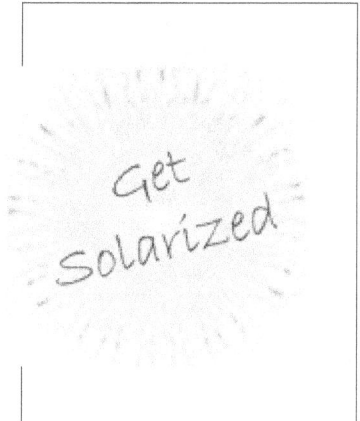

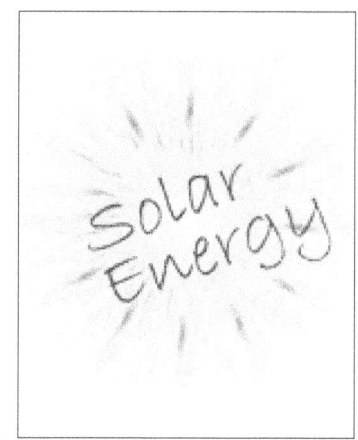

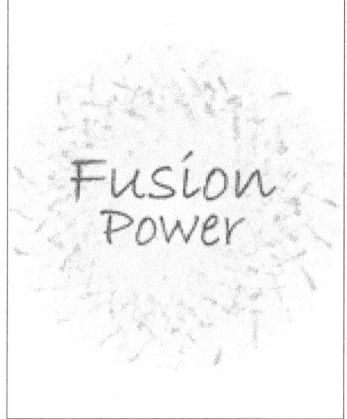

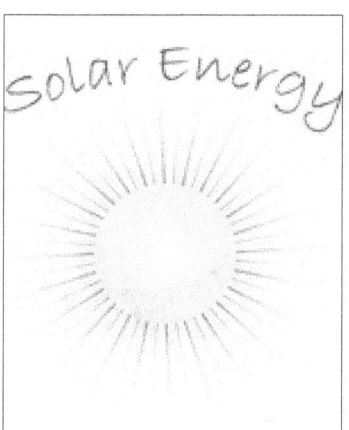

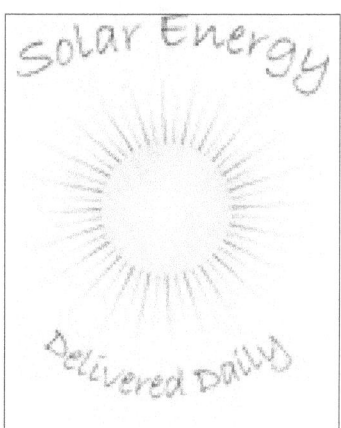

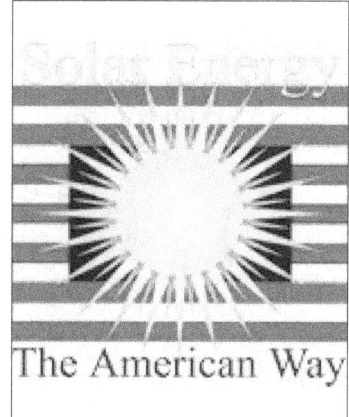

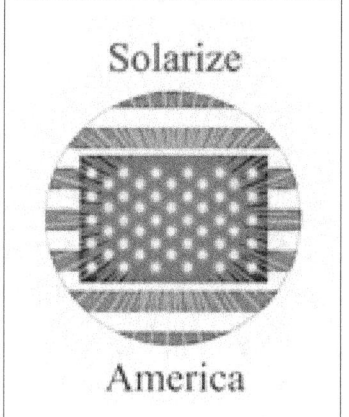

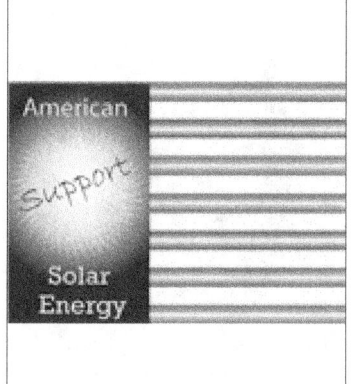

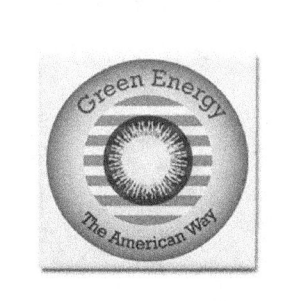

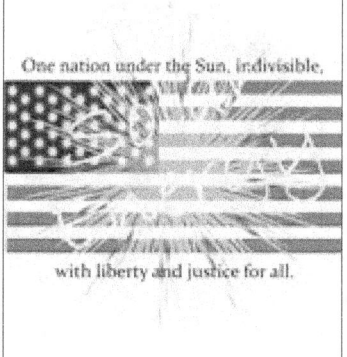

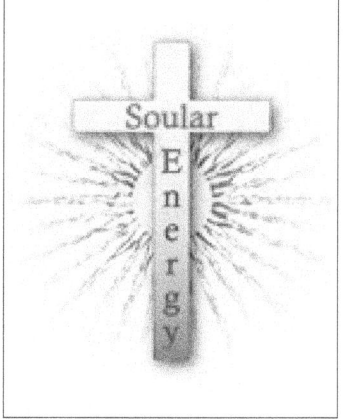

M7

45

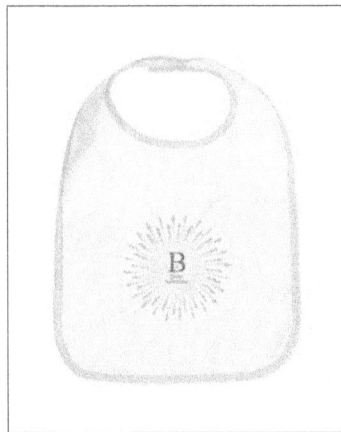
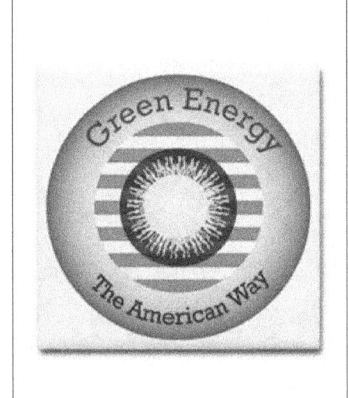
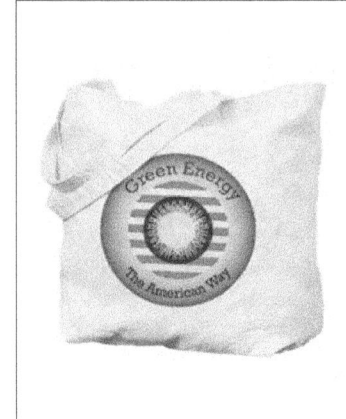

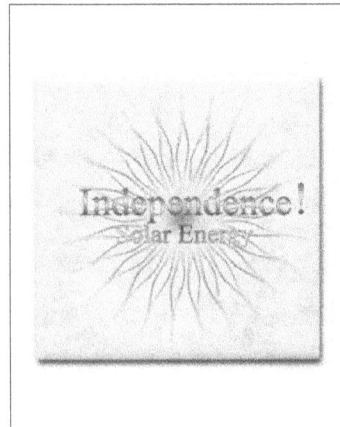
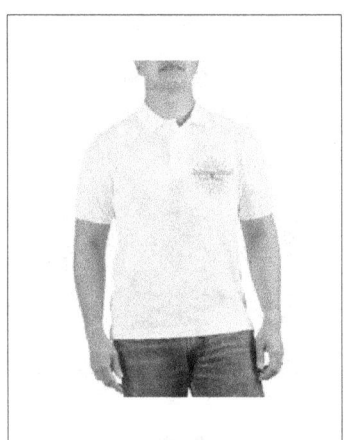
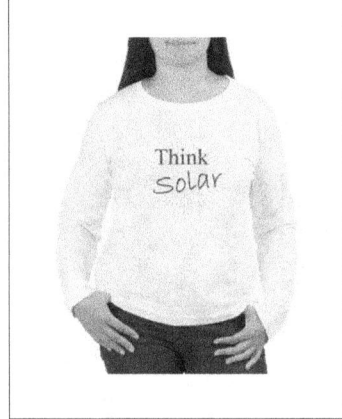
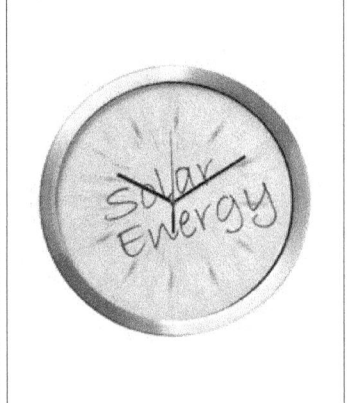
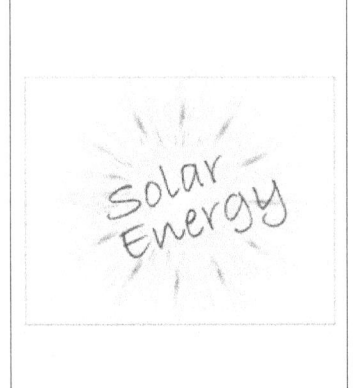
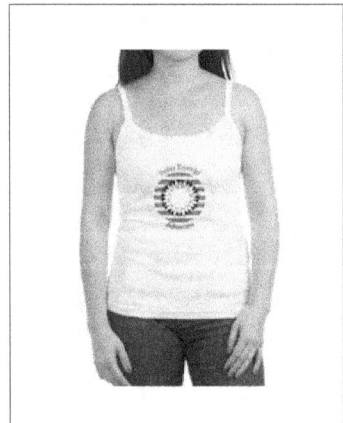
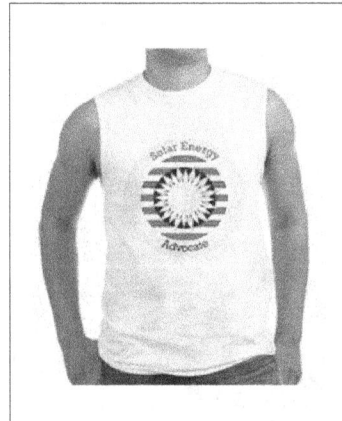
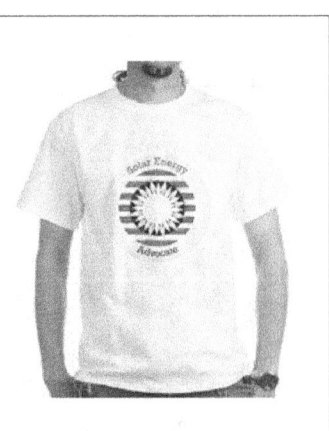
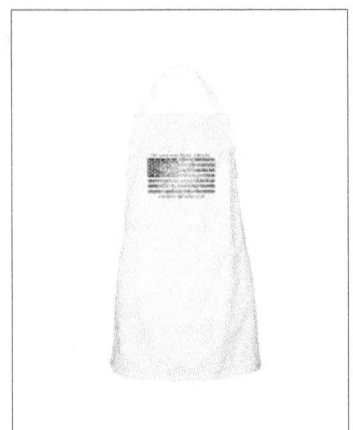
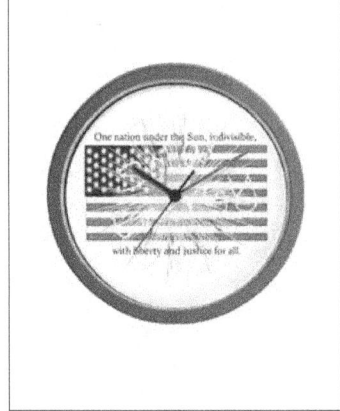
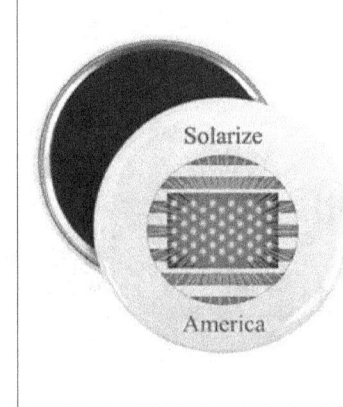
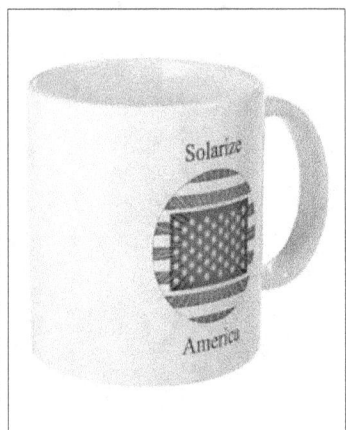

THE SOLAR ADVOCATE

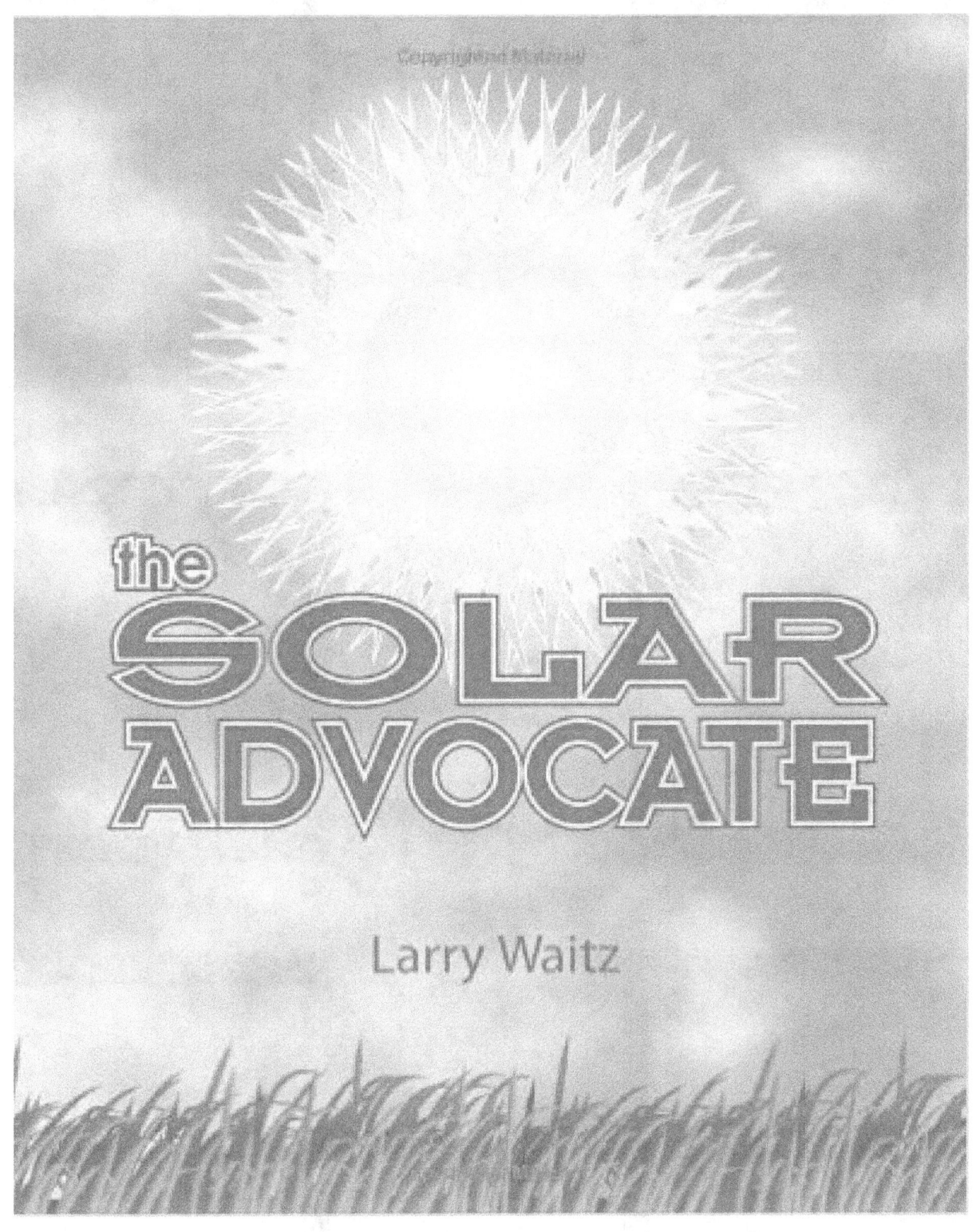

AVAILABLE ON AMAZON

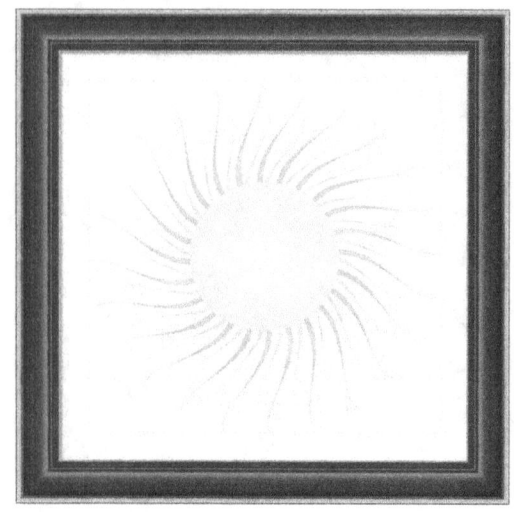

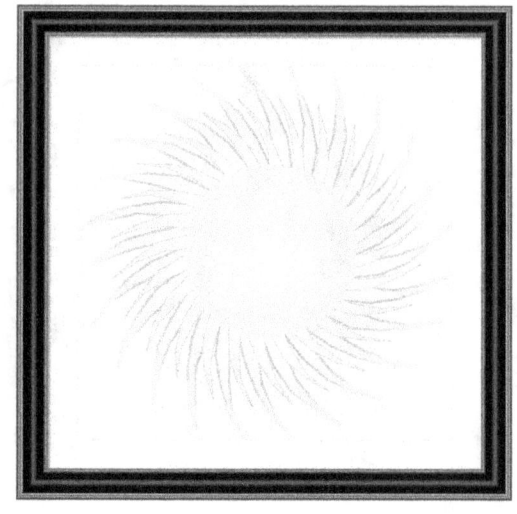

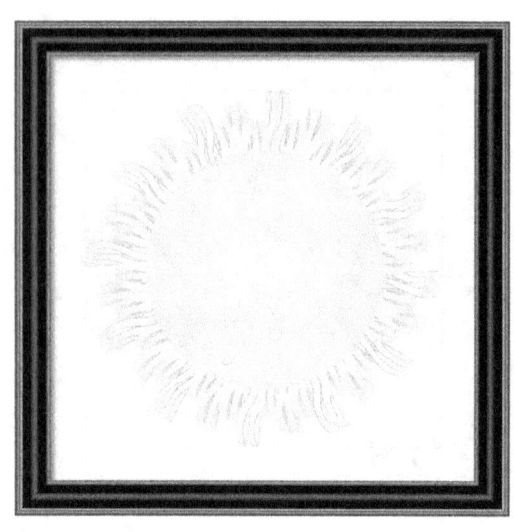

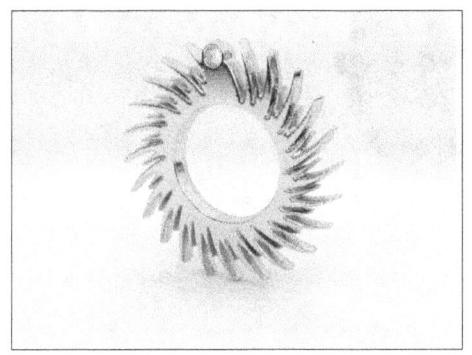

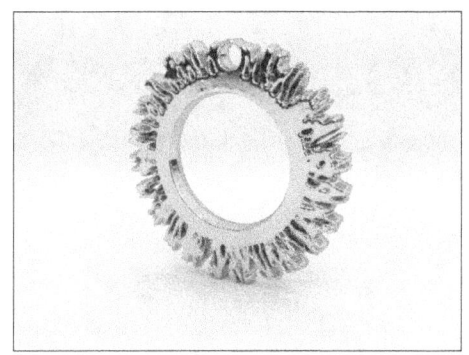

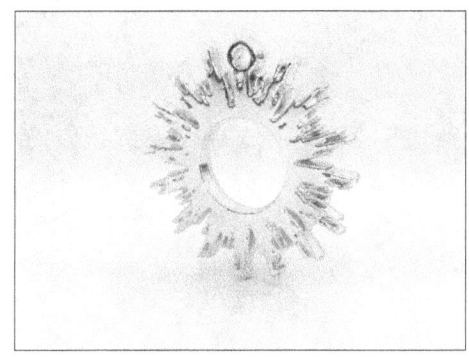

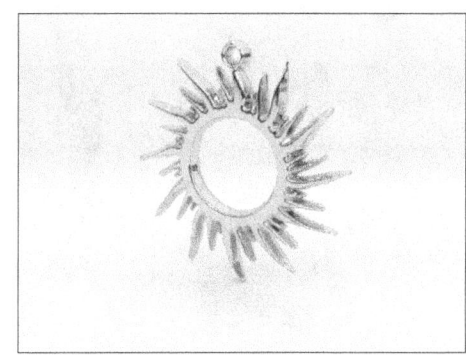

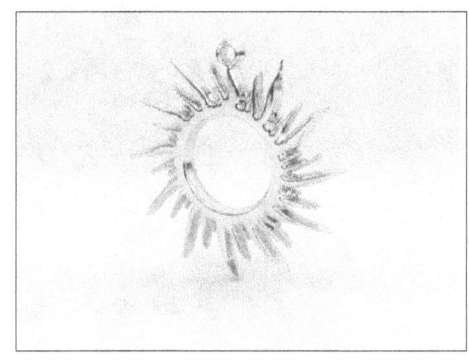

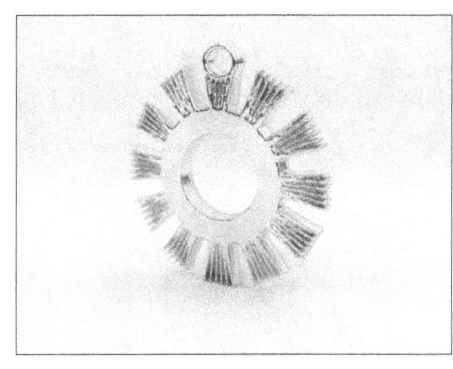

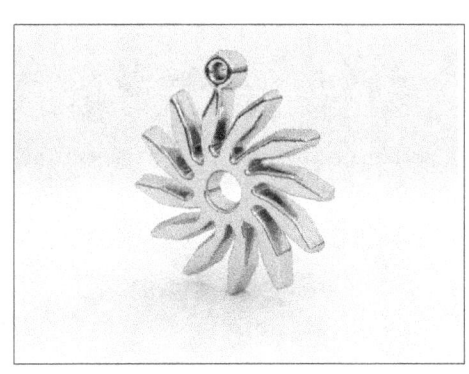

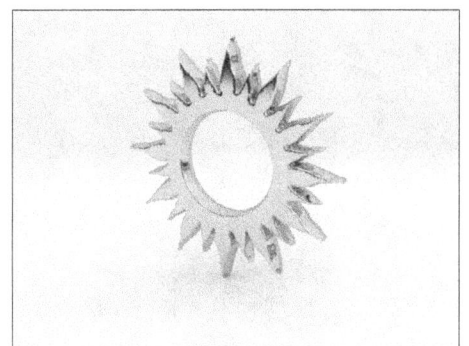

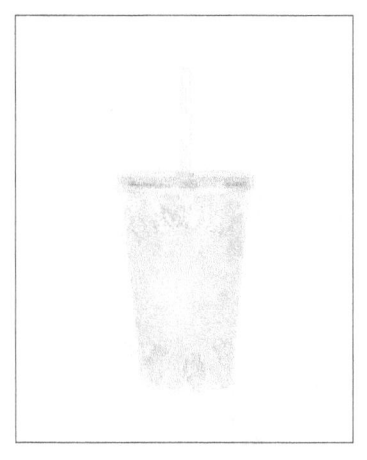 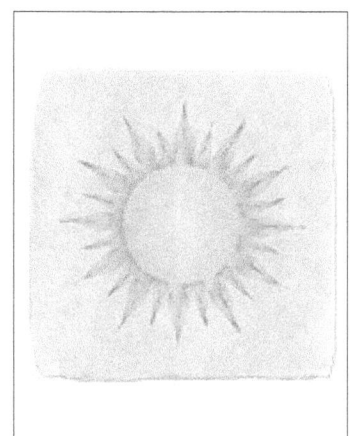 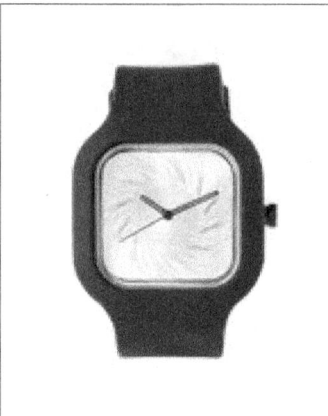 

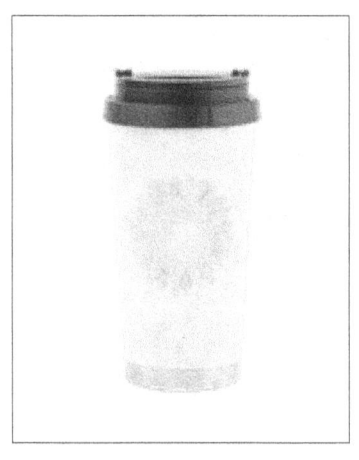 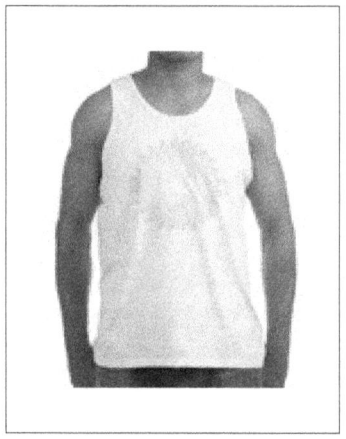 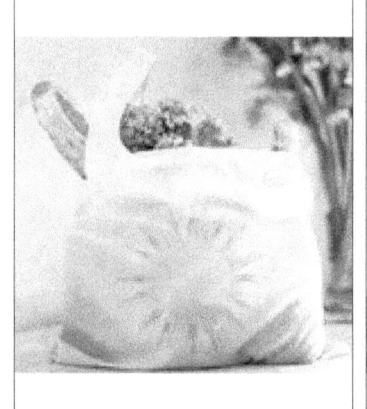 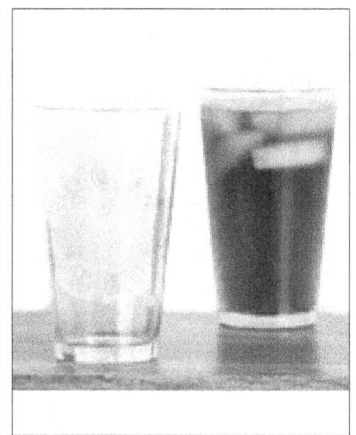

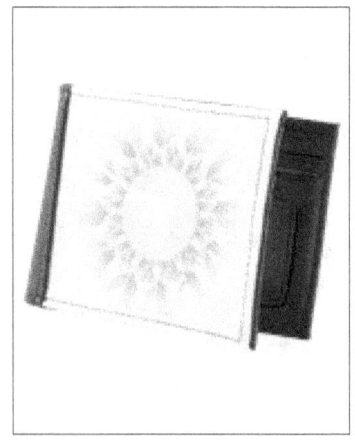 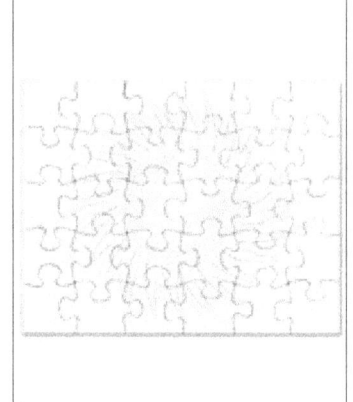  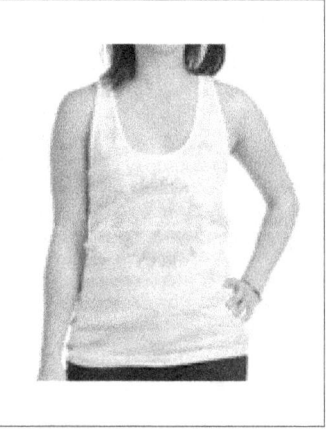

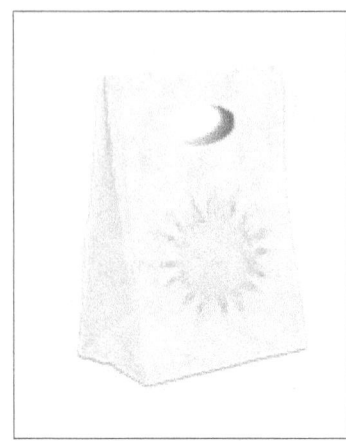 

GEOGEMS 19

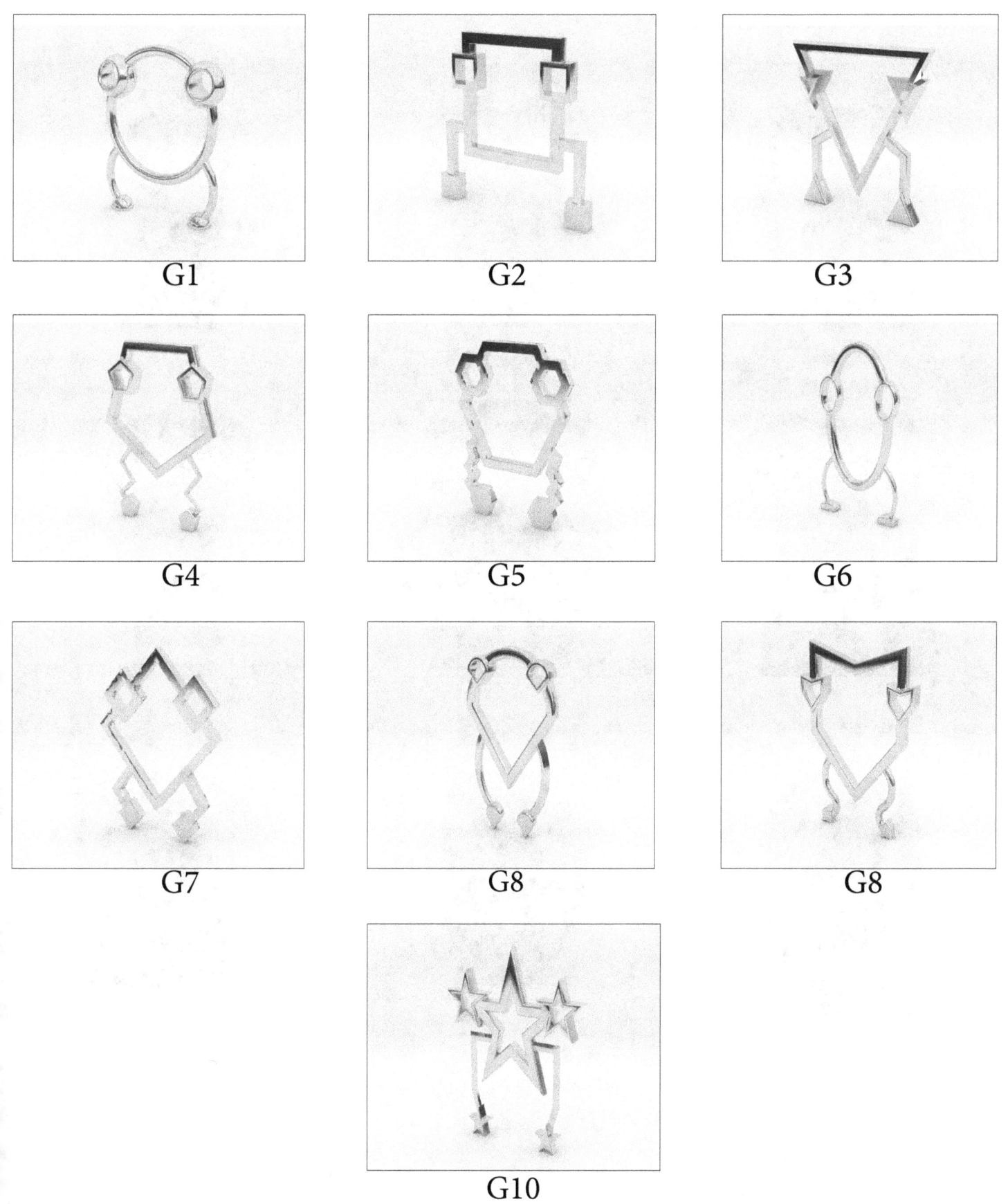

G1

G2

G3

G4

G5

G6

G7

G8

G8

G10

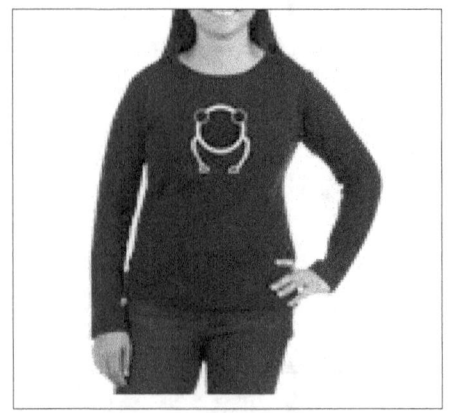 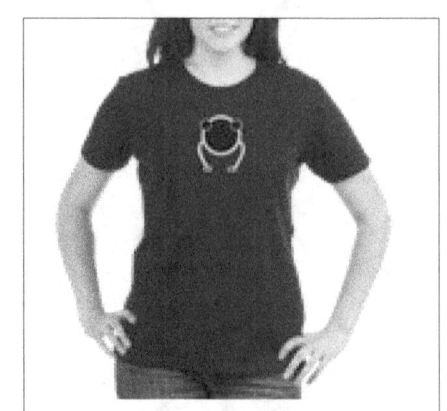 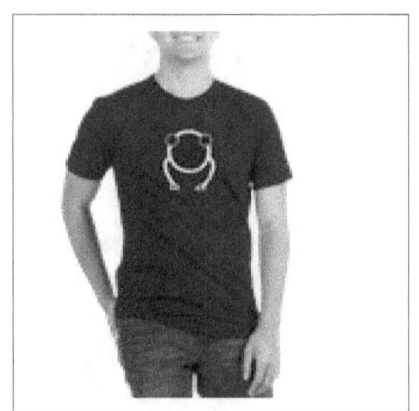

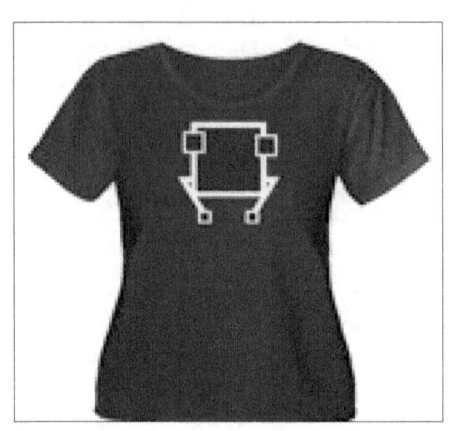 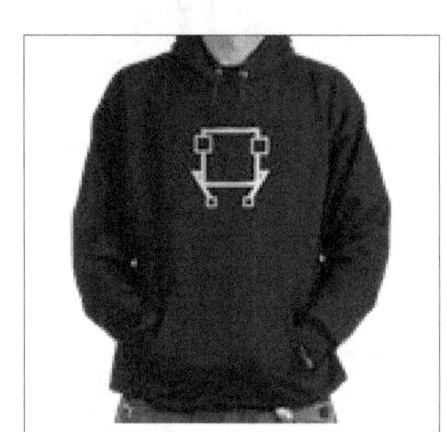 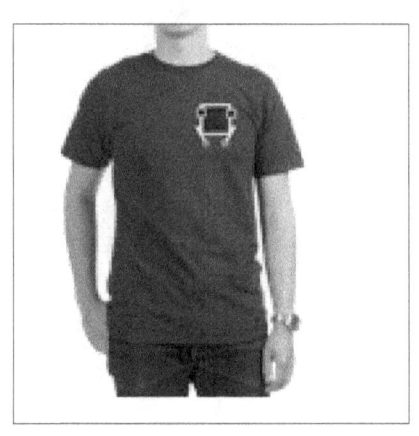

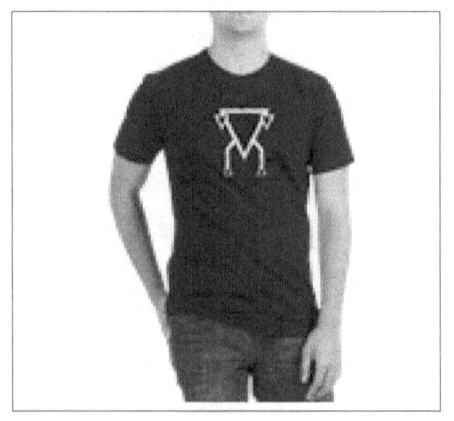 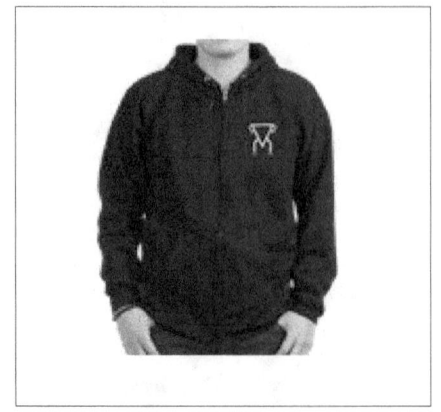 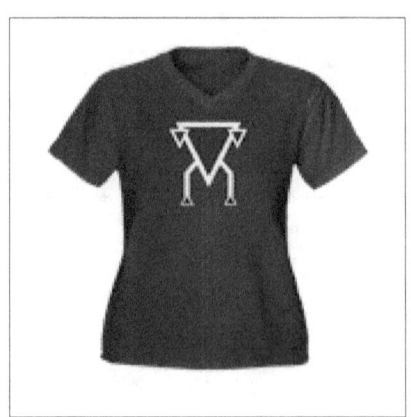

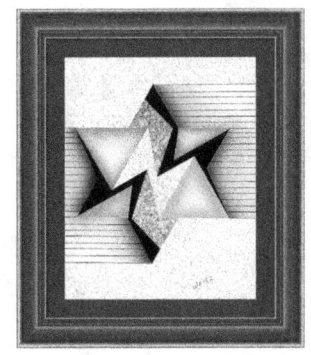

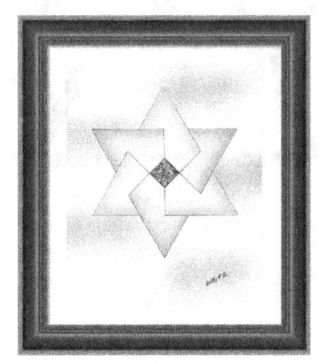

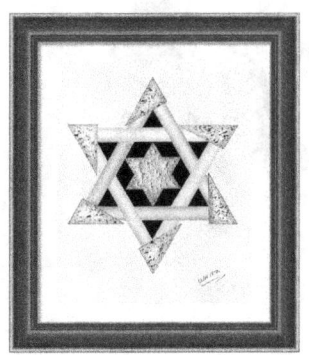

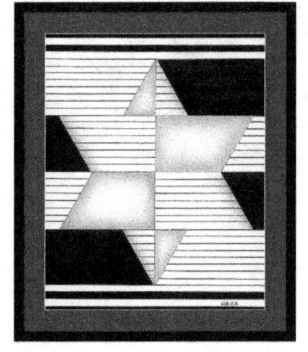

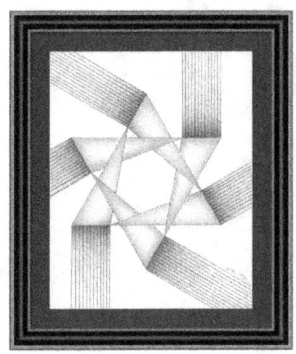

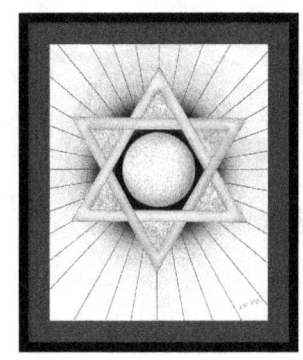

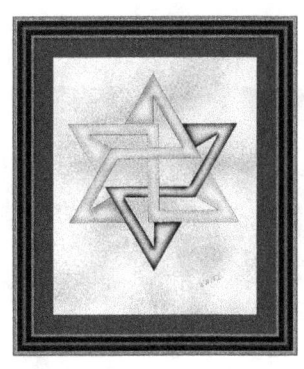

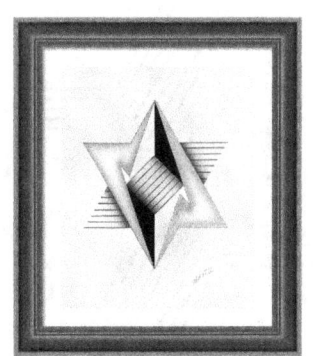

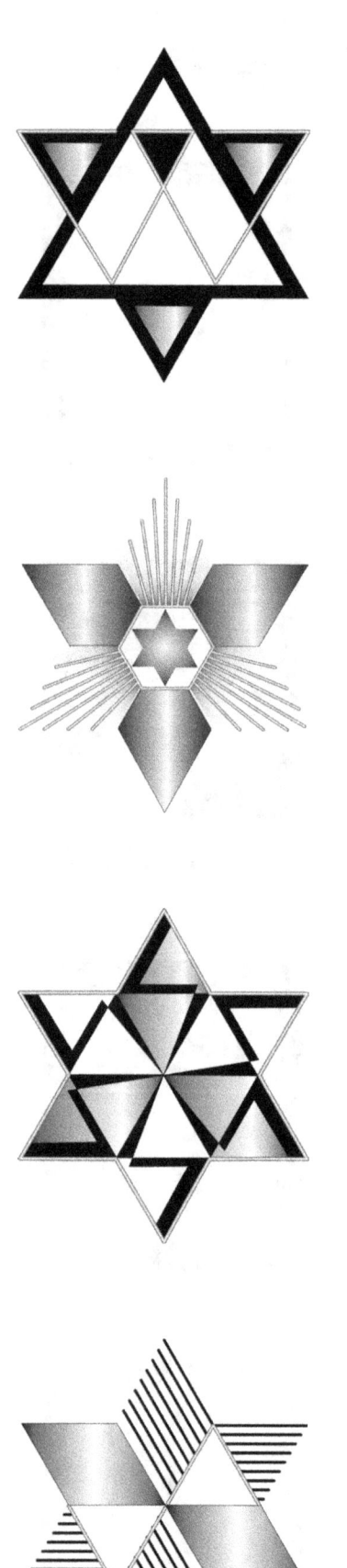
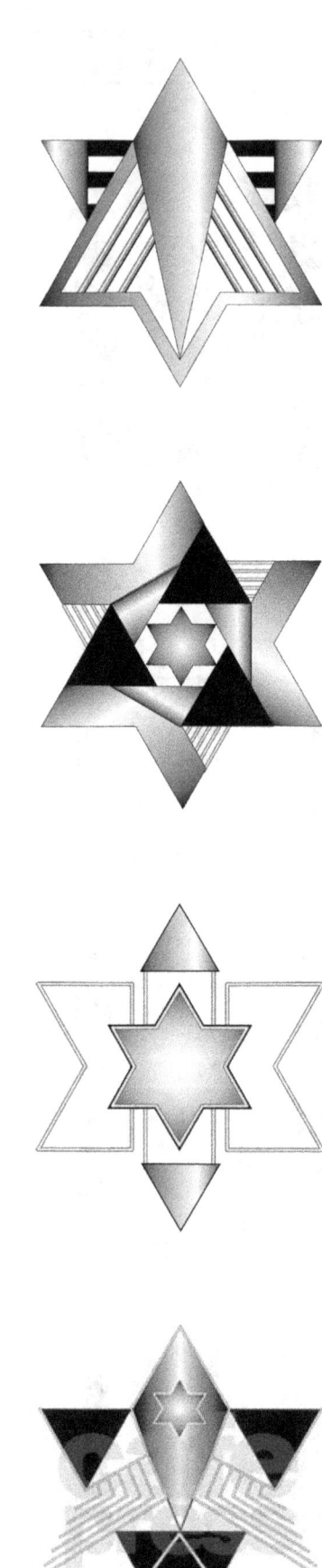

M7

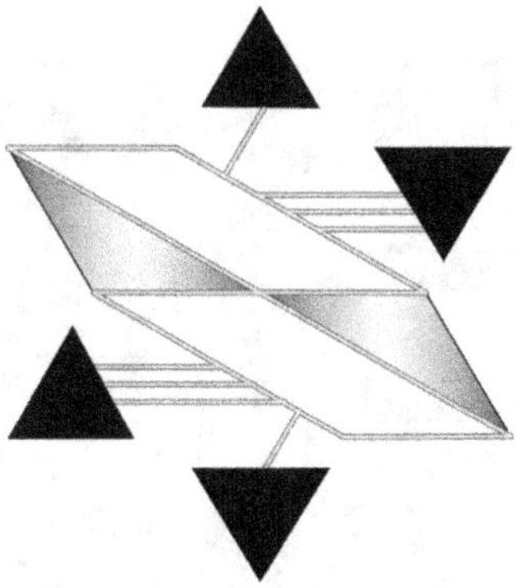

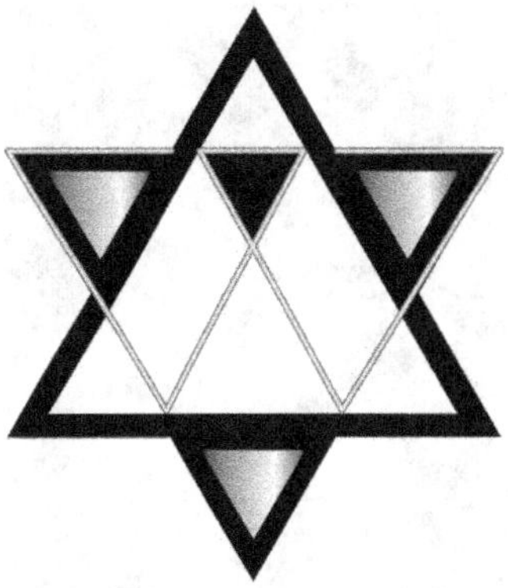

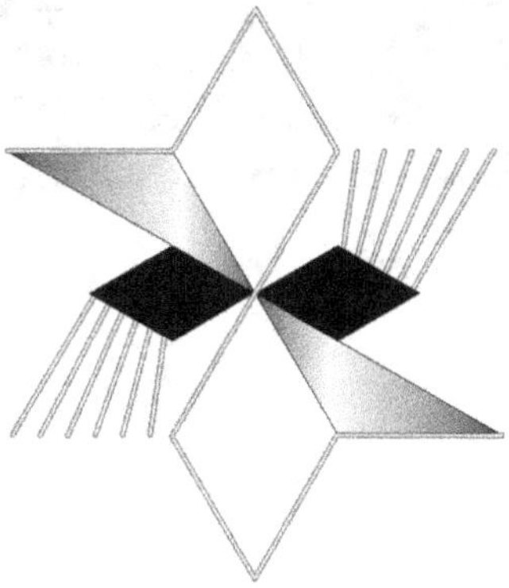

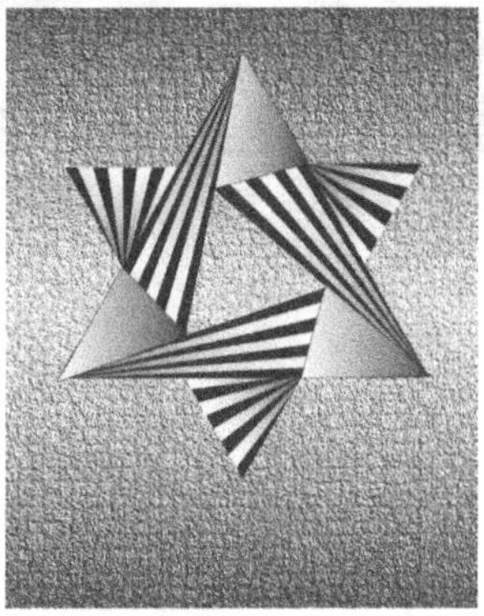

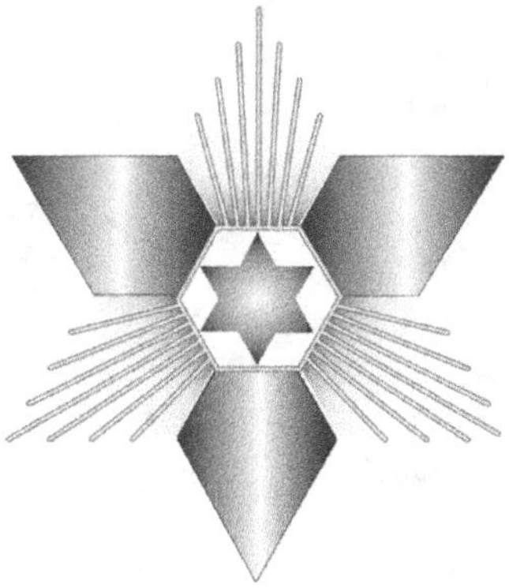

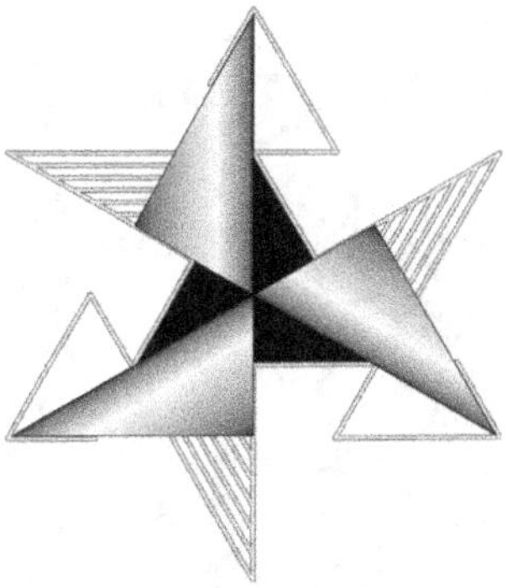

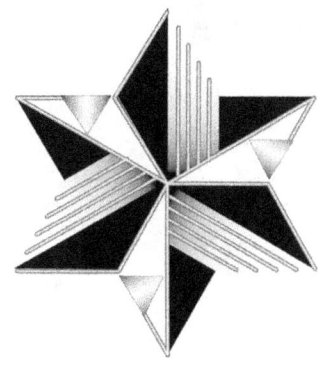

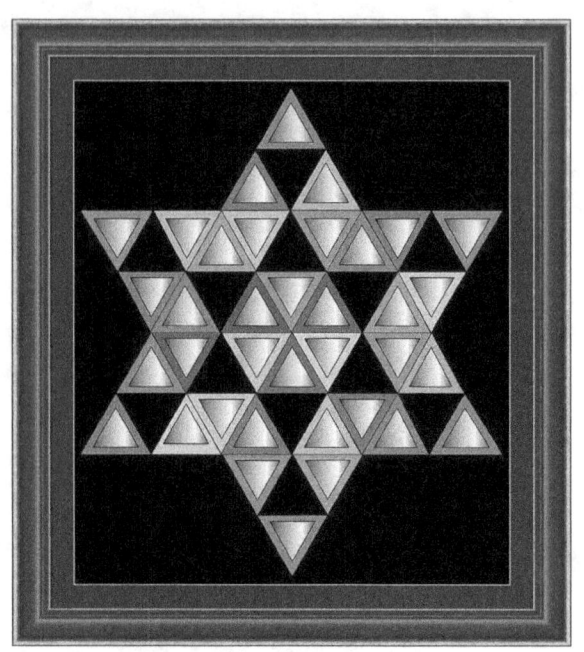

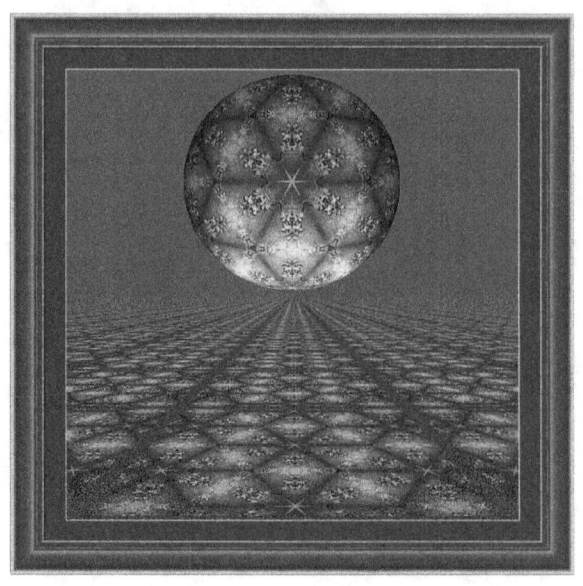

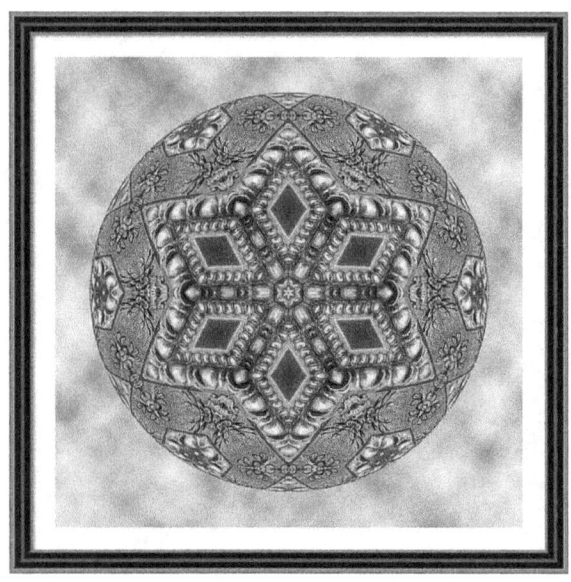

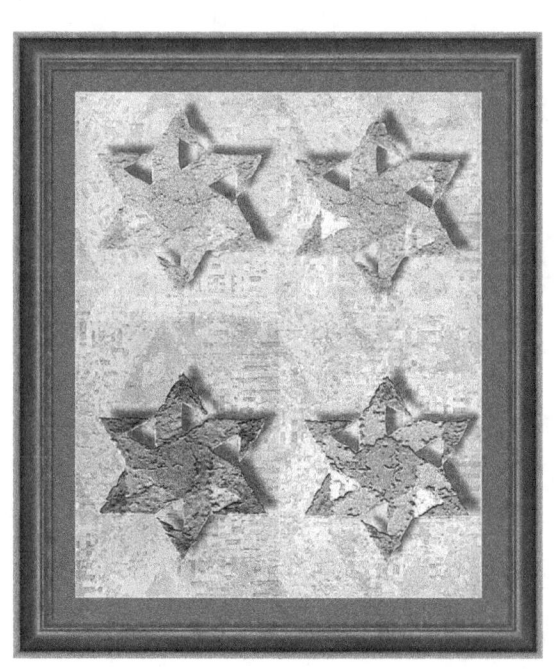

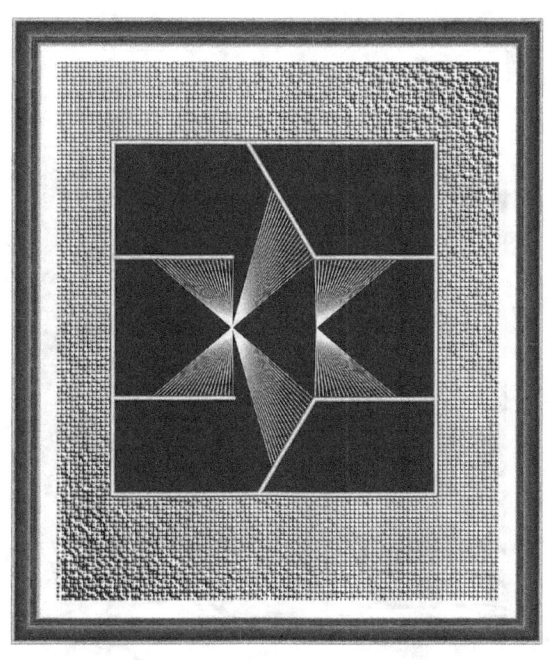

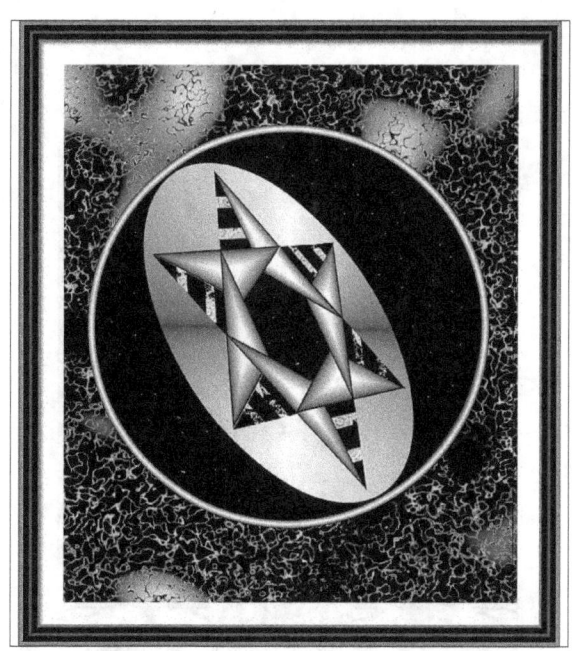

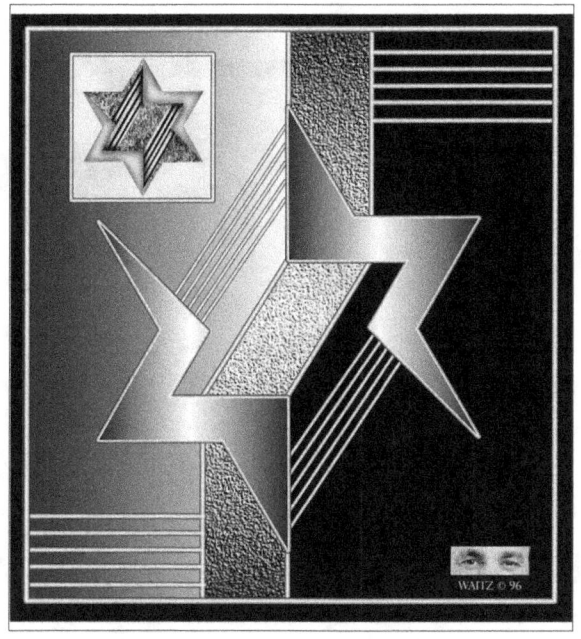

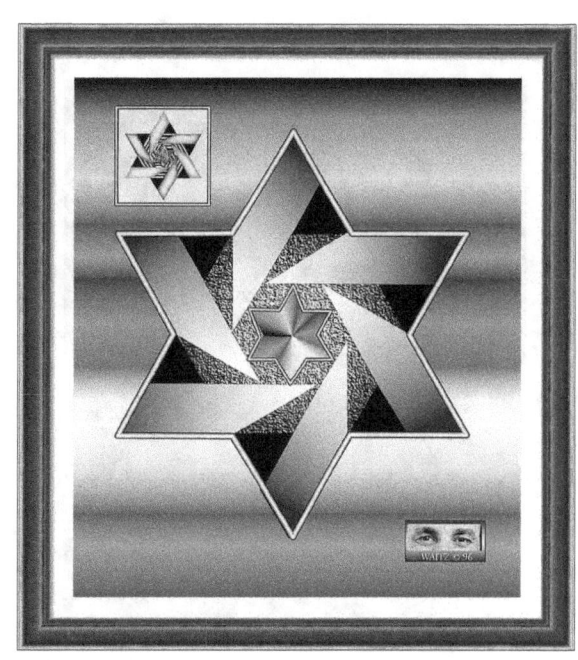

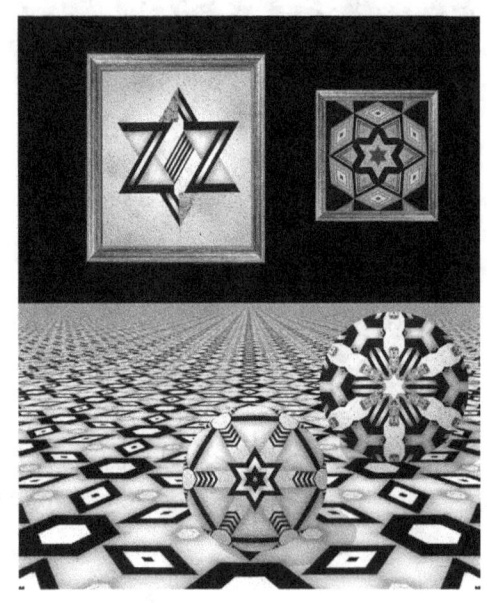

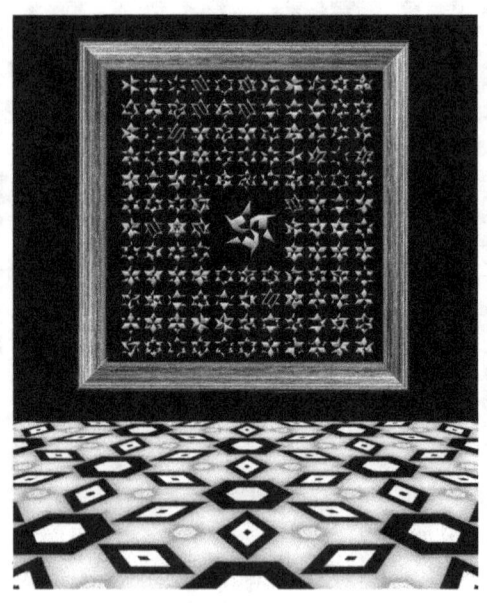

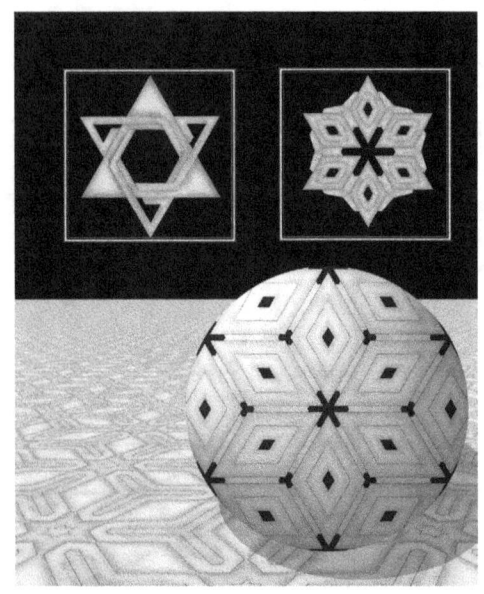

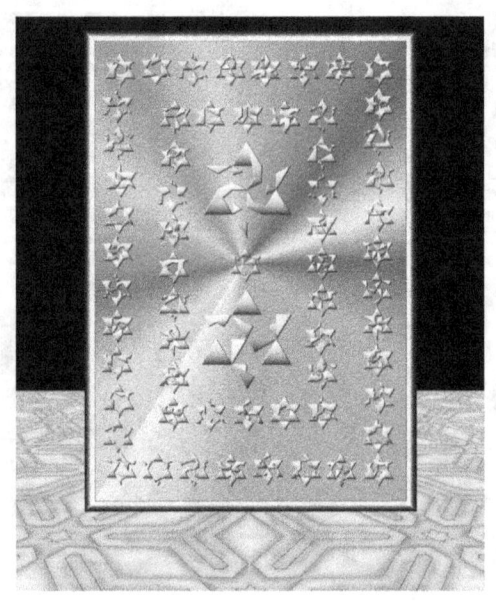

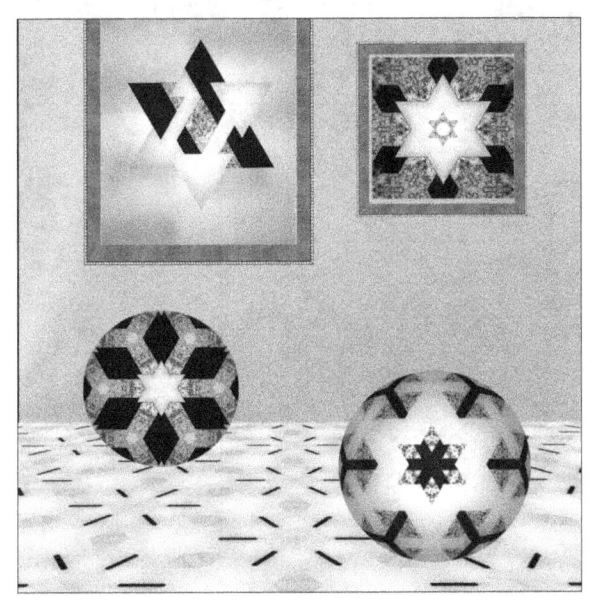

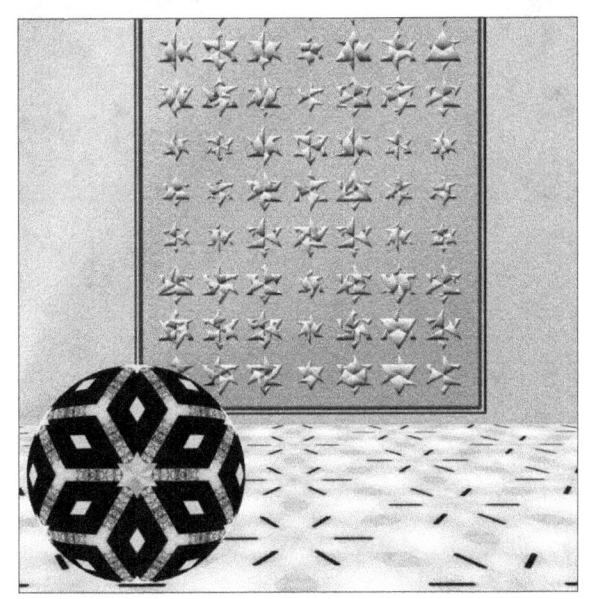

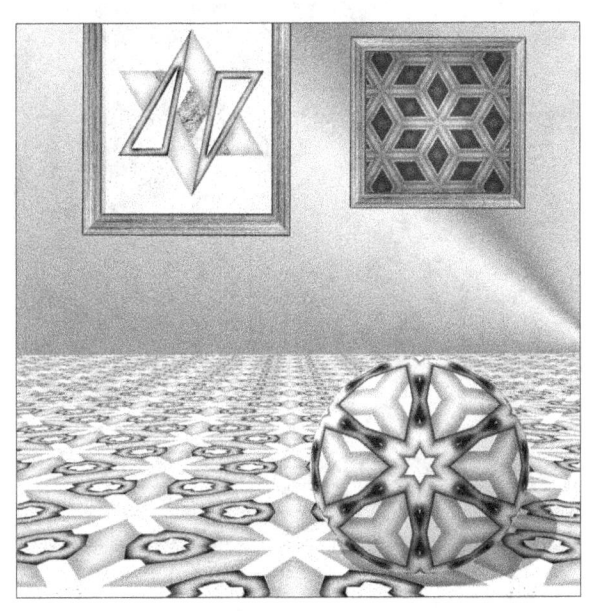

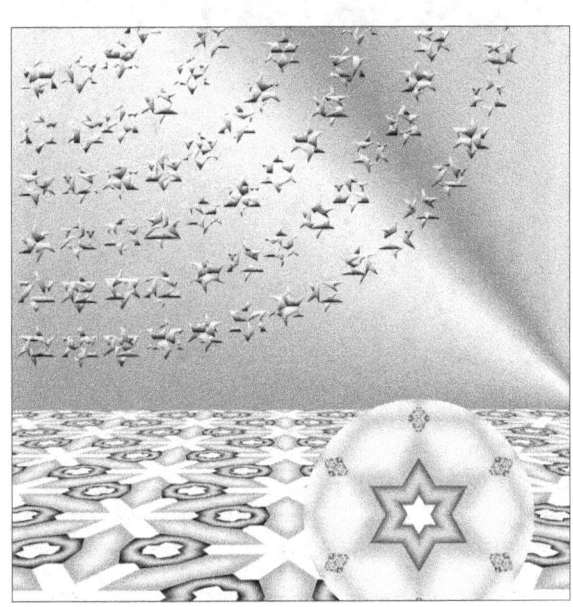

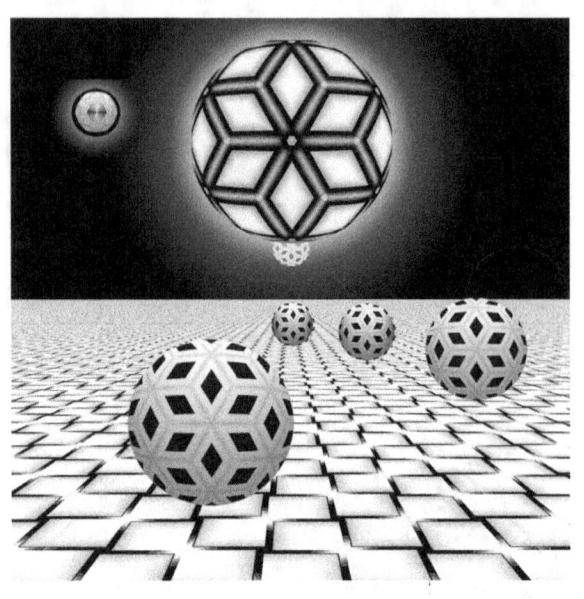 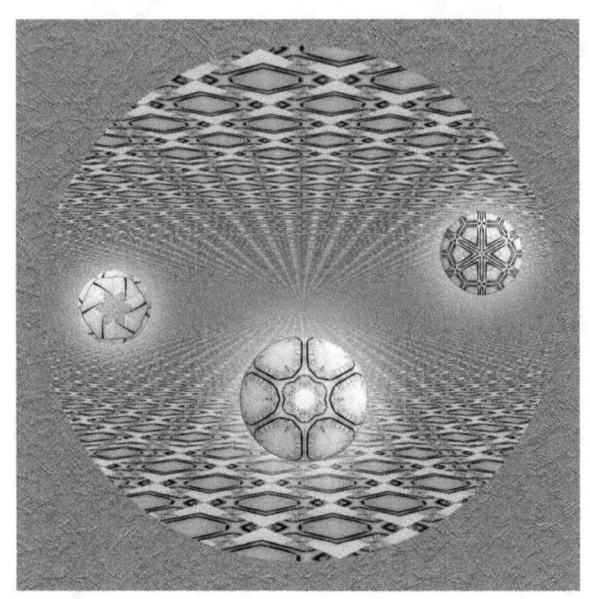

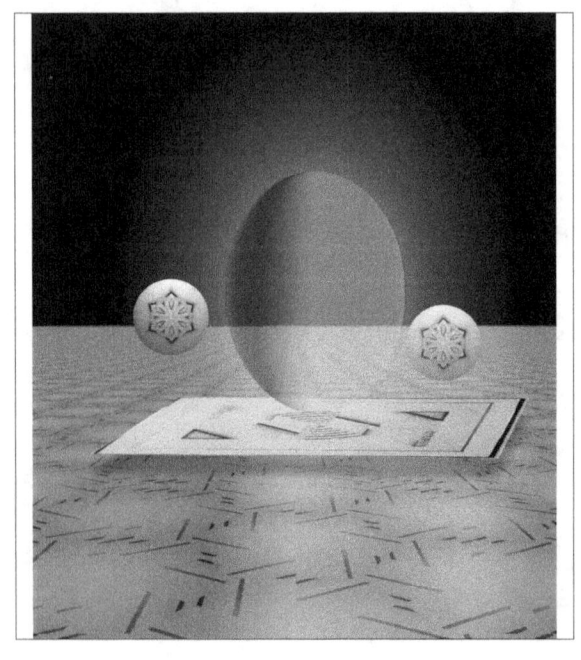 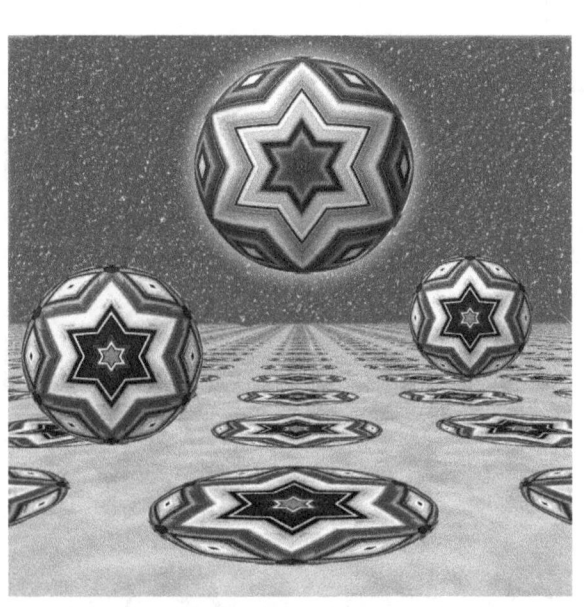

M7

STAR OF DAVID - ROUND

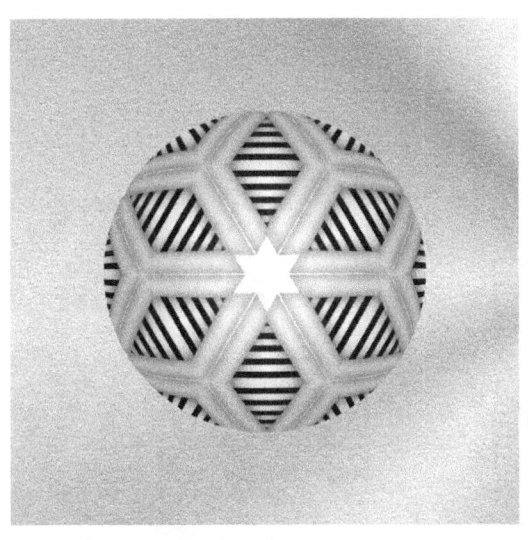

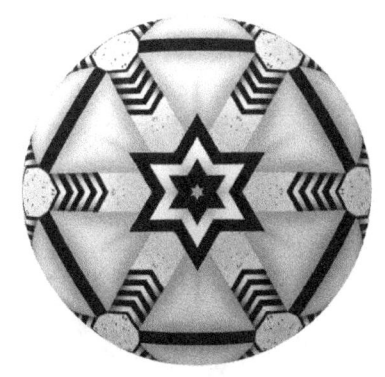

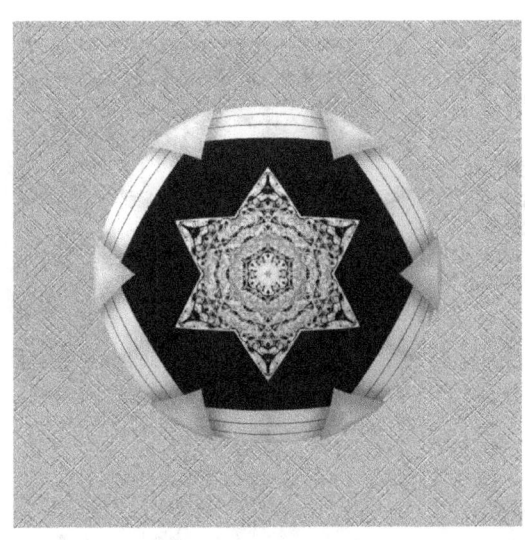

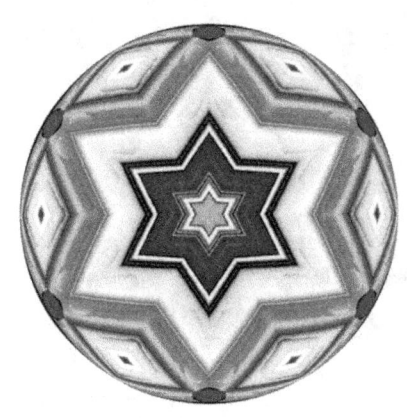

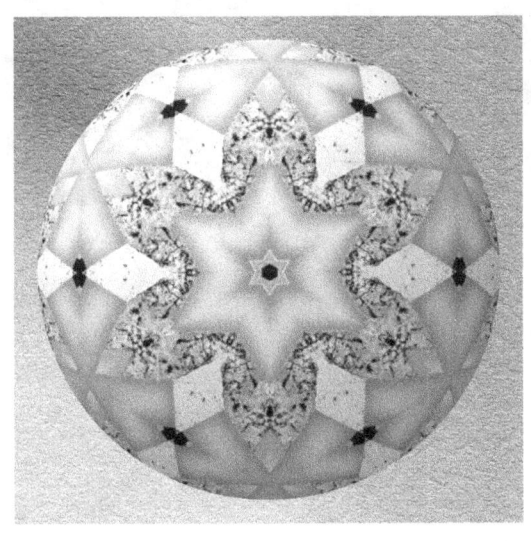

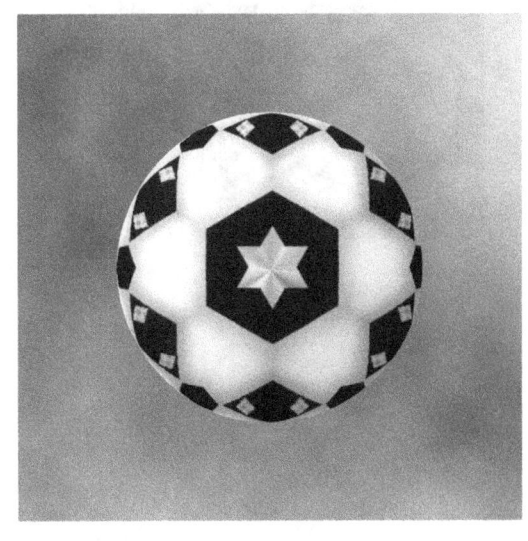

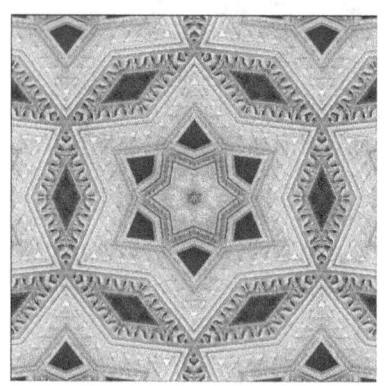
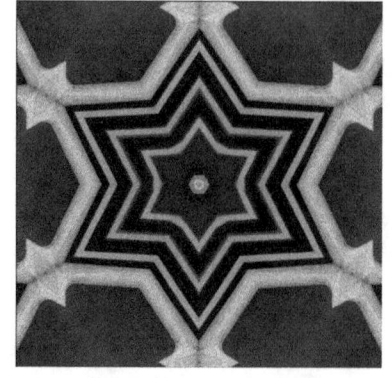
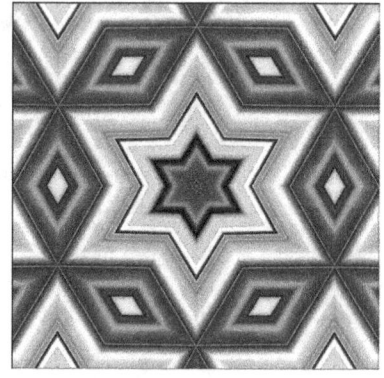

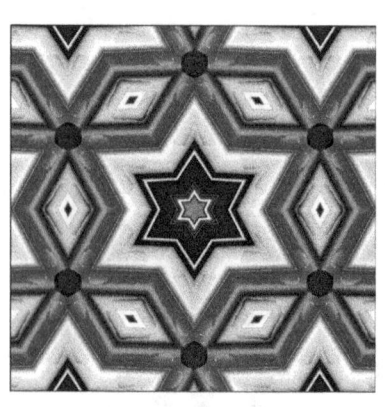
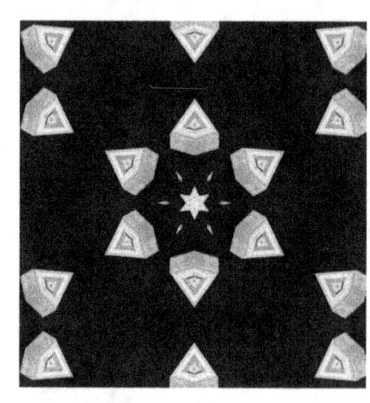
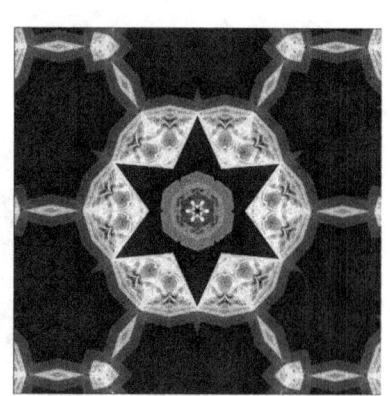

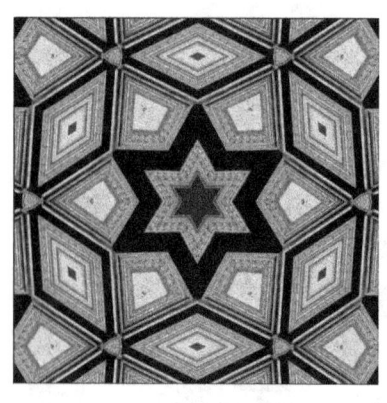
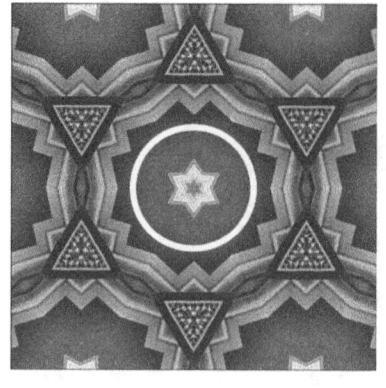
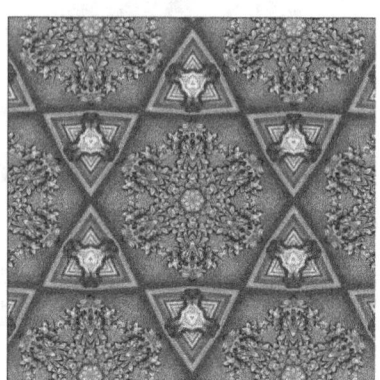

STAR OF DAVID JEWELRY

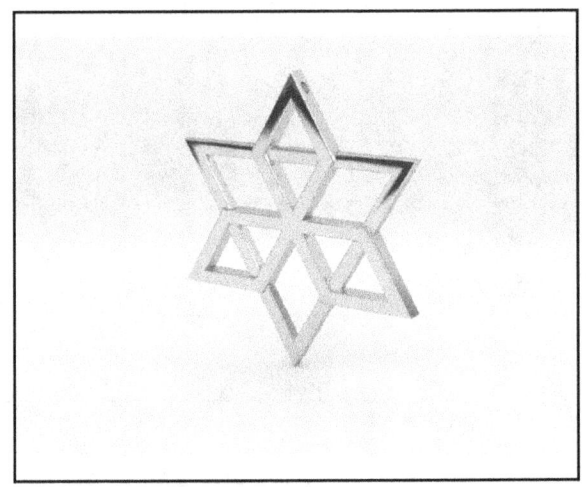

SOD-2

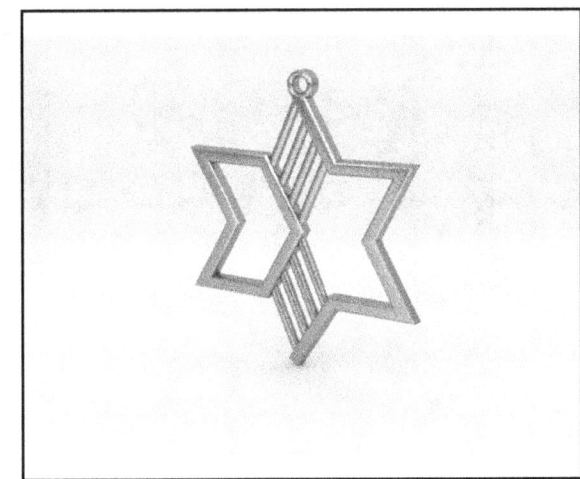

SOD-4

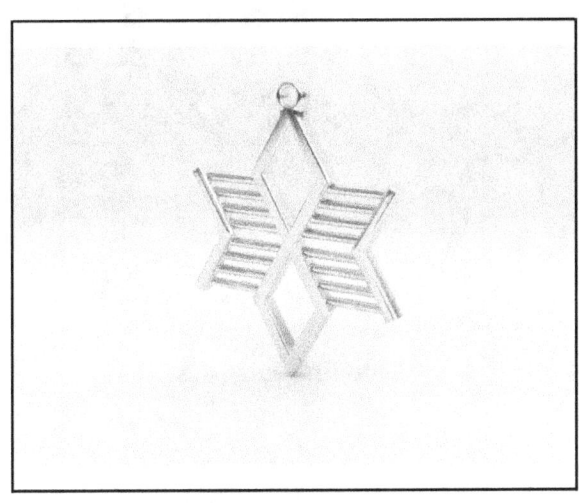

SOD-7

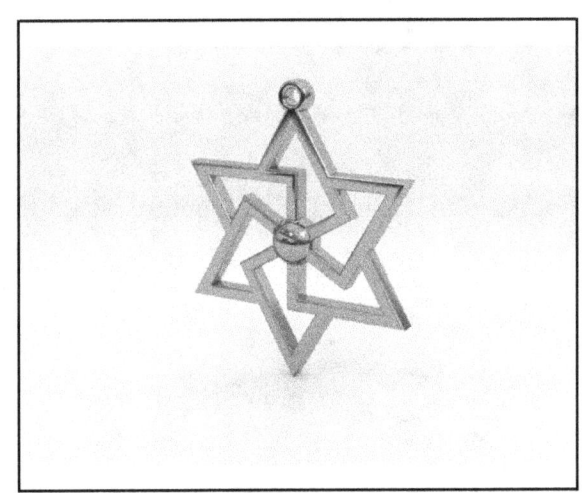

SOD-11

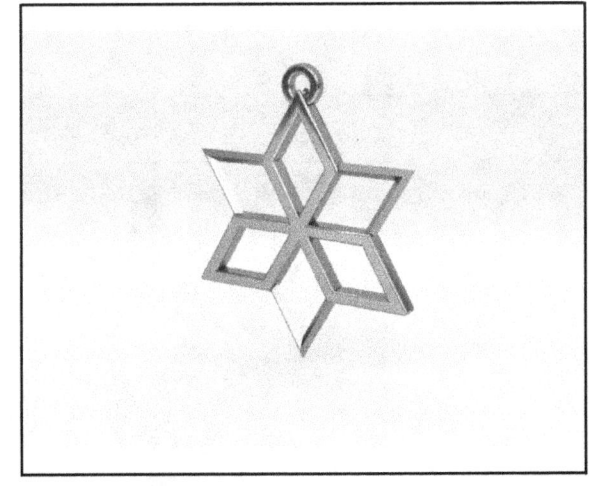

SOD-9

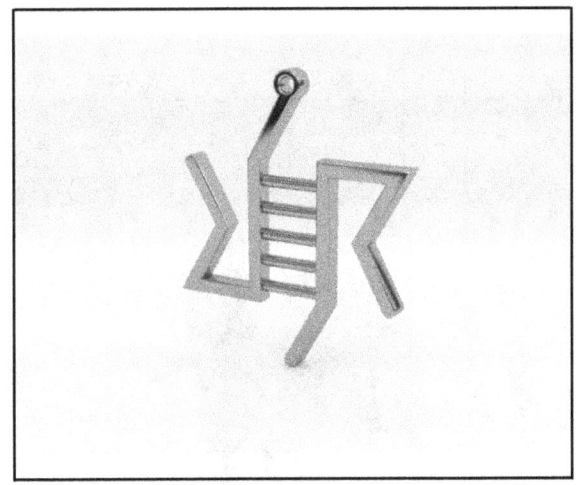

SOD-16

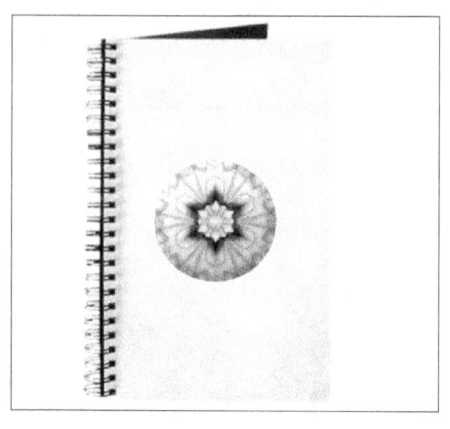
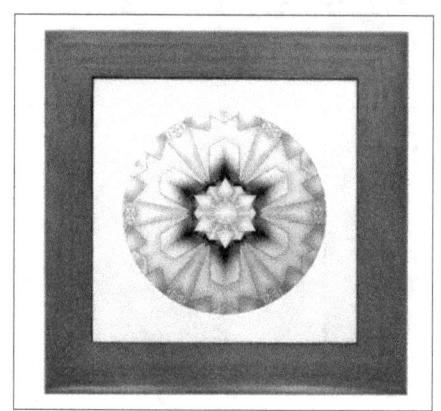
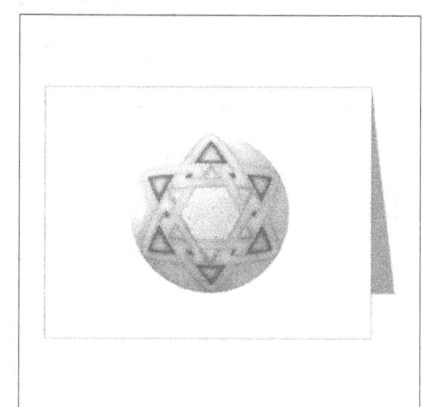
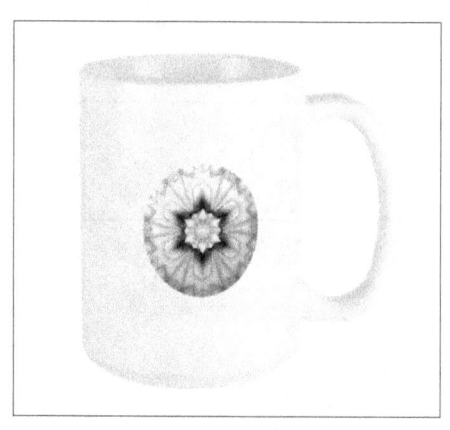
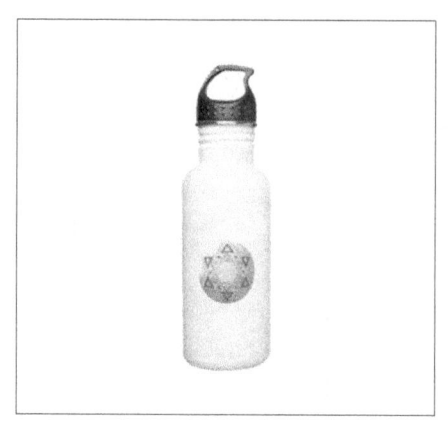
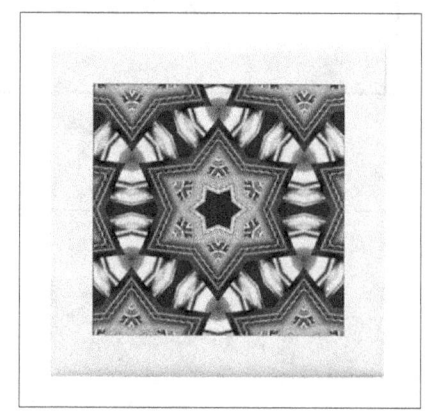
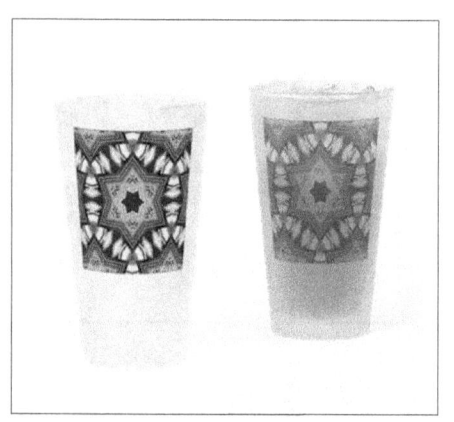
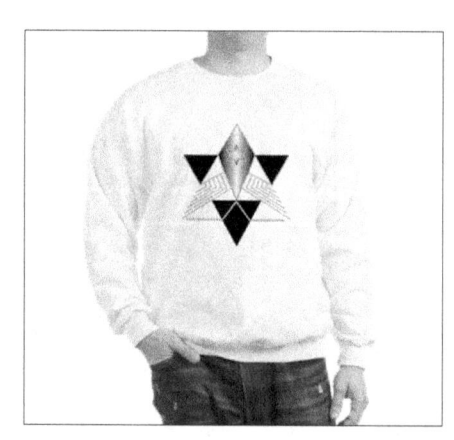
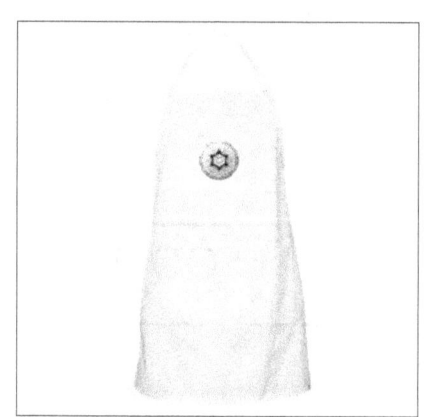
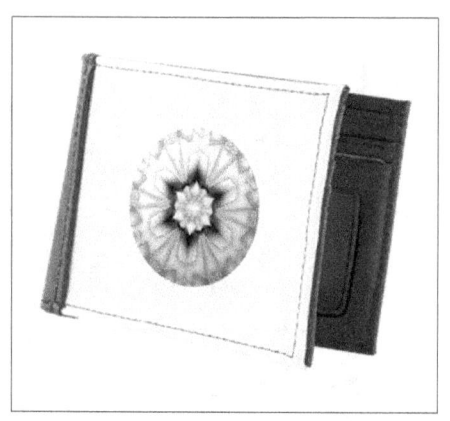
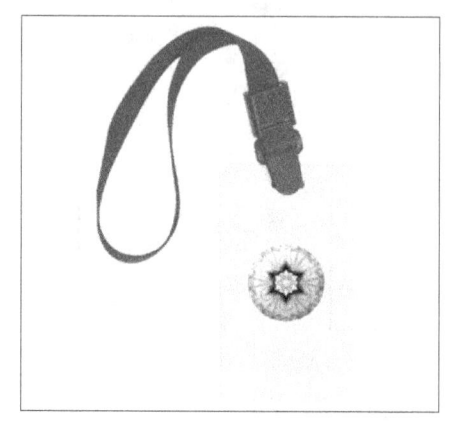
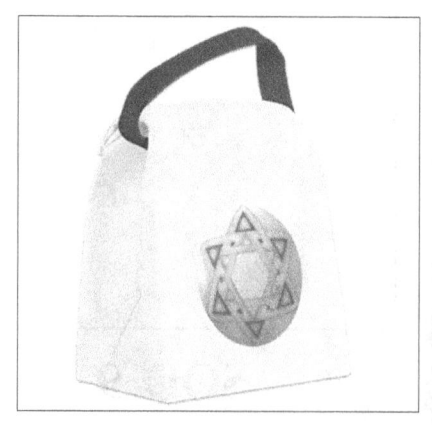

STAR OF DAVID - BOOK

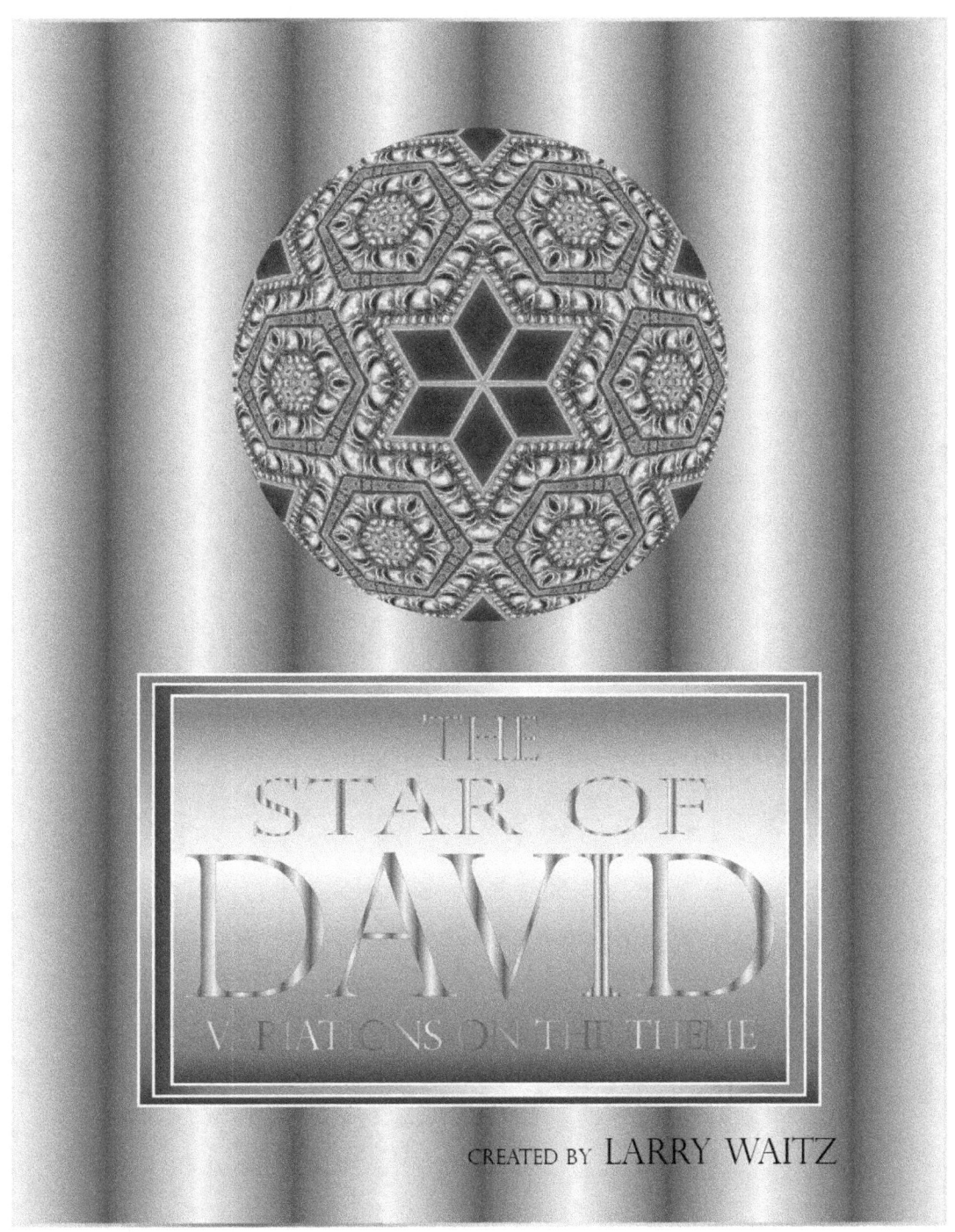

AVAILABLE ON AMAZON

2 PART COFFEE CUPS

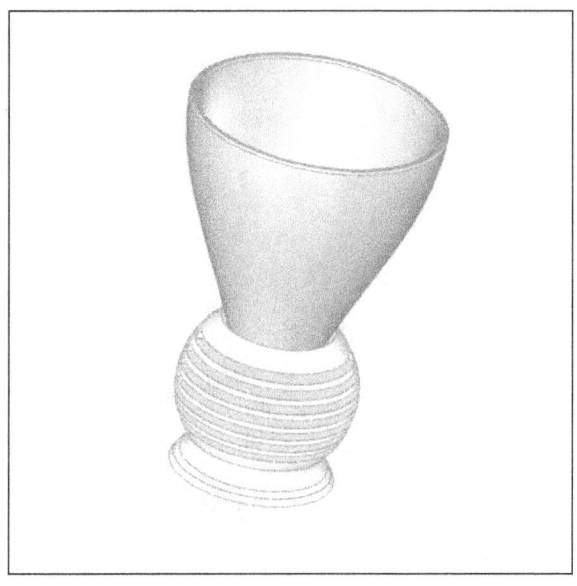

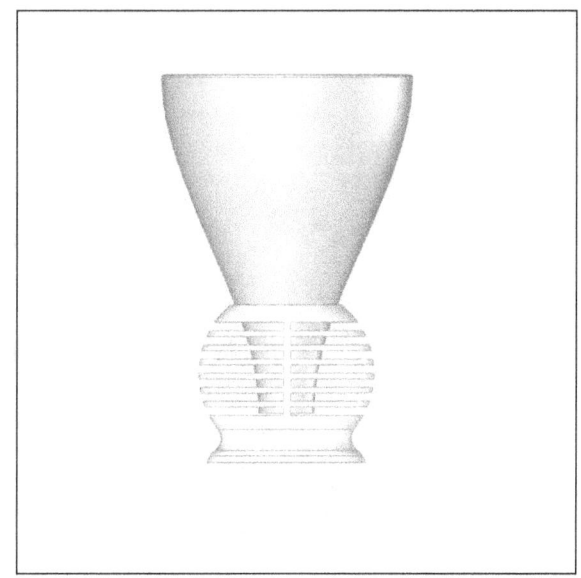

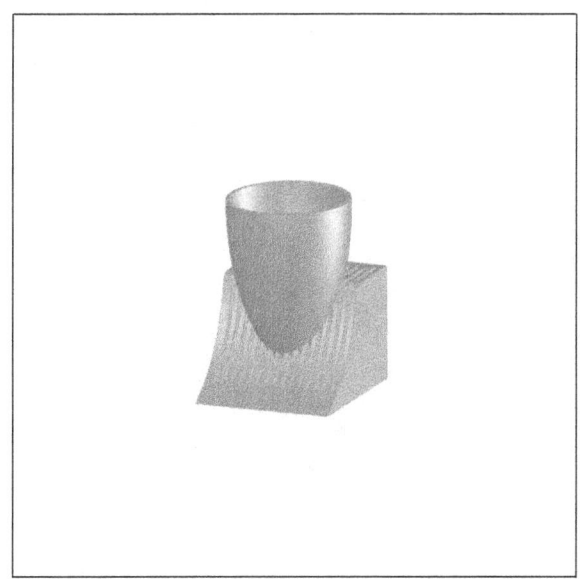

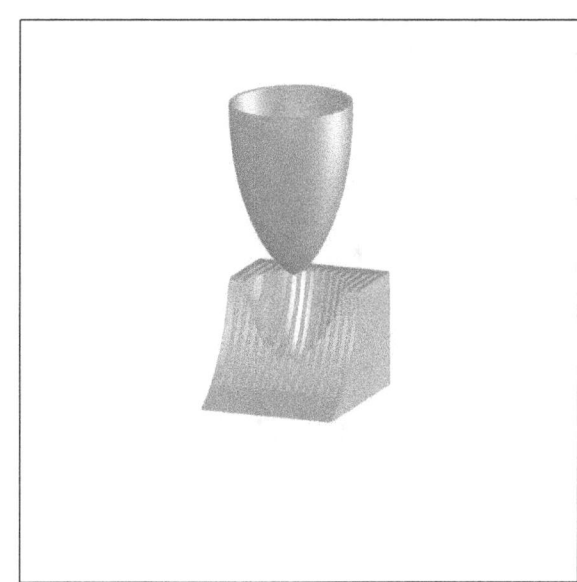

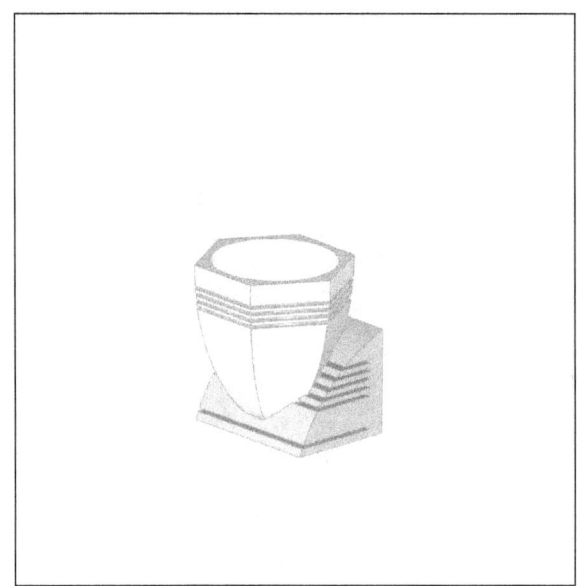

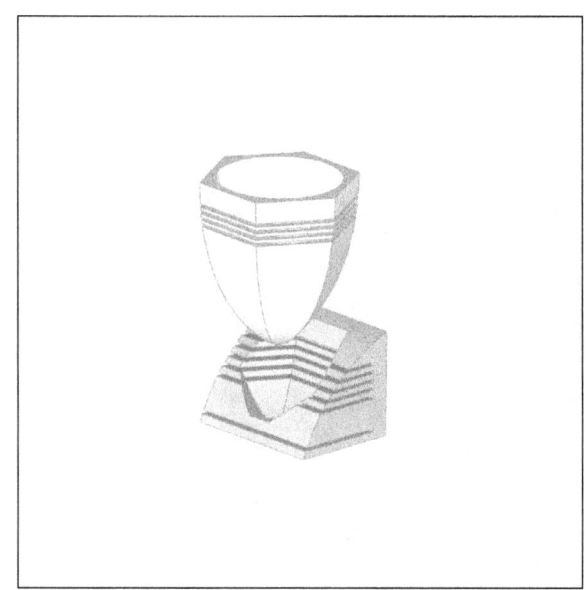

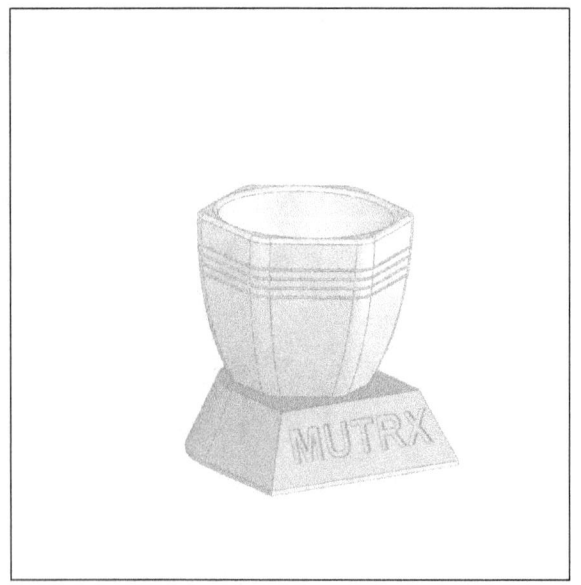

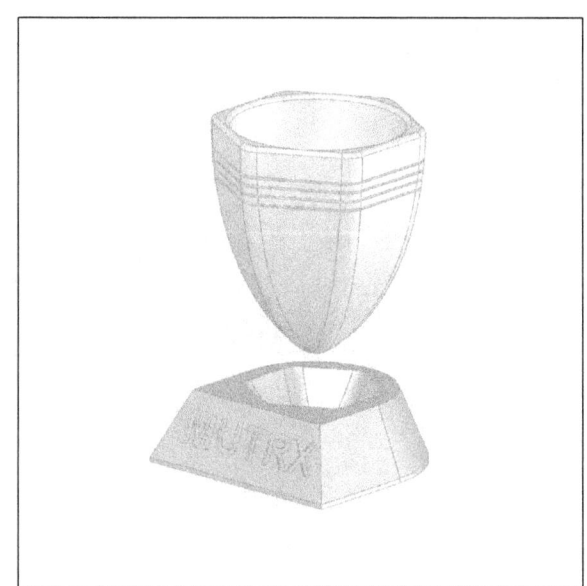

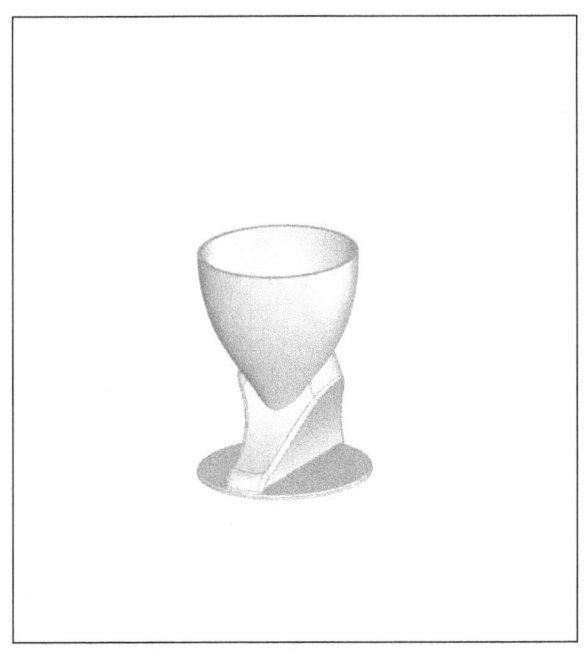
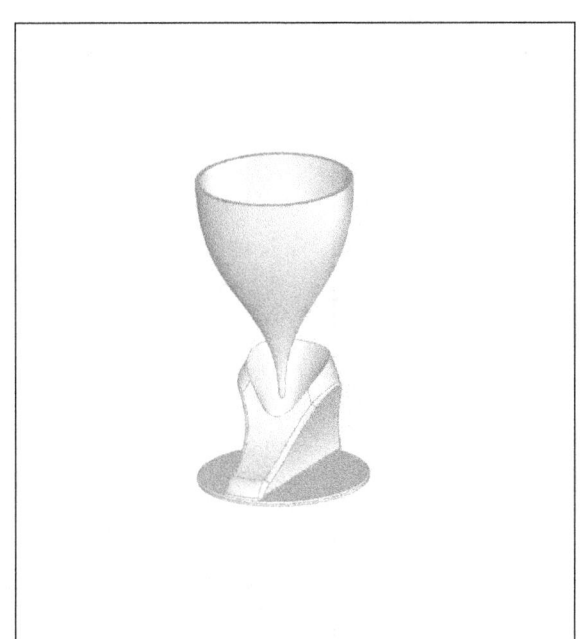
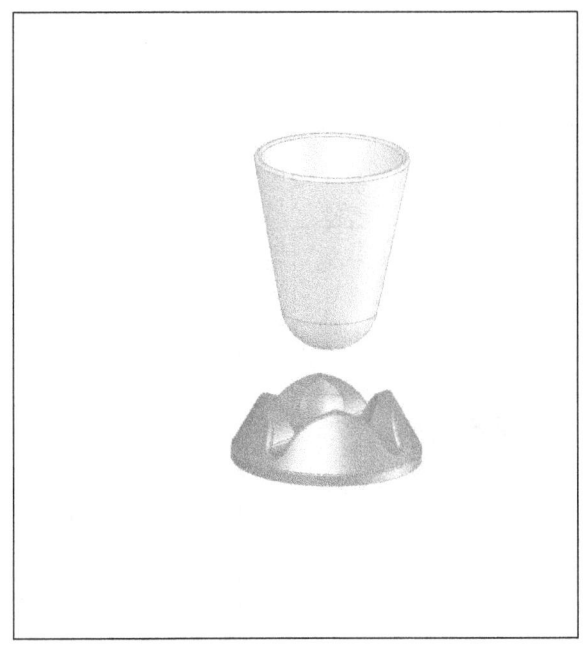
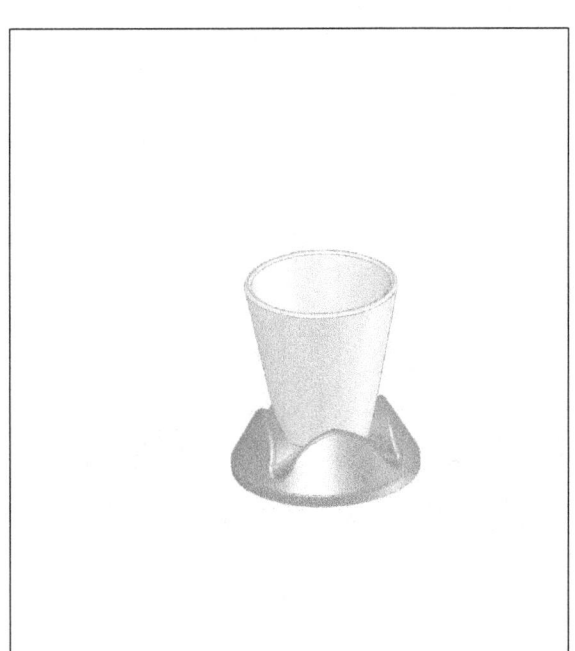

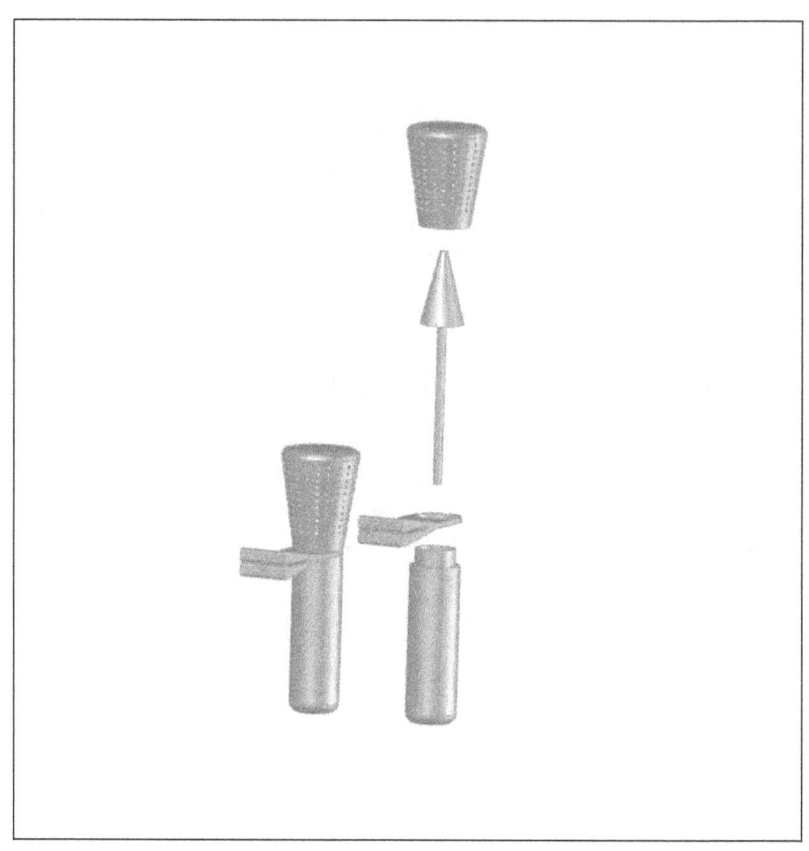

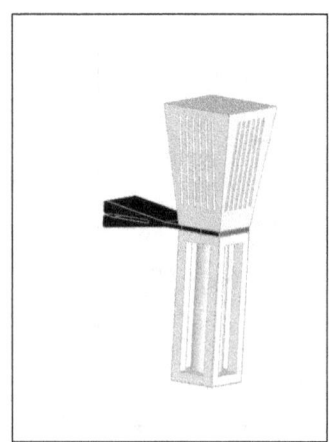
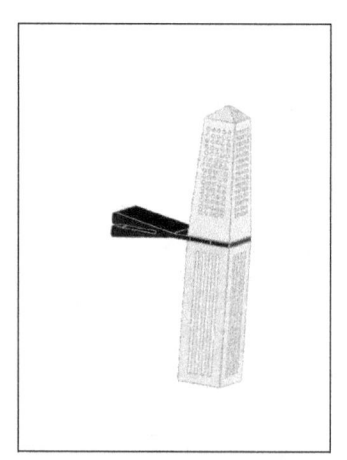
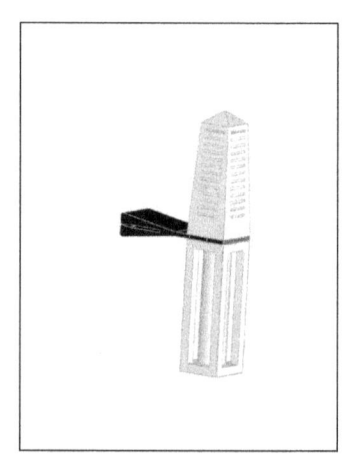
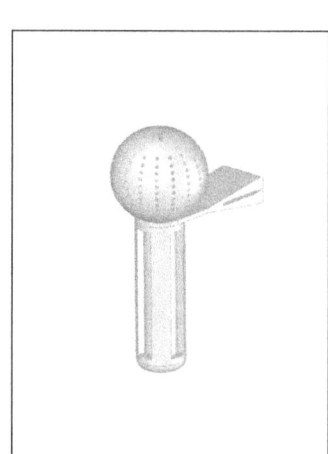

AUTO AIR FRESHNERS FLAT

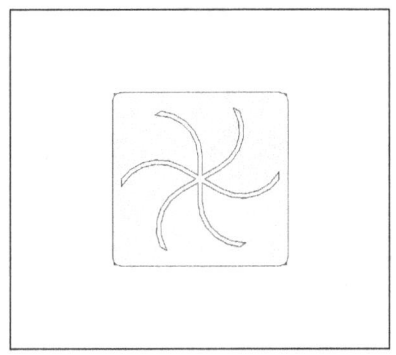

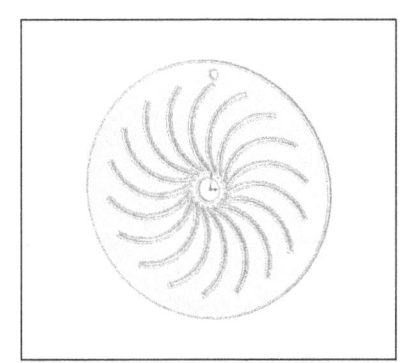

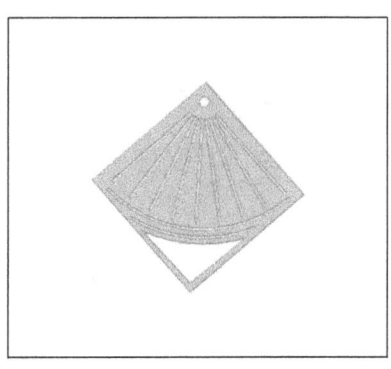

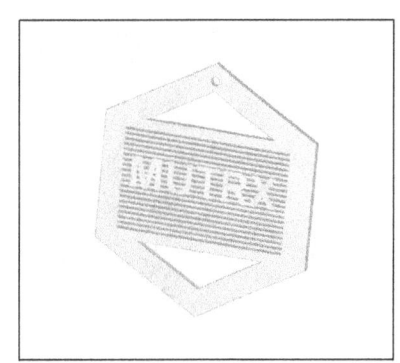

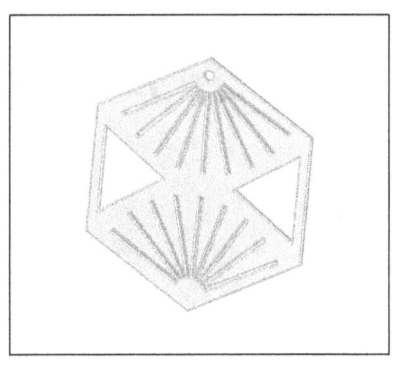

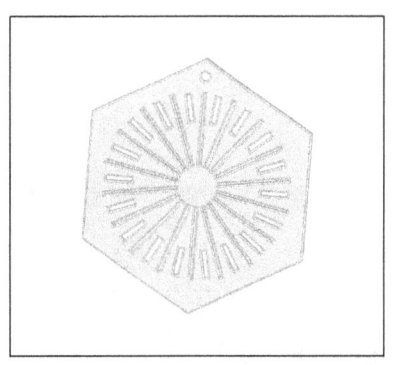

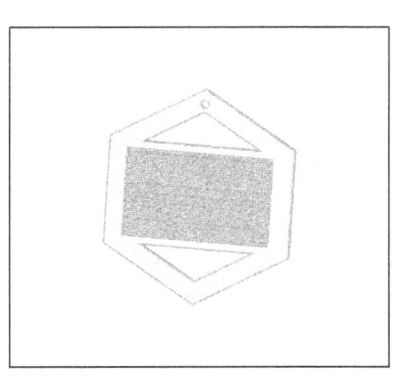

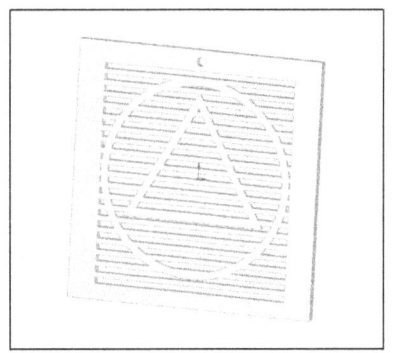

BACK OF DOOR ORGANIZER

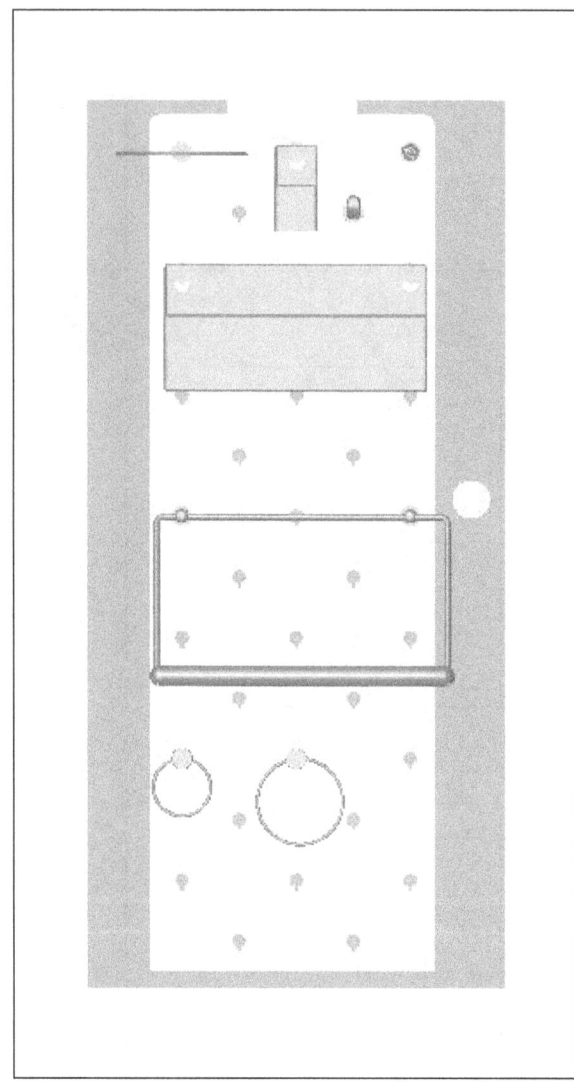

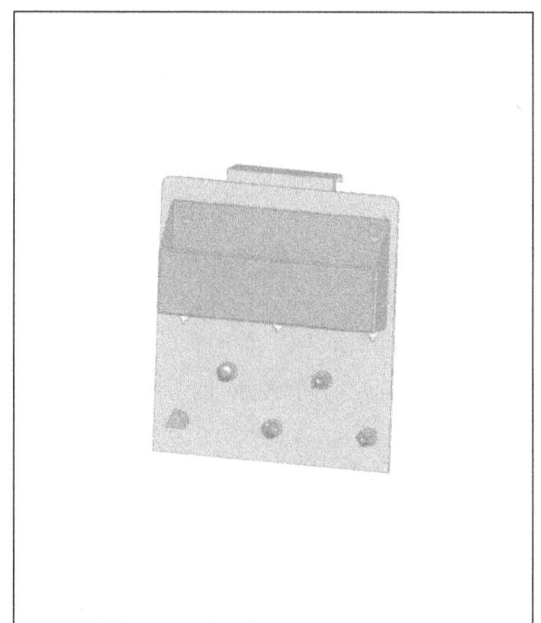

OFFICE CUBY ARRANGER

RESIDENTIAL DOOR

BEHIND THE DOOR REMOVABLE BRACKETS

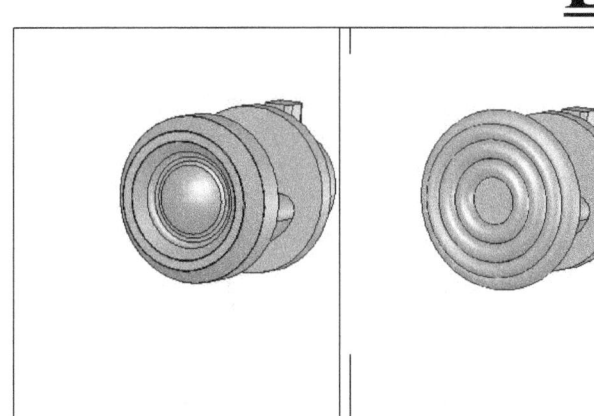

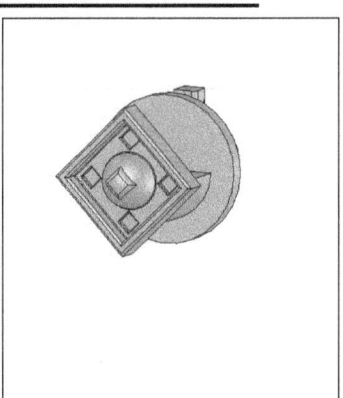

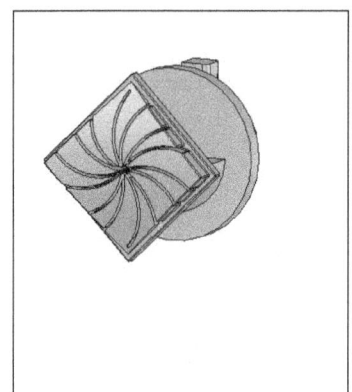

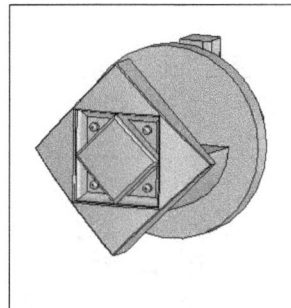

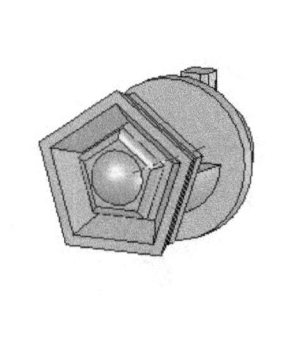

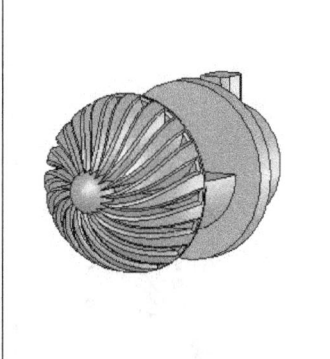

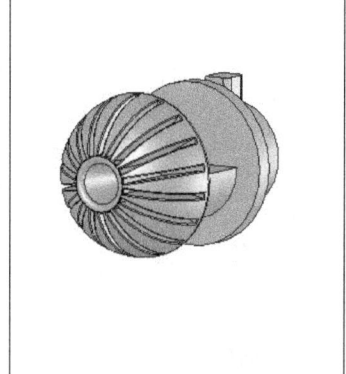

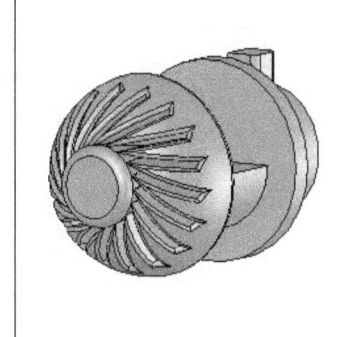

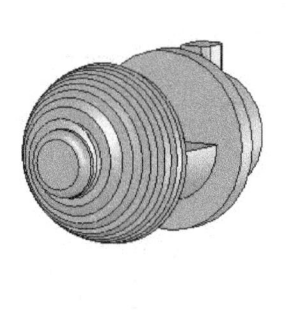

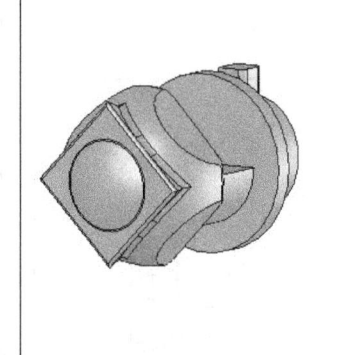

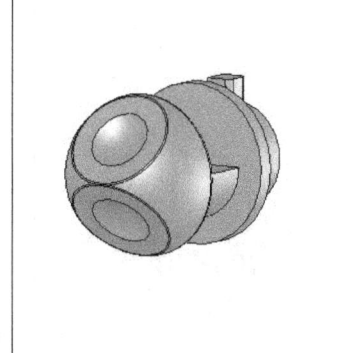

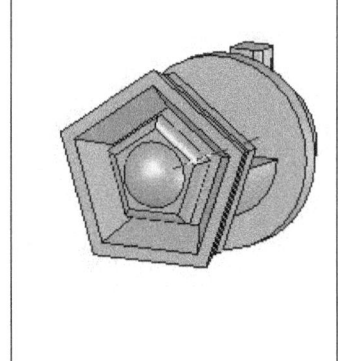

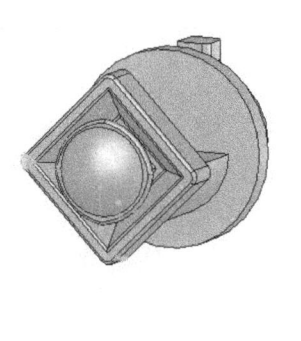

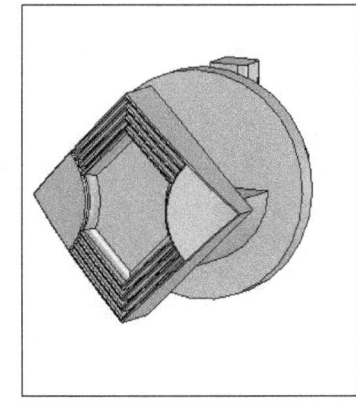

M7

WATCH BELTS

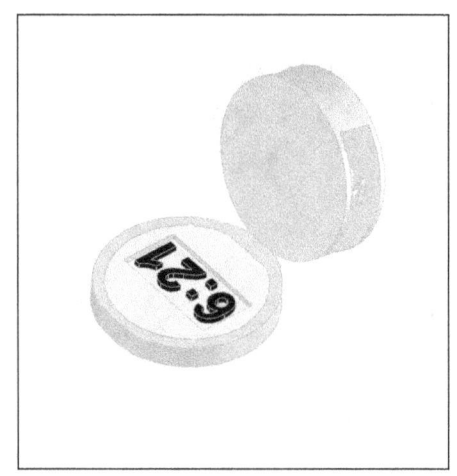 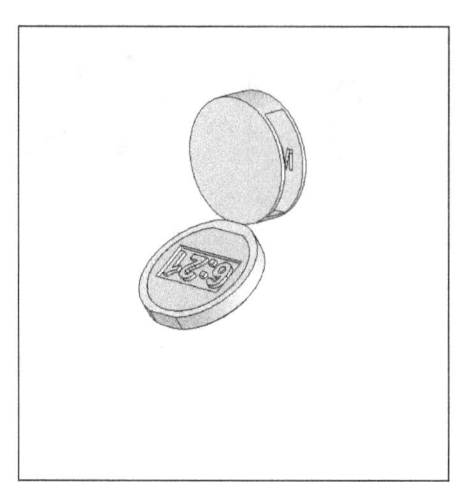 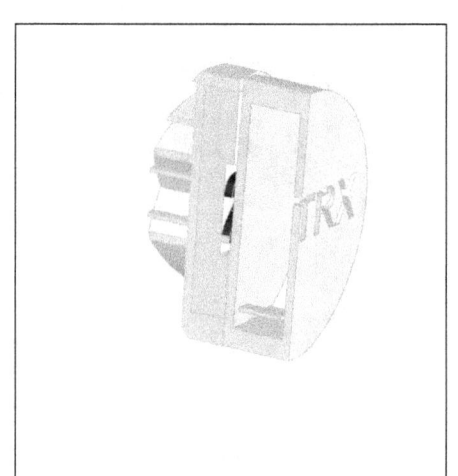

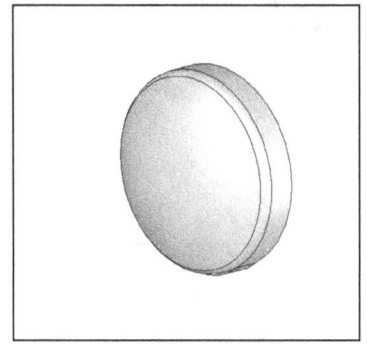 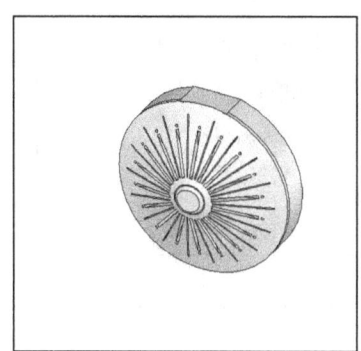 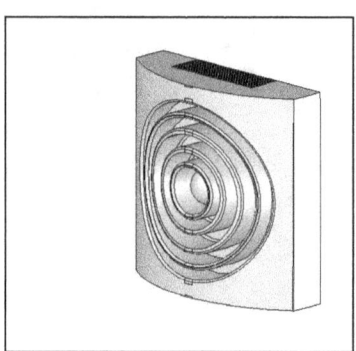 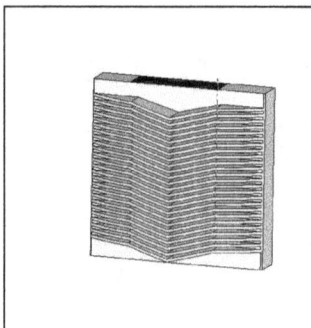

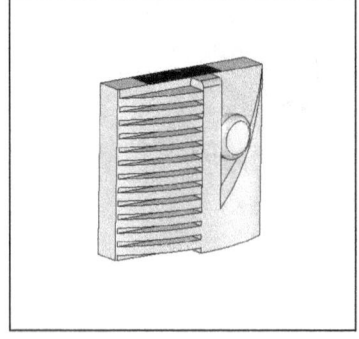 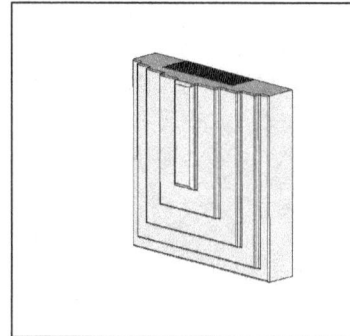 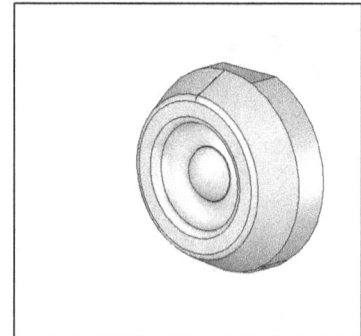 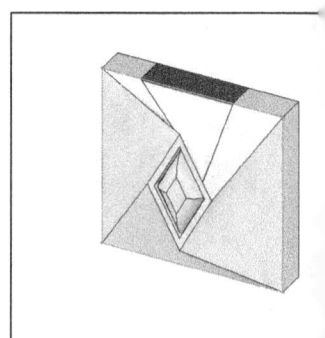

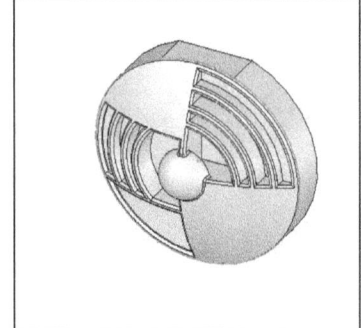 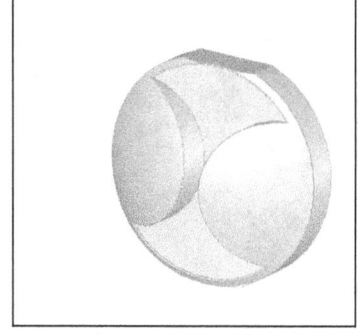 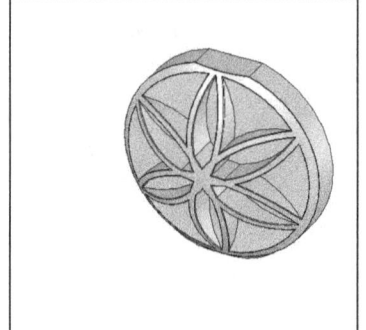 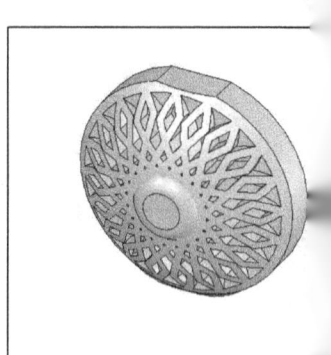

CEREAL TO GO

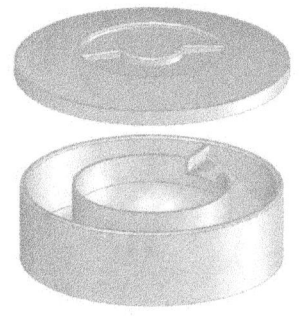

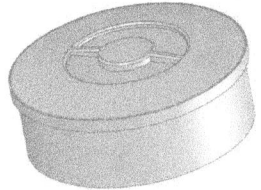

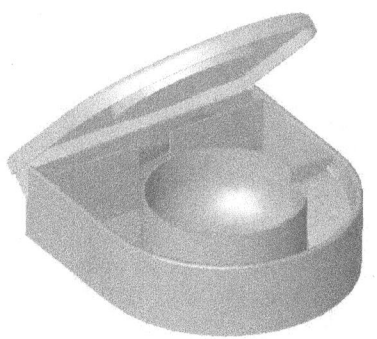

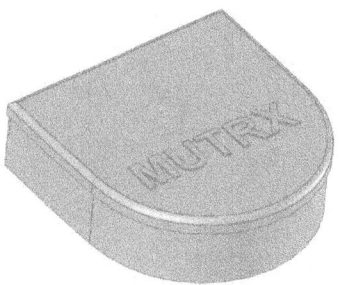

CRUNCHY CEREAL BOWL

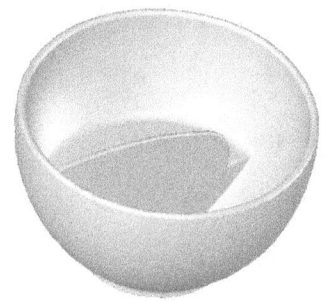

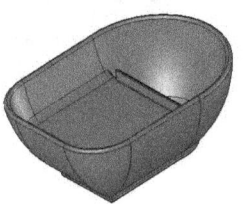

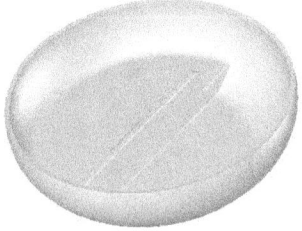

BUTTON WRAPS

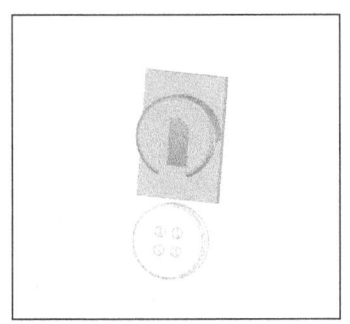
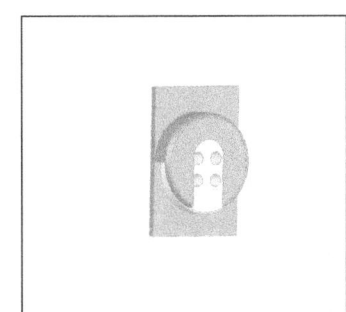

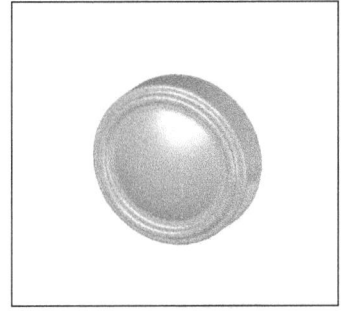
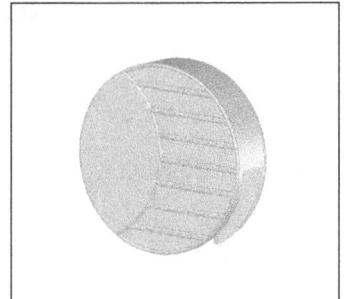
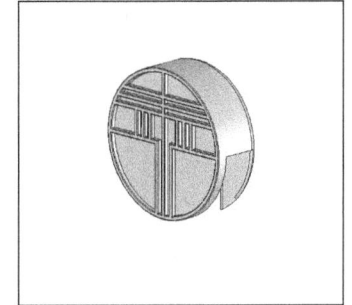
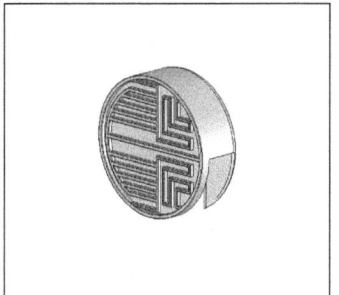

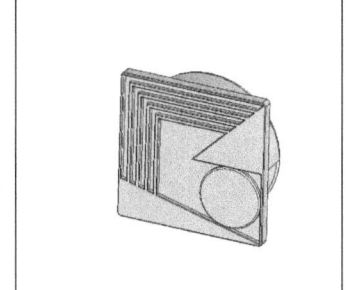
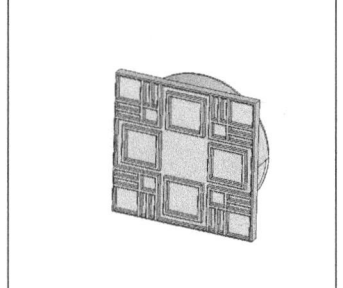
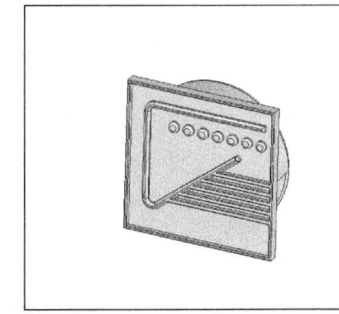
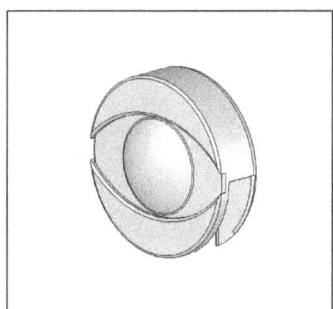

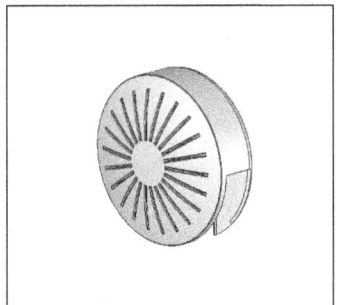
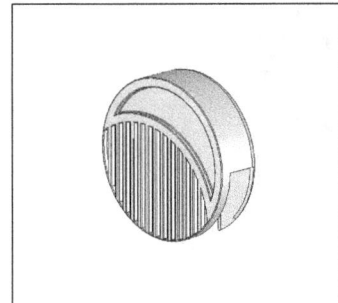
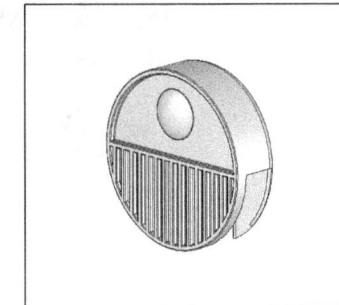
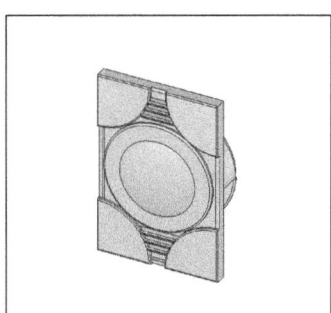

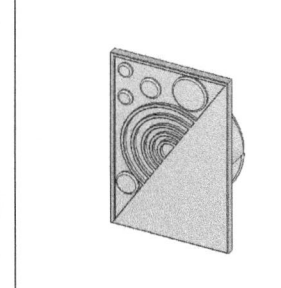
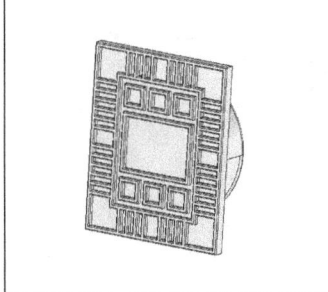
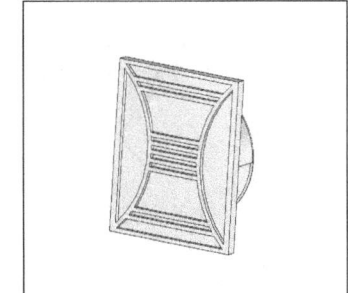
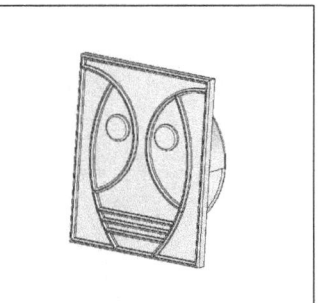

CHECKERS

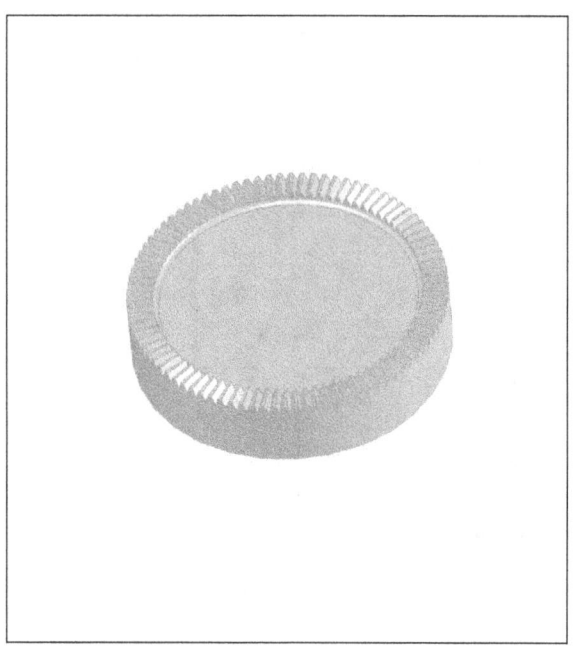

Get to the other side of board

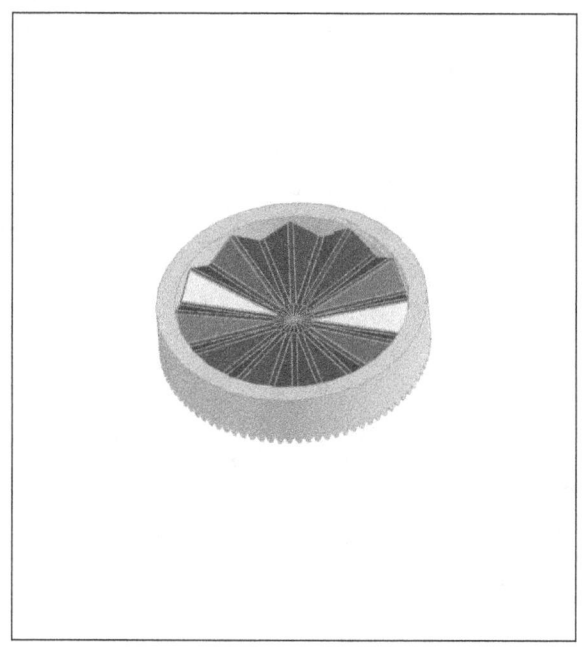

TURN YOUR CHECKER OVER

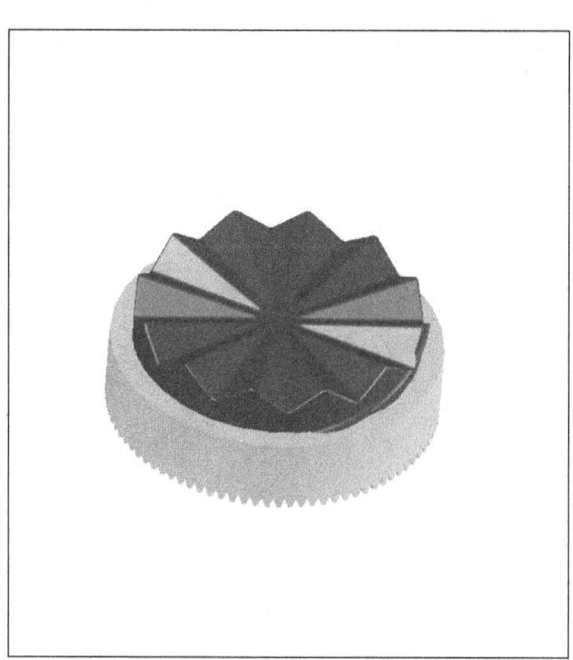

YOUR KING!

TRAVELING CHESS SET

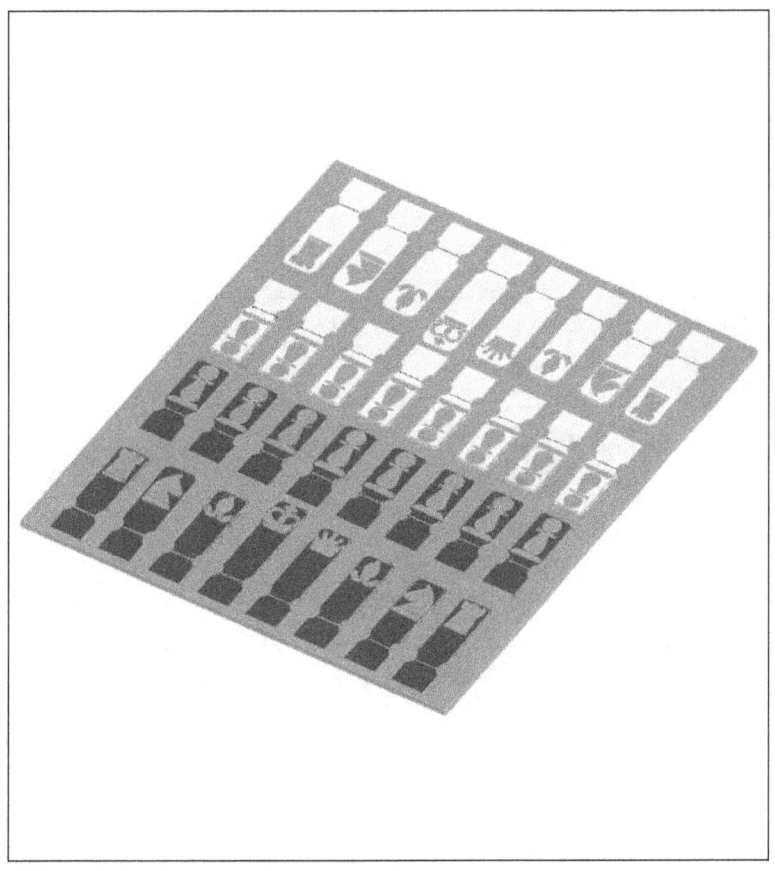

THINNEST CHESS SET IN WORLD

EACH PIECE LESS THEN 1/16
INCH THICK

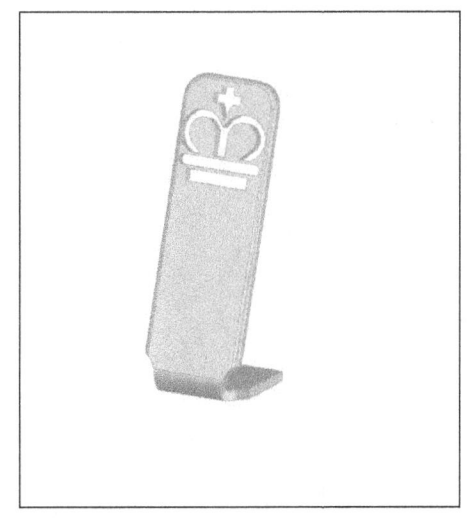

CLOSED FOLDED SET ONLY 1/8
THICK

BAG CLIPS

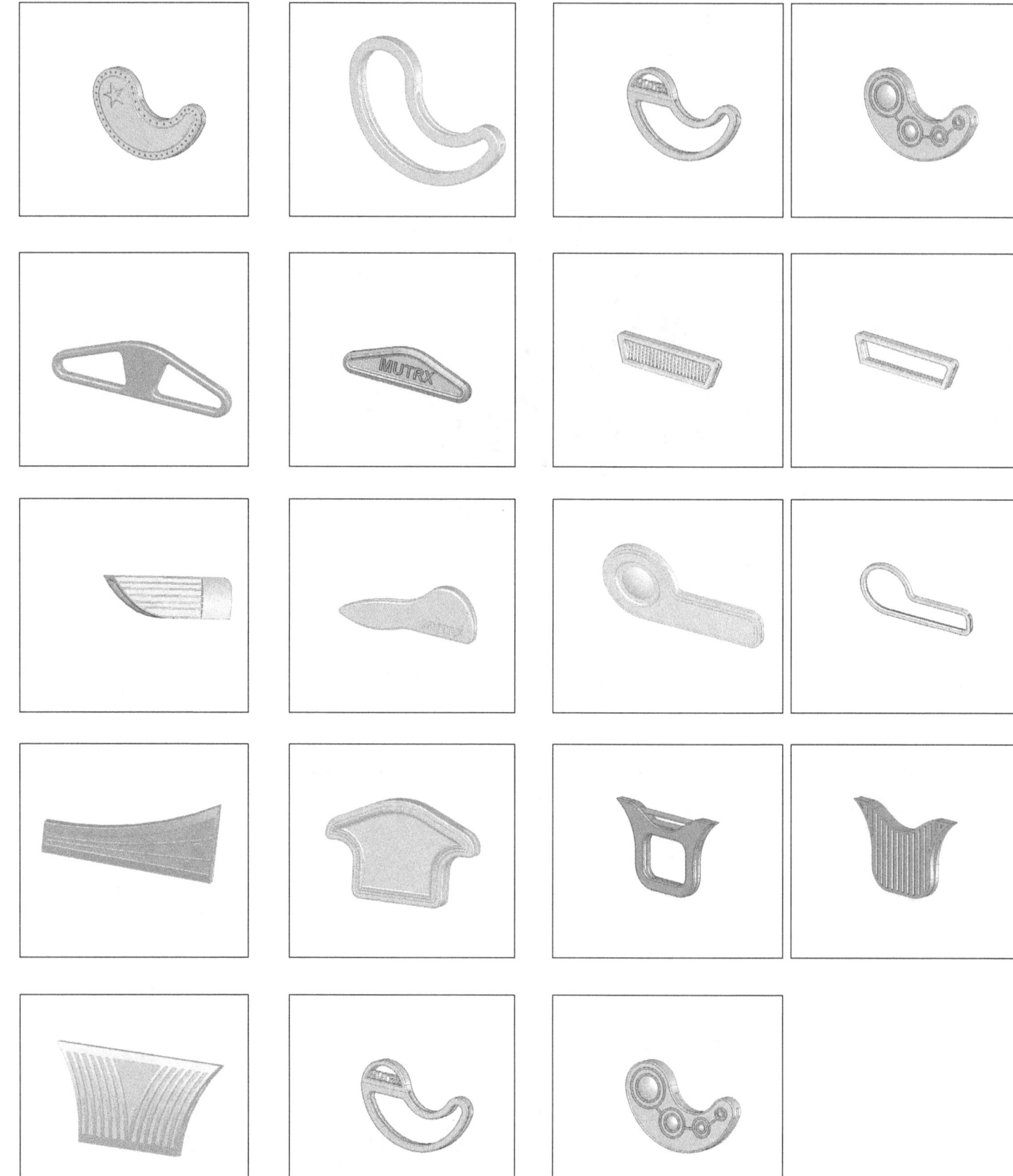

COFFEE DISPENSERS AND STORAGE

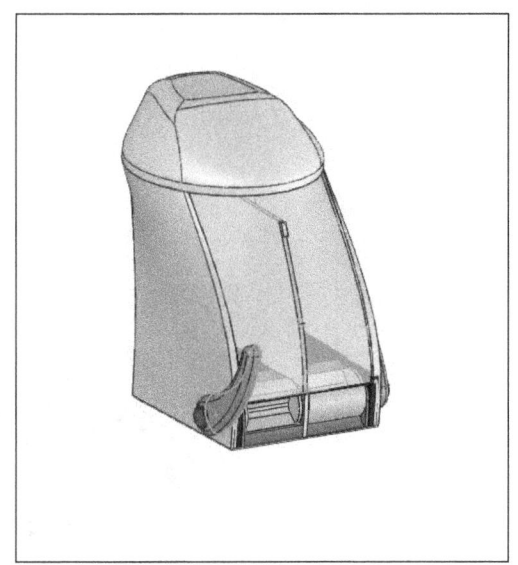

YOU MIX BEANS?

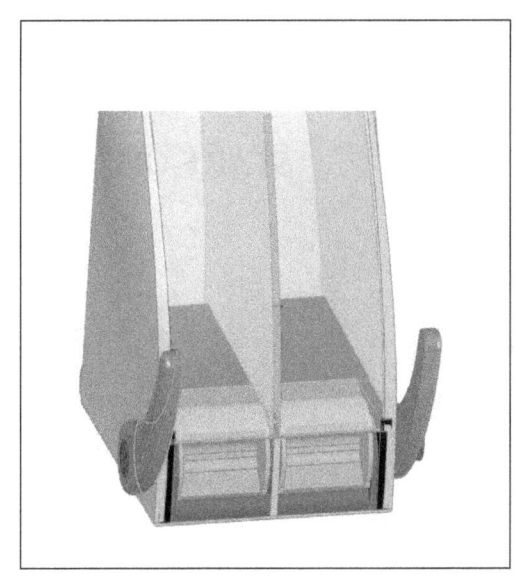

YOU WILL OPEN NEW FRONTIERS

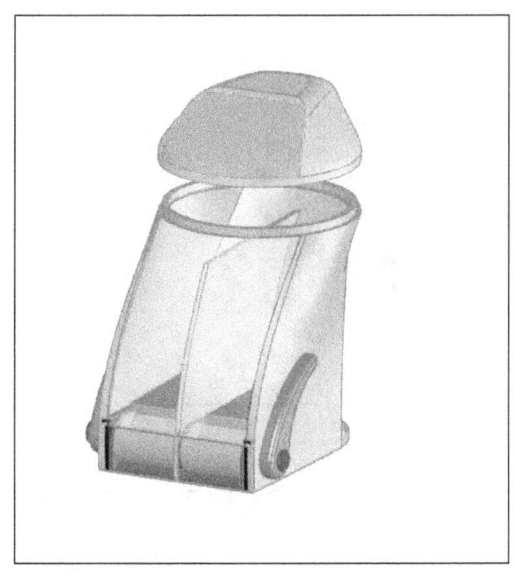

MAYBE REG. AND DECAF.

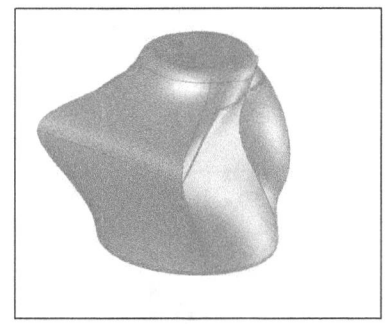

STORAGE

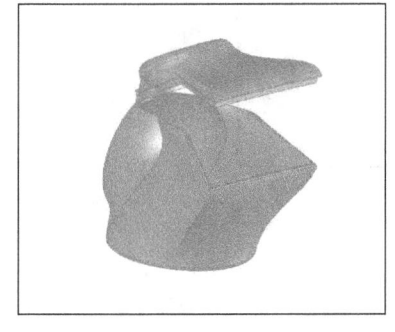

REGULAR BEANS ONLY

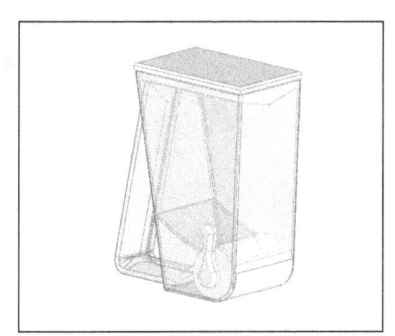

ASJUSTABLE CUP AMOUNTS

M7

COMPASS JEWELY KIT

START OFF WITH A BASE

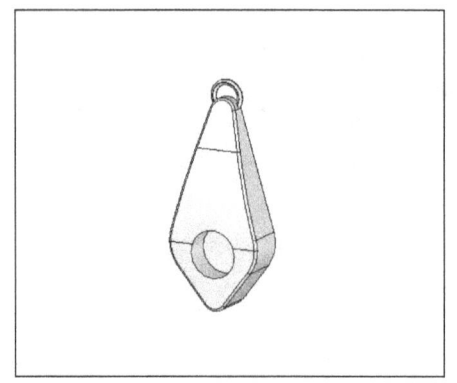
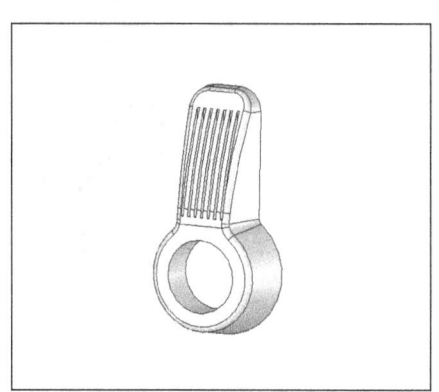
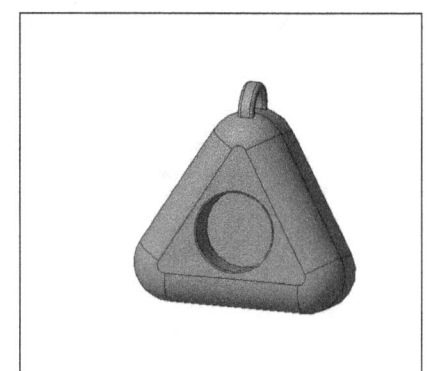

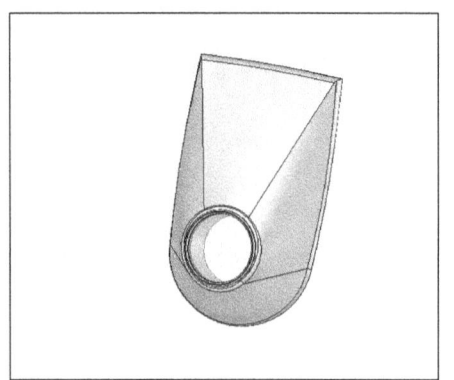
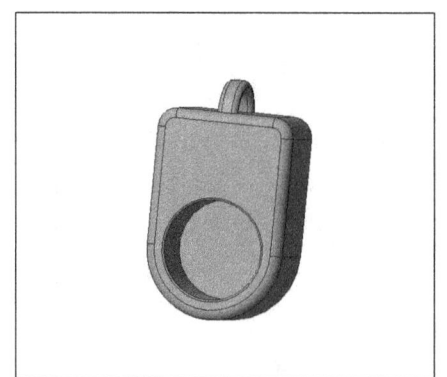
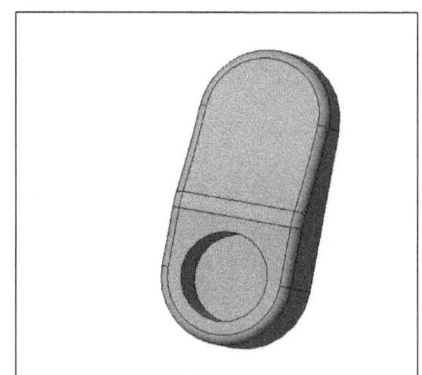

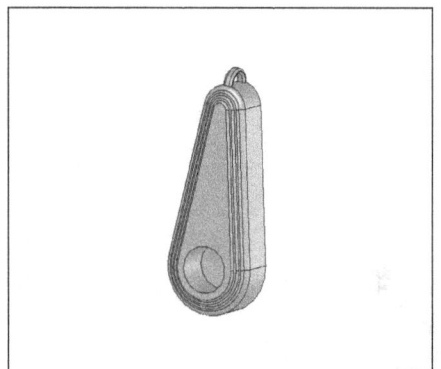
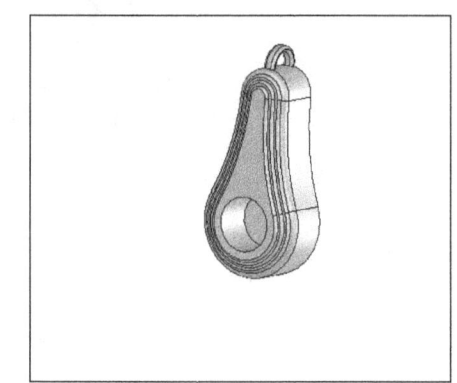

ADD REPLACABLE ACCECORY

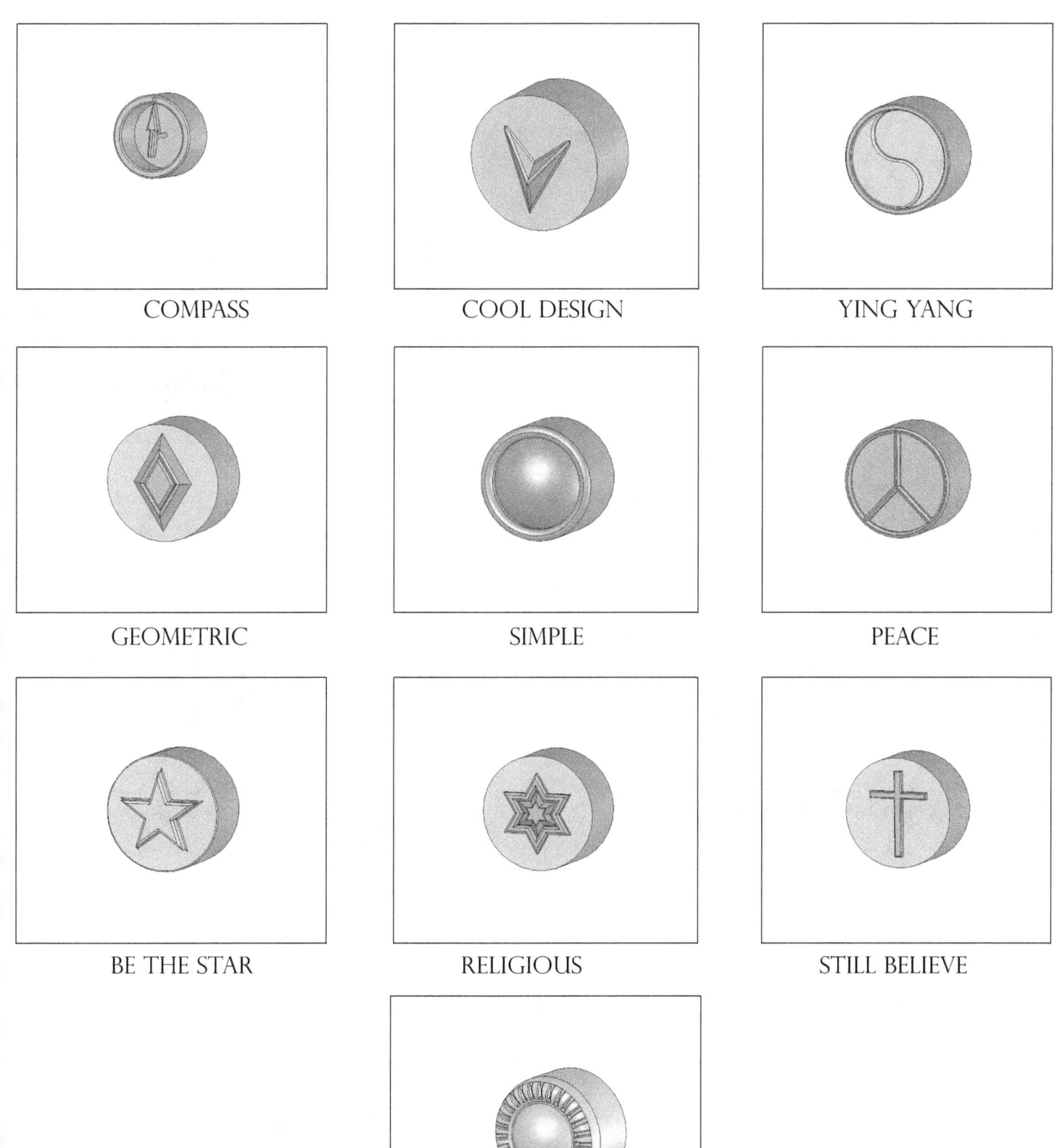

COMPASS

COOL DESIGN

YING YANG

GEOMETRIC

SIMPLE

PEACE

BE THE STAR

RELIGIOUS

STILL BELIEVE

SIMPLE WITH A TWIST

M7

LOOKING STYLIST

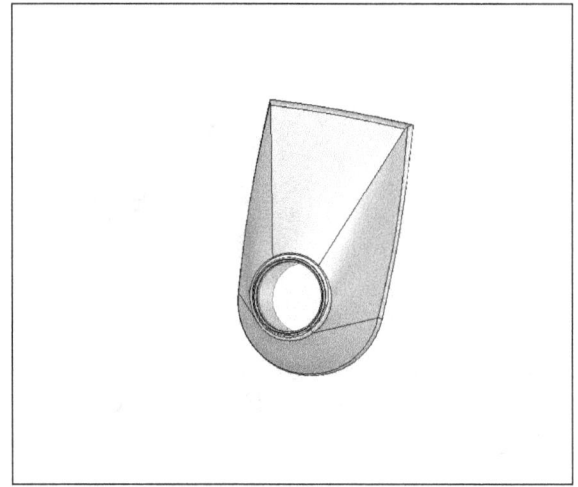

DAILY CHANGES

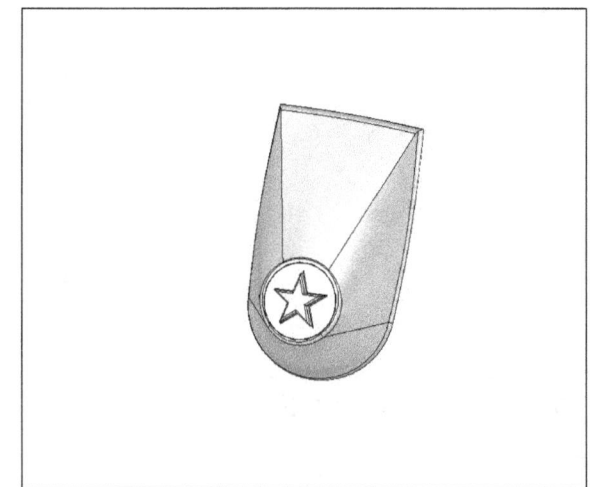

REPRESENTING SELF

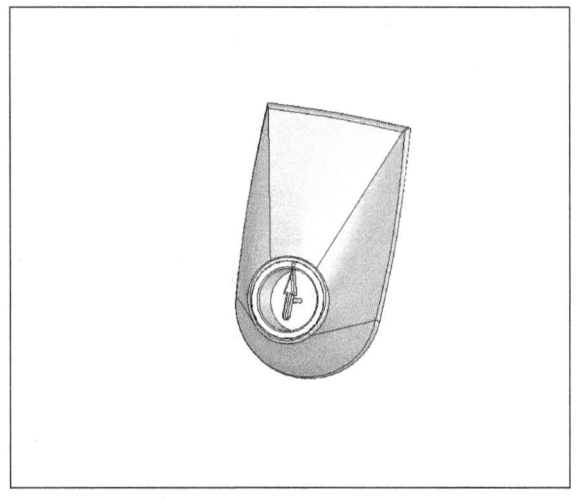

YOU KNOW WHERE YOU ARE?

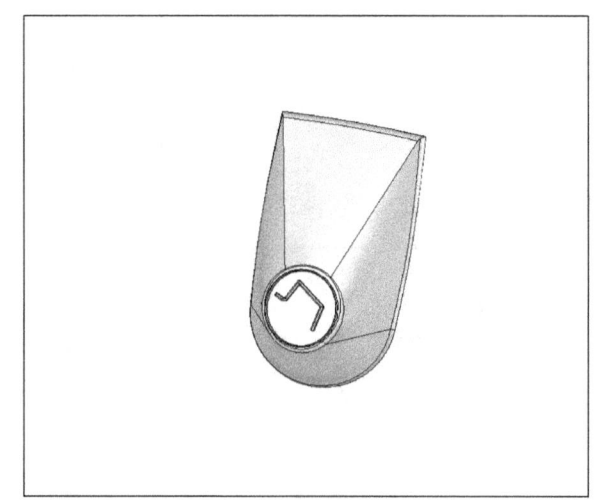

YOU BELIEVE

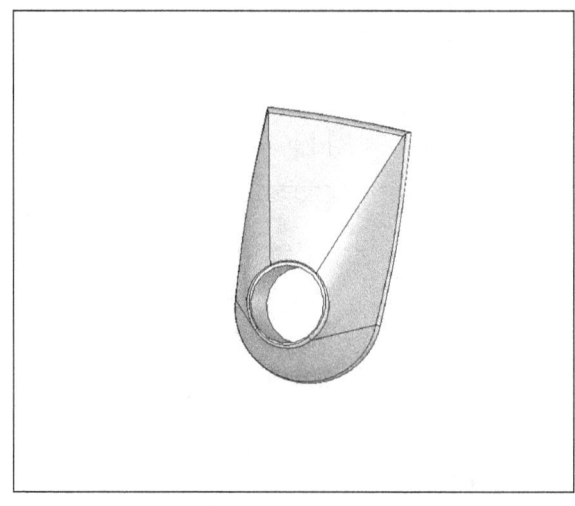

PHOTOS

MEZUZAHS

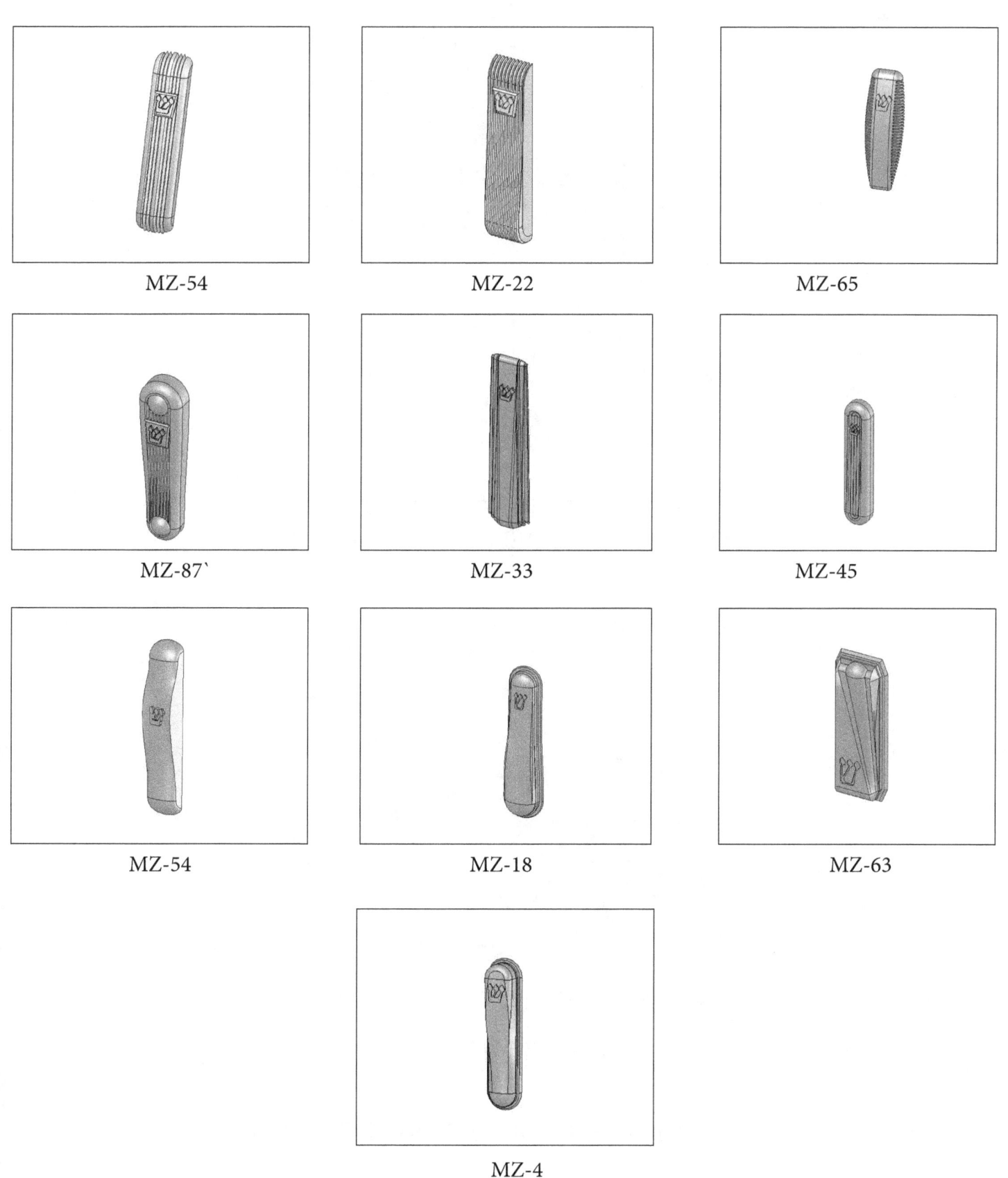

MZ-54

MZ-22

MZ-65

MZ-87`

MZ-33

MZ-45

MZ-54

MZ-18

MZ-63

MZ-4

M7

FORTUNE CUBE

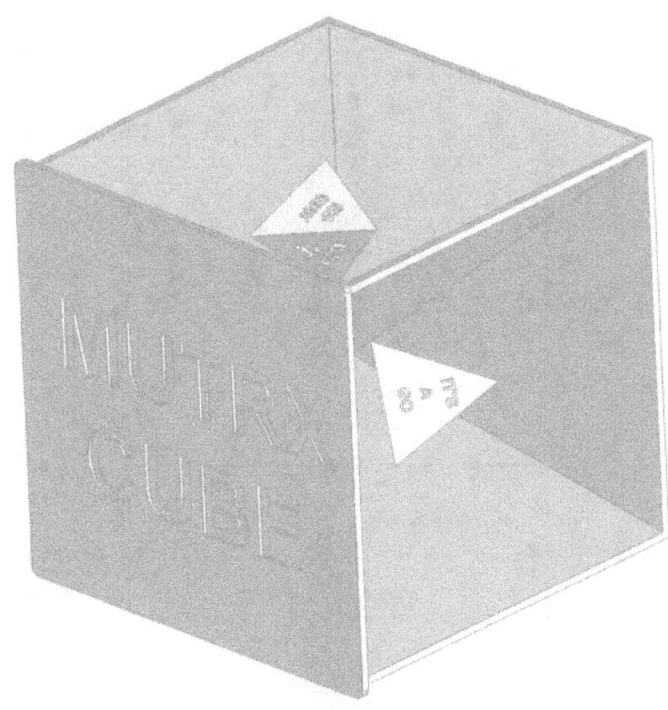

GET 5 DIFFERENT PREDICTIONS
LOVE,MONEY,CAREER,PERSONAL,SCHOOL

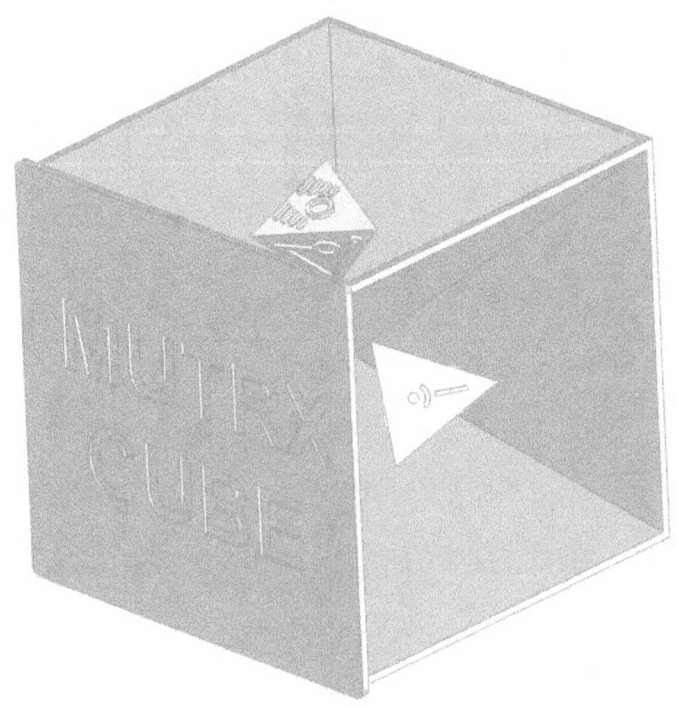

PAINT EACH SIDE AND INVENT A GAME

CONDOM HOLDERS

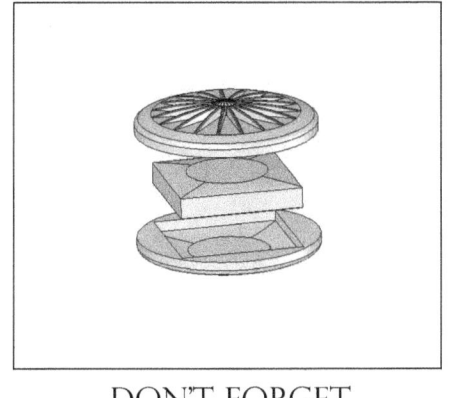

DON'T FORGET

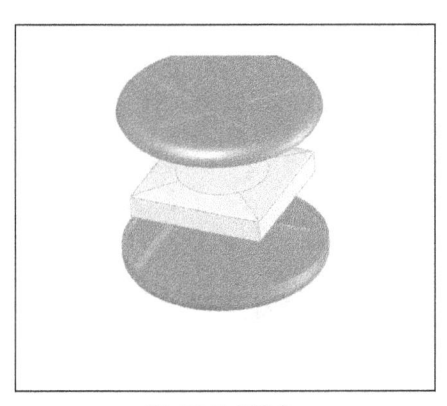

IMPRESS

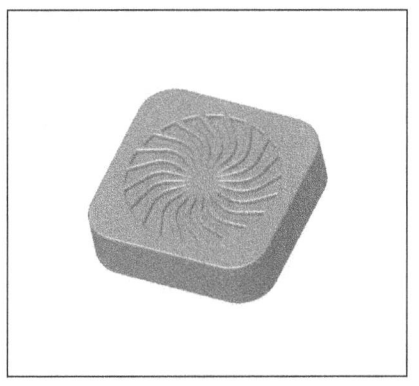

ENJOY

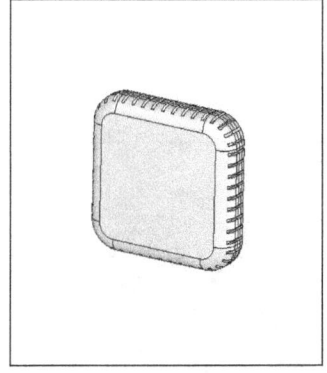
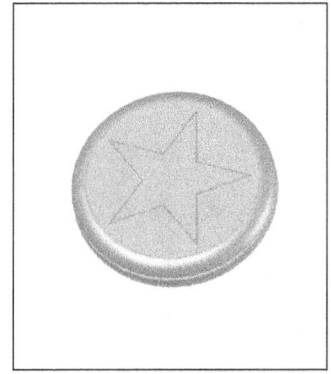
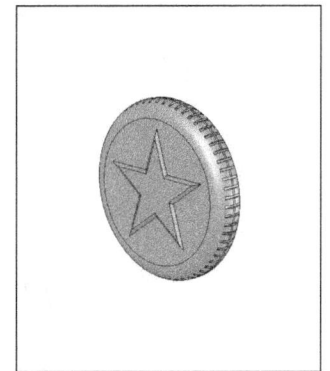
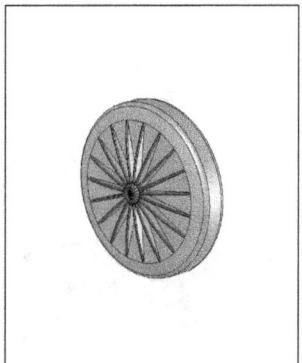

CHOICES IN STYLE

THE WEEKENDER

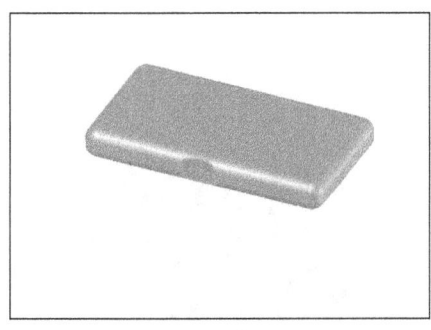
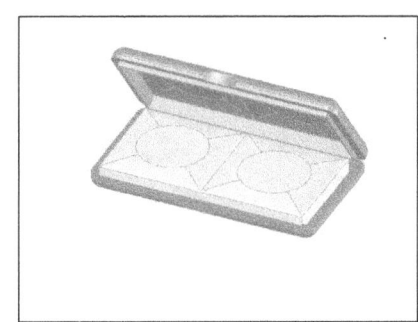

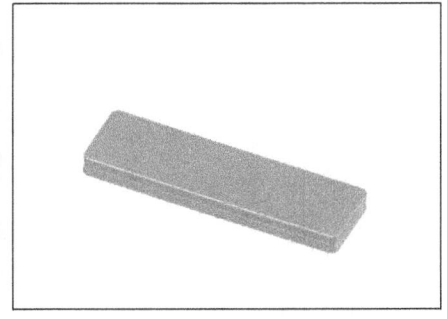
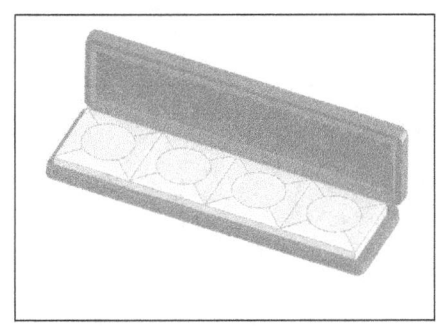

COLLEGE GIFT

DECORATIVE INTERCHANGABLE

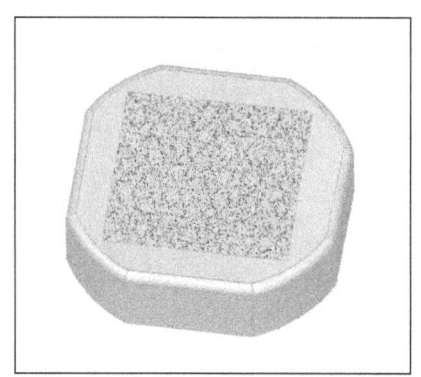

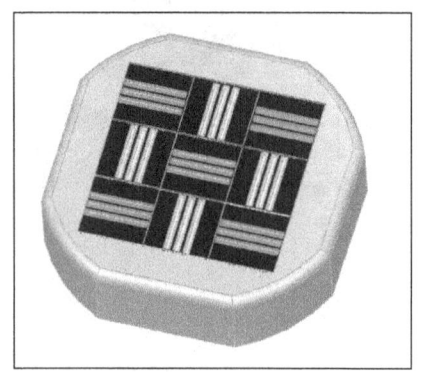

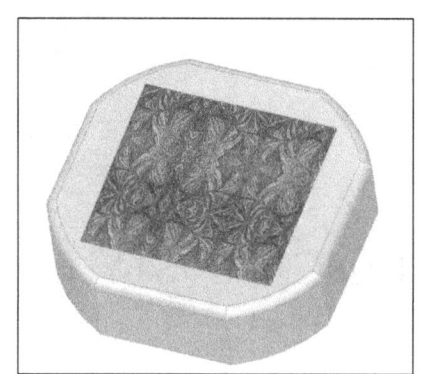

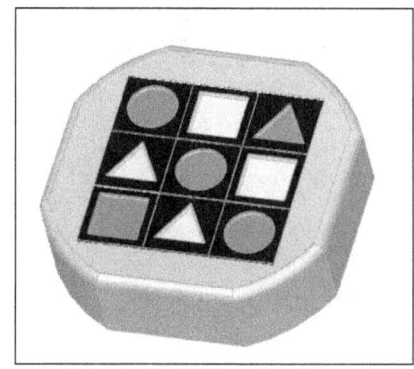

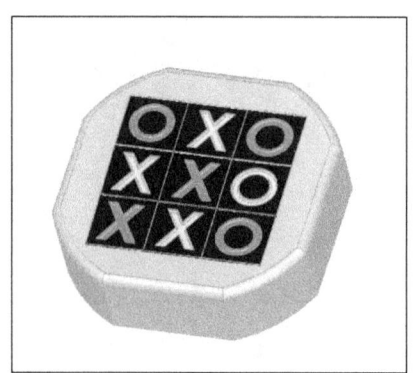

CYLINDERS ???

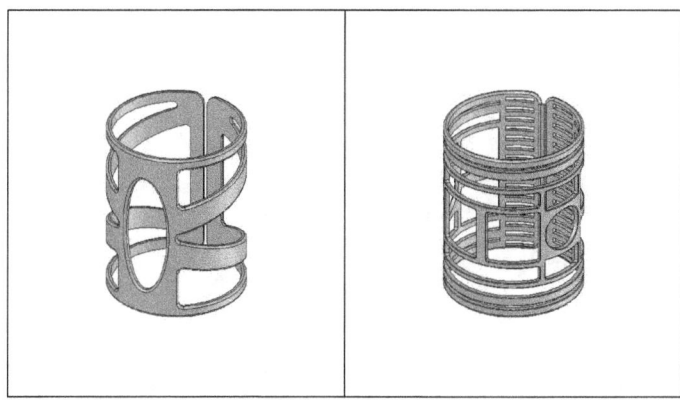
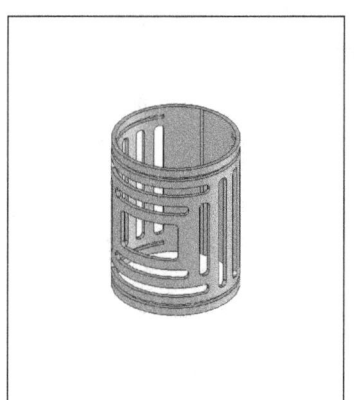
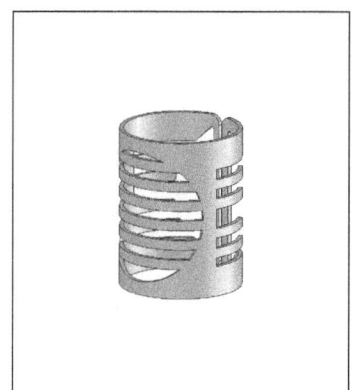

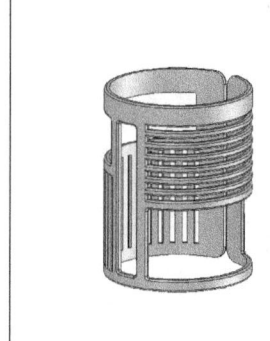
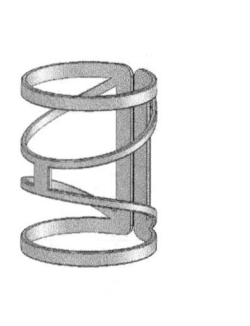
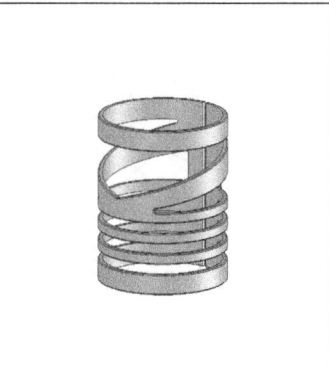
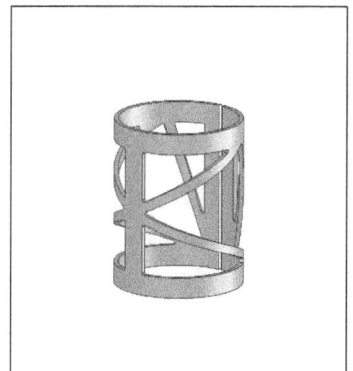

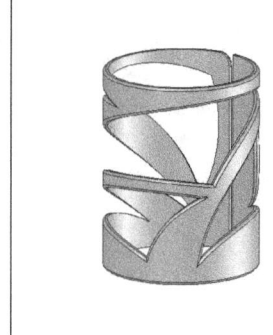
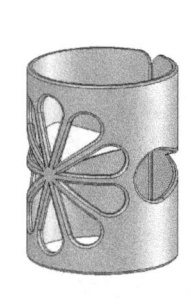
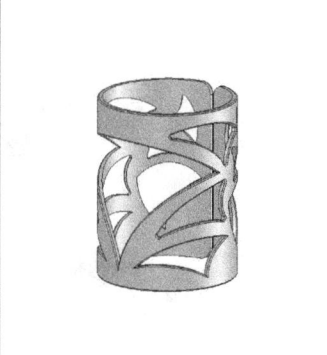
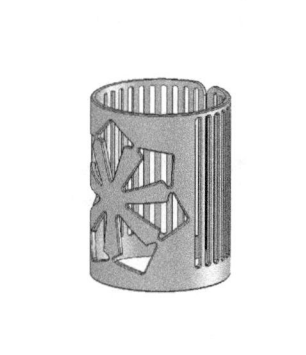

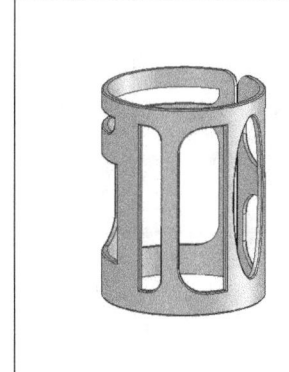
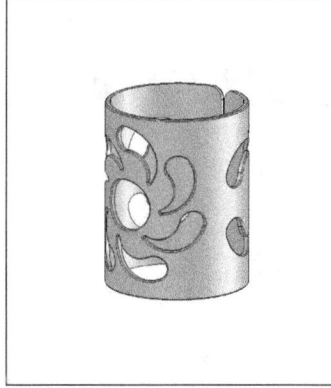
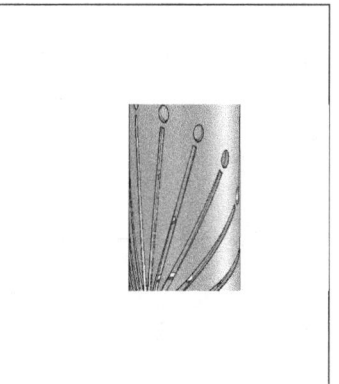

M7

89

DOMINOS

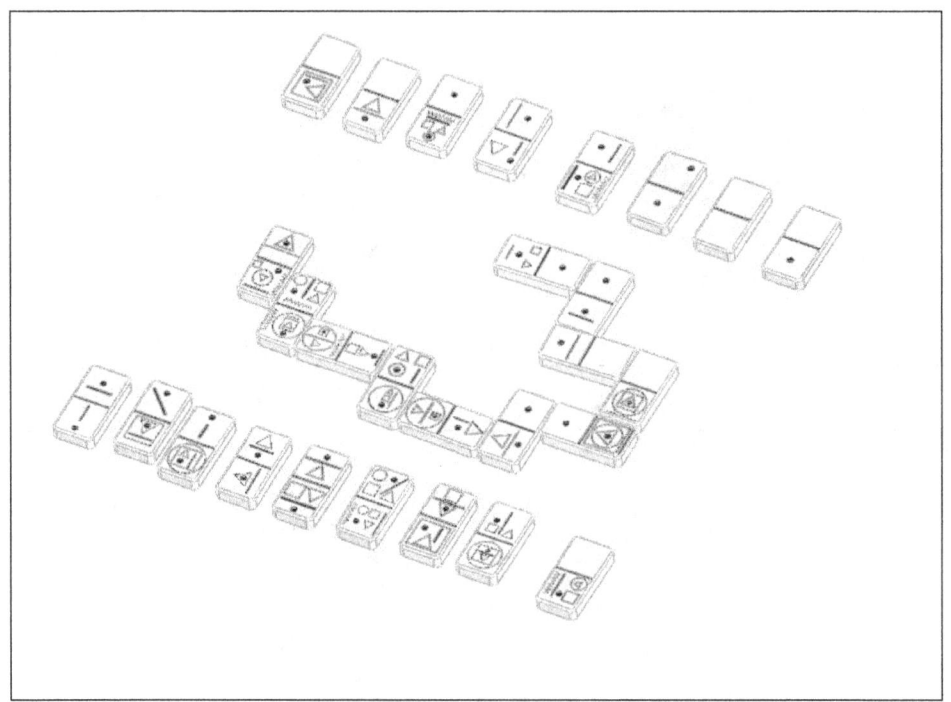

SYMBOLS

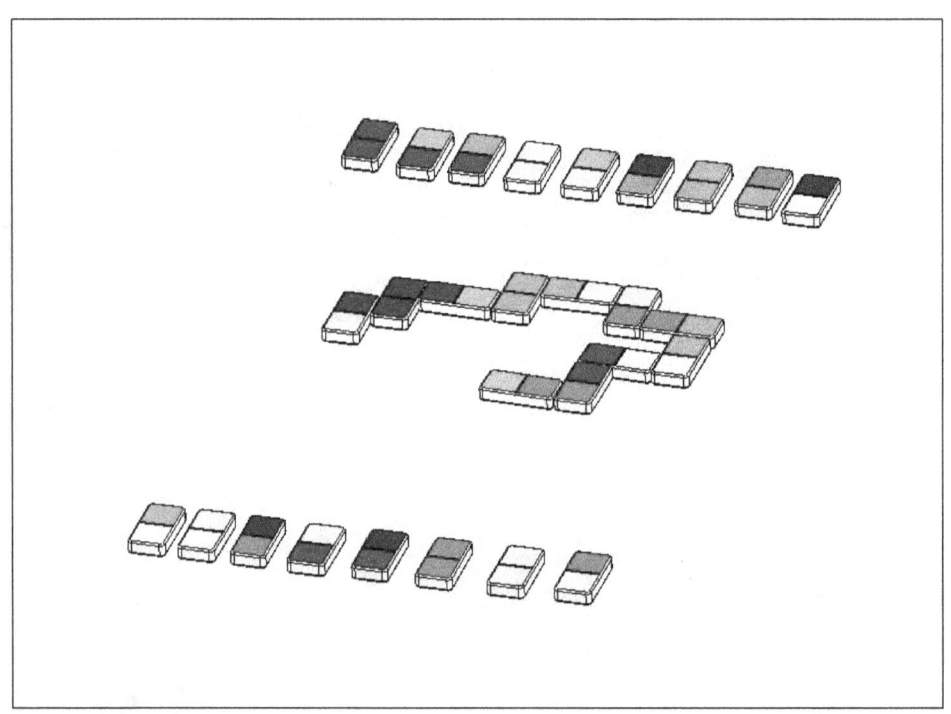

COLOR

M7

DRINKING STRAW ADD ONS

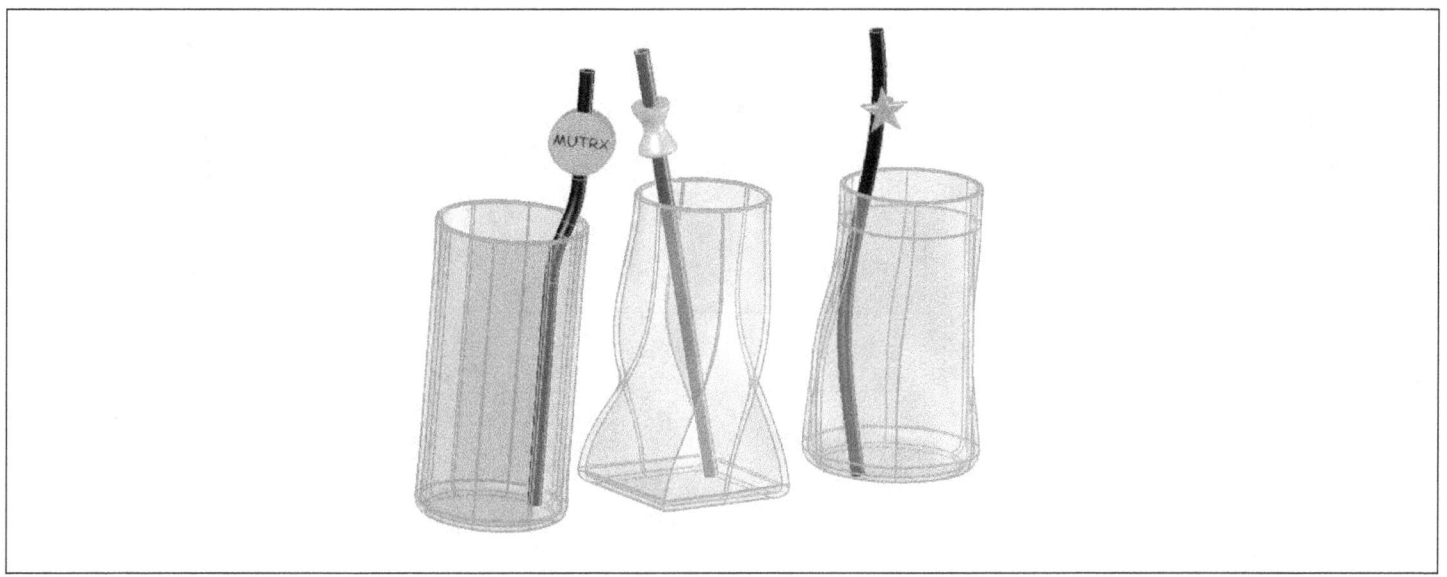

HANDSOME GLASS ACCESORIES

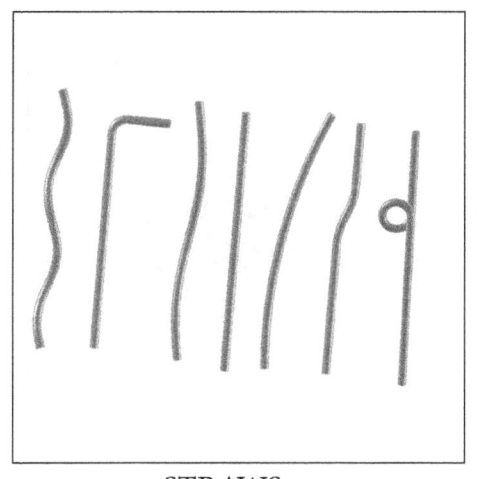

STRAWS

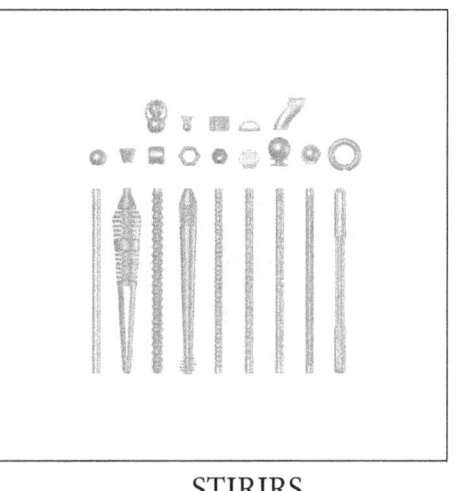

STIRIRS

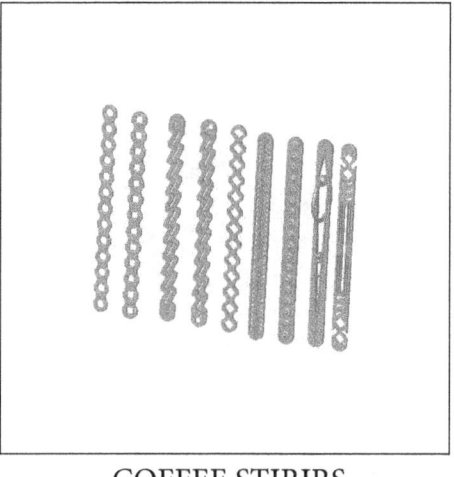

COFFEE STIRIRS

M7

HUGS FOR STRAWS!

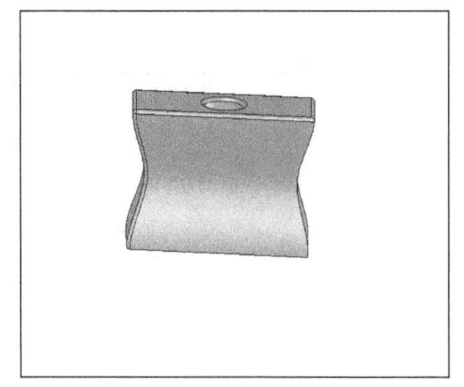
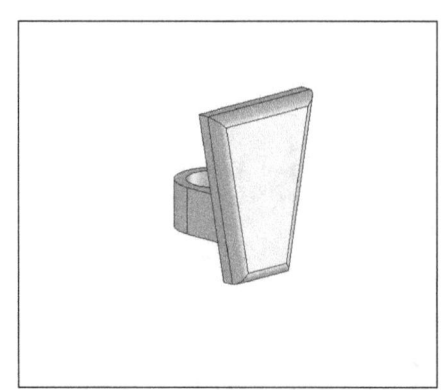
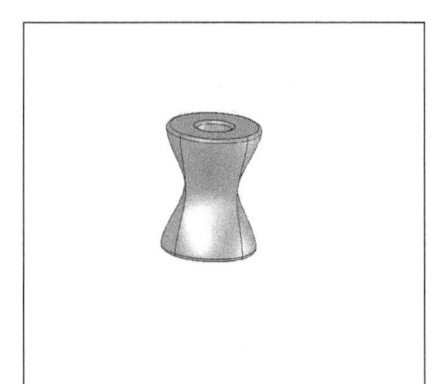
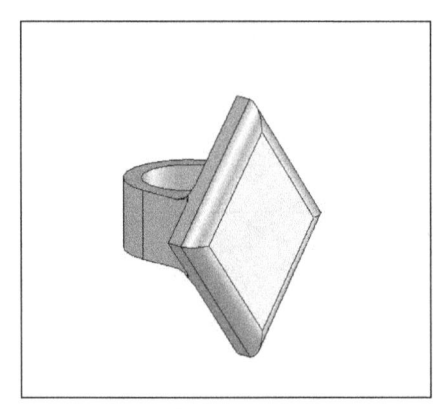
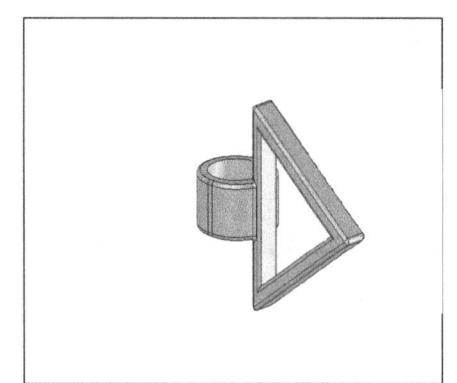
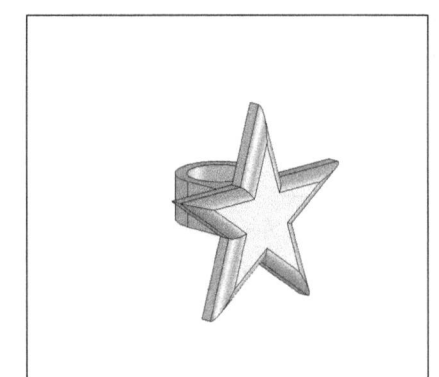
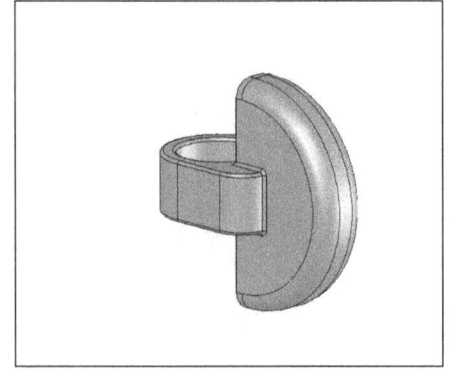
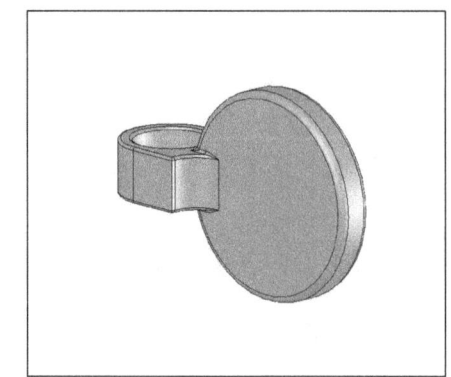
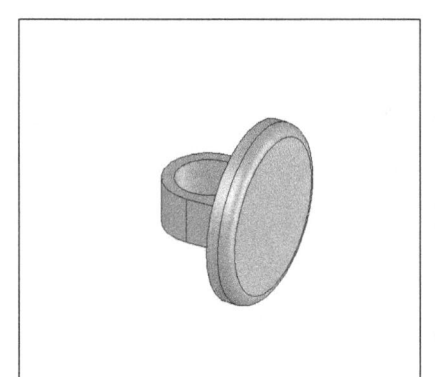
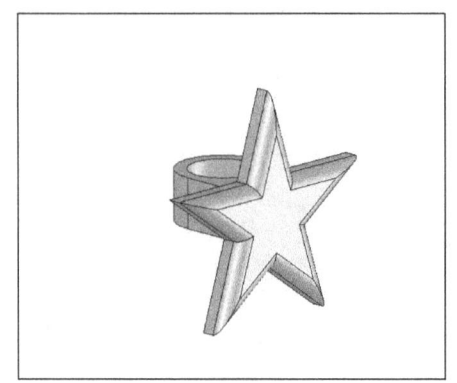
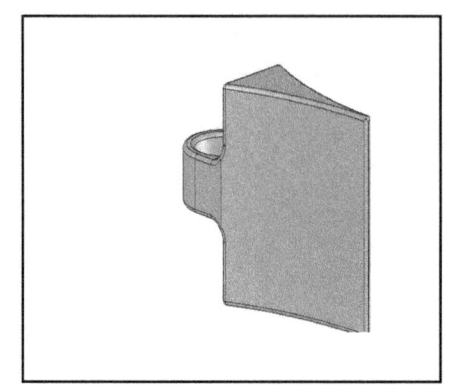
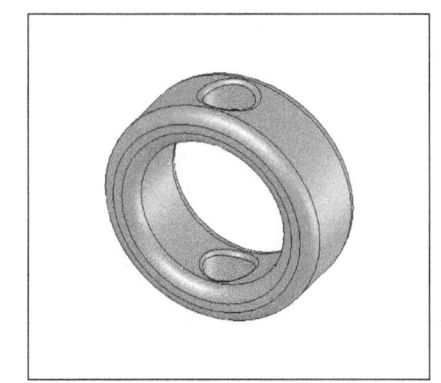

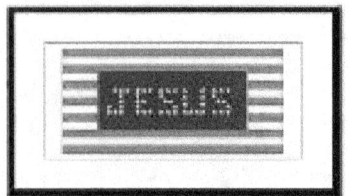

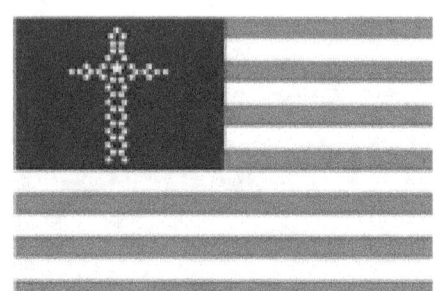

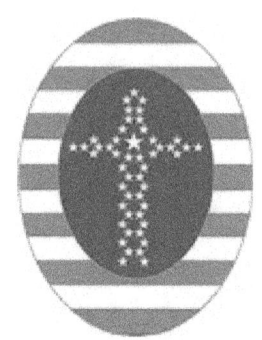

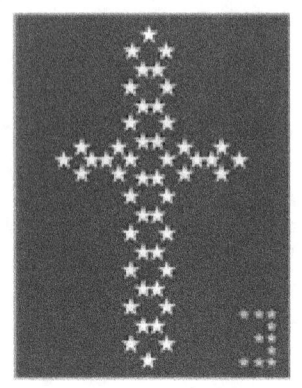

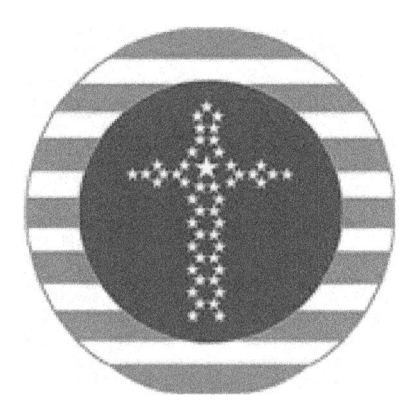

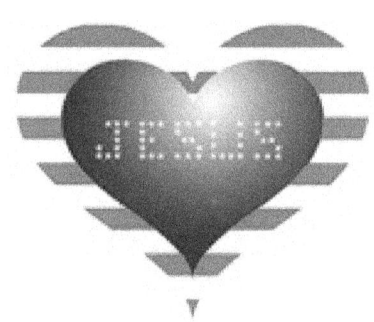

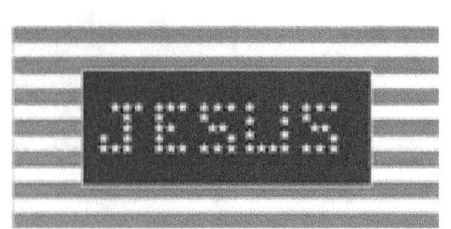

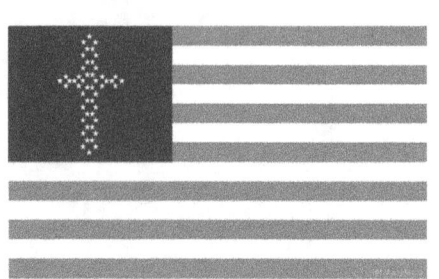

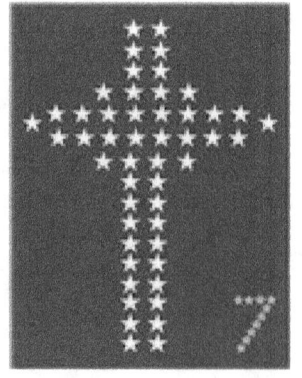

JESUS JEWELRY

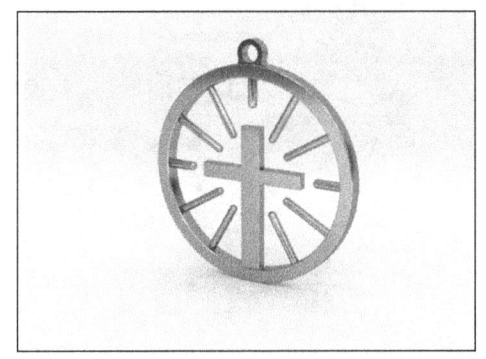
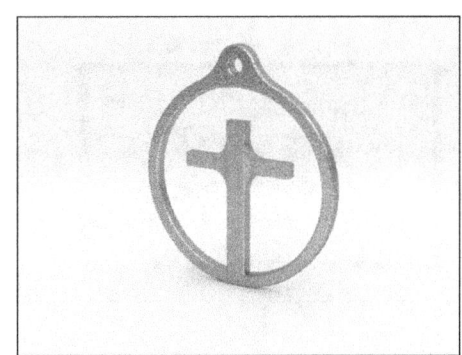

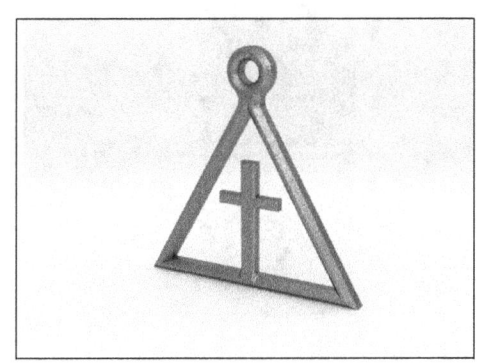
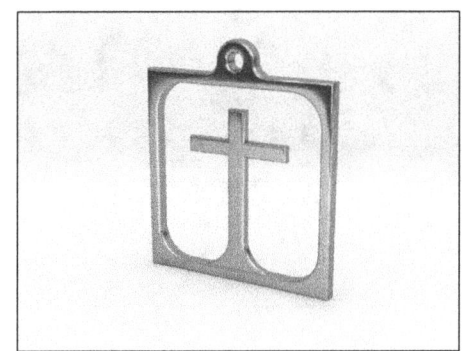

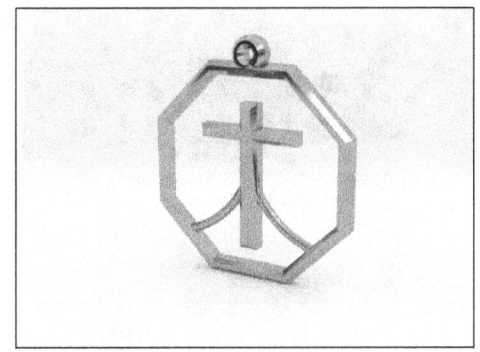
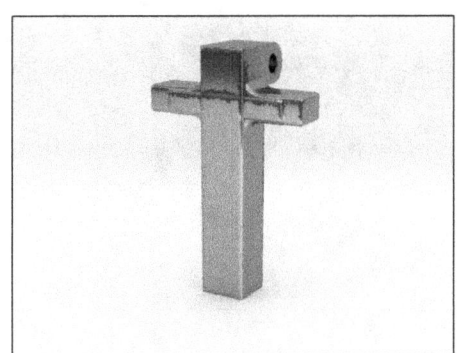

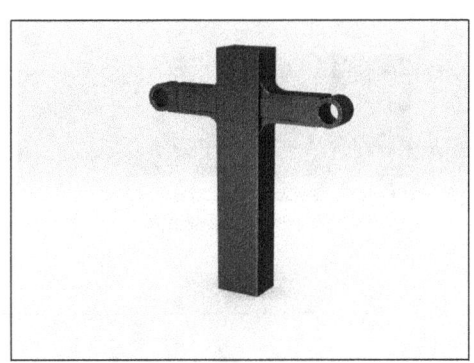

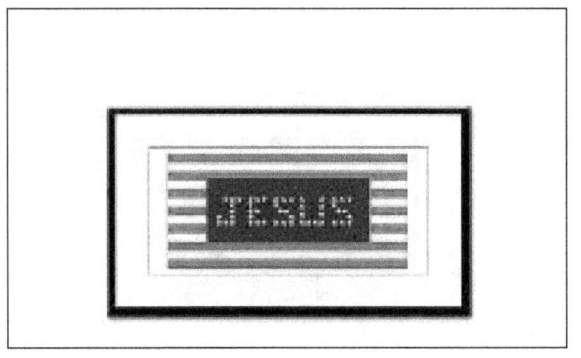

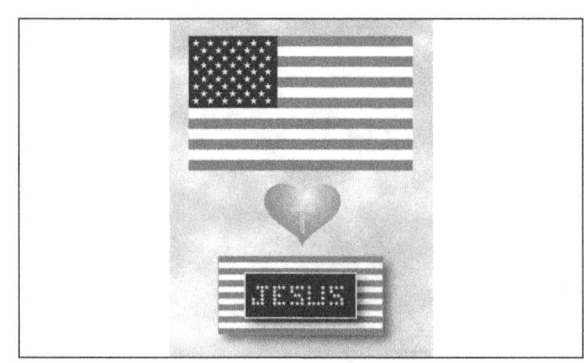

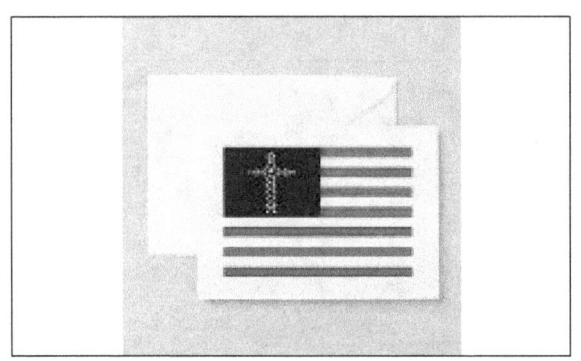

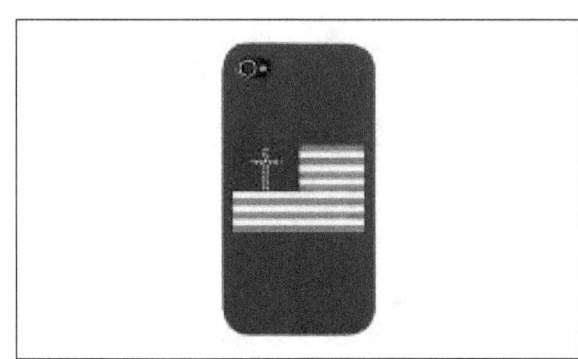

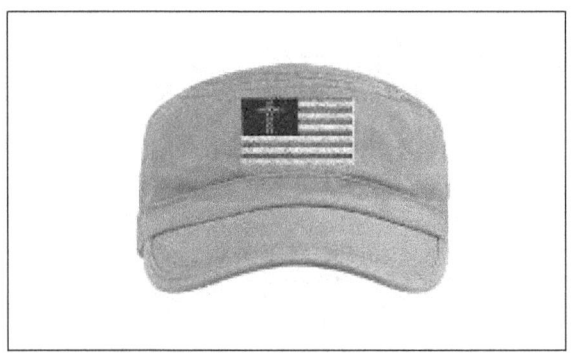

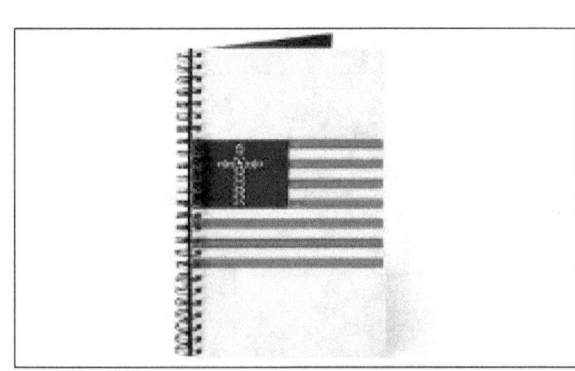

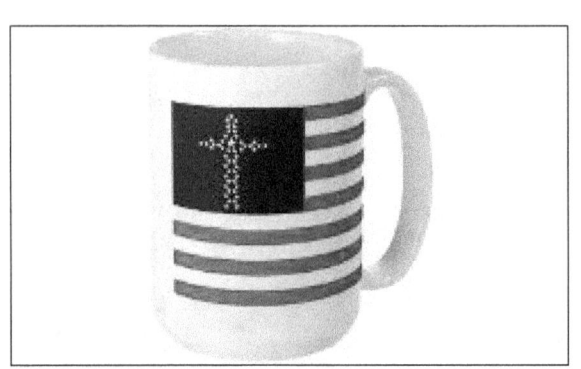

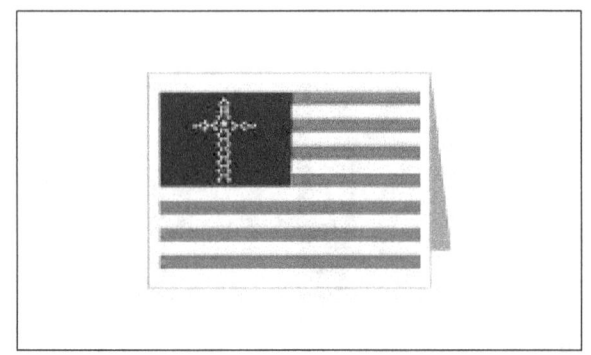

M7

FINGER TOYS

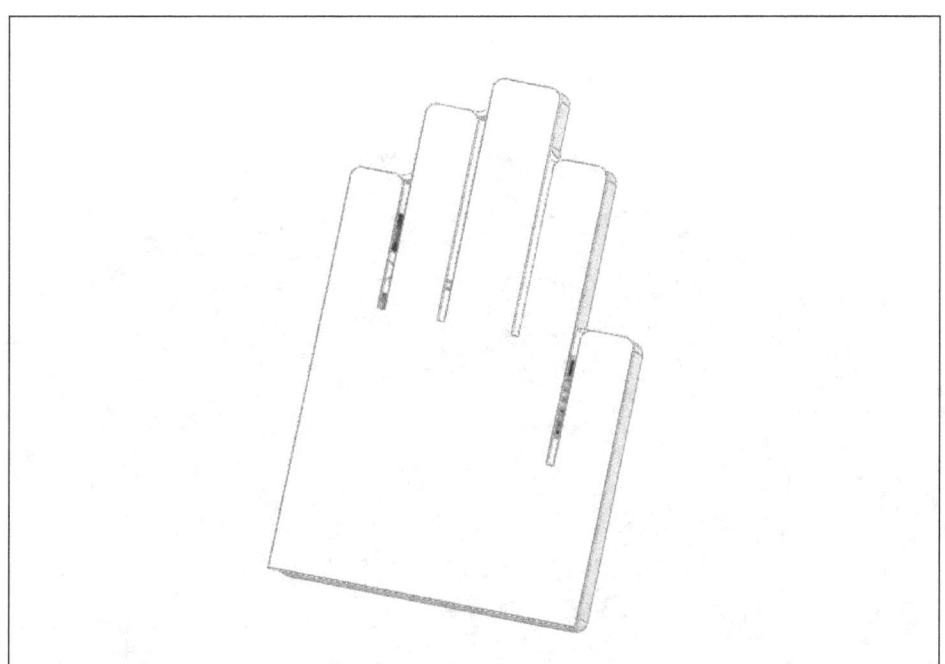

BORED HANDS ?

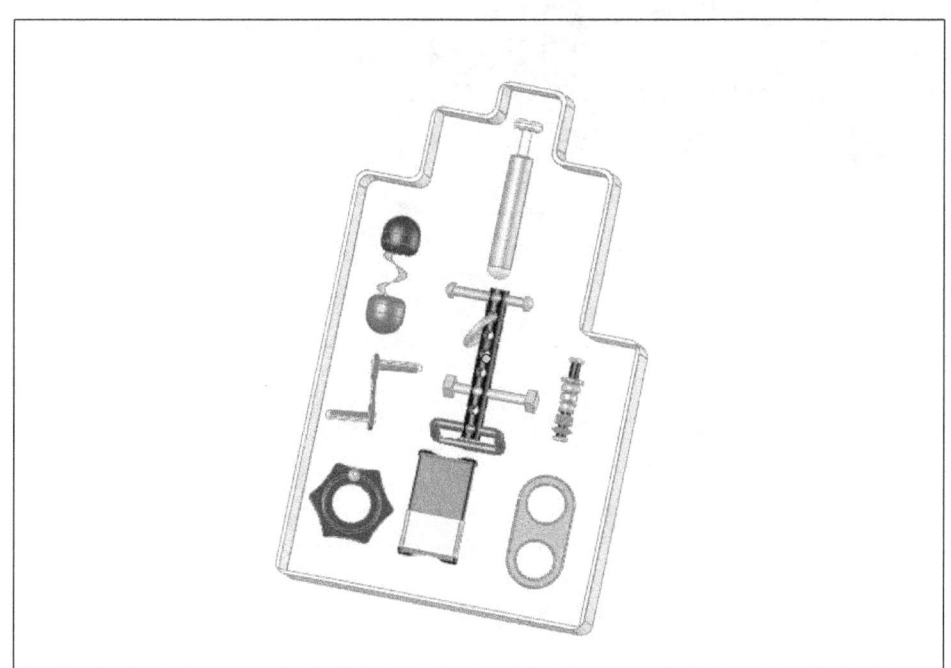

Have Fun !

M7

MUTRX GARDEN

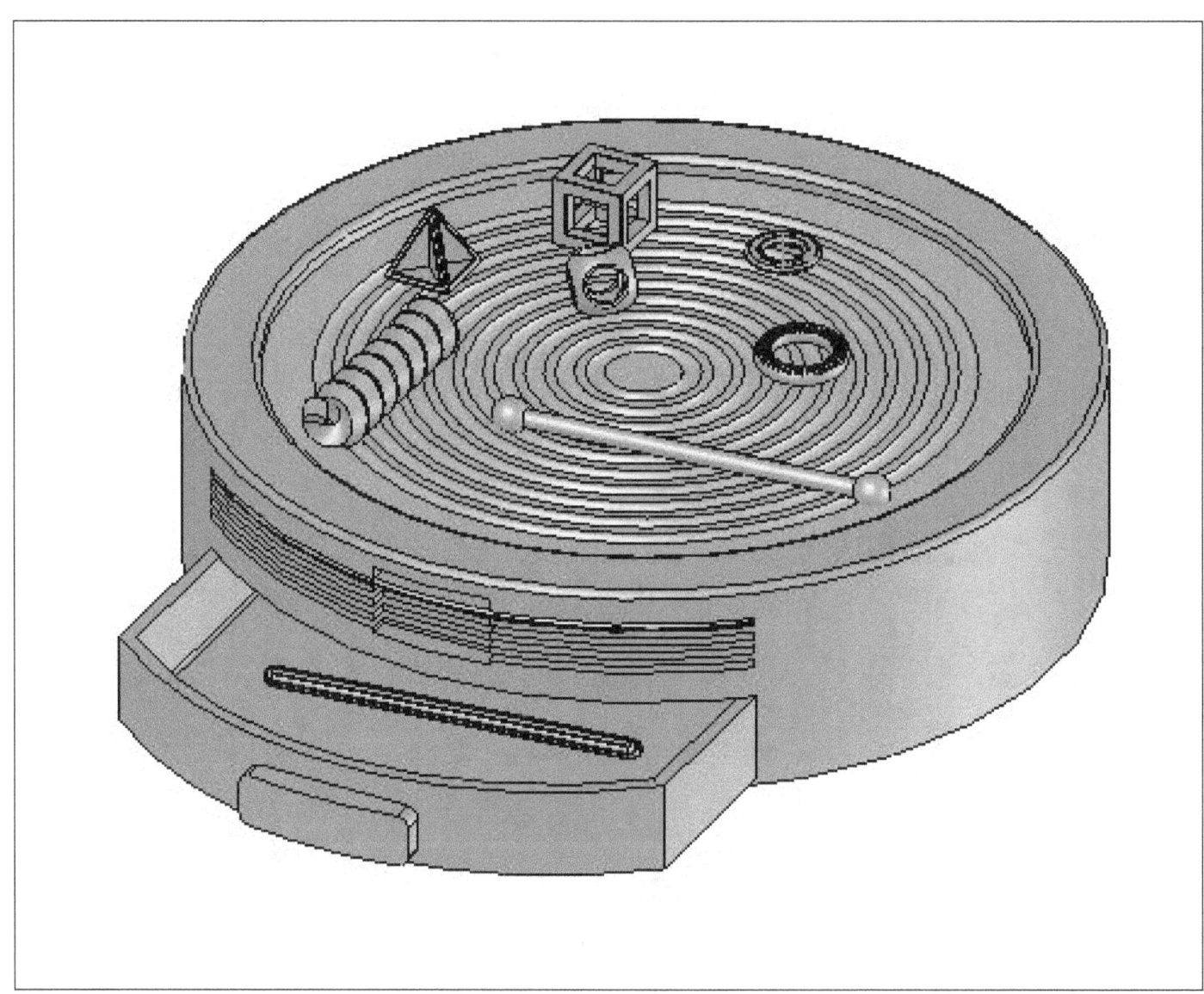

FUTURE PARTS

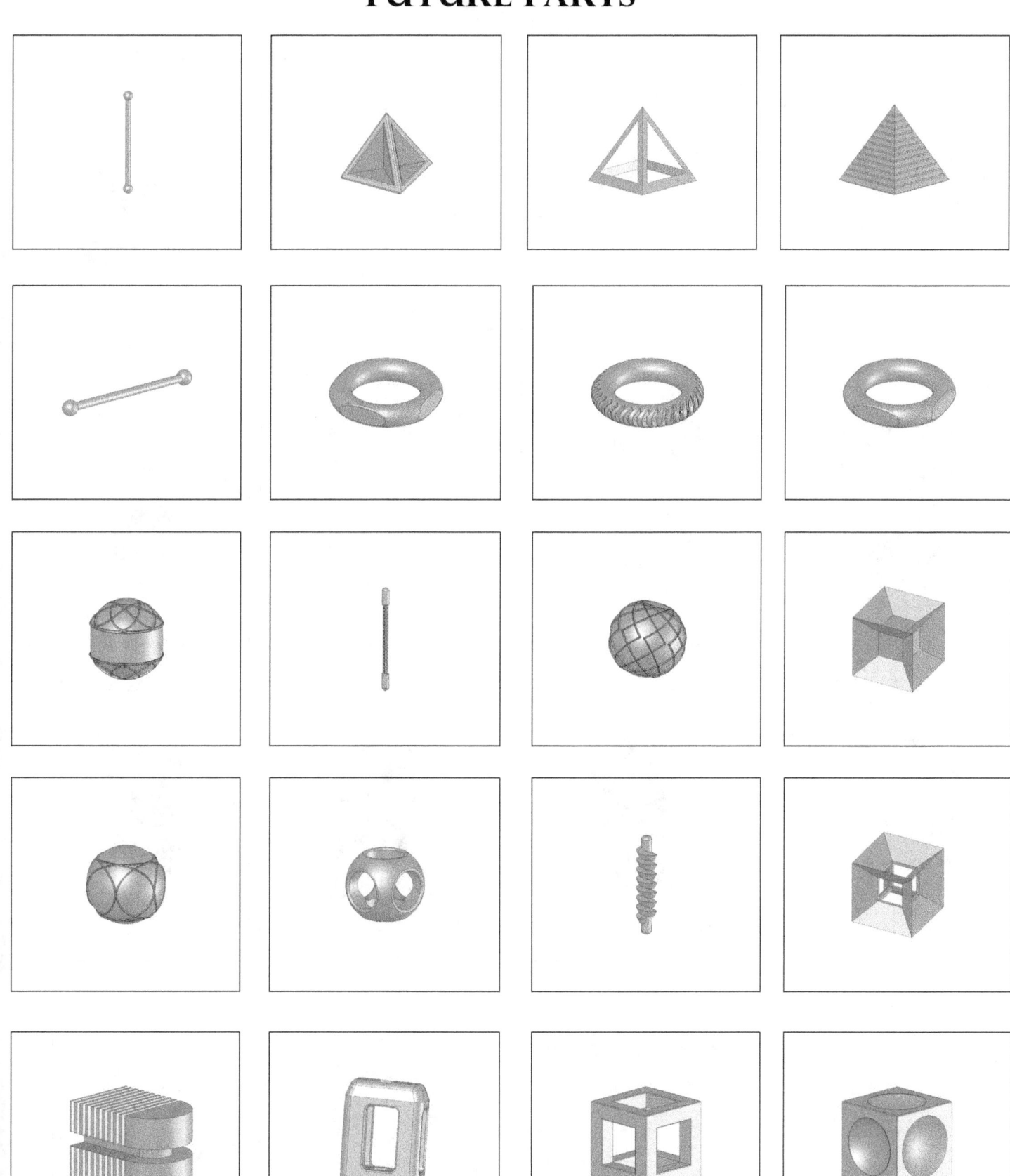

GLASSWARE

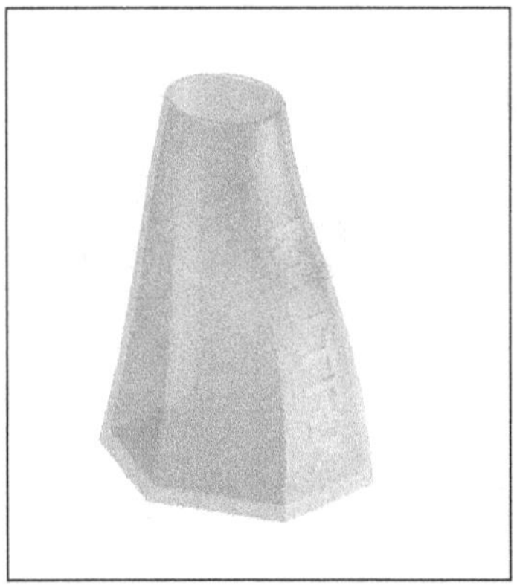

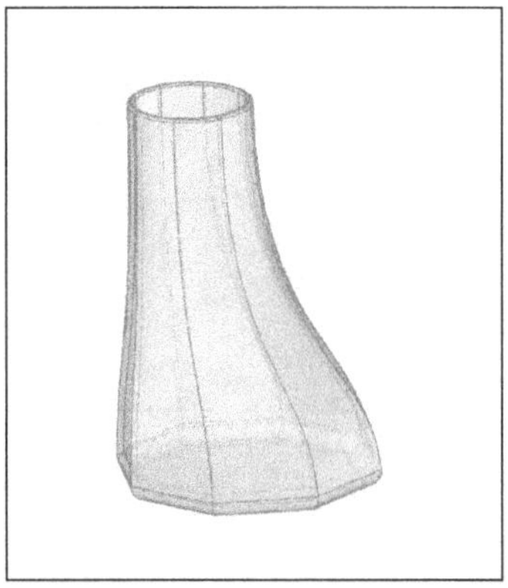

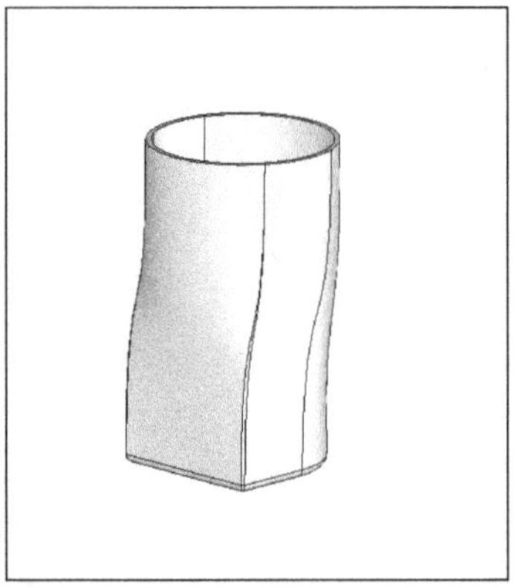

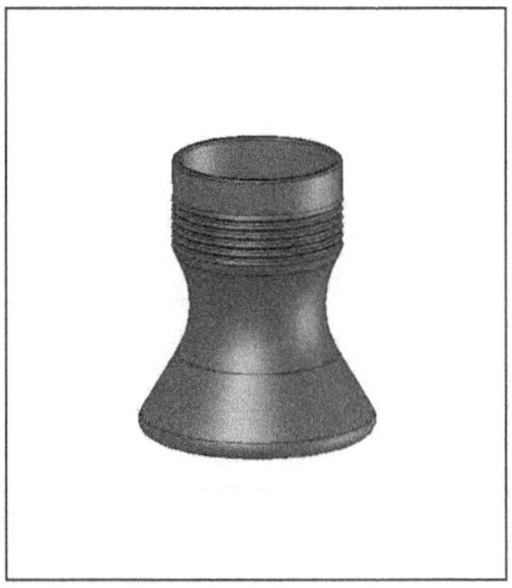

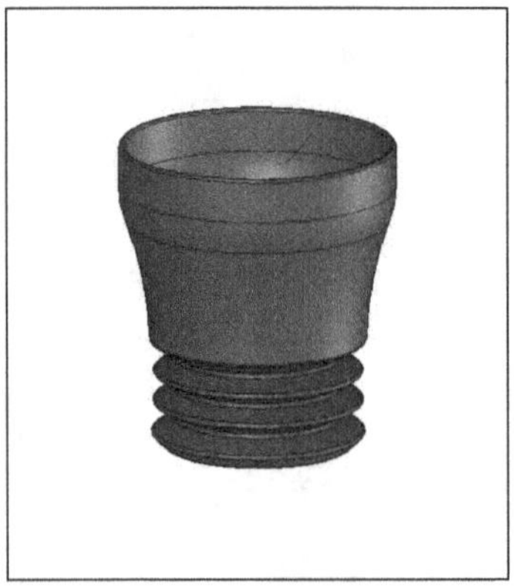

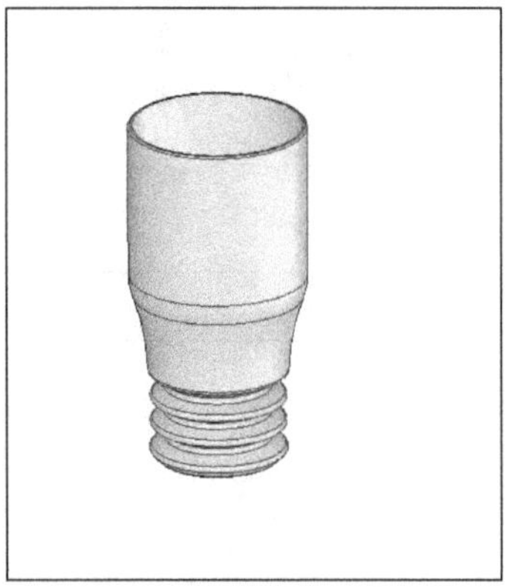

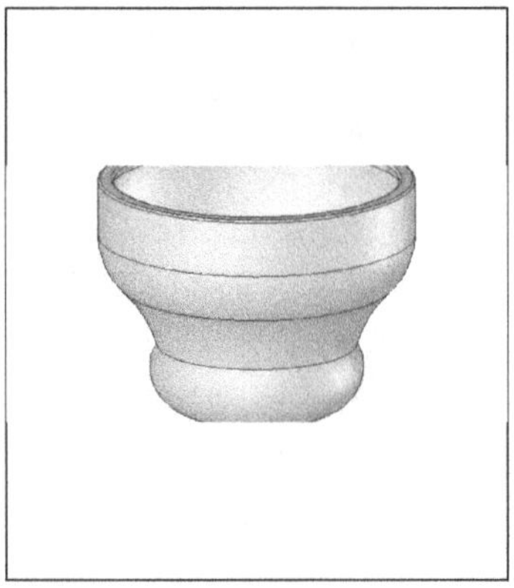

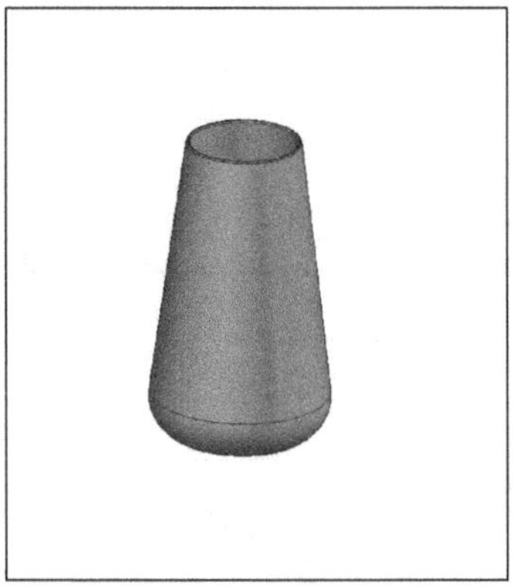

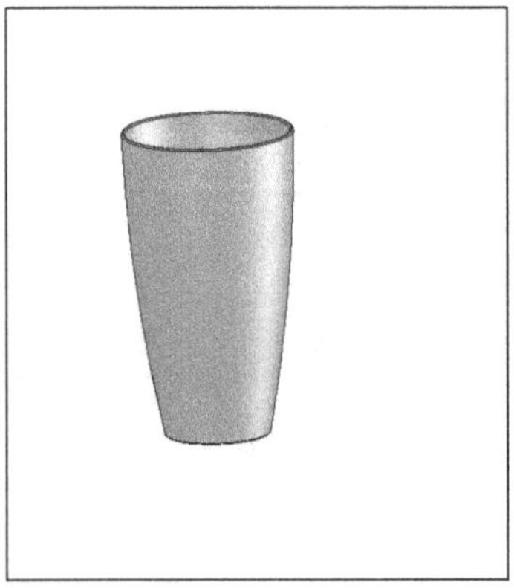

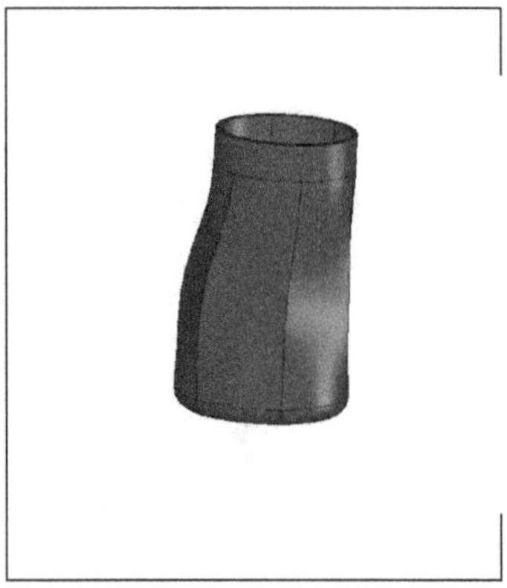

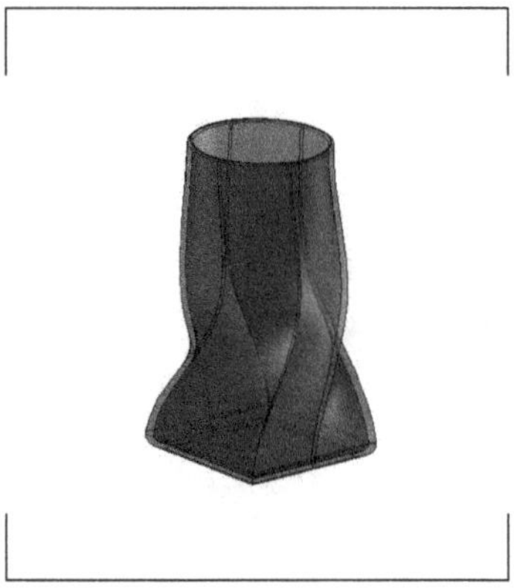

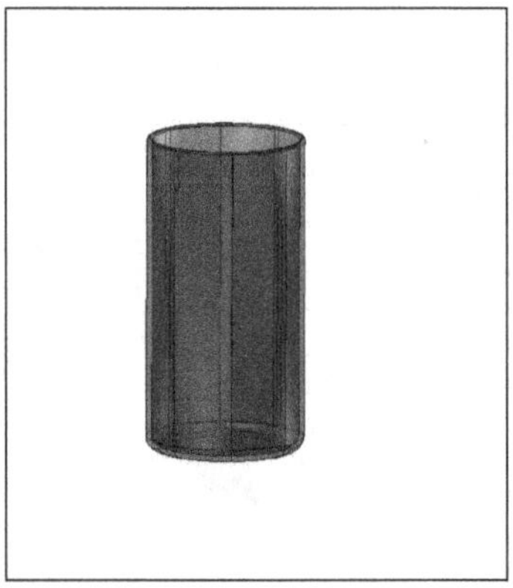

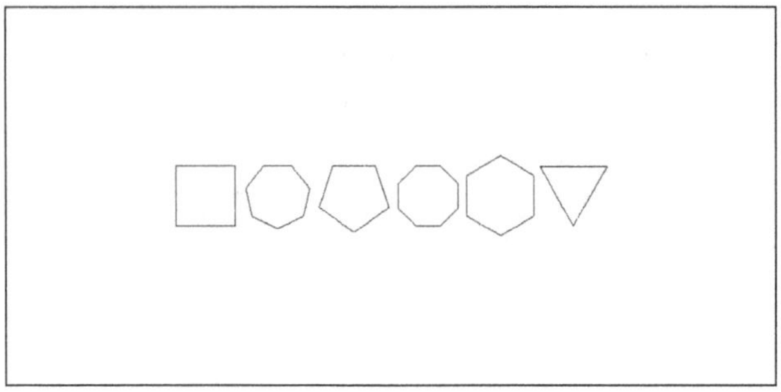

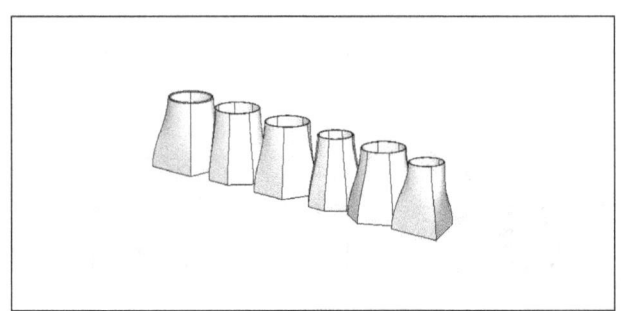

ICE CREAM CONTAINER

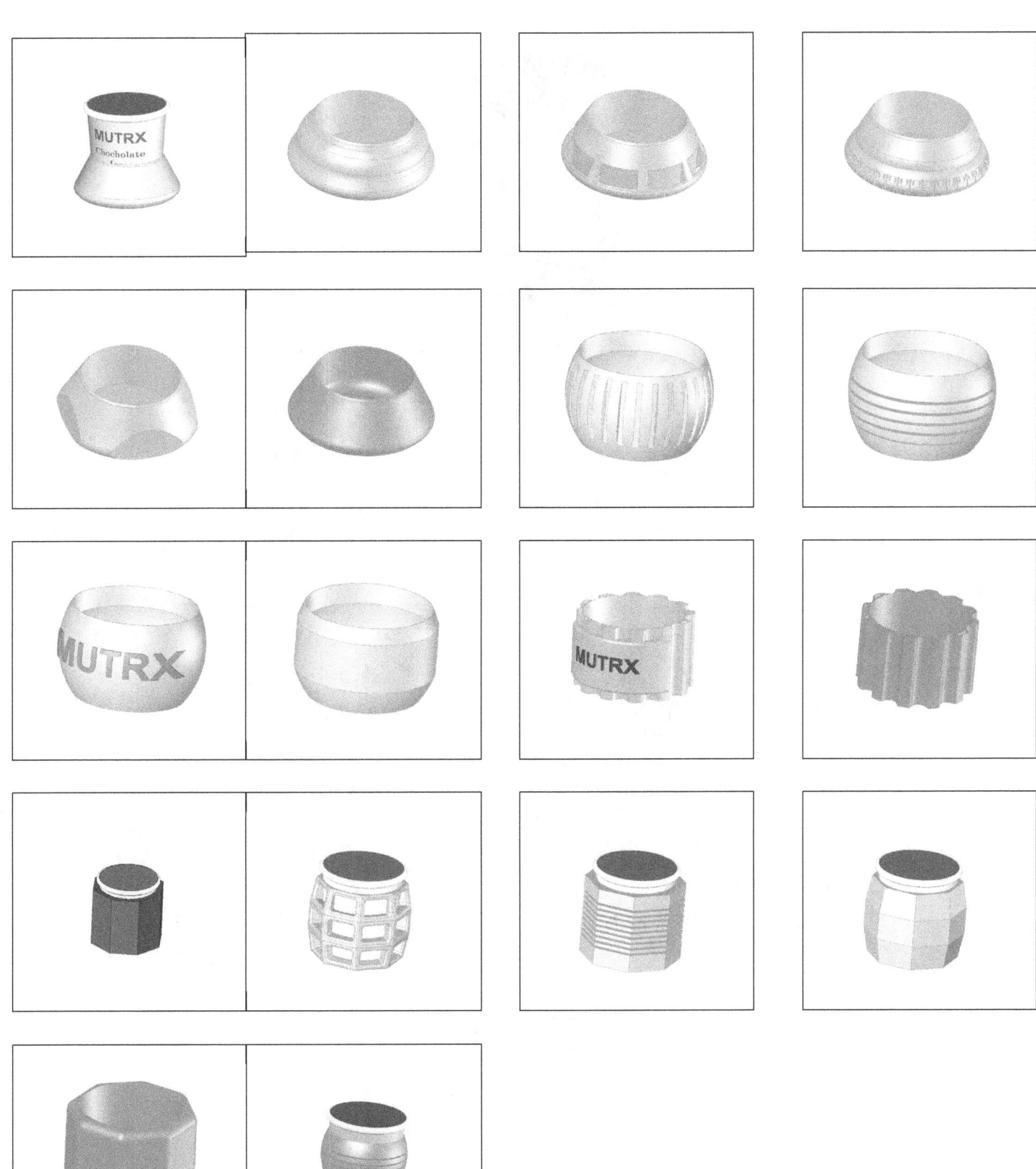

ICE CUBE TRAYS

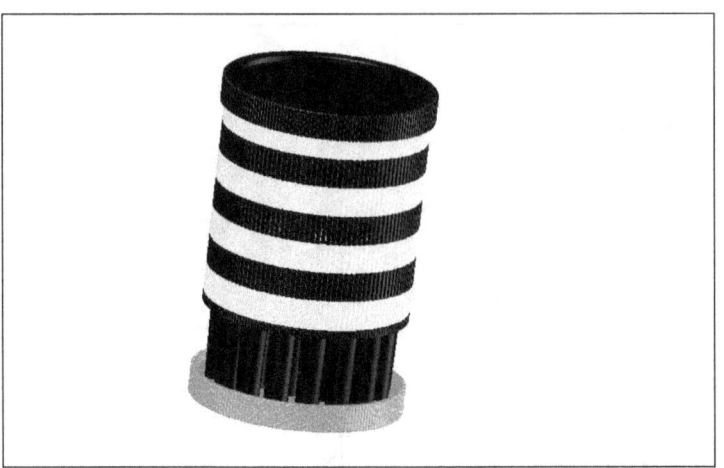

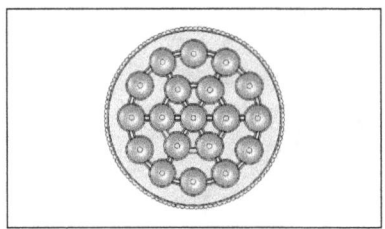

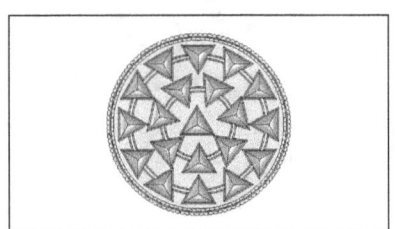

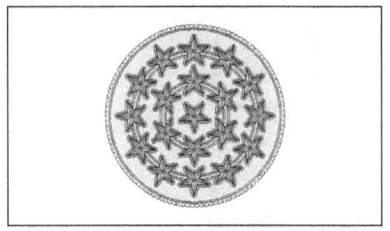

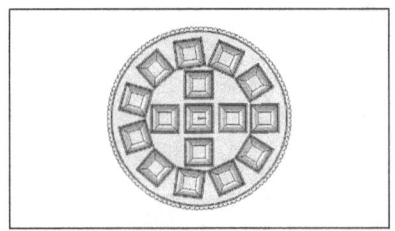

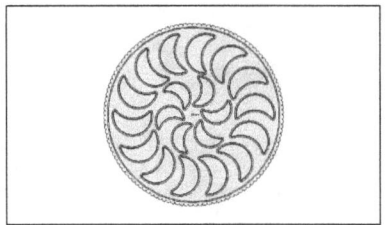

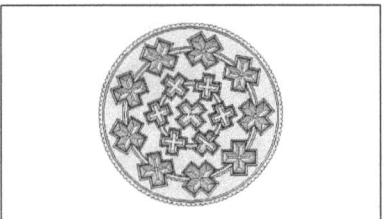

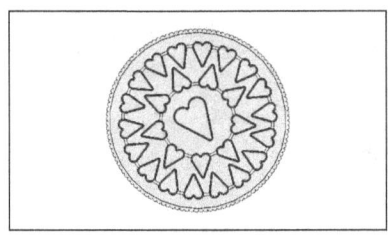

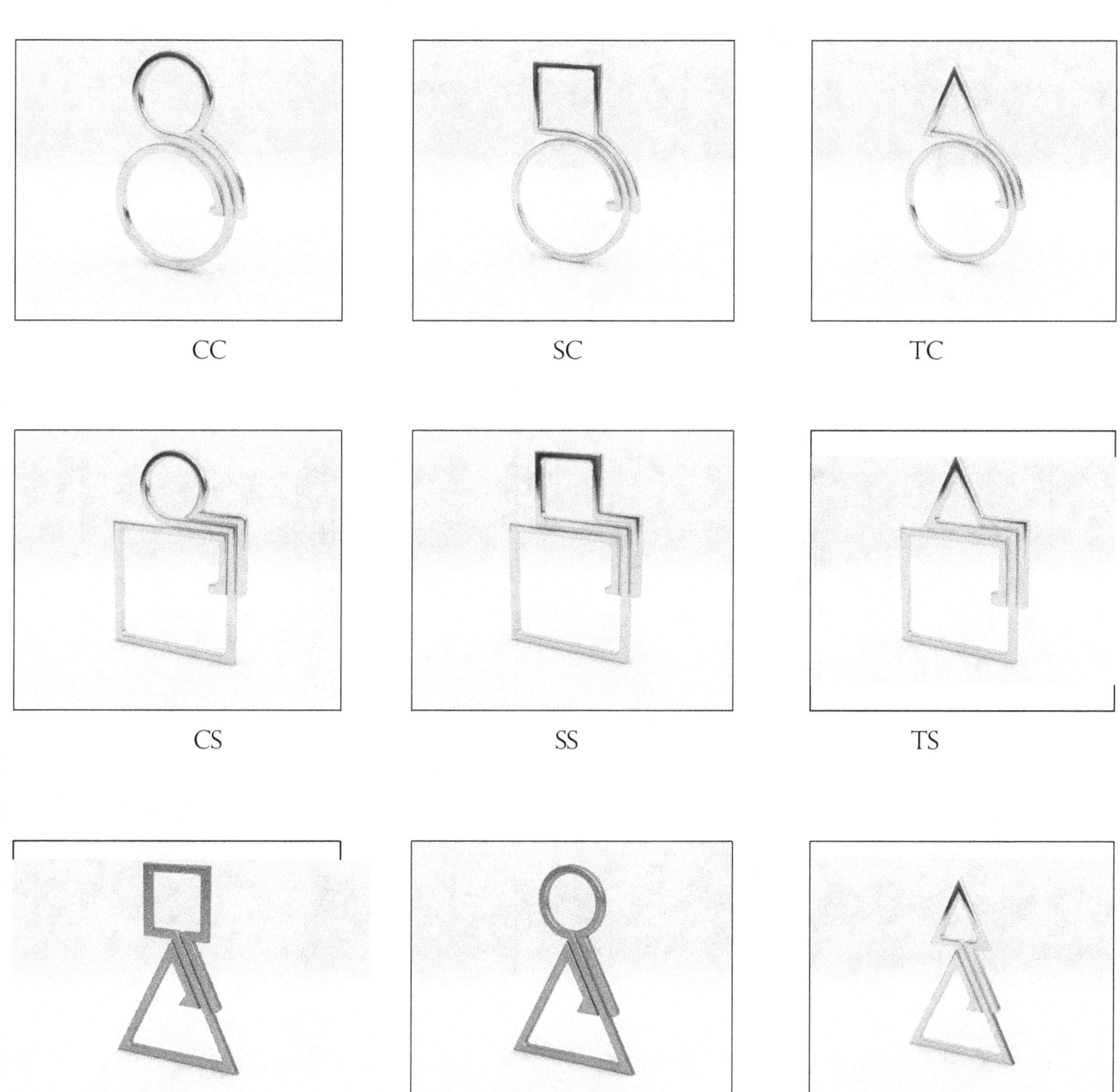

CC   SC   TC

CS   SS   TS

ST   CT   TT

ADDITIONAL KEYCHAINS

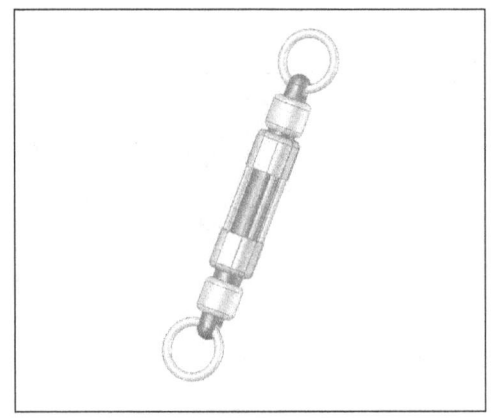
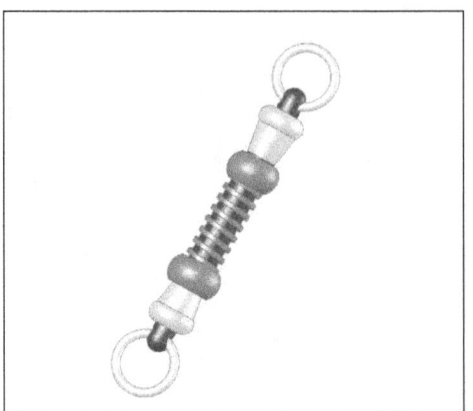
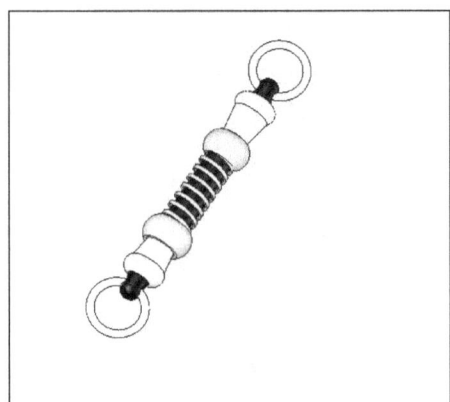
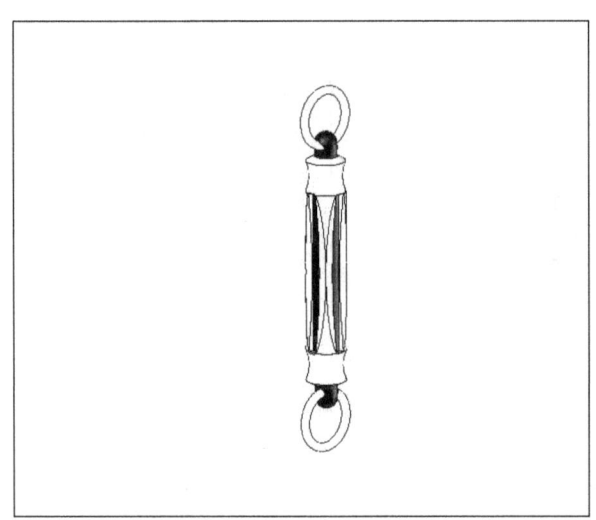
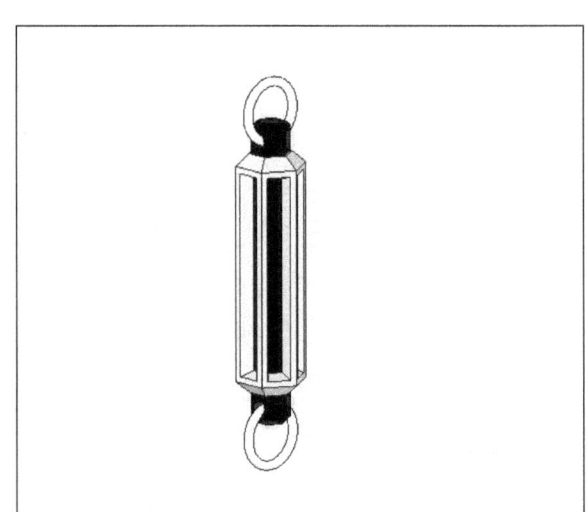
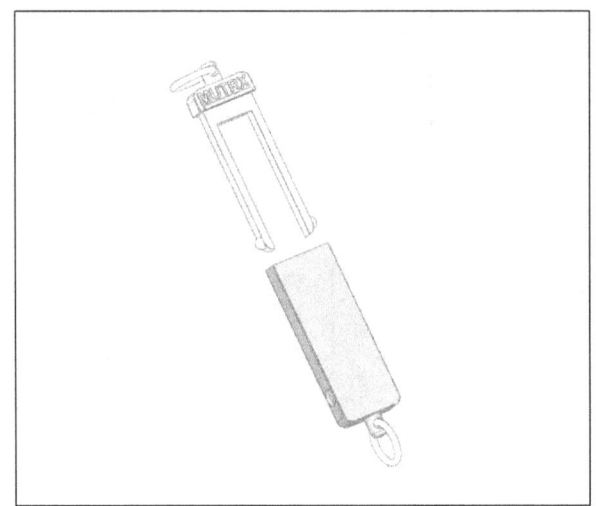
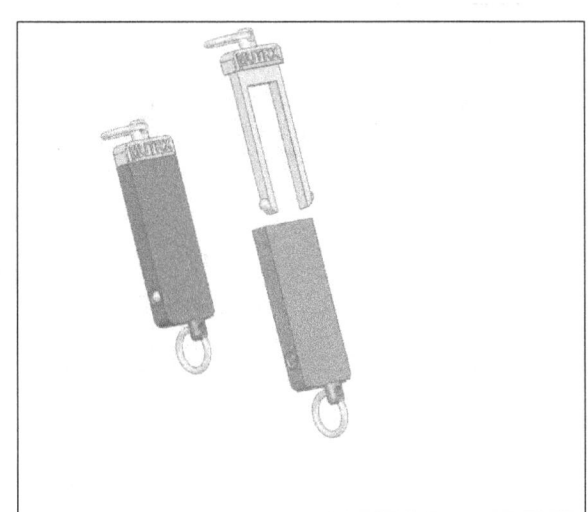

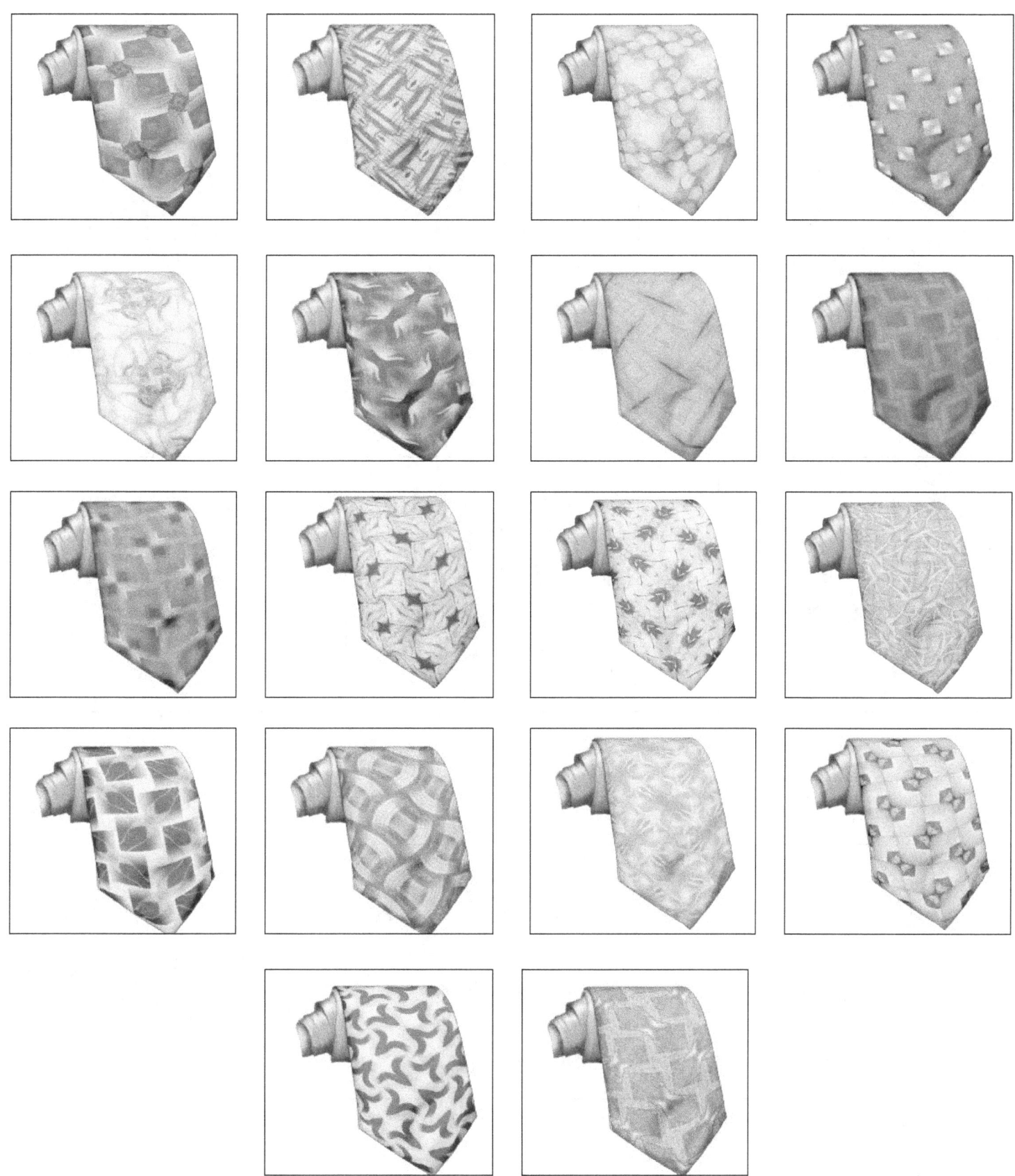

TIE KNOTS 4

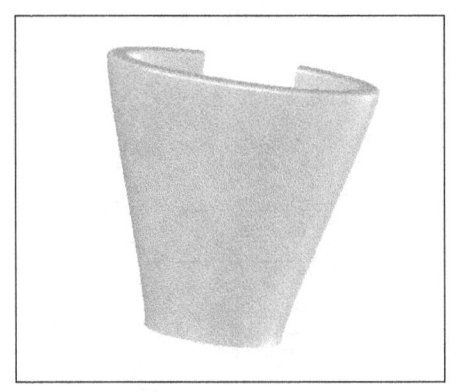 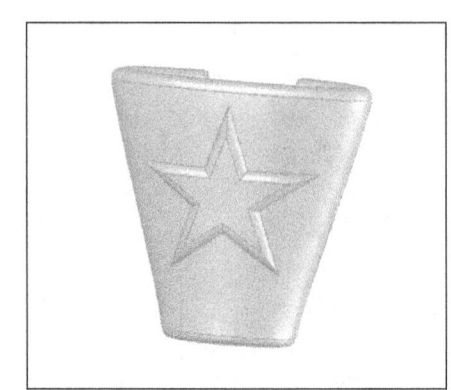 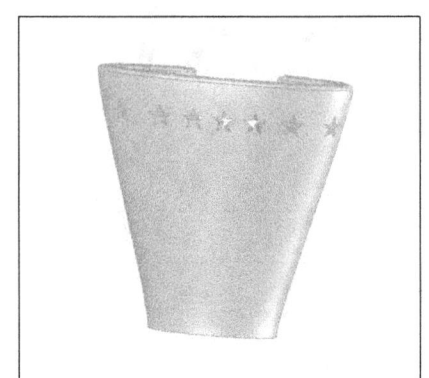

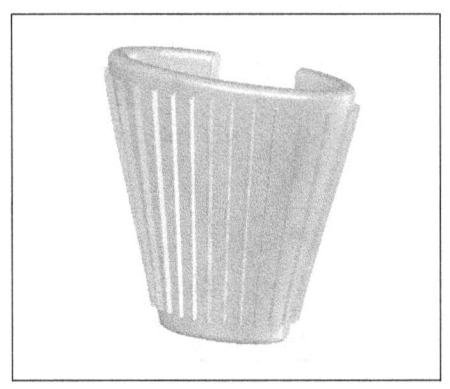 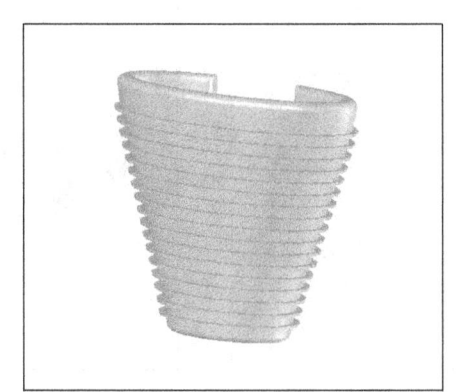 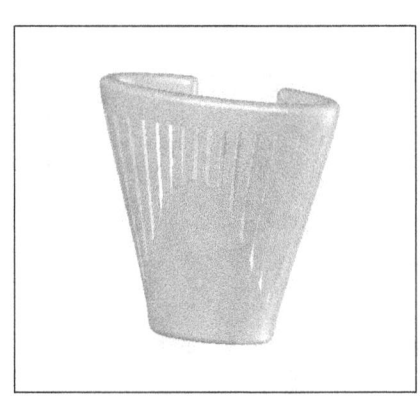

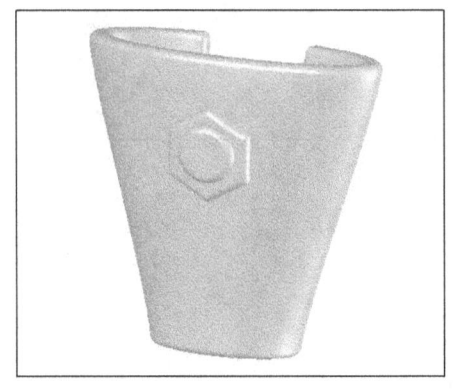 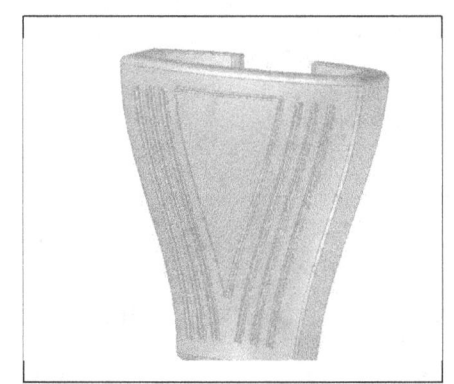 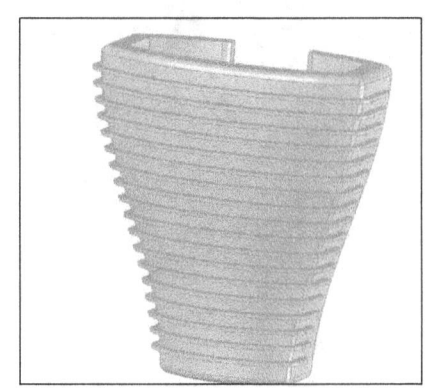

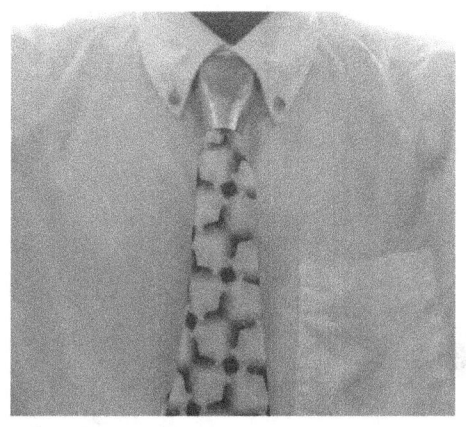 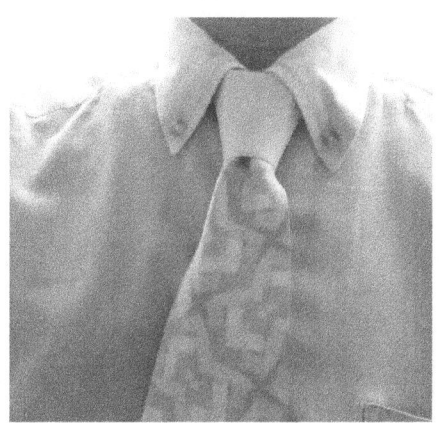 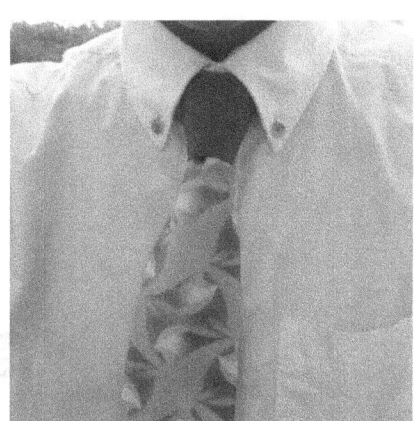

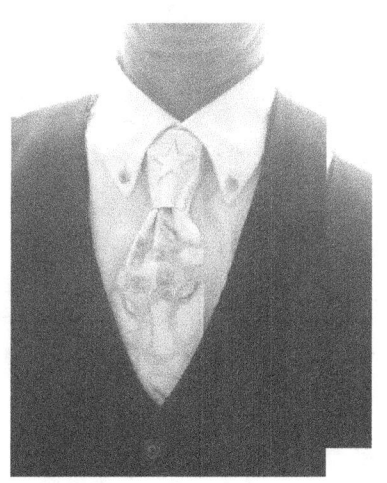 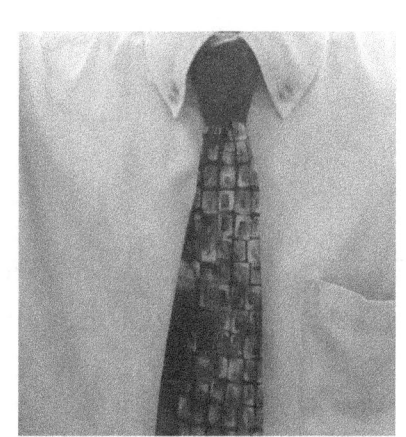 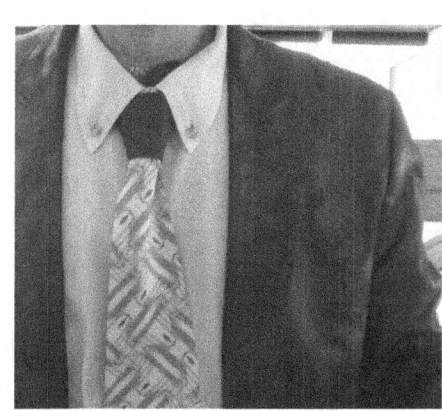

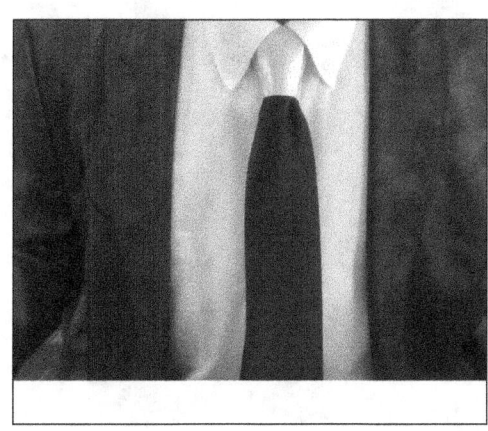 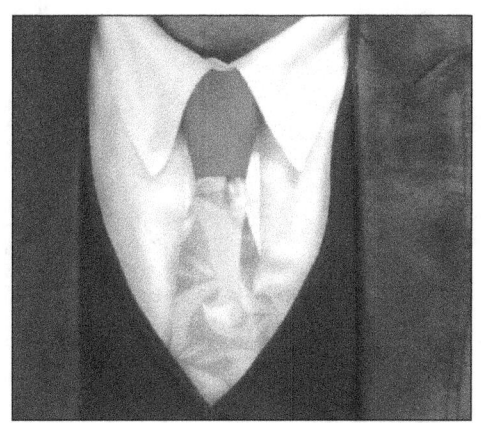

KYGA STICK

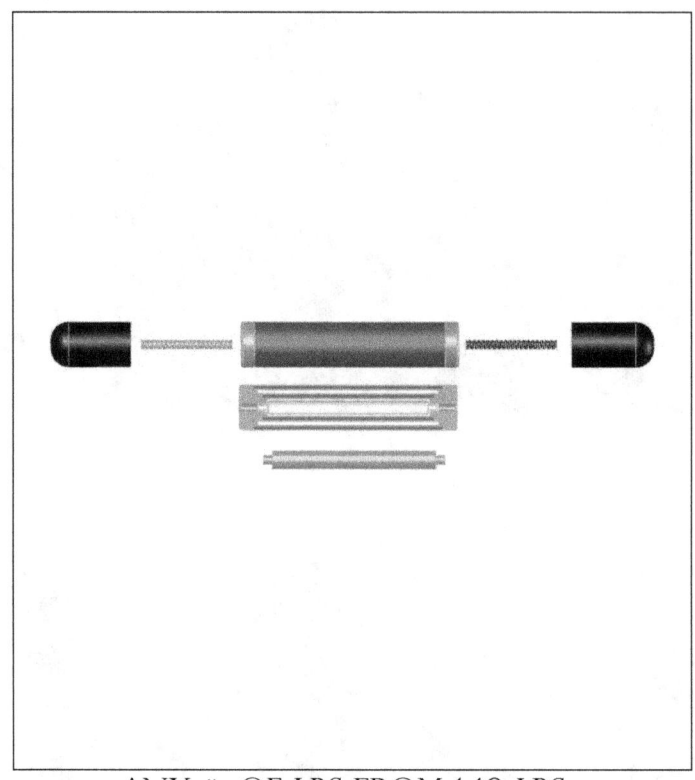

ANY # OF LBS FROM 1-10 LBS
2 PER SET

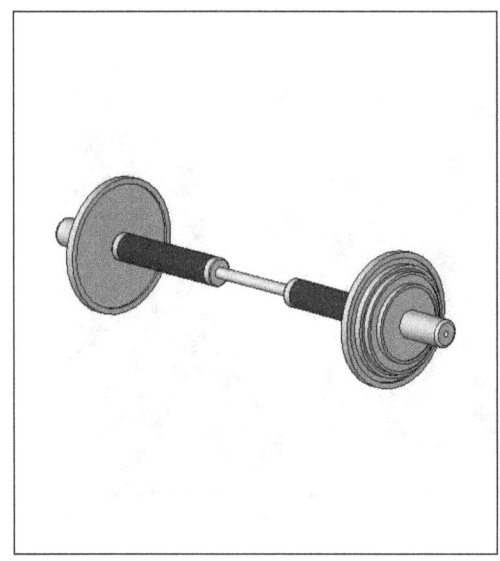

BARBELL ACCESSORIES

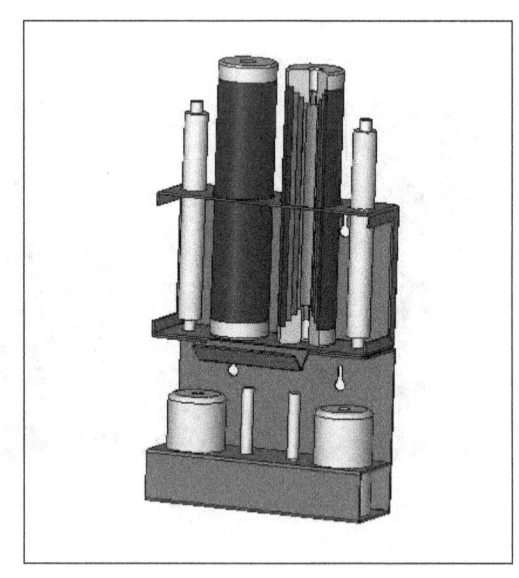

HOME STORAGE

M7

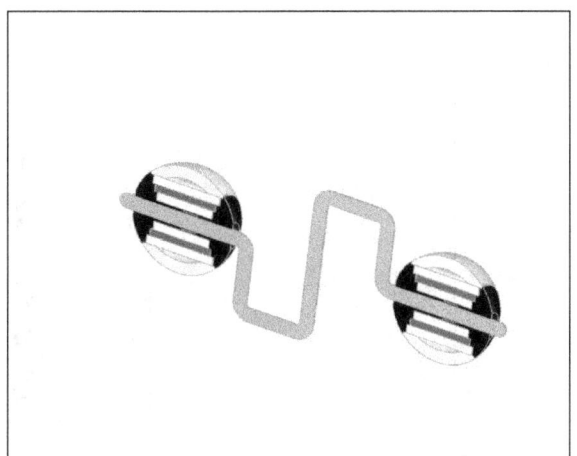

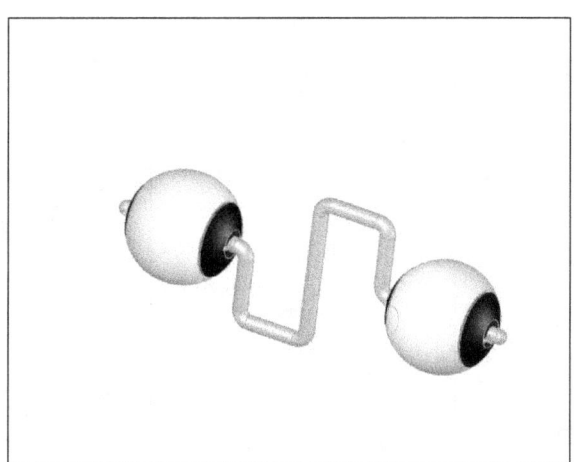

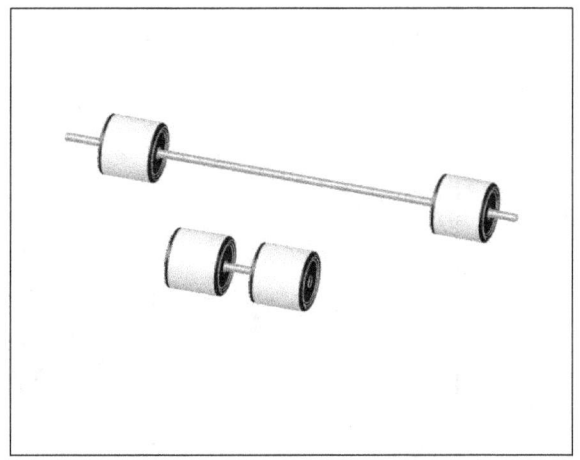

M7

MENORAHS

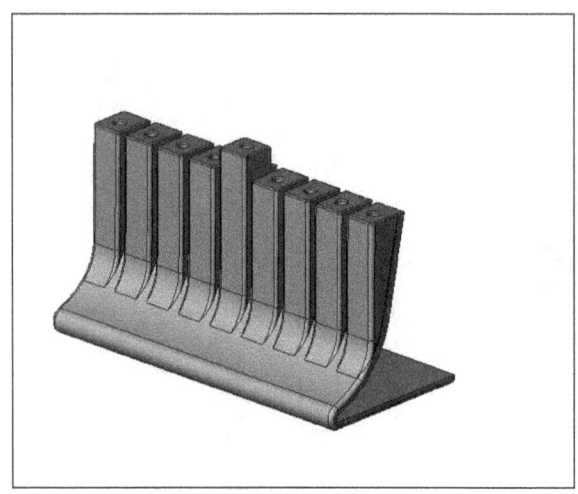

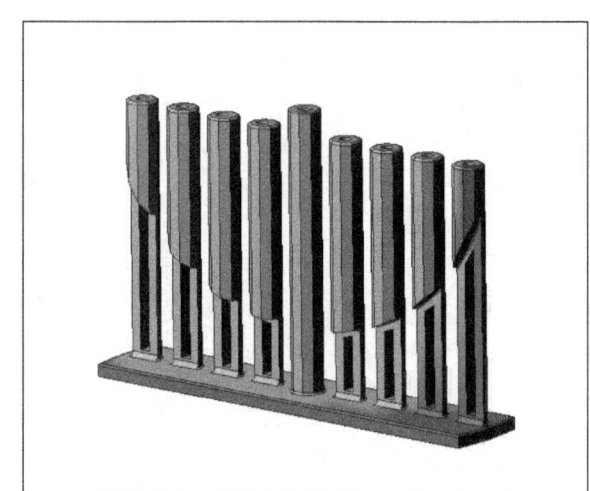

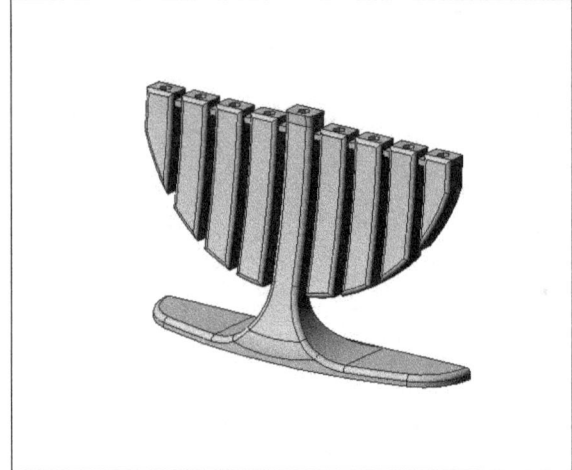

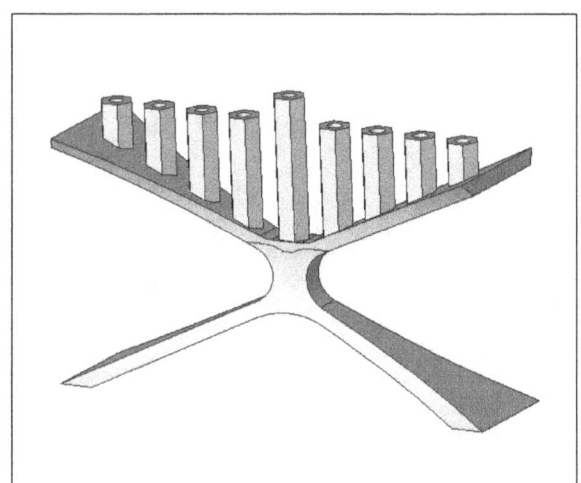

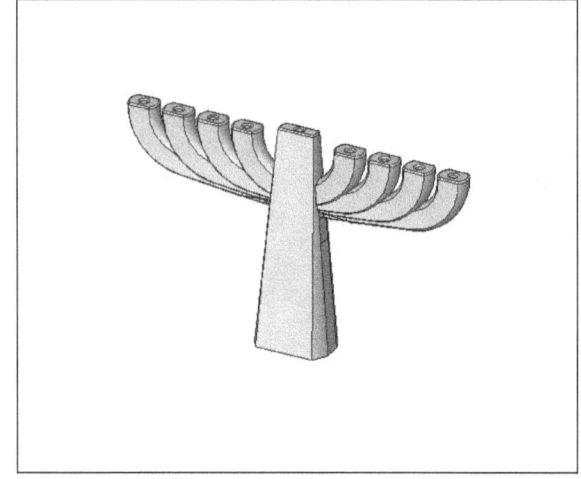

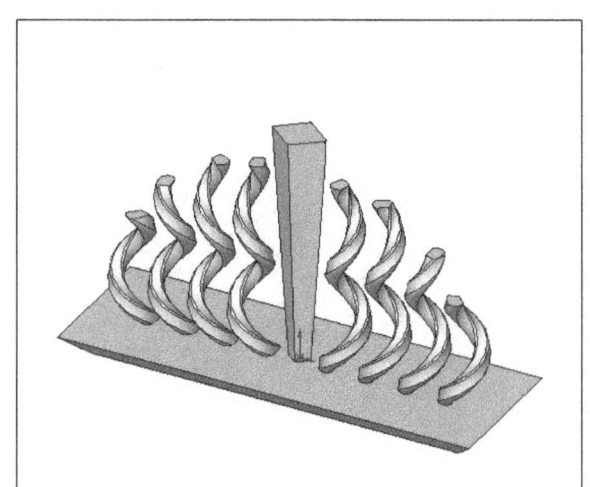

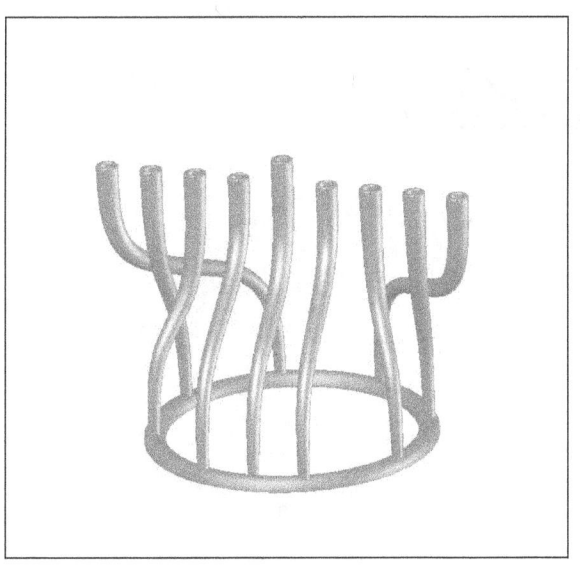 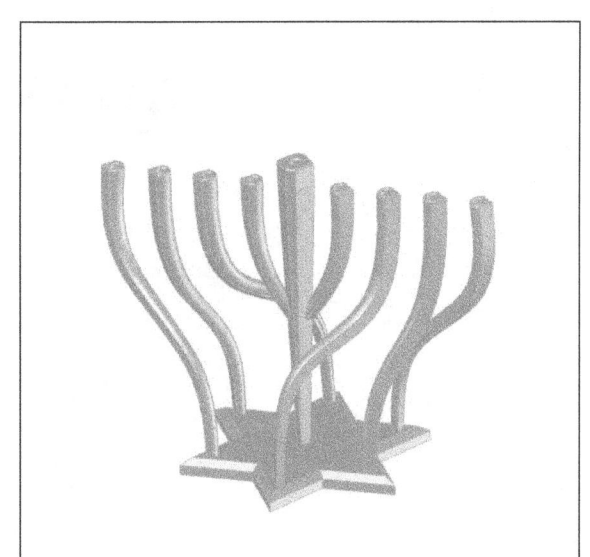

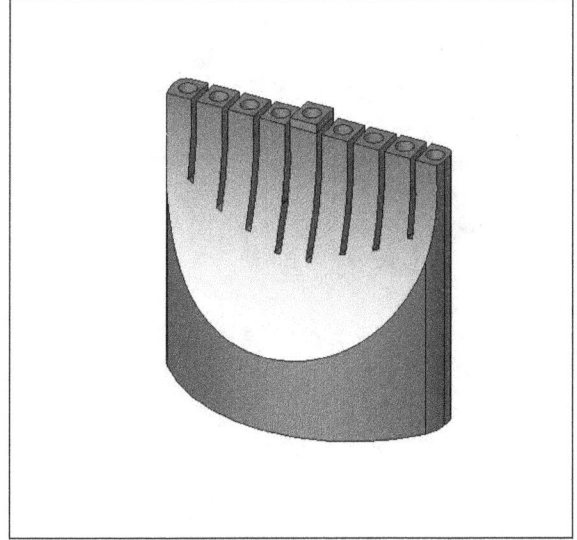 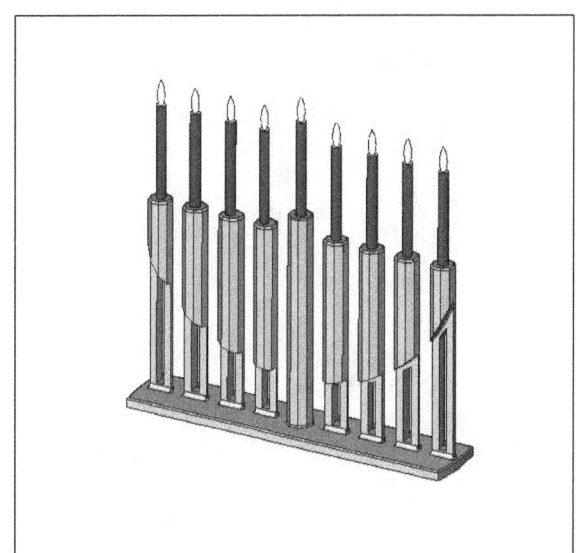

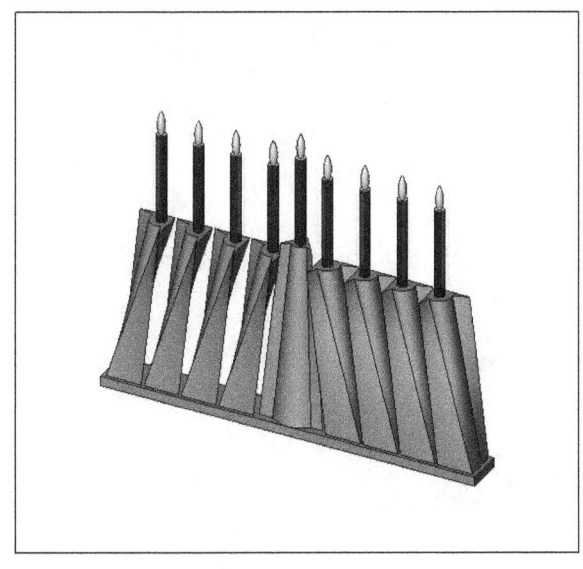 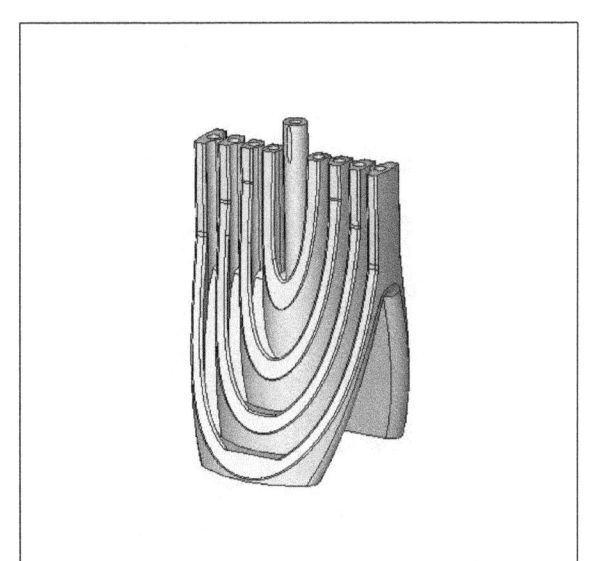

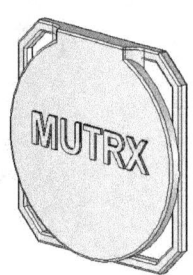

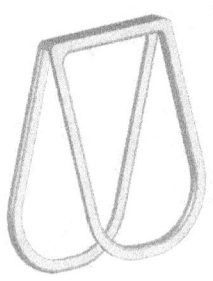

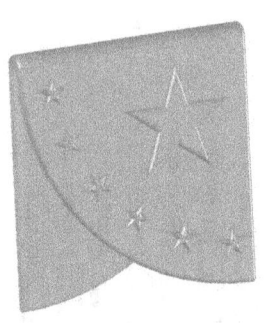

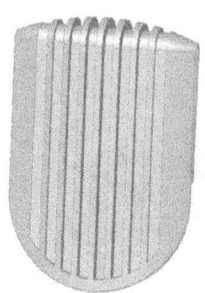

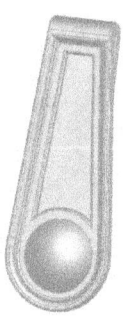

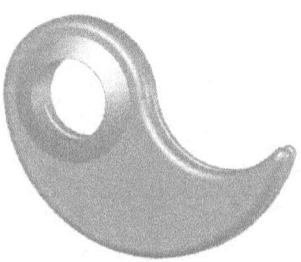

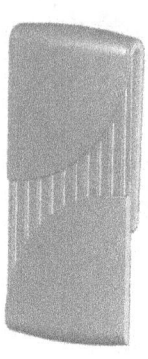

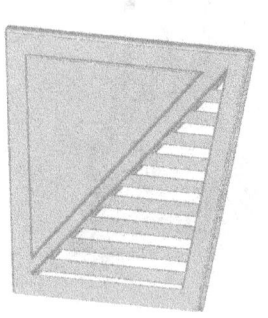

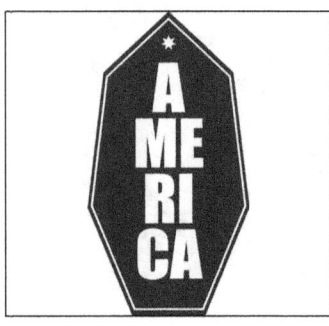
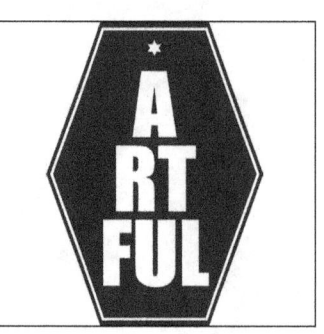
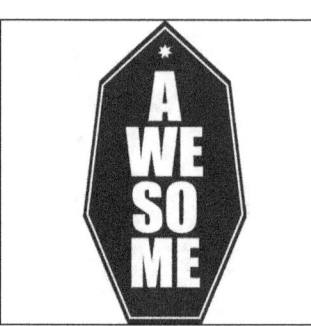
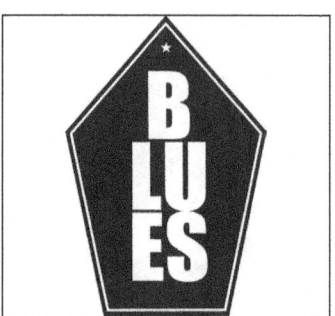

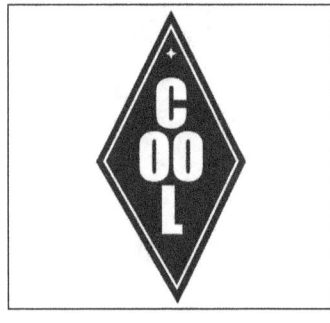
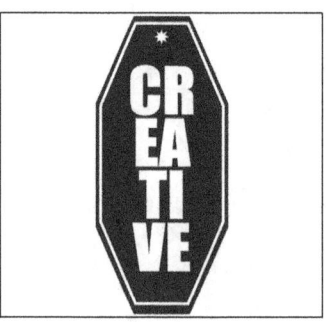
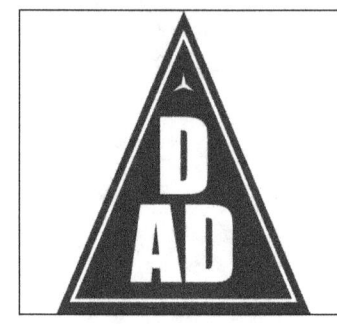
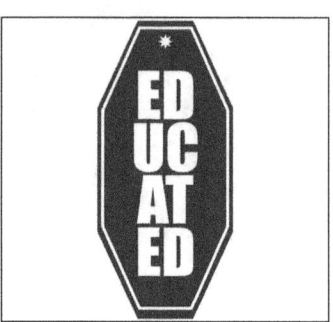

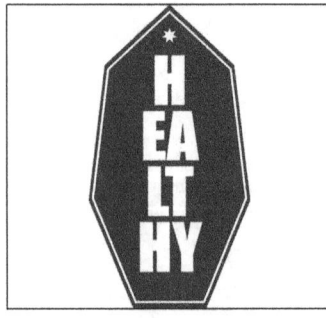
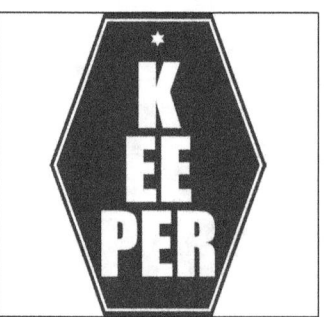
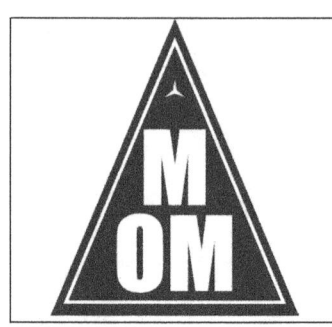
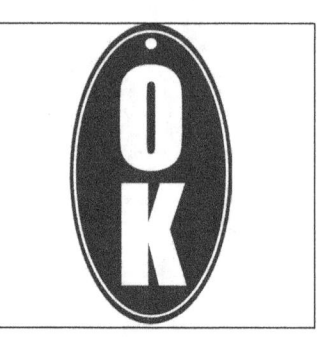

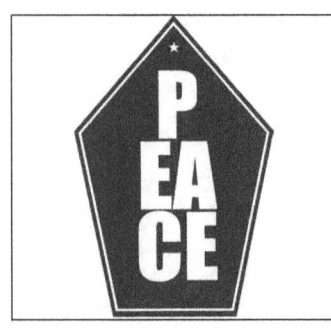
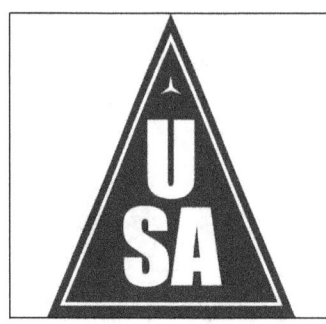
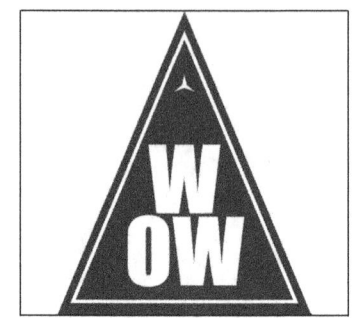
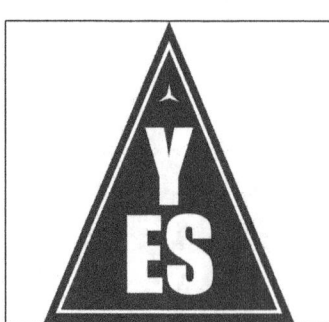

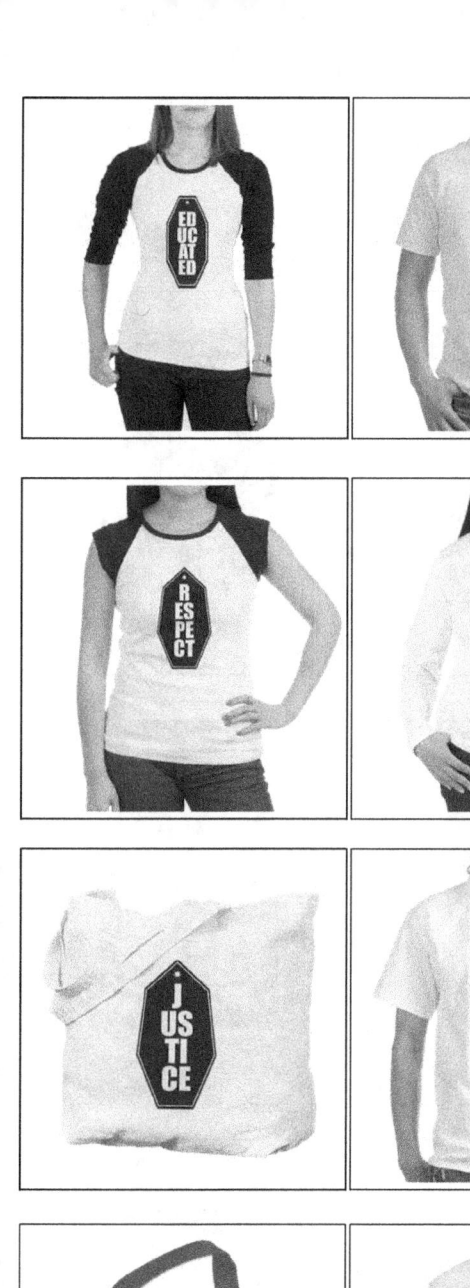 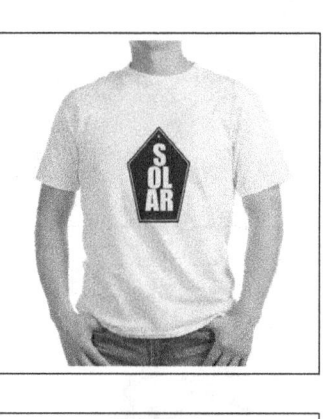 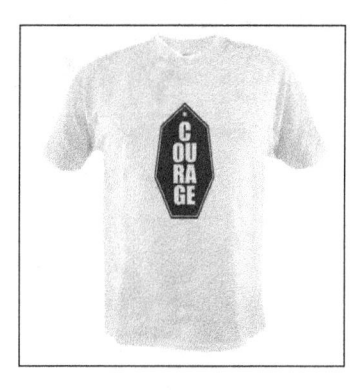 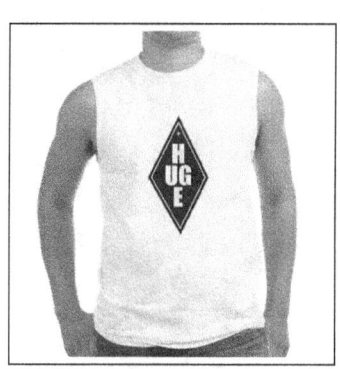

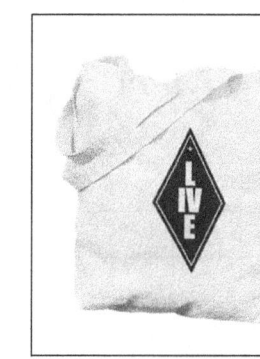 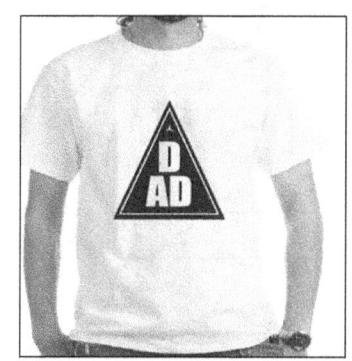

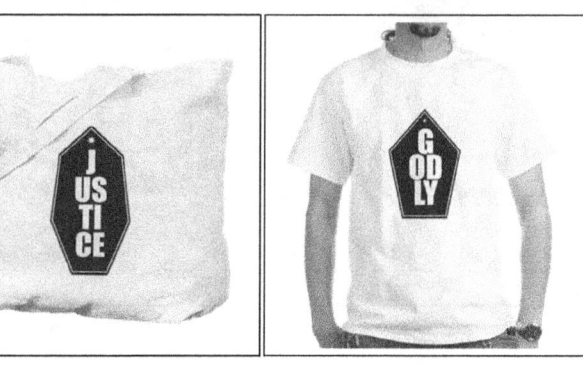 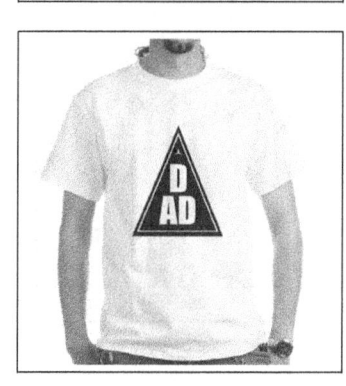 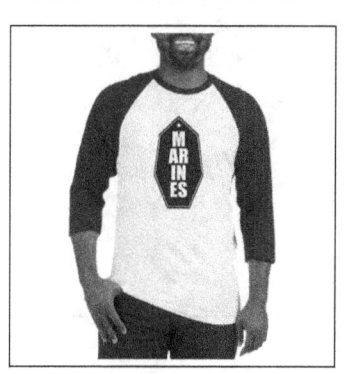

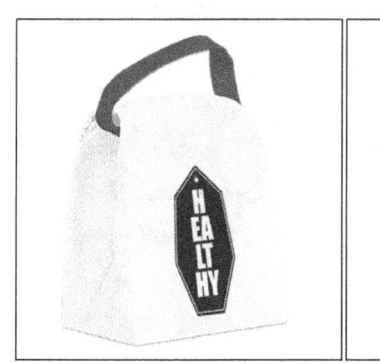 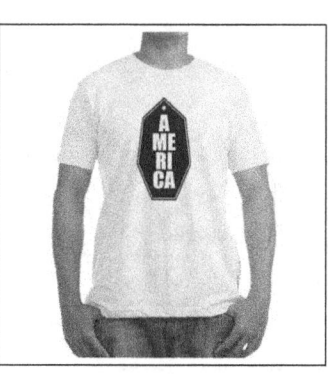 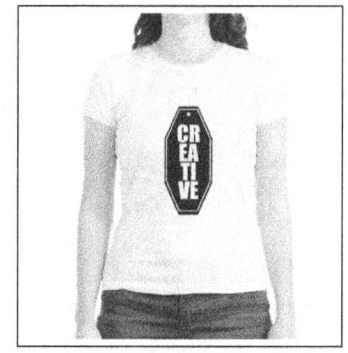 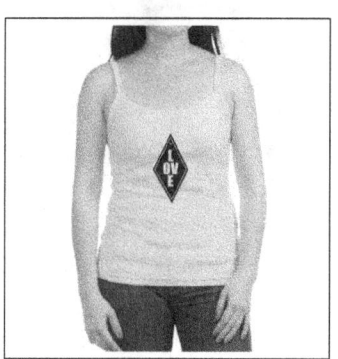

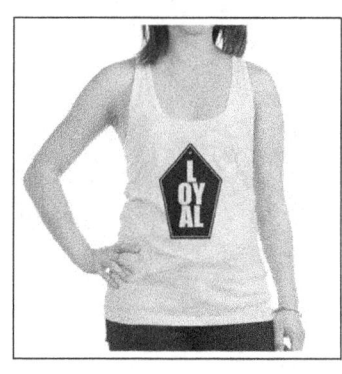 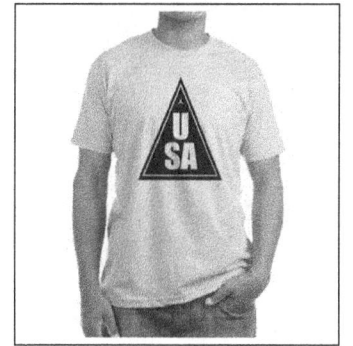

MUGS

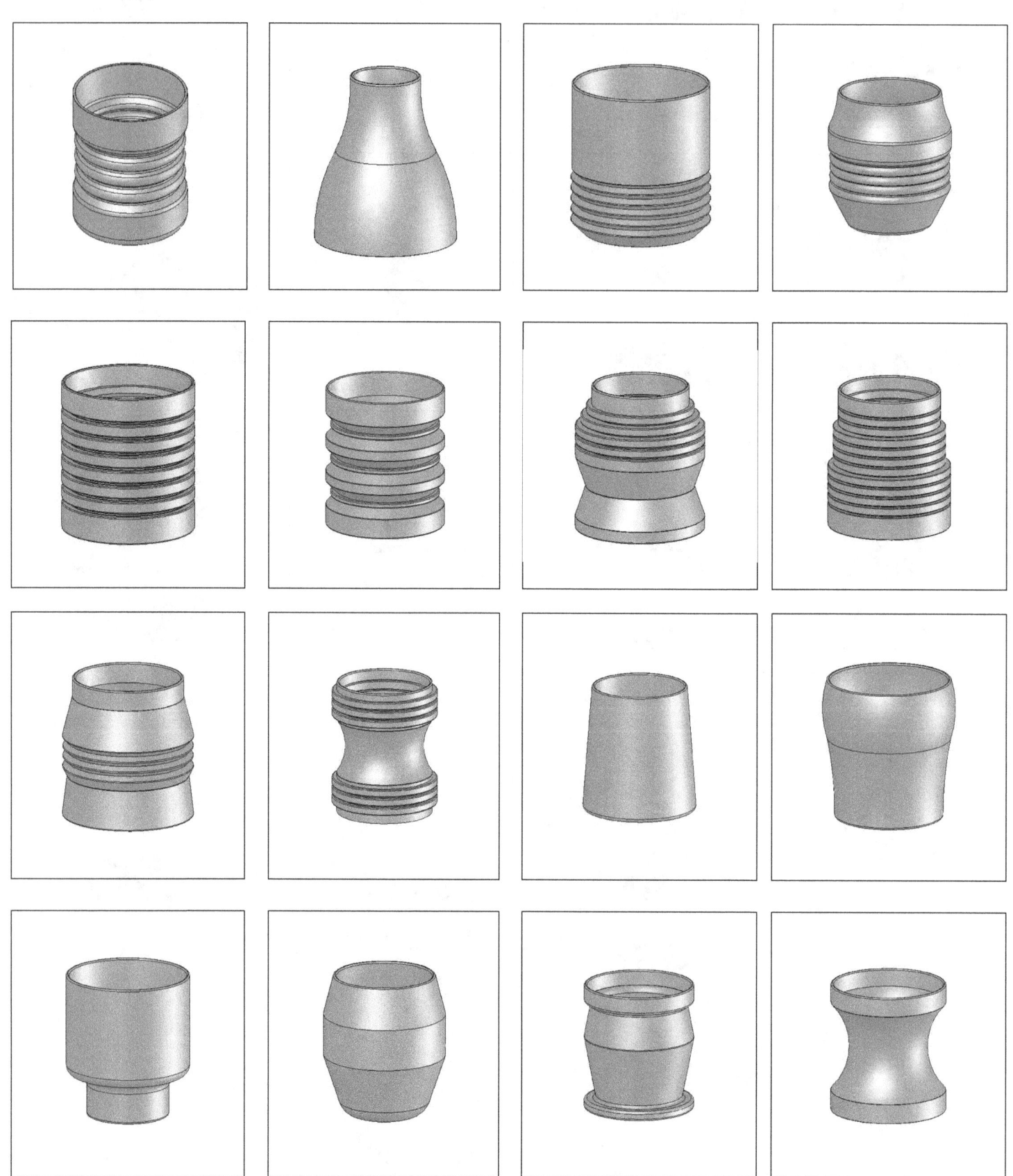

M7

OIL / VINEGAR

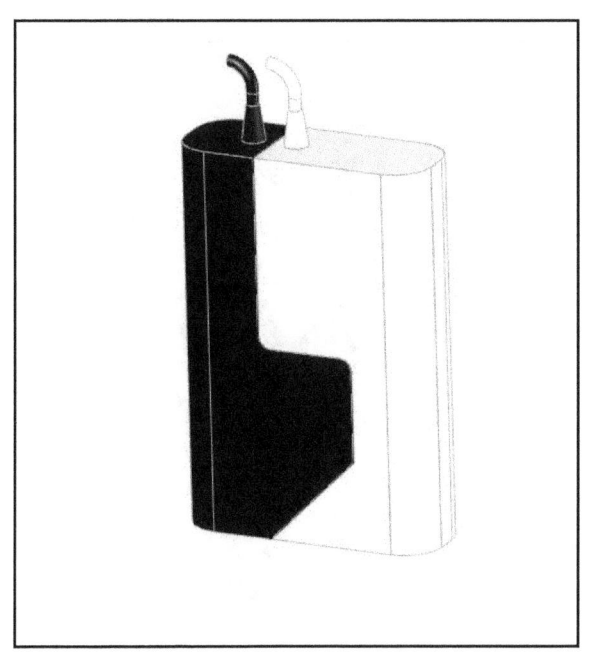

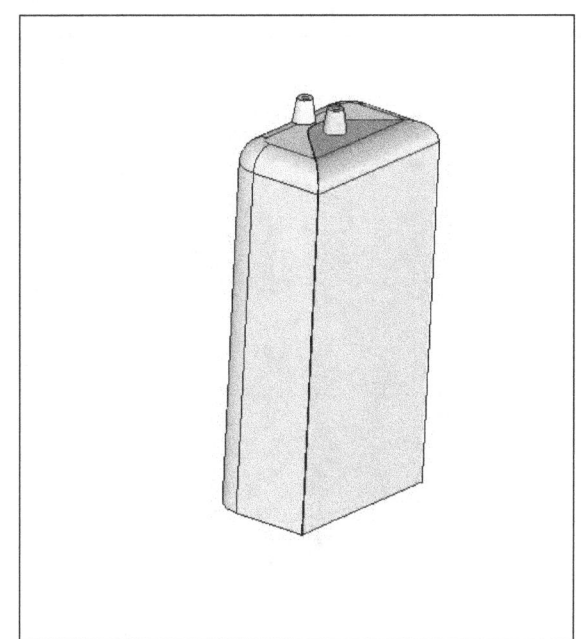

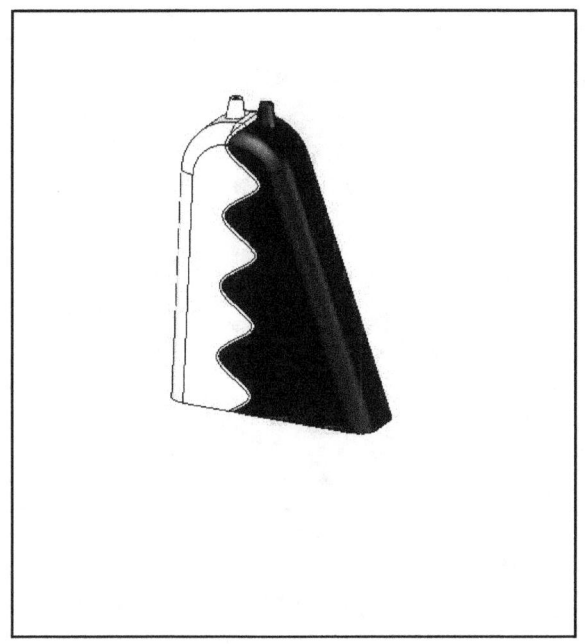

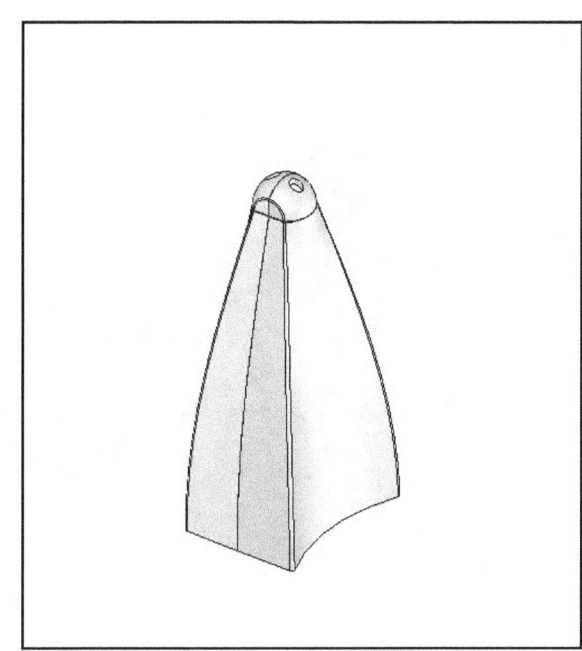

SPRAY/ PAPER TOWEL COMBO

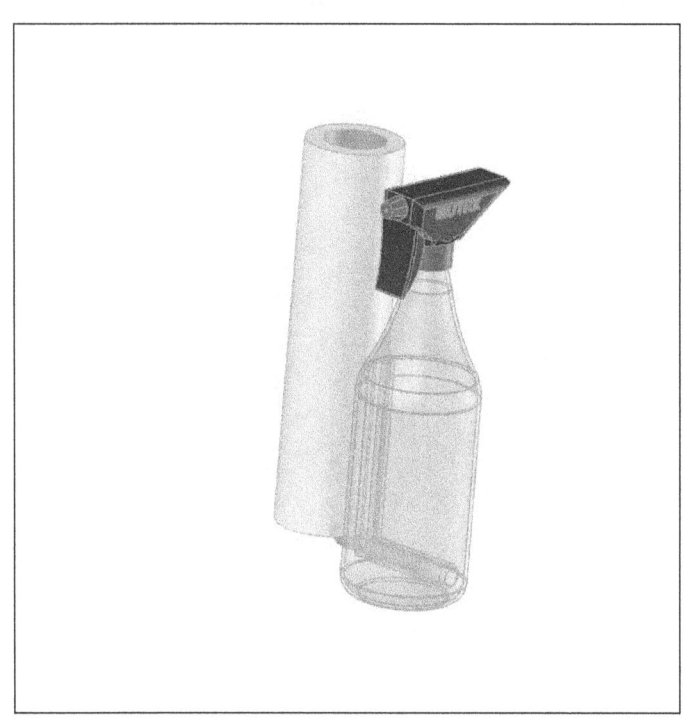

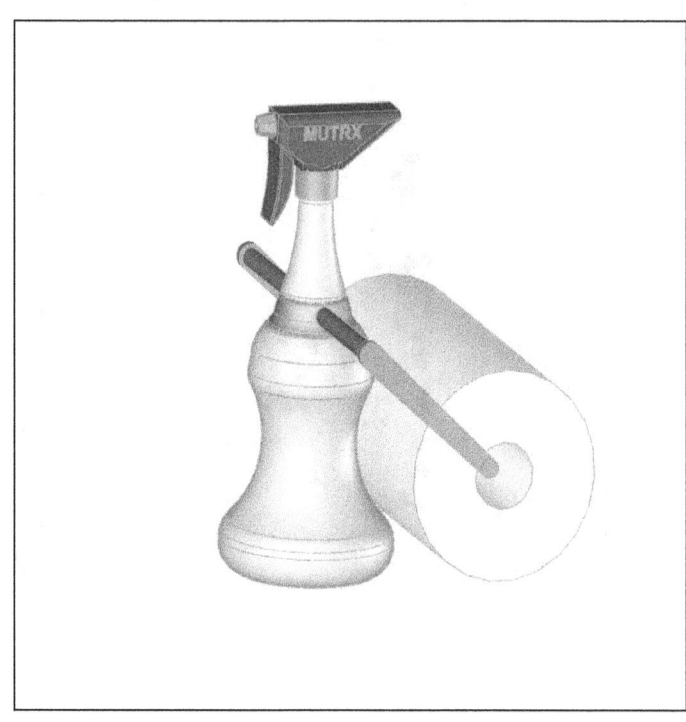

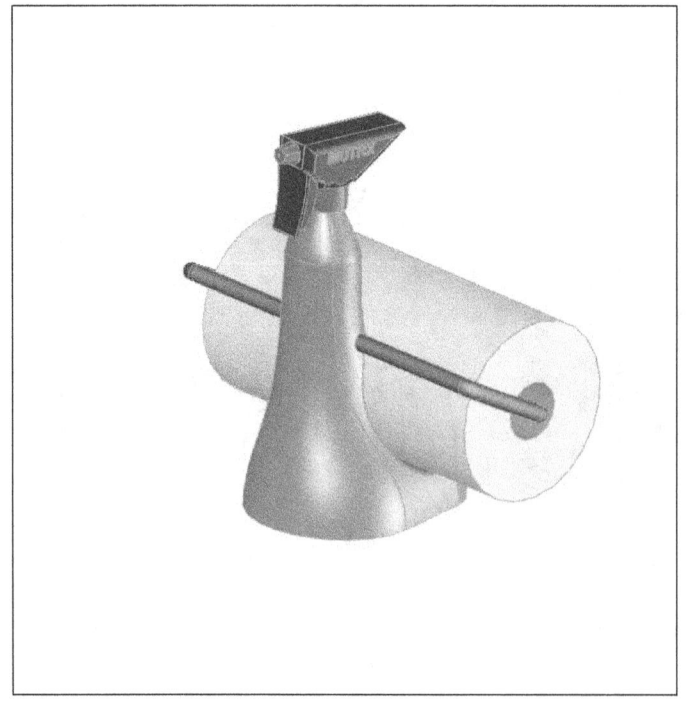

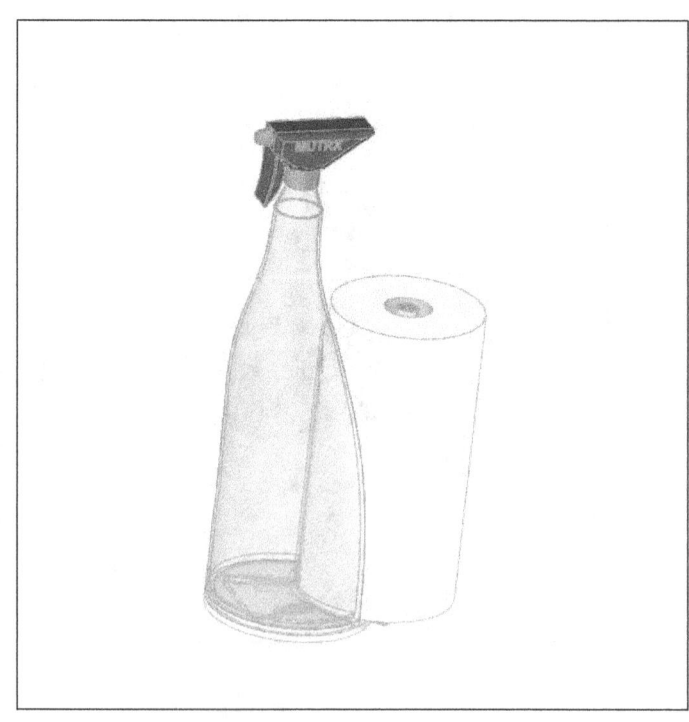

222
TWO
TWENTY
TWO
222

A VOWEL
AEIOU
PLEASE

DANCE

DREAM BIG!

MAN UP
SHUT UP

KISS
KEEP
IT
SIMPLE
STUPID

JAZZMAN

HUGS
RULE

REALLY!?

ON
A
MISSION

NO
GIVING
UP.

*SO AWESOME
IT HURTS*

TRY
(HARDER)

VIRTUAL
PERFECTION

YES, YOU
CAN

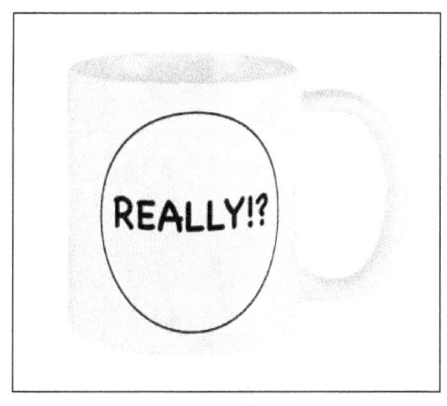

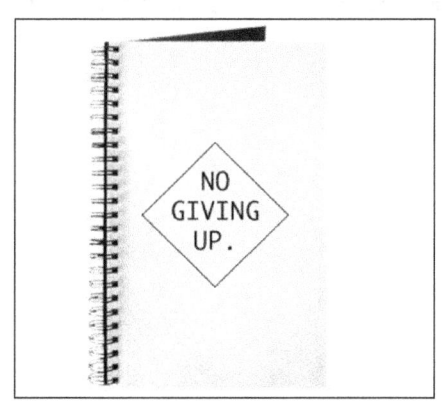

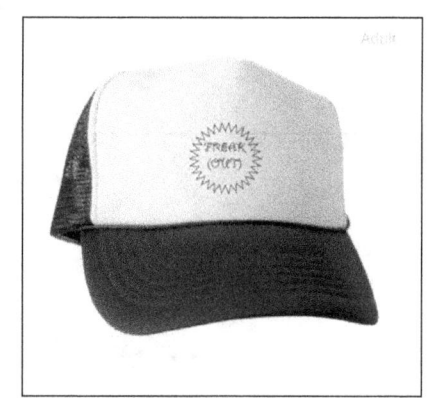

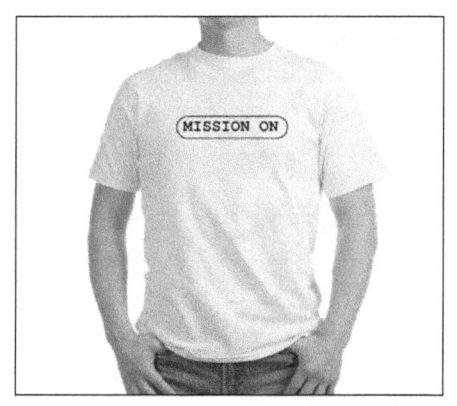

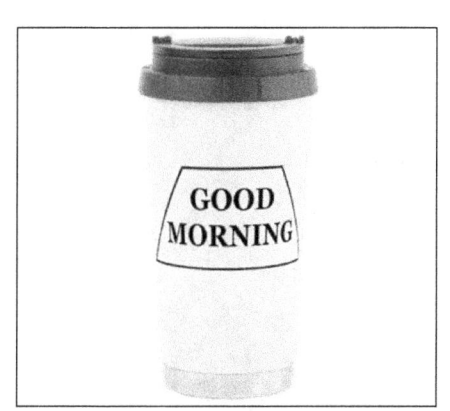

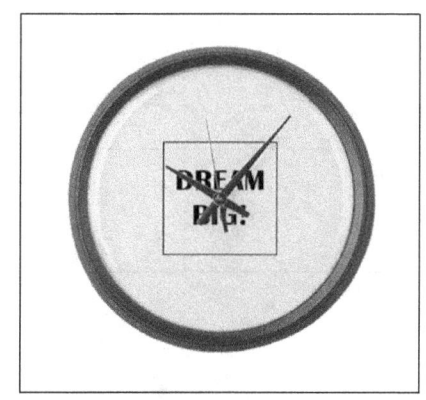

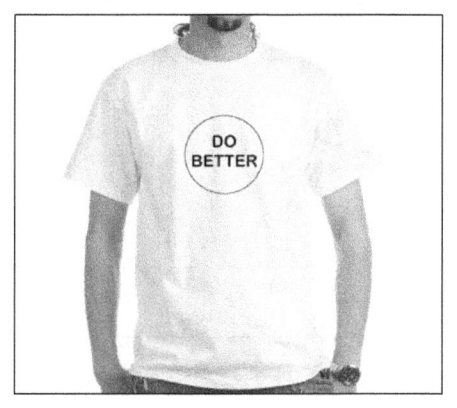

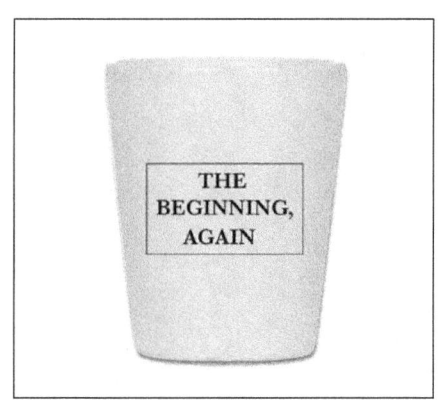

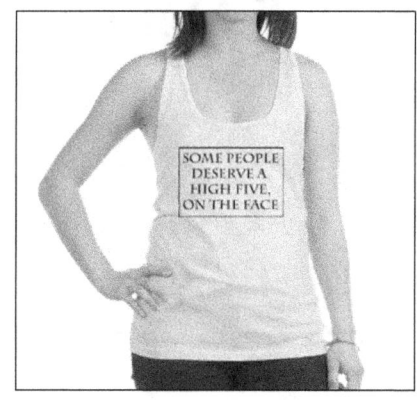

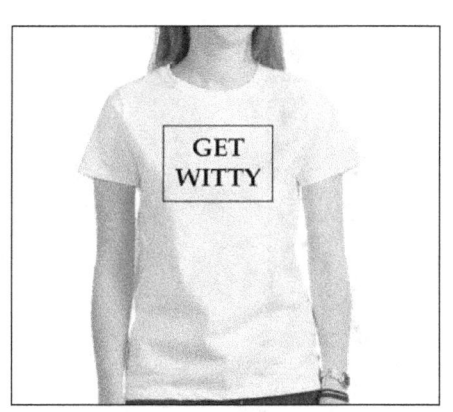

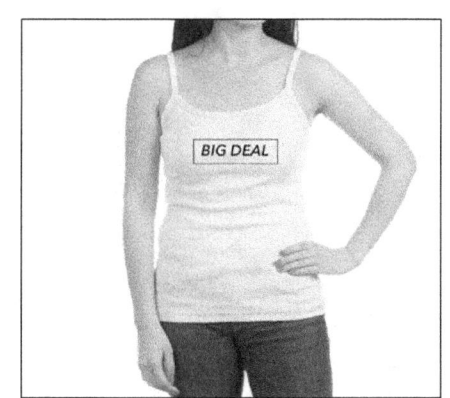

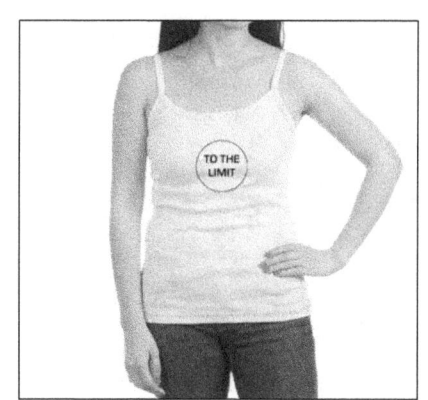

PAPER BINDING

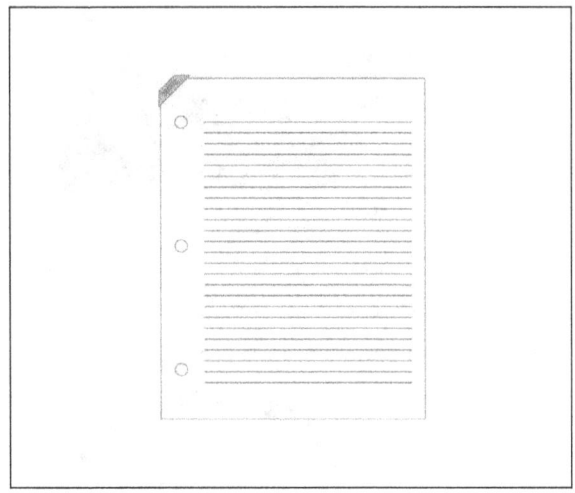

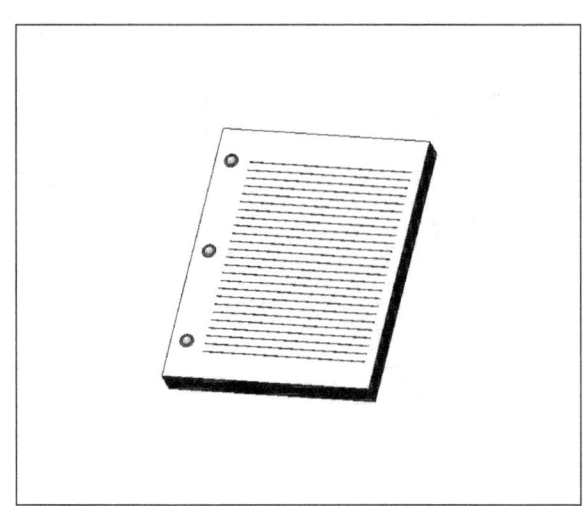

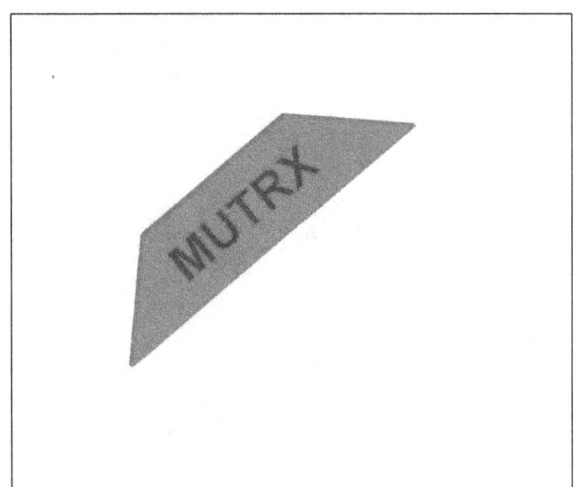

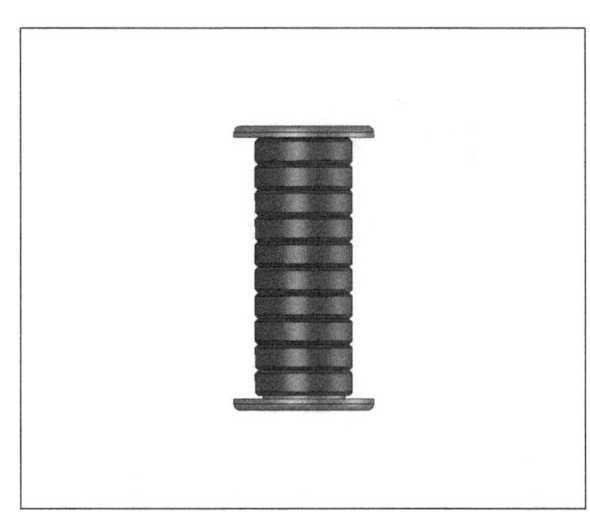

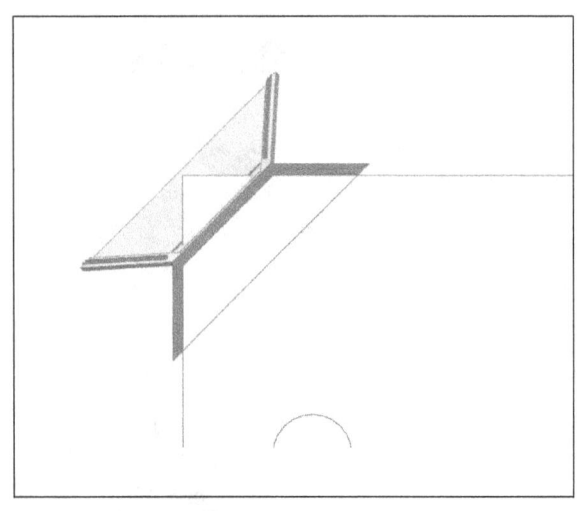

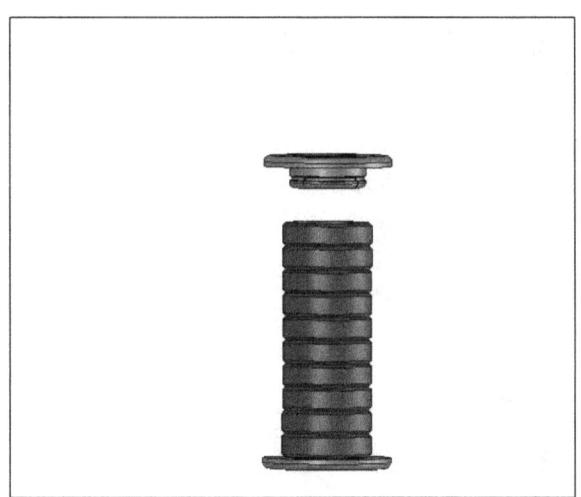

PAPER CLIPS

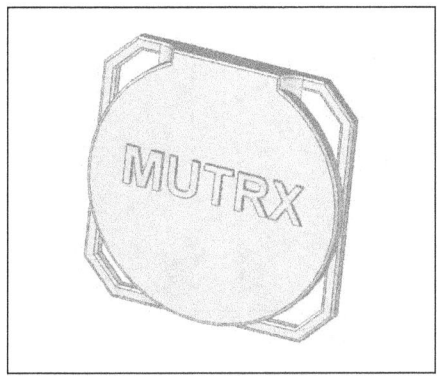

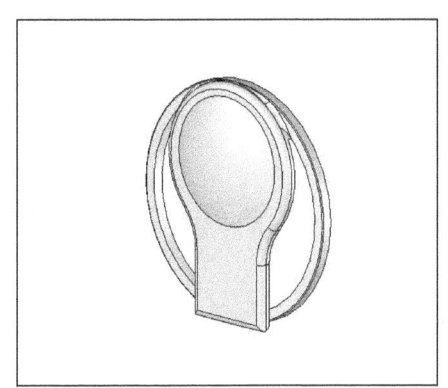

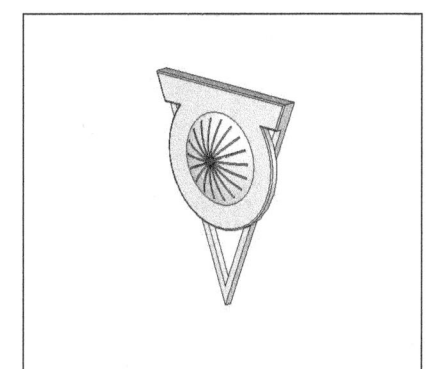

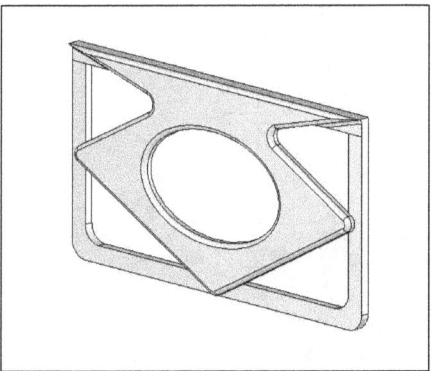

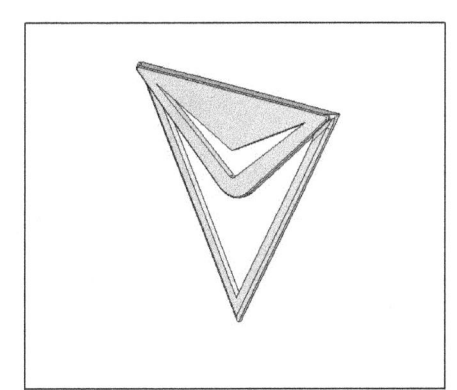

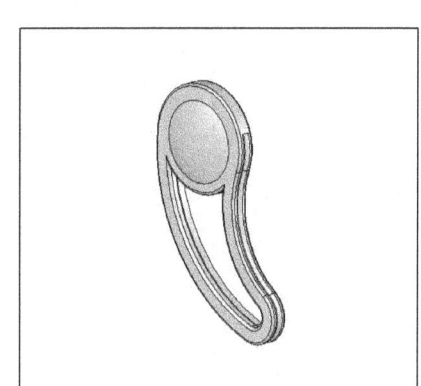

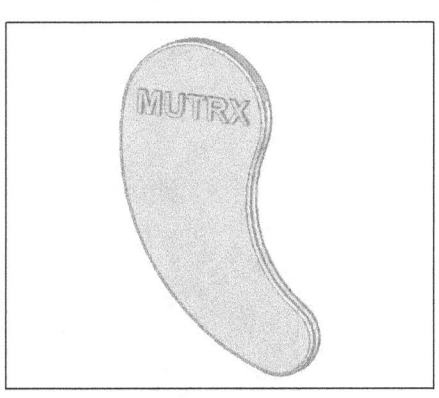

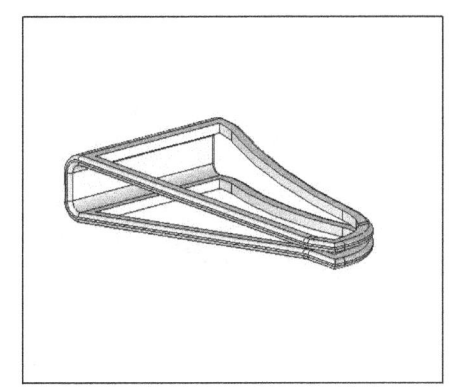

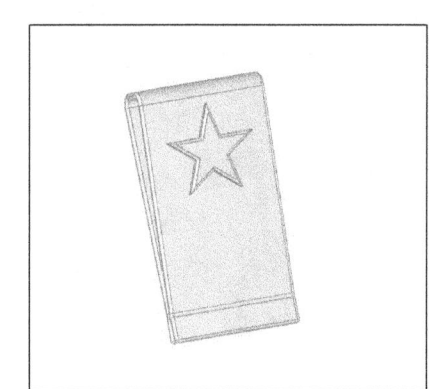

PAPER WEIGHTS

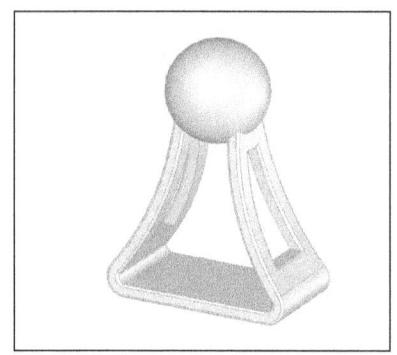
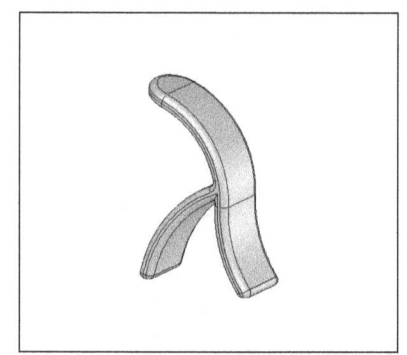
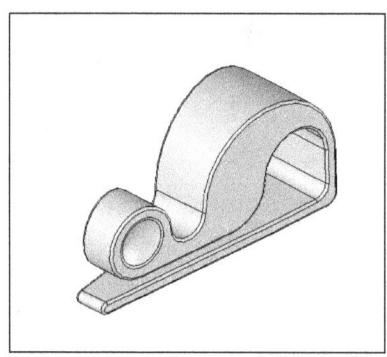
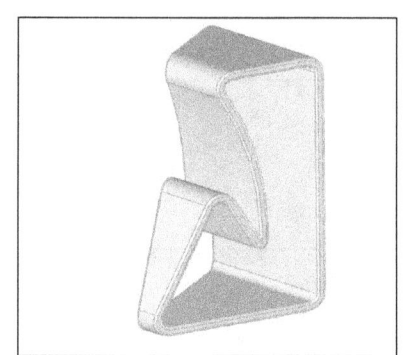
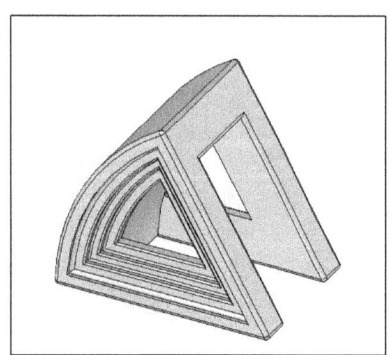
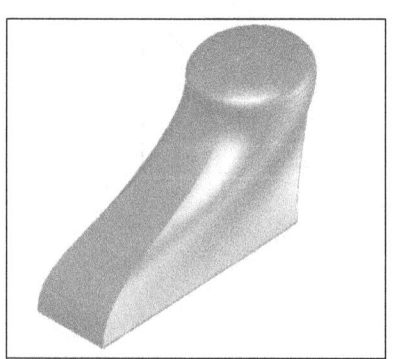
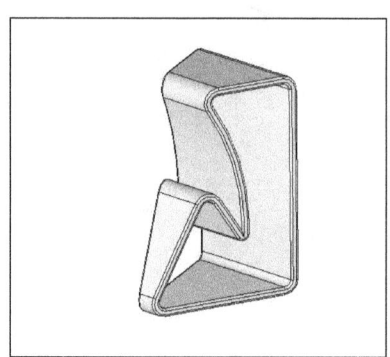

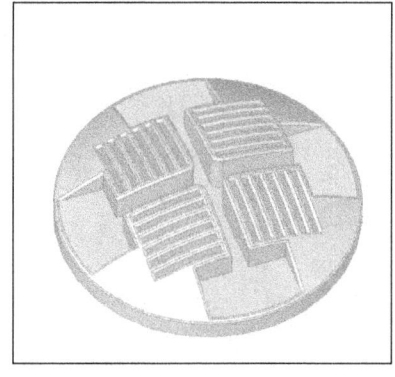

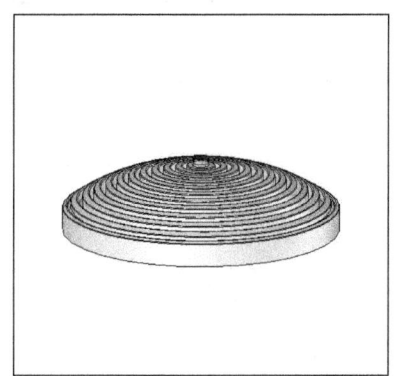

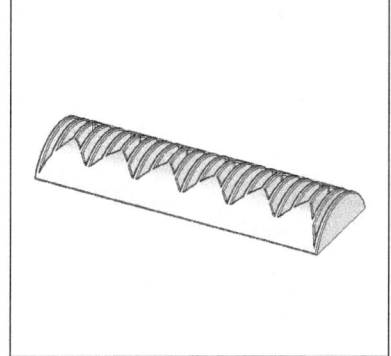

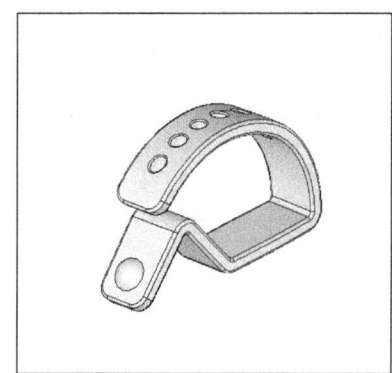

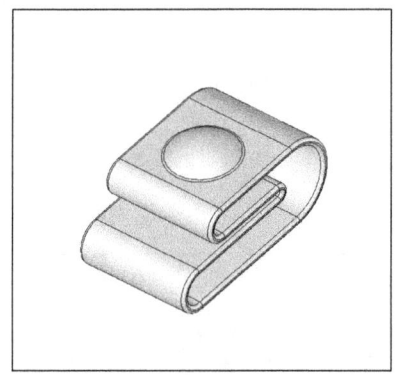

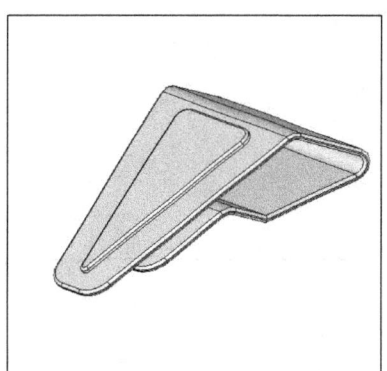

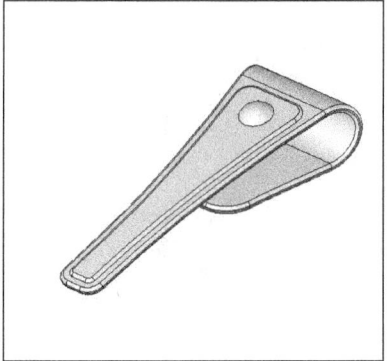

PHOTO FRAMES

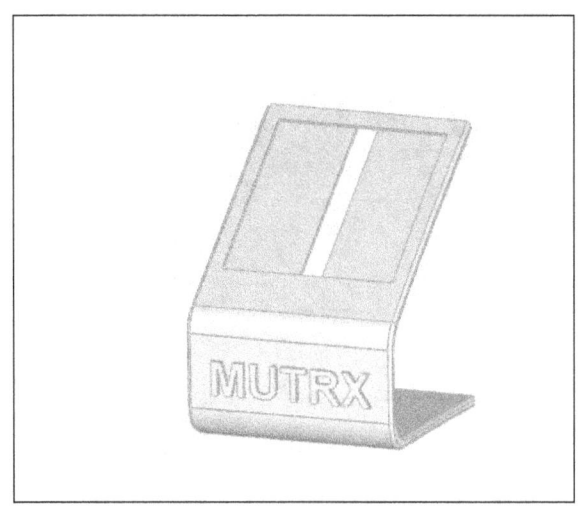

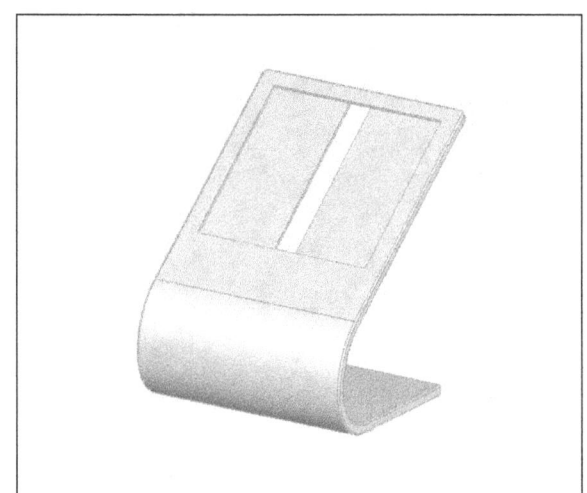

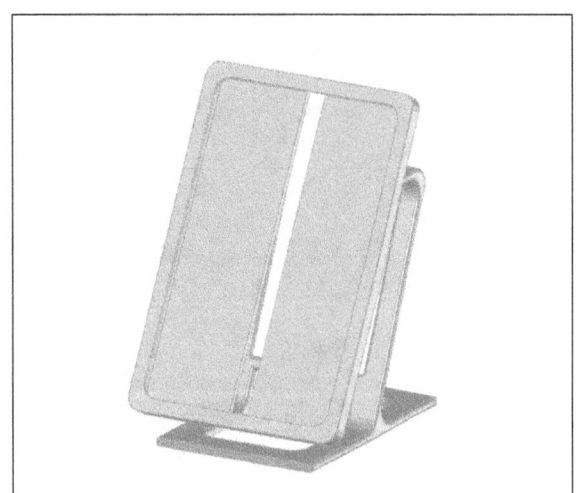

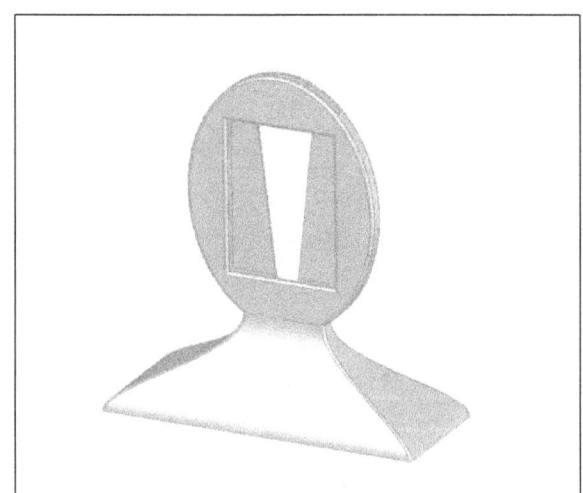

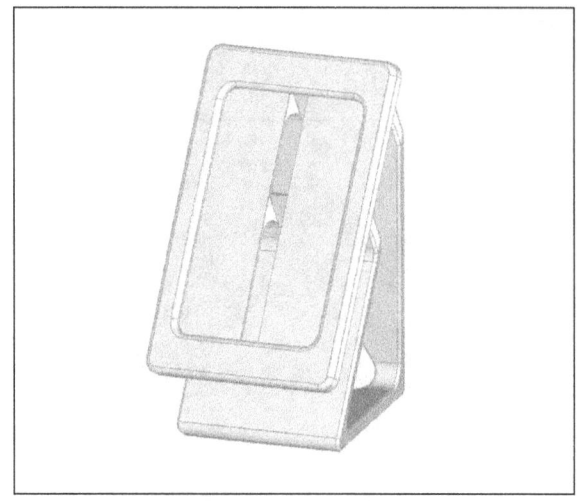

SNACK HOLDERS

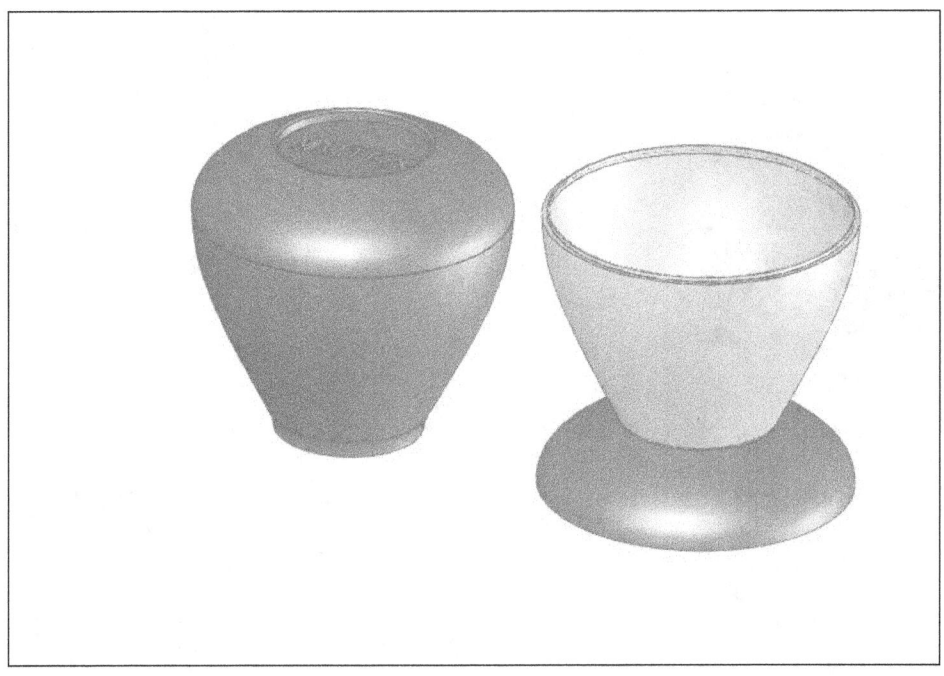

TO GO

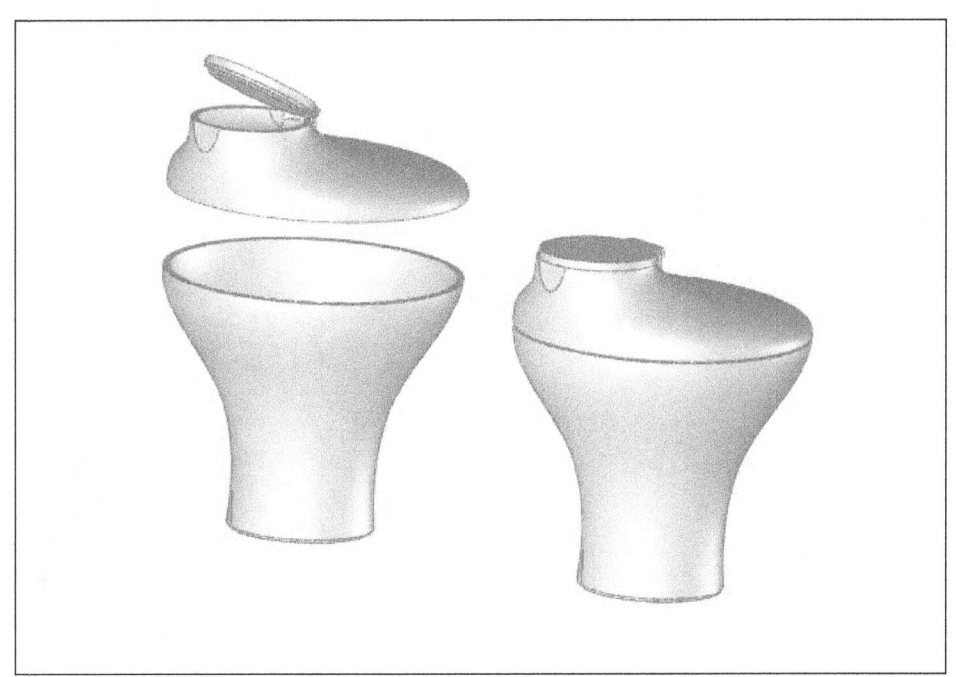

FOR YOUR AUTO

M7

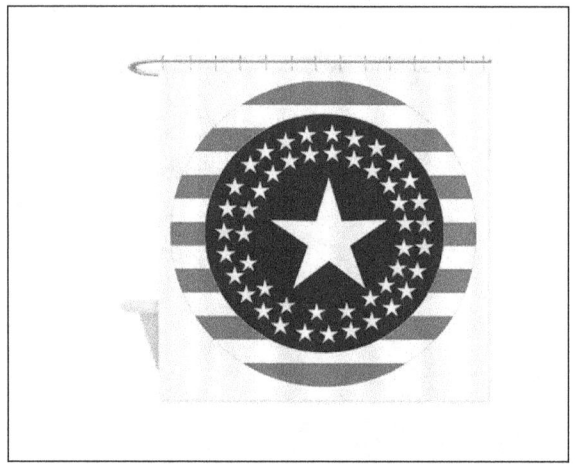

PATRIOTIC

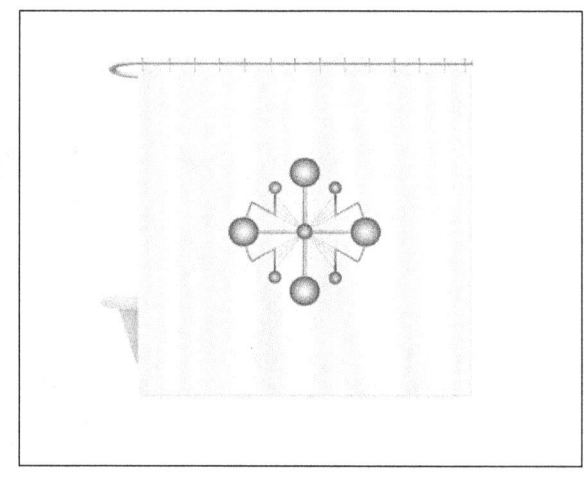

NEW DESIGN

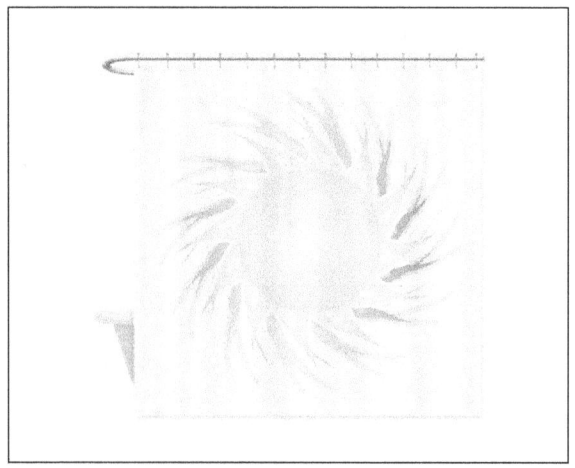

SUN DESIGNS

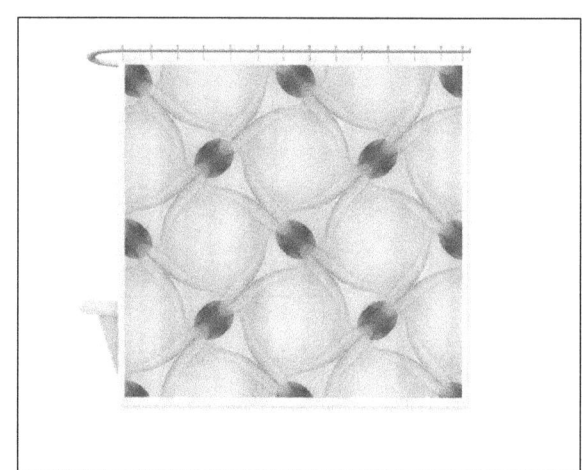

PATTERNS

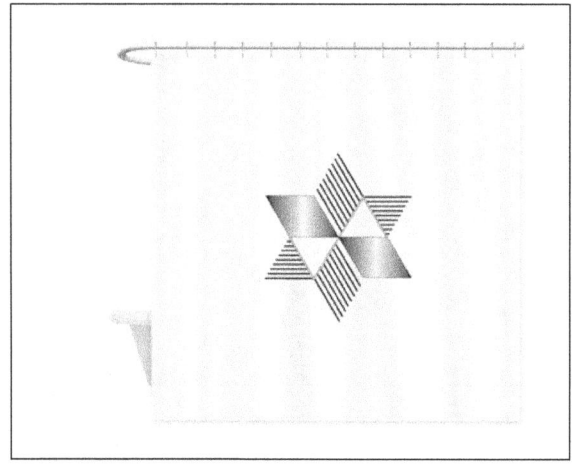

RELIGION BOUND

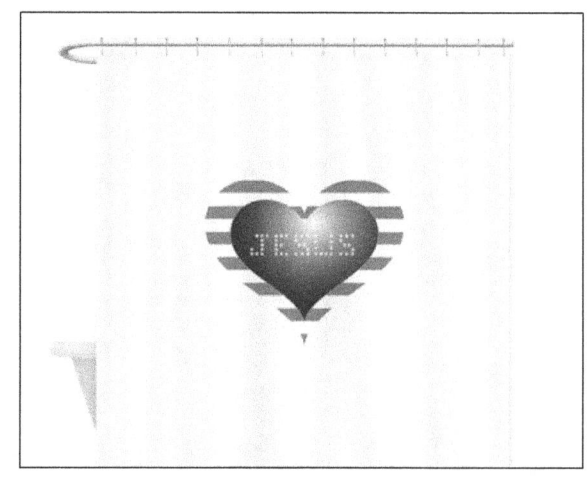

RELIGION BOUND

SHOWER HOOKS

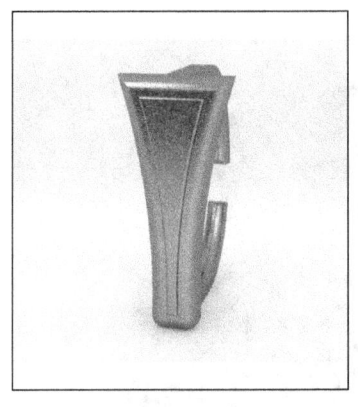 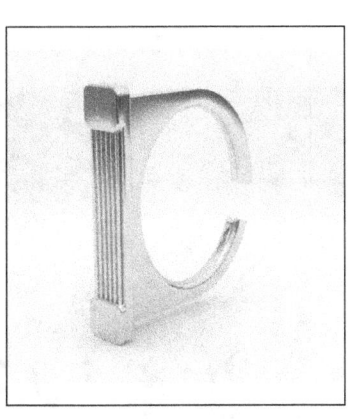 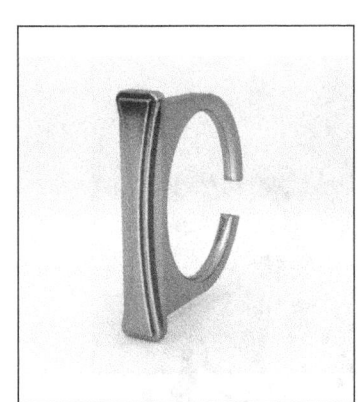 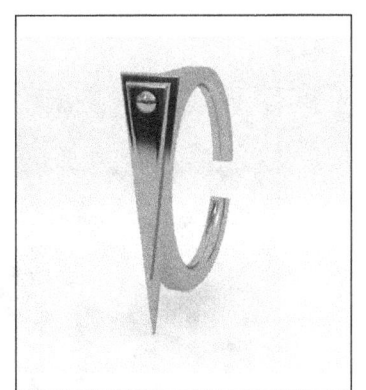

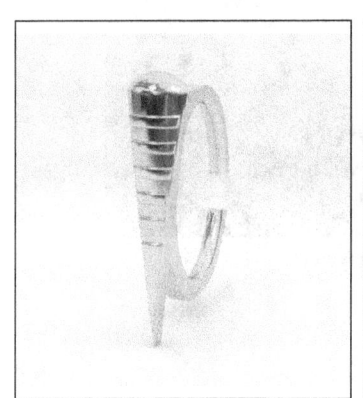 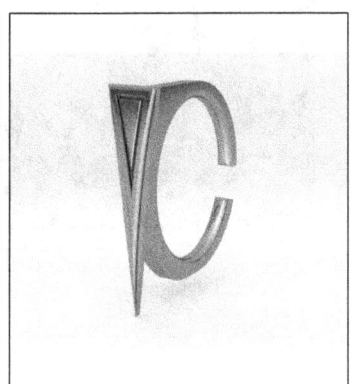 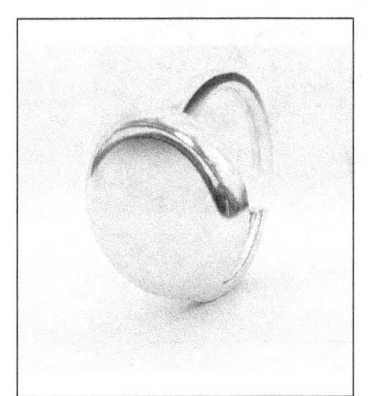 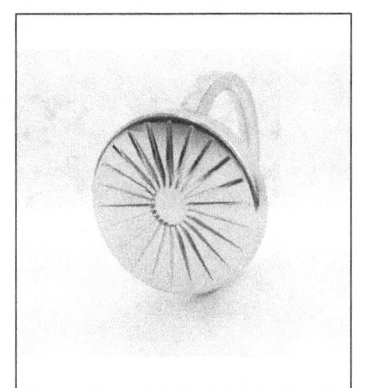

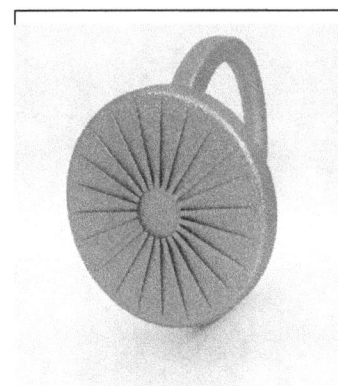 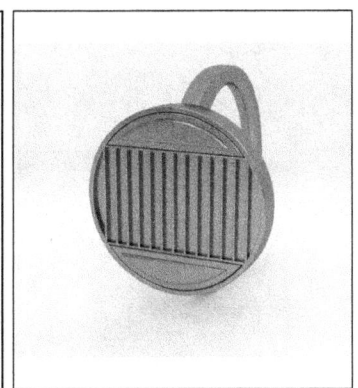 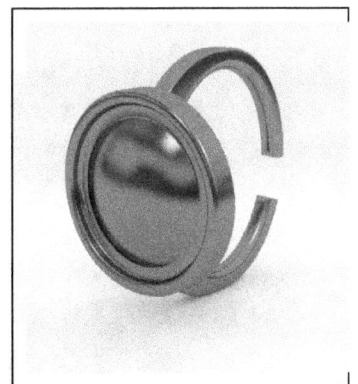 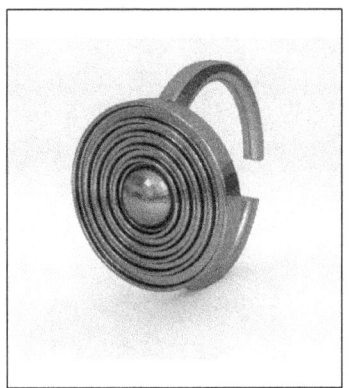

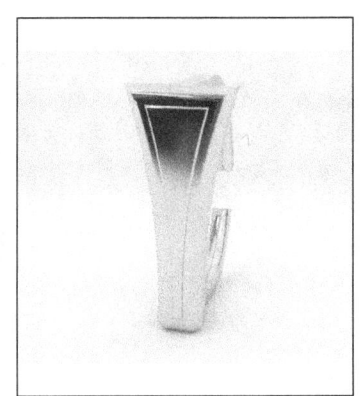 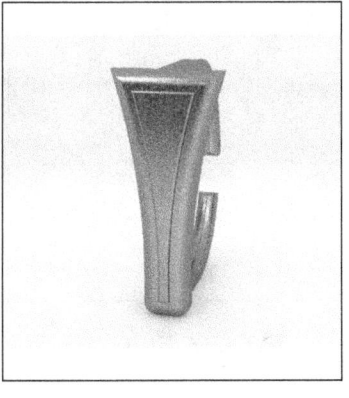 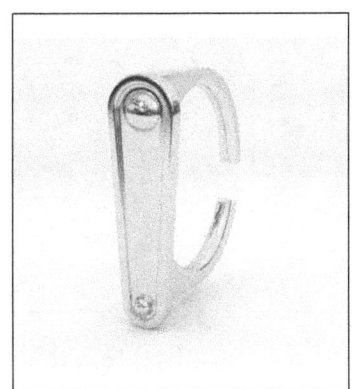 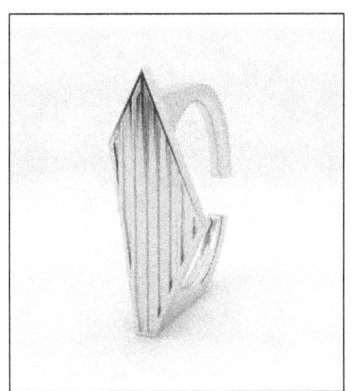

STAMPING

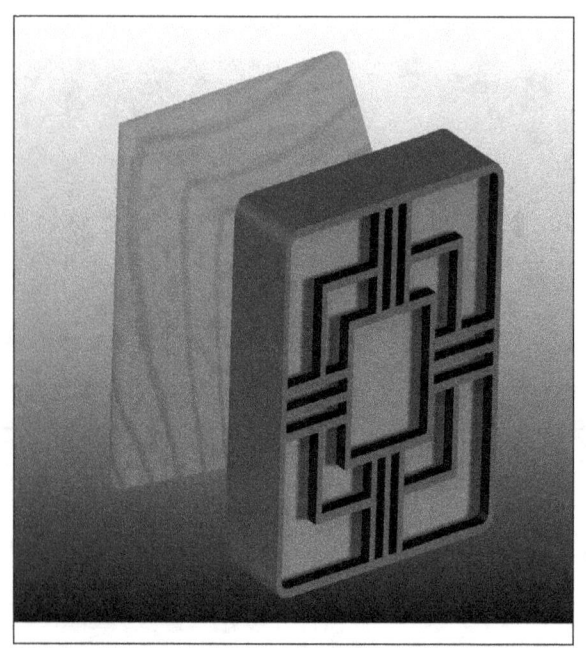

DESIGNS

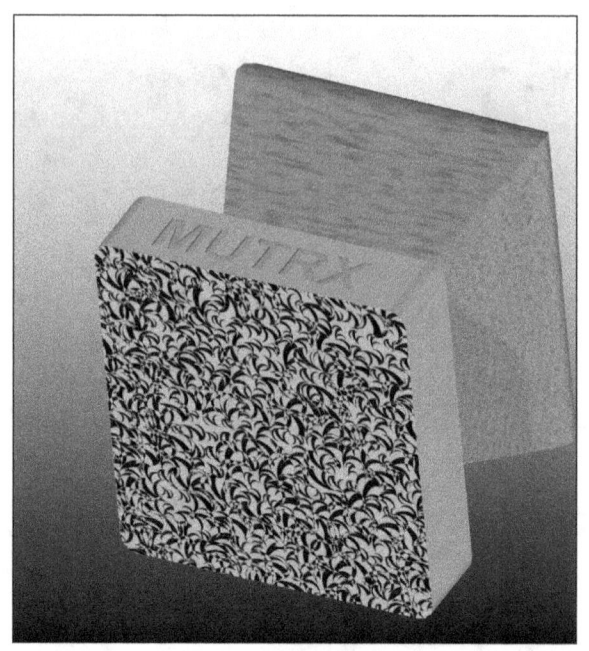

TEXTURES

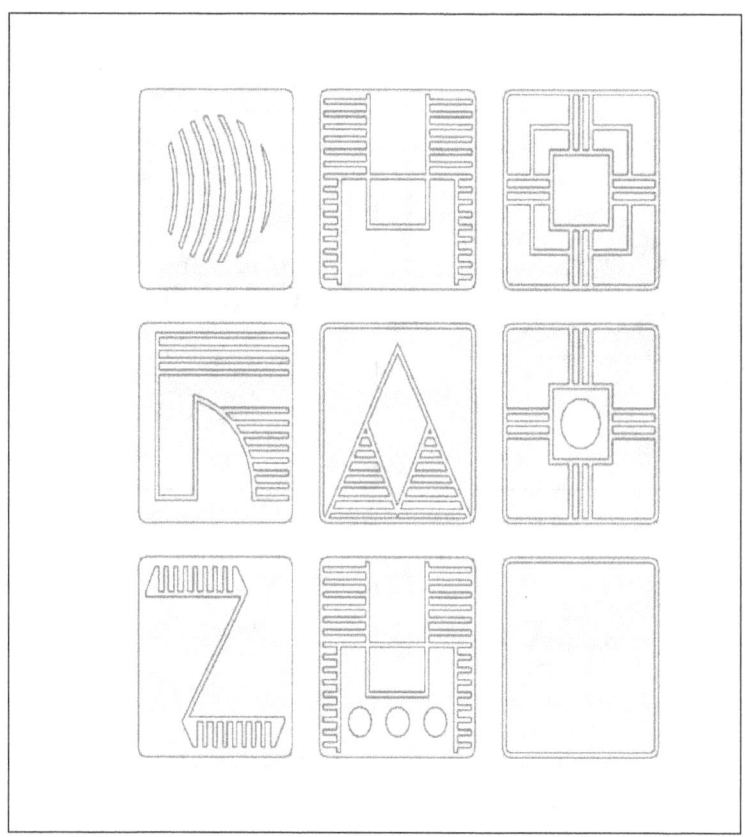

LIBRARY OF DESIGNS

THIN WALLET

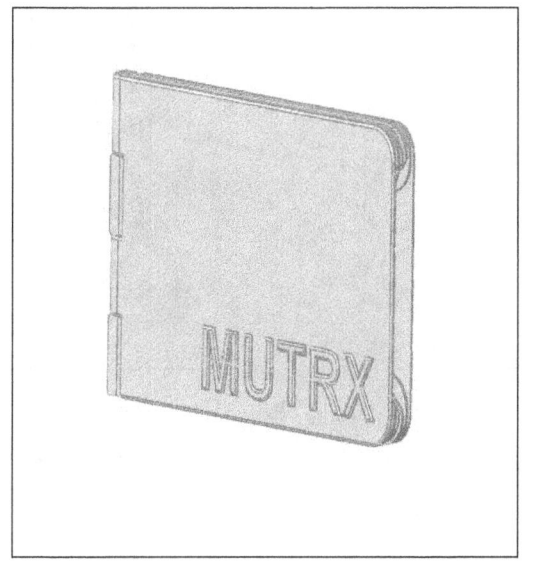

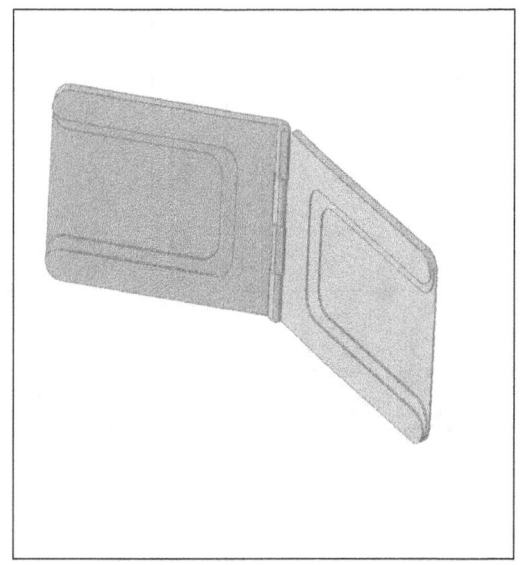

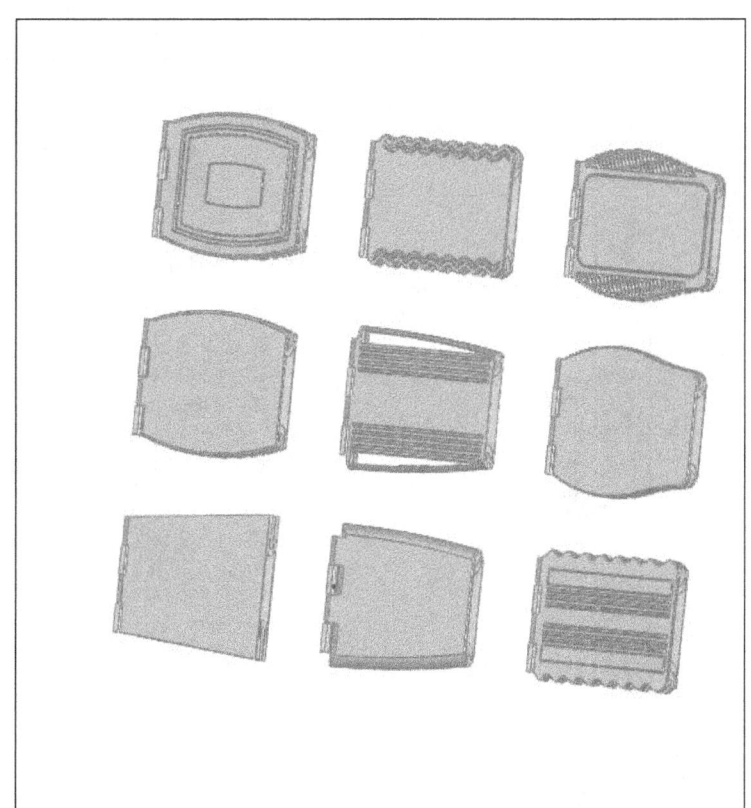

STYLES

M7

WATER BOTTLES

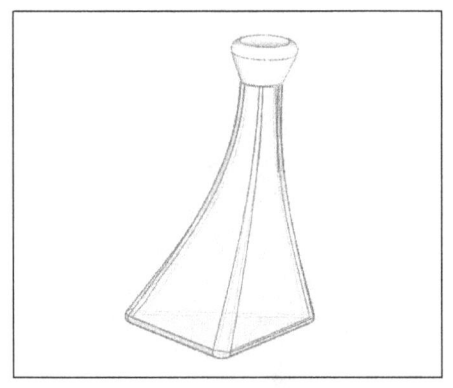 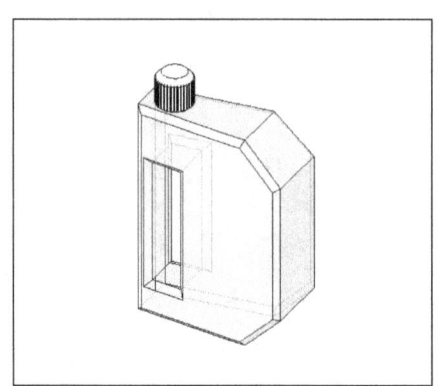 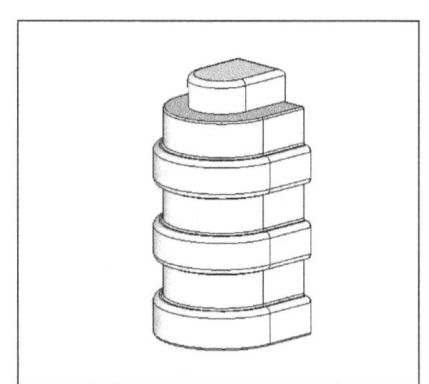

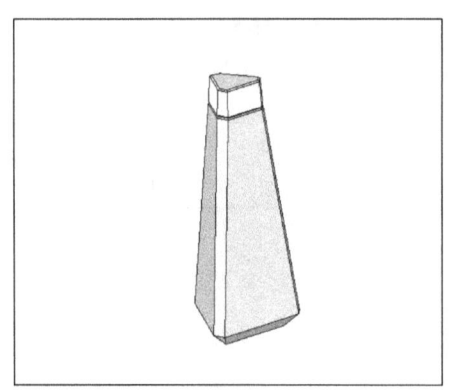 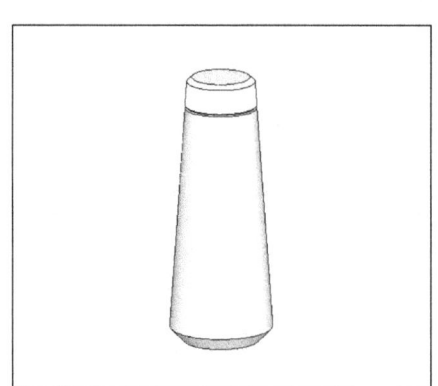 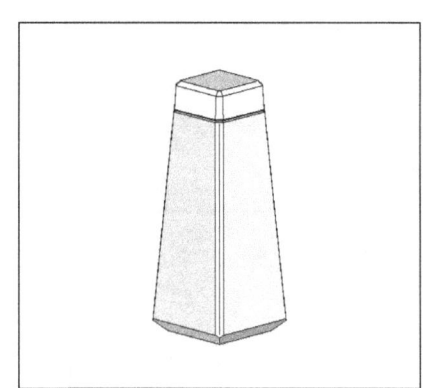

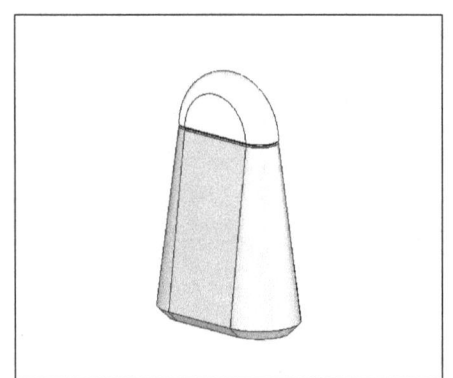 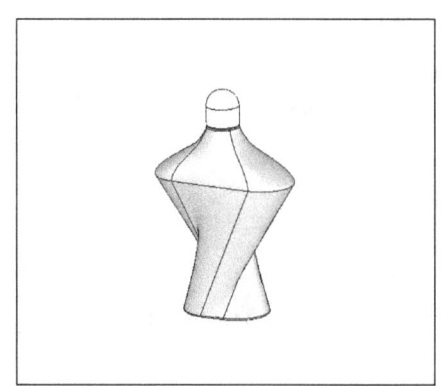 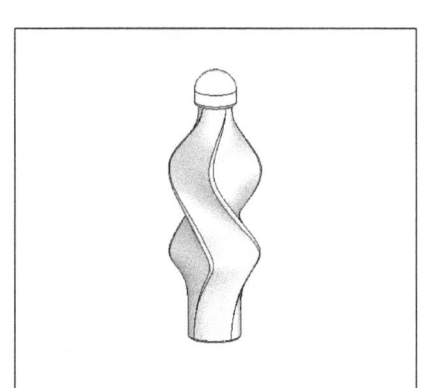

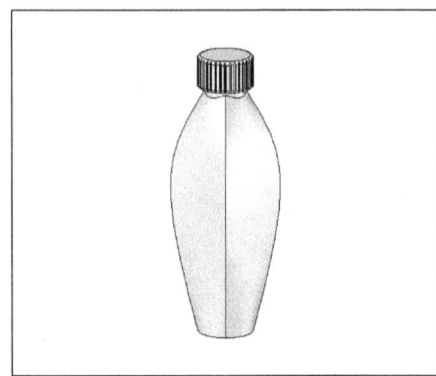

TABLE TOP WATER DISPENSER

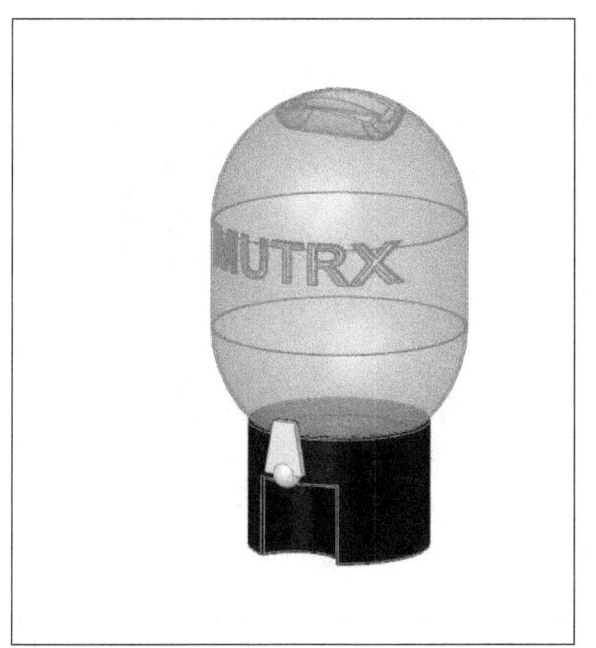

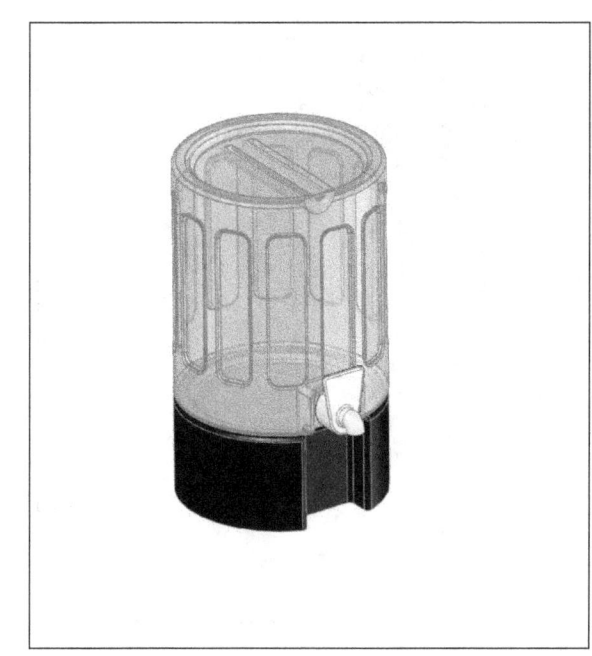

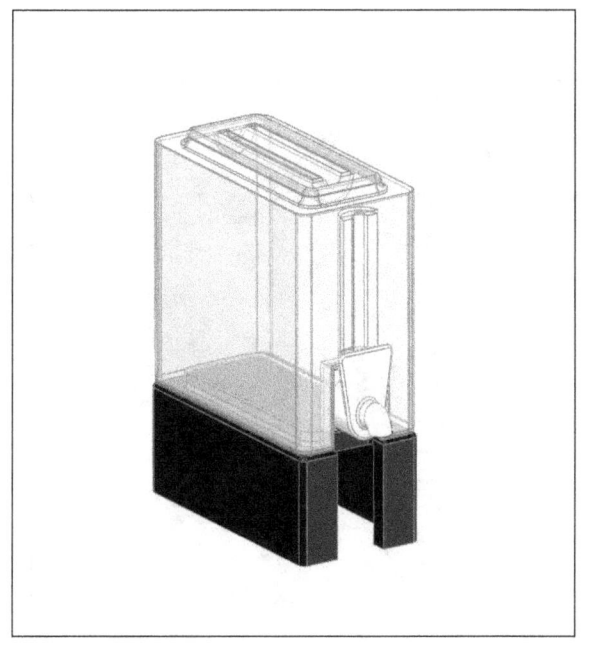

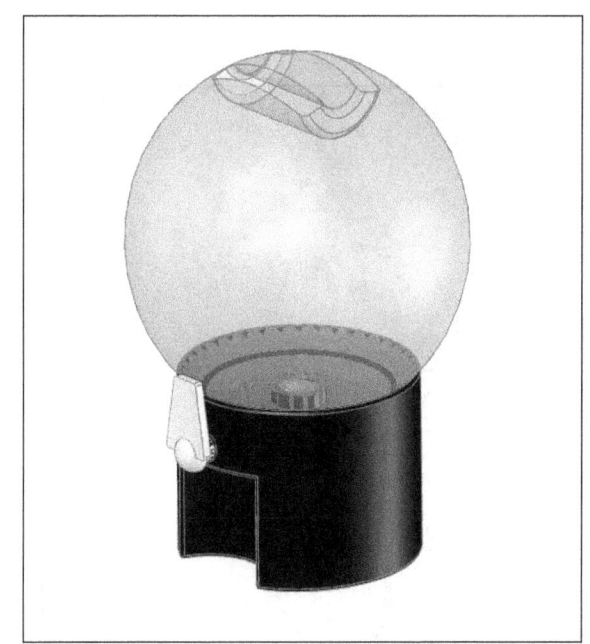

BELT LOOPER 4

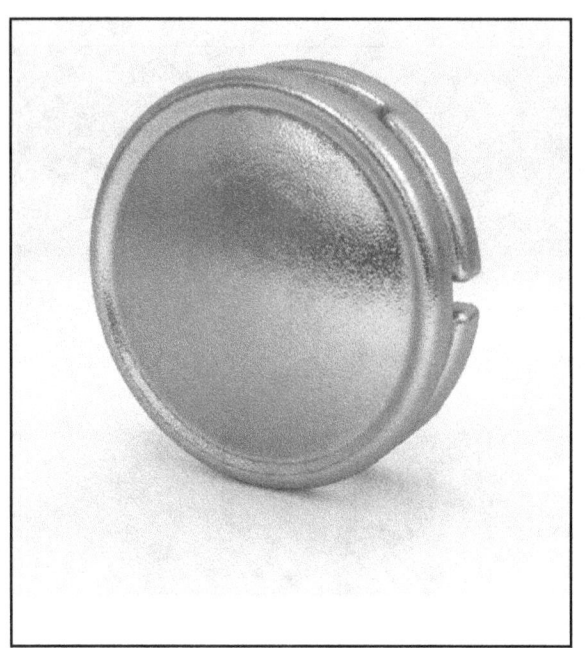

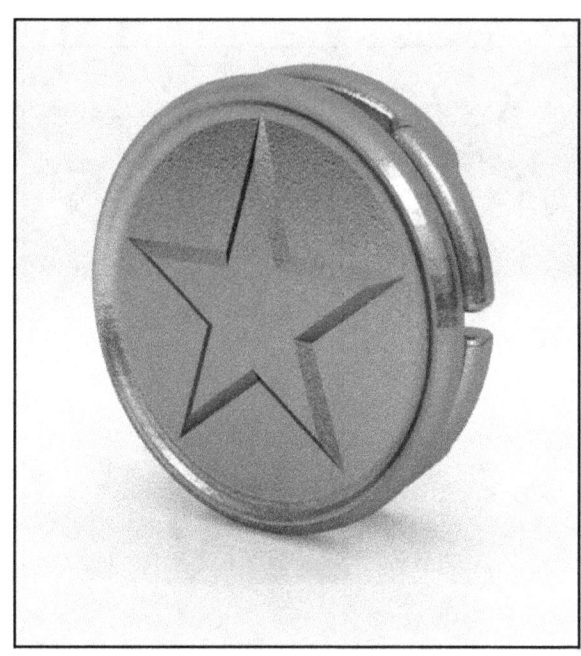

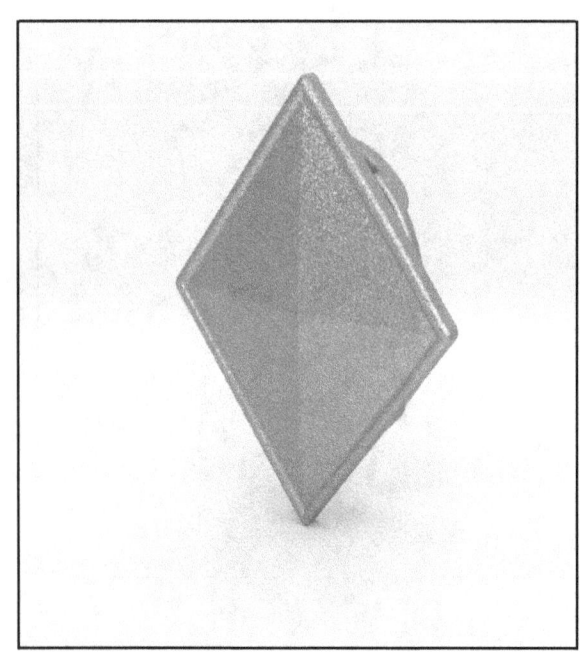

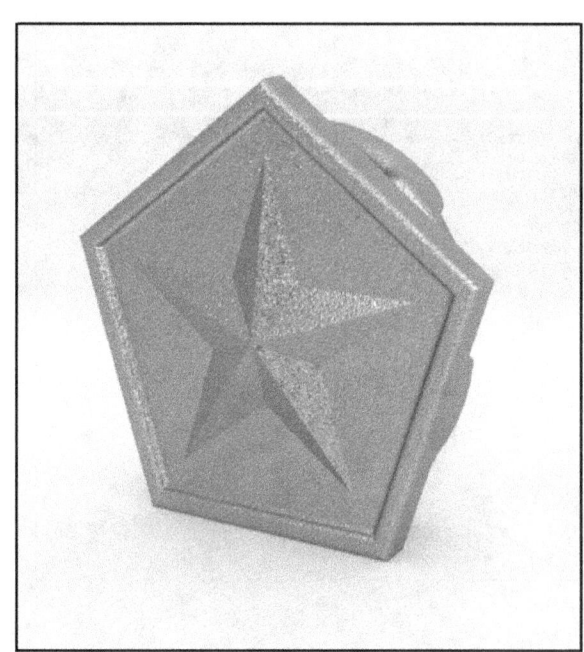

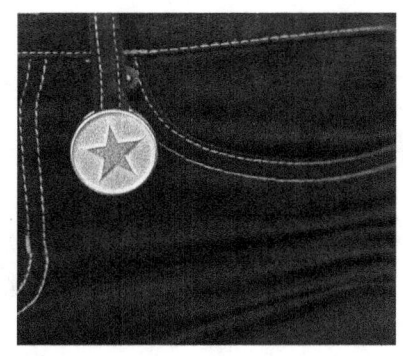

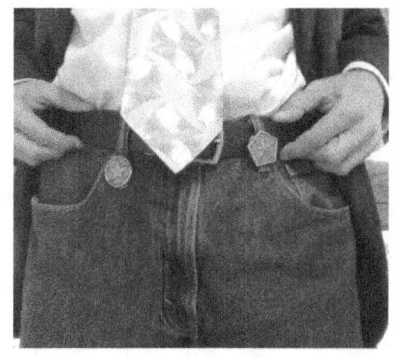

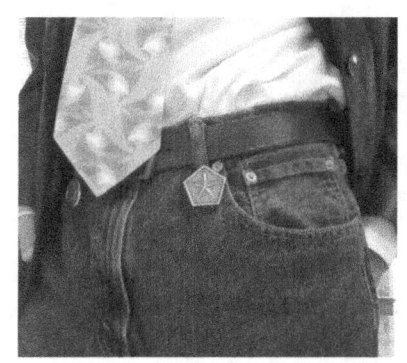

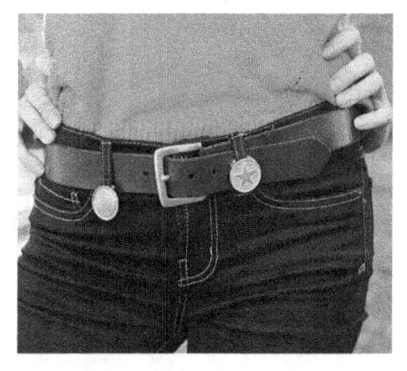

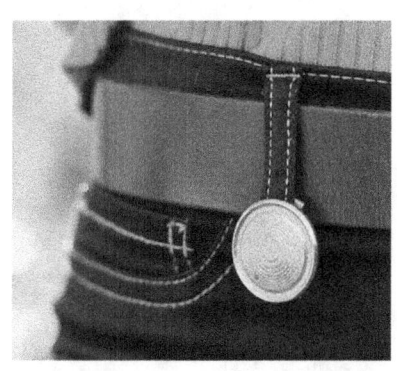

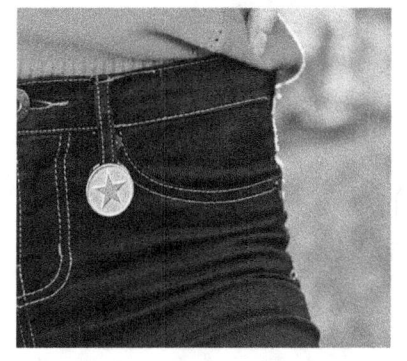

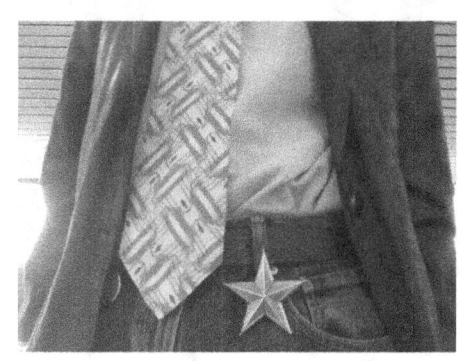

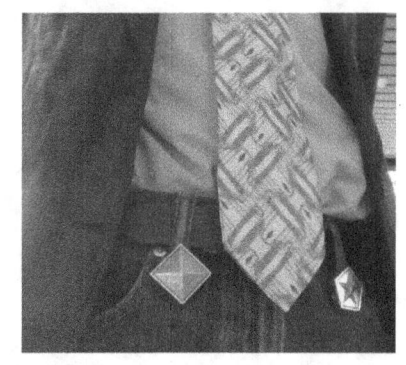

BOWLS

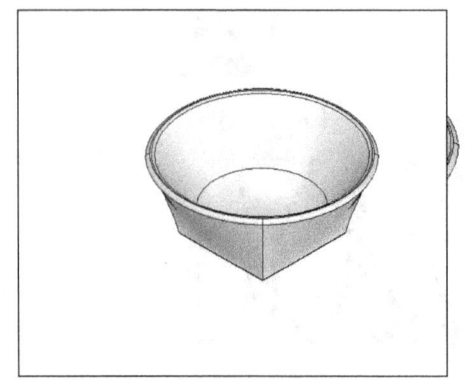
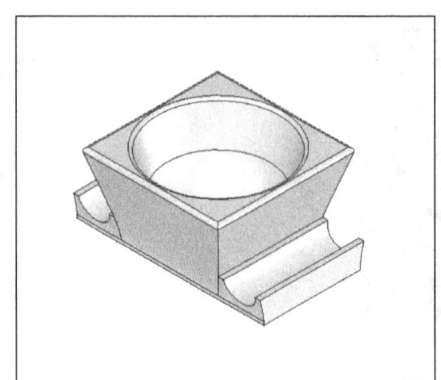
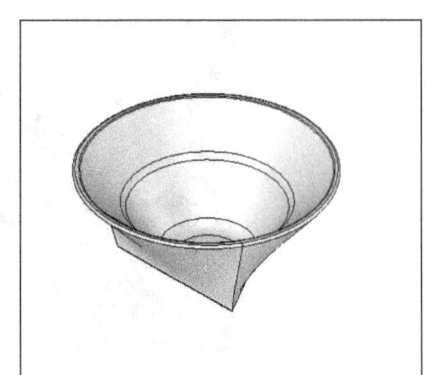

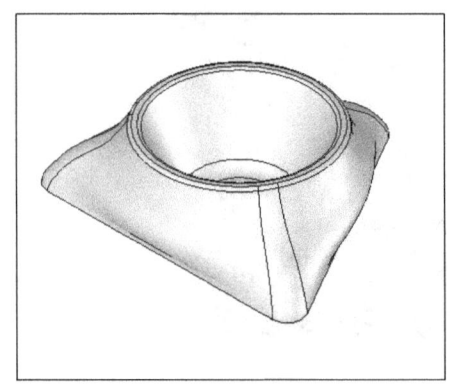
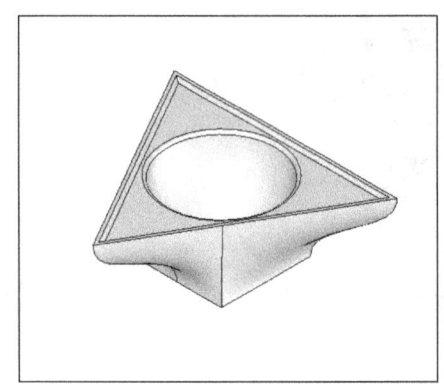
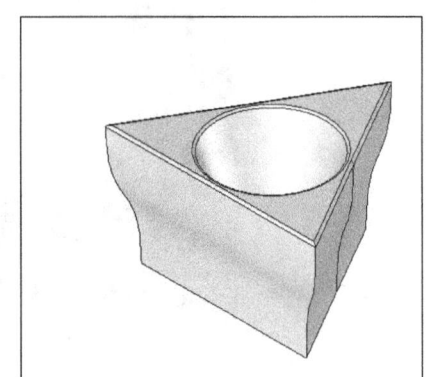

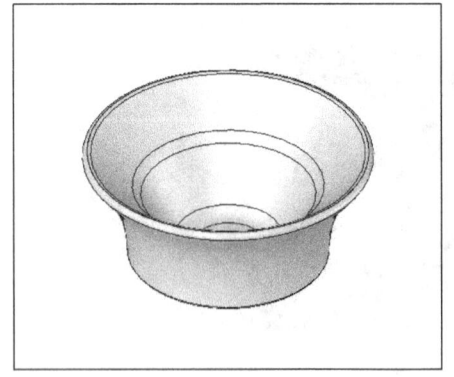
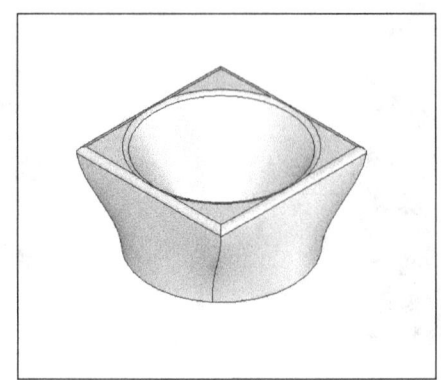
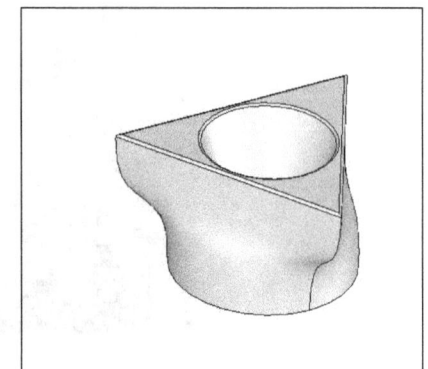

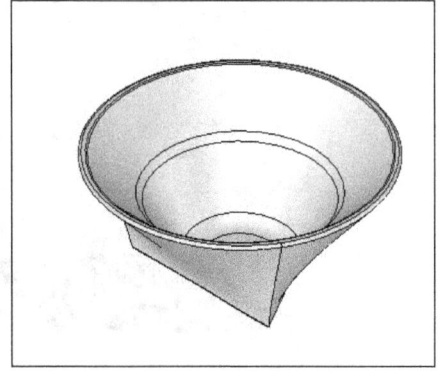
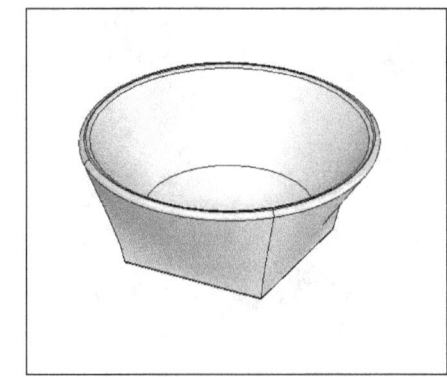

WONDERFUL *amazing, brilliant, excellent, marvelous, tremendous, devine, miraculous, stupendous, astonishing, cool, fabulous, incredible, outstanding, dynamite, peachy, super, awesome, fantastic, phenomenal, remarkable, terrific, groovy, swell*

★ ★ ★ **GIVEN.** ★ ★ ★

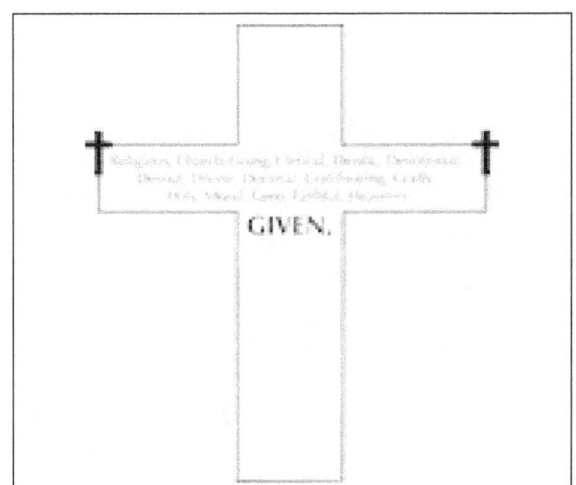

★ **Ceo, VIP, Big-Wheel, Bass, Brass, Chief, Commander, Director, Exec, Head, Head-Honcho, Head Guy, Heavyweight, Leader, Manager, Top Brass, Top Dog** ★

GIVEN.

Better, *Exceeding, Finer, Greater, High Quality, Improved, Larger, More Desirable, Superior, A Cut Above, Expert, Choice, Five Star, Noteworthy*

★ ★ ★ **GIVEN.** ★ ★ ★

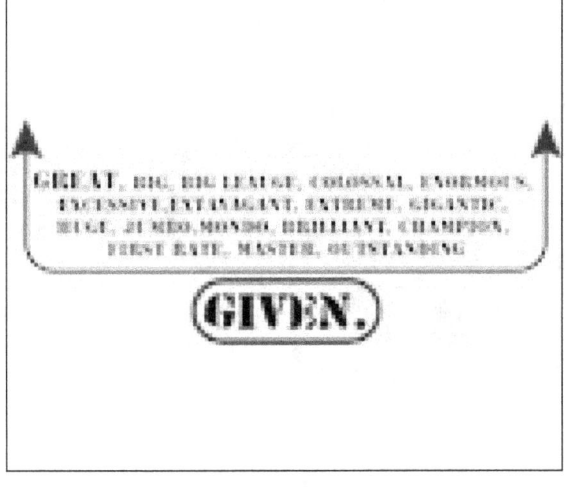

GREAT, BIG, BIG LEAGUE, COLOSSAL, ENORMOUS, EXCESSIVE, EXTRAVAGANT, EXTREME, GIGANTIC, HUGE, JUMBO, MONDO, BRILLIANT, CHAMPION, FIRST RATE, MASTER, OUTSTANDING

GIVEN.

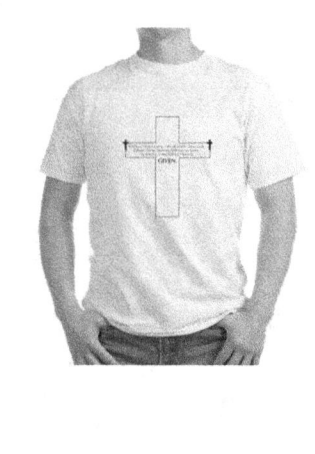
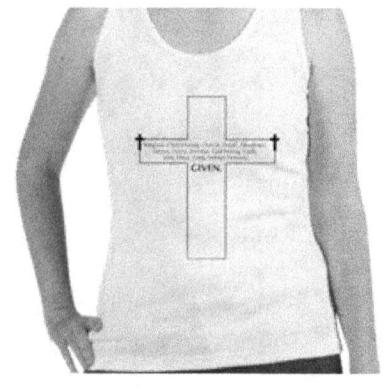
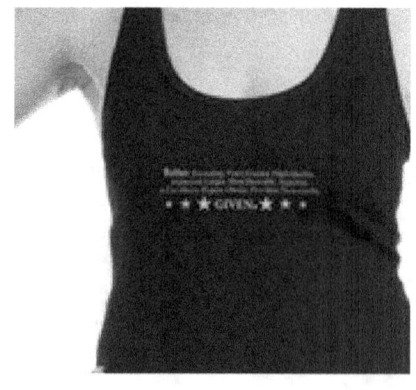
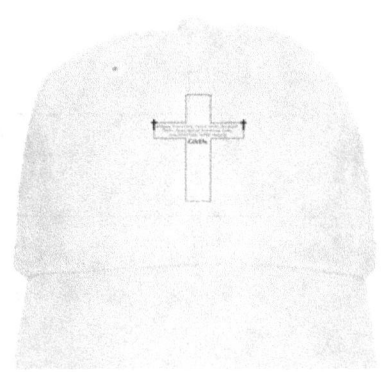
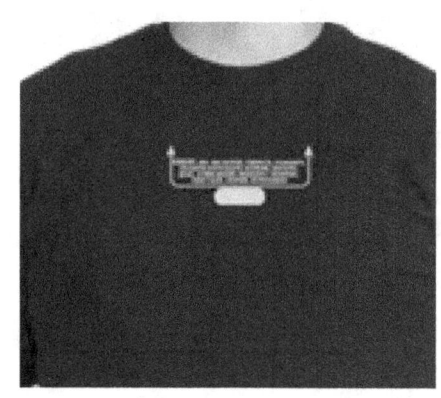
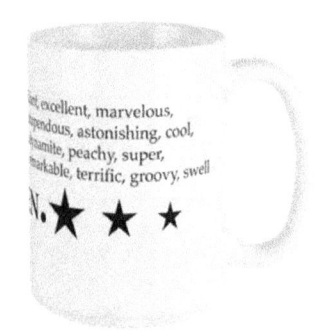
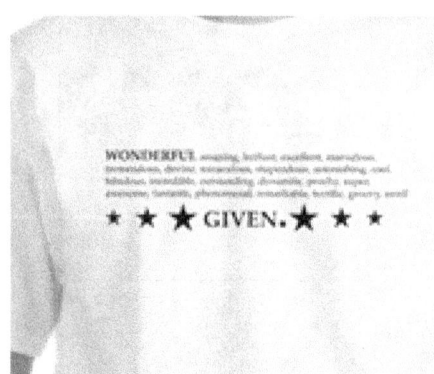
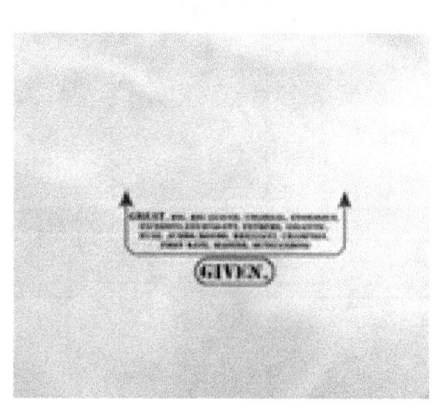
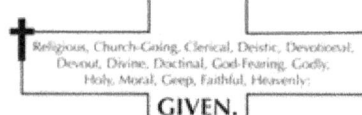

Religious, Church-Going, Clerical, Deistic, Devotional, Devout, Divine, Doctrinal, God-Fearing, Godly, Holy, Moral, Geep, Faithful, Heavenly:

GIVEN.

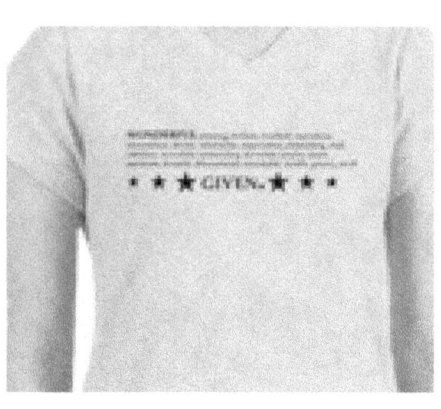
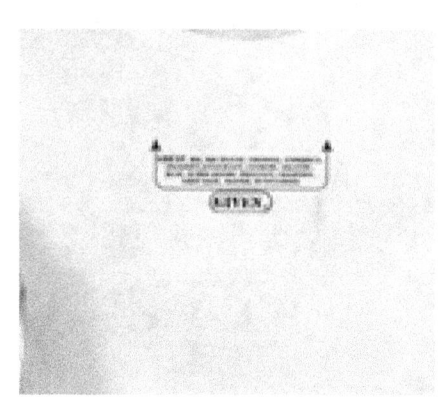
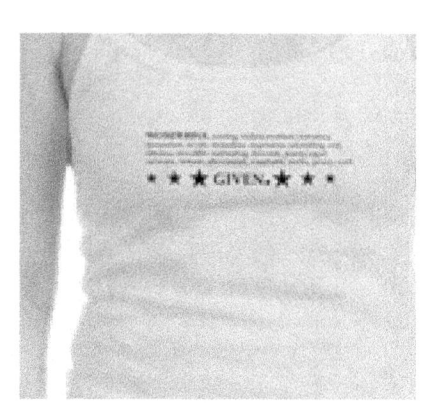

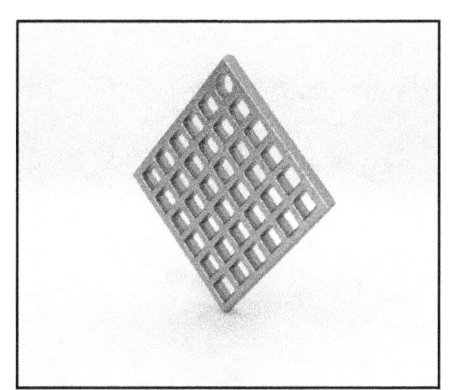
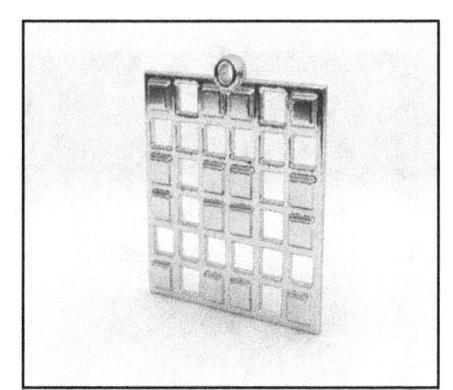
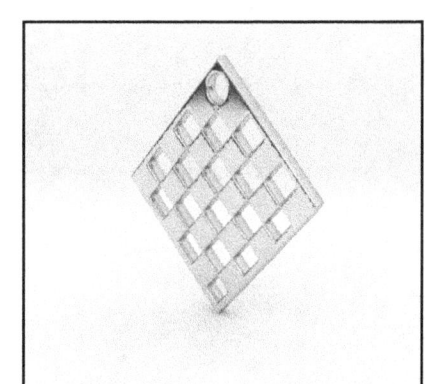
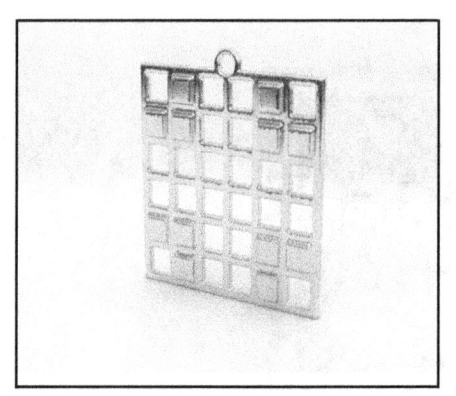
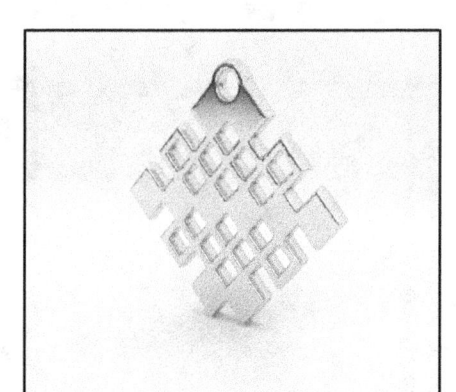
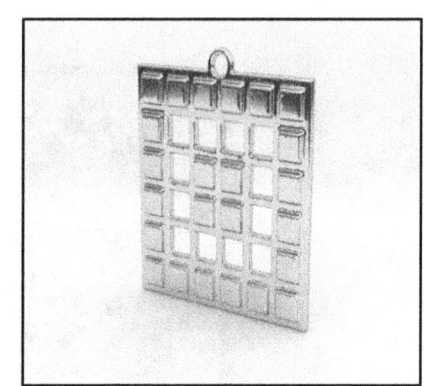
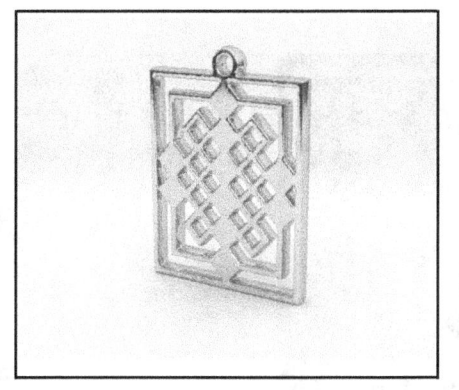
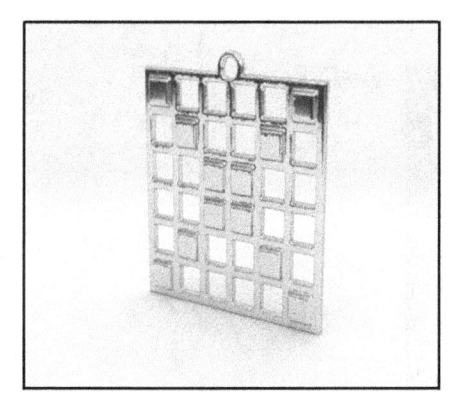
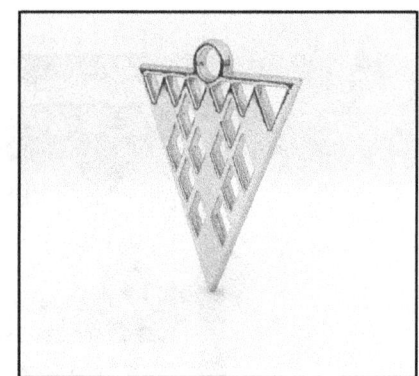
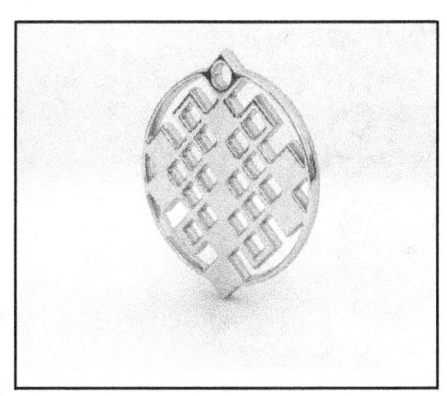
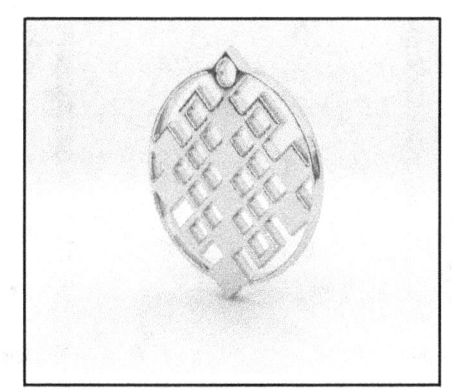
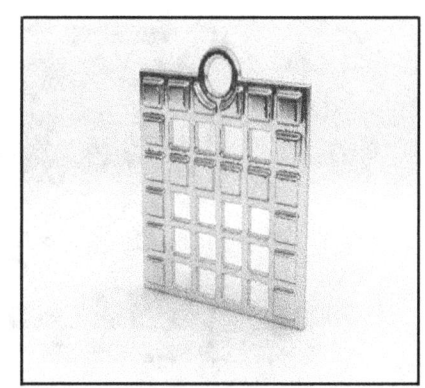

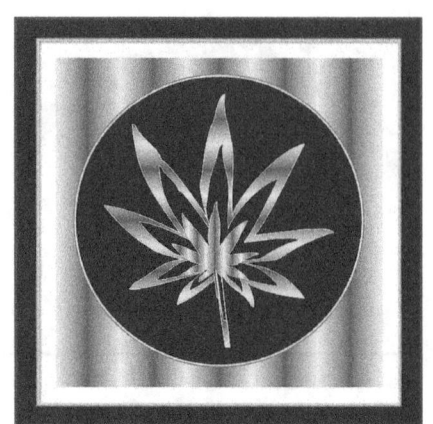

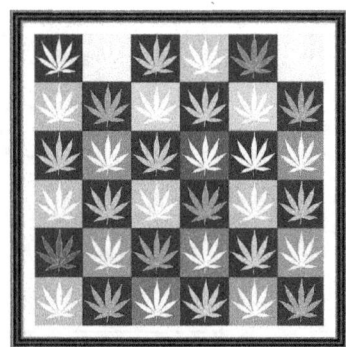

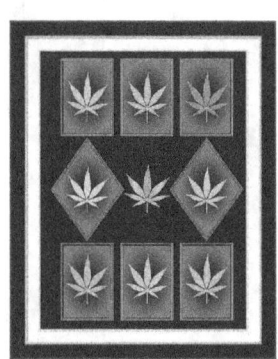

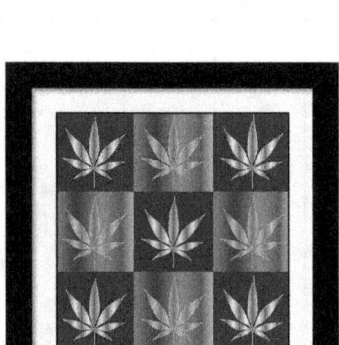

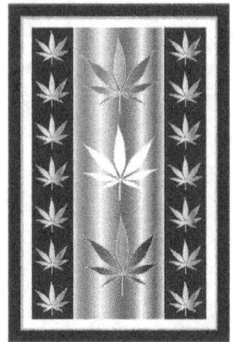

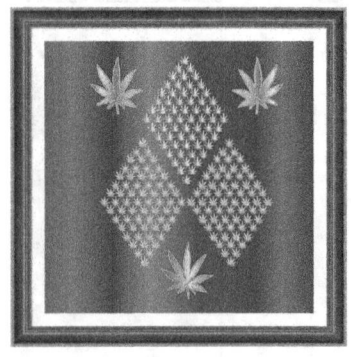

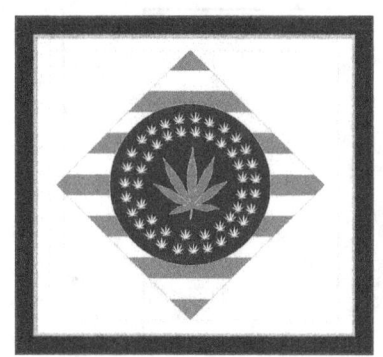

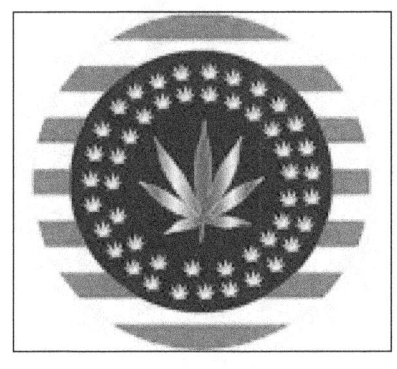

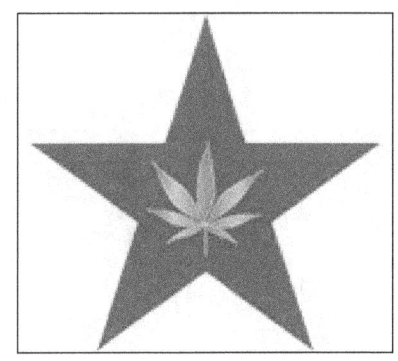

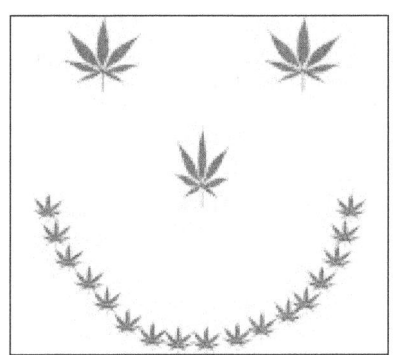

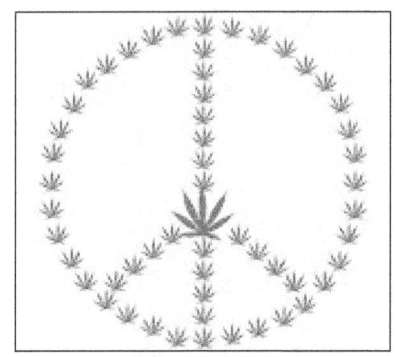

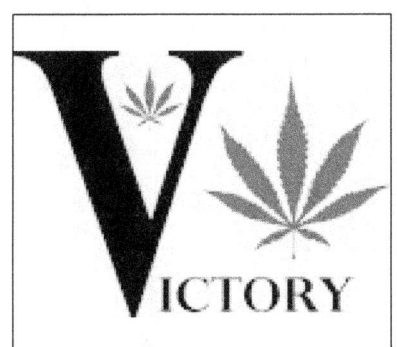

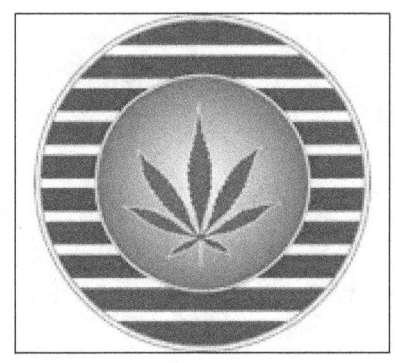

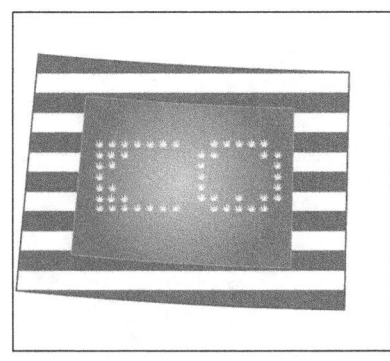

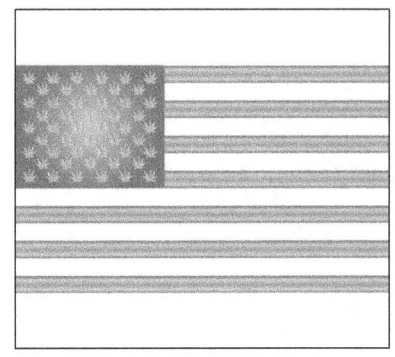

M7

The "MOBILE"

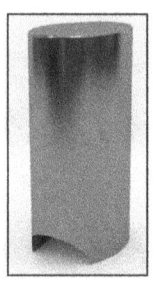 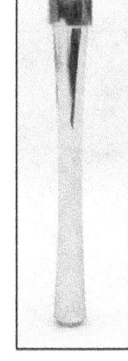 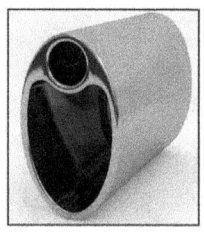

AVAILABLE MATERIALS
White Gold, 14K Gold, Stainless Steel, Gold Steel, Platinum, Black Steel
PLUS 14K Gold, Premium Silver, Raw Silver, Polished Silver, Brass, Bronze,
Silver Plated, Rose Gold Plated

THE TABLETOP WITH "LOAD ASSIST"

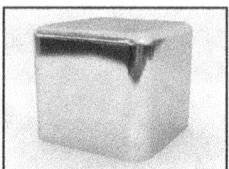

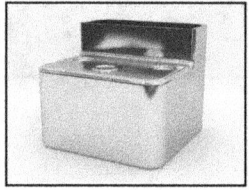

PLUS 14K Gold, Premium Silver, Raw Silver, Polished Silver, Brass, Bron
Silver Plated, Rose Gold Plated

THE "MOUTHPIECE"

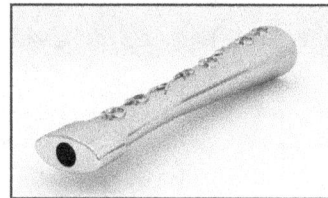

*Personalized or Not?
*Added Surface area for added
  Filtering
*Flat Mouthpiece for added Draw
*Spiral Design for Joint stability

AVAILABLE STYLES

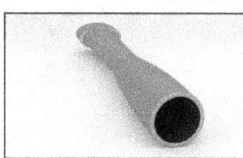

The "Mouthpiece"

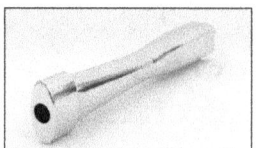

The "Mouthpiece Squared"

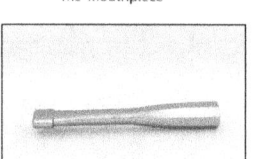

The "Mouthpiece 9"

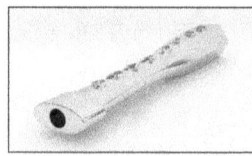

"My Mouthpiece"

COLORADO HITZ - THE BOOK

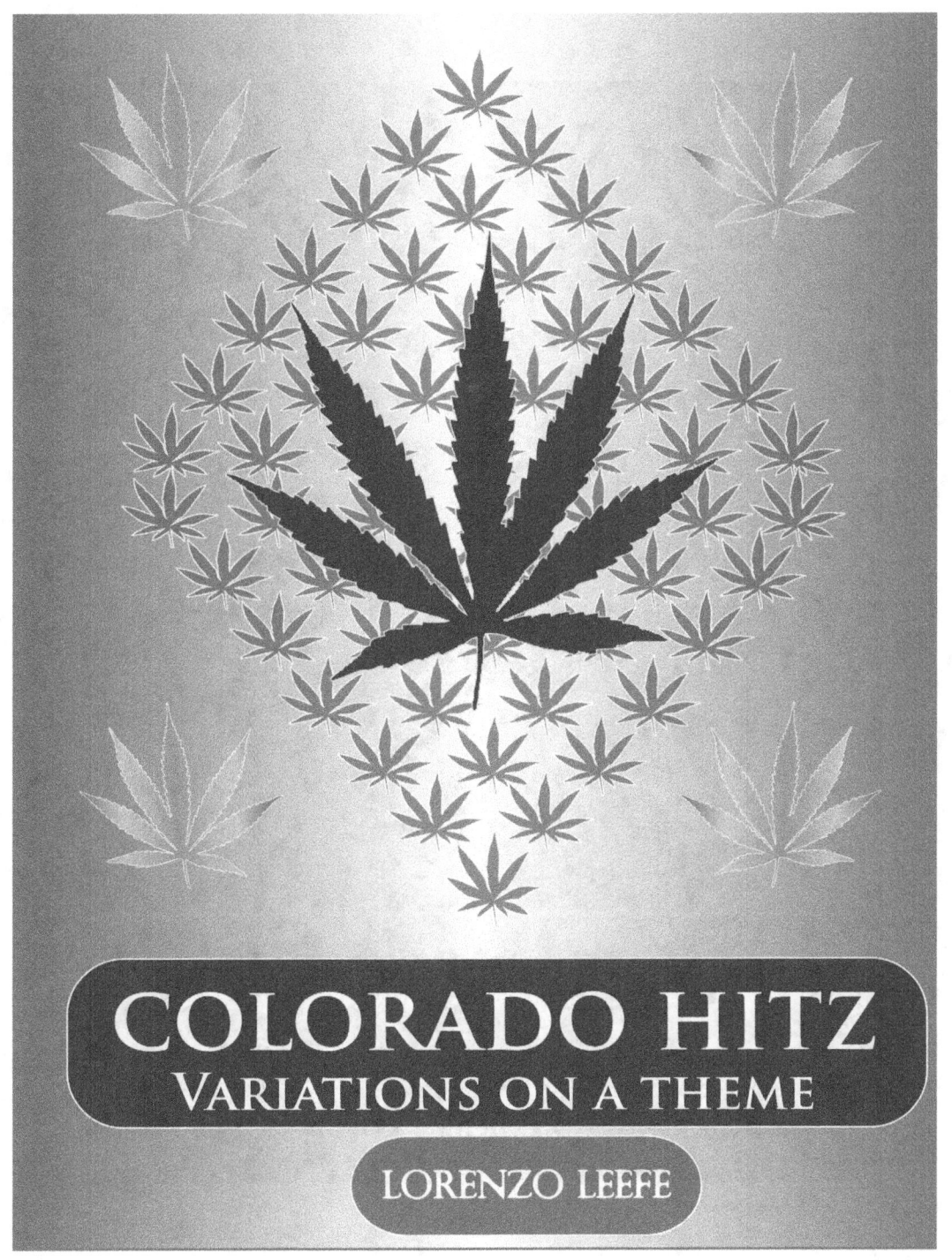

AVAILABLE ON AMAZON

THE COLORADO HITZ - THE COLORING BOOK

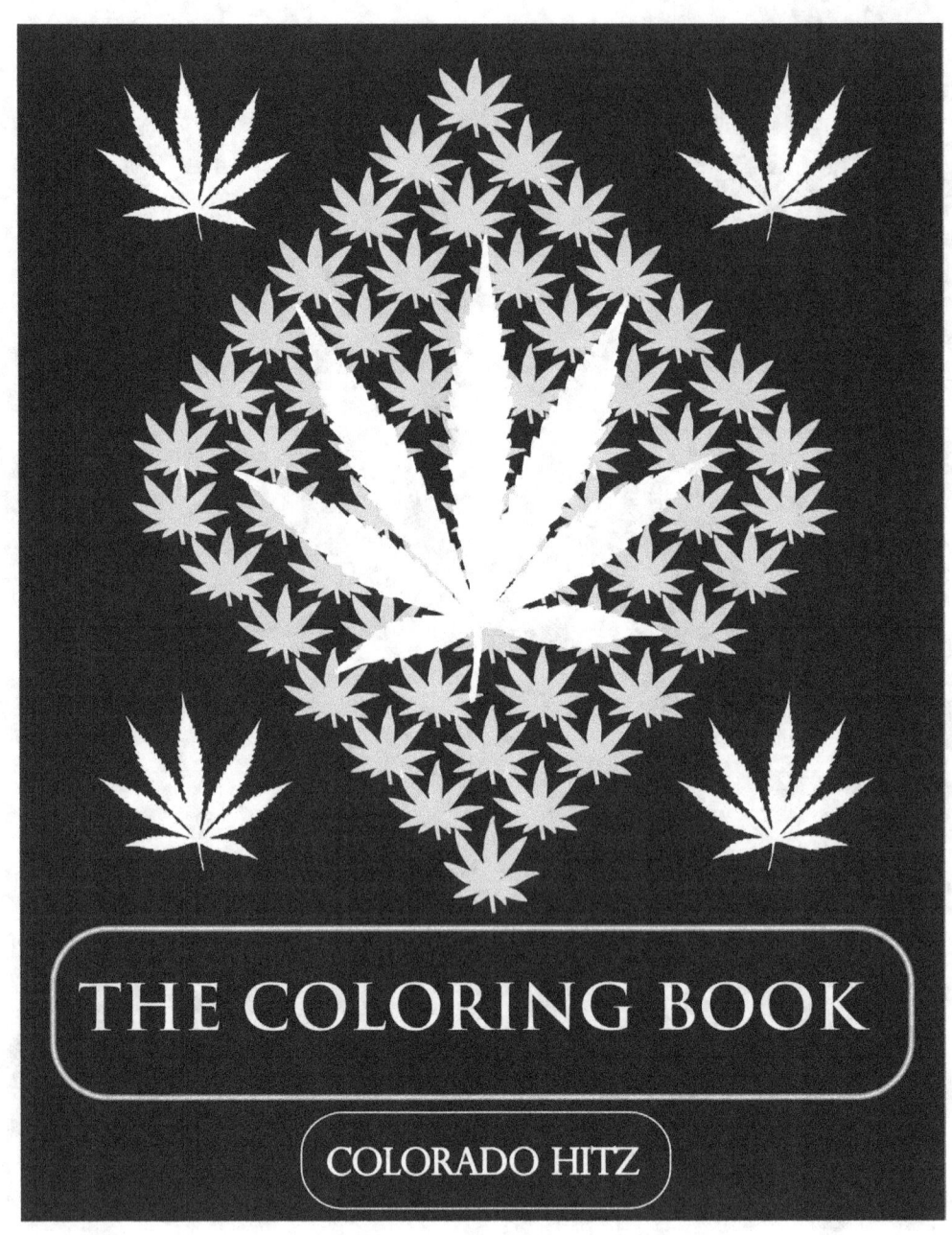

AVAILABLE ON AMAZON

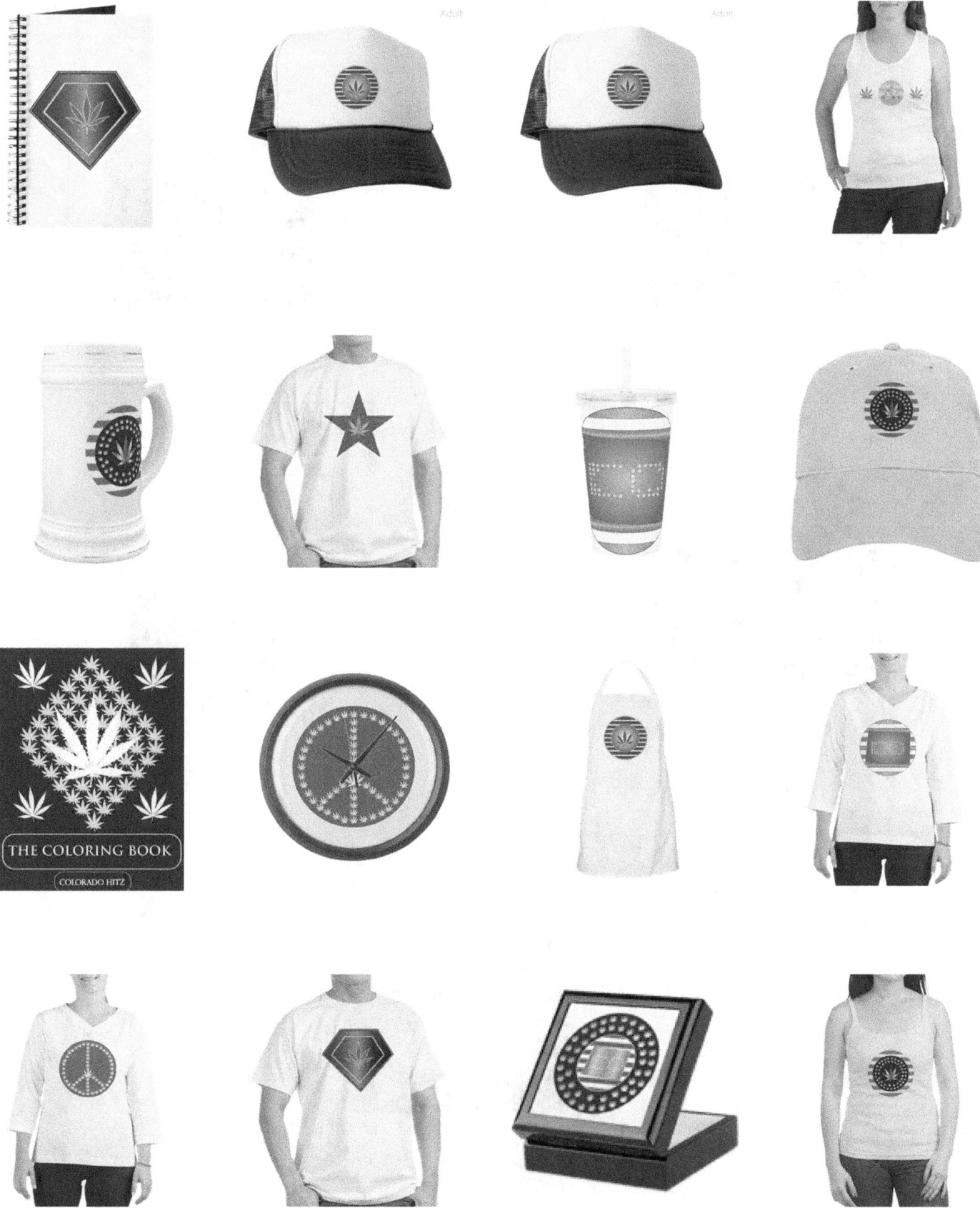

COLORING BOOKS

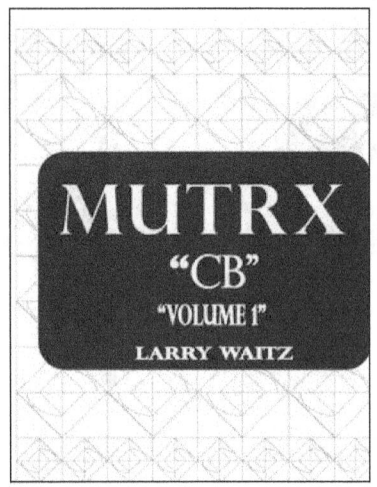

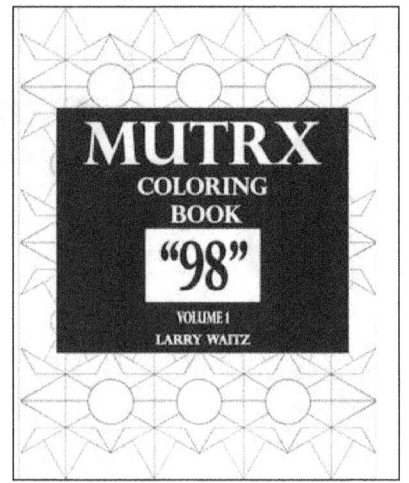

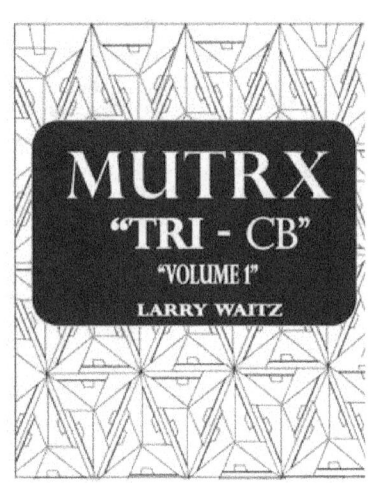

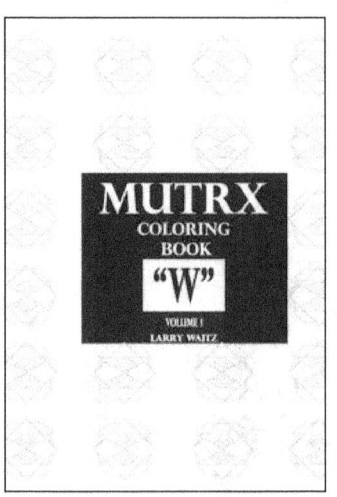

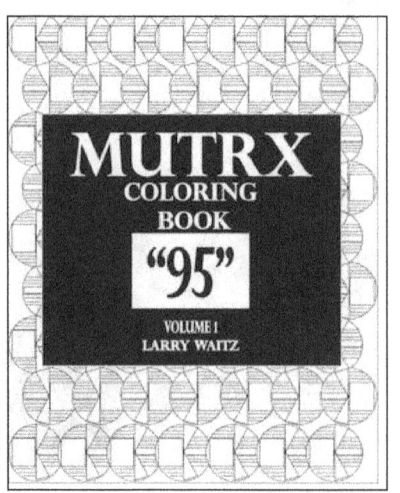

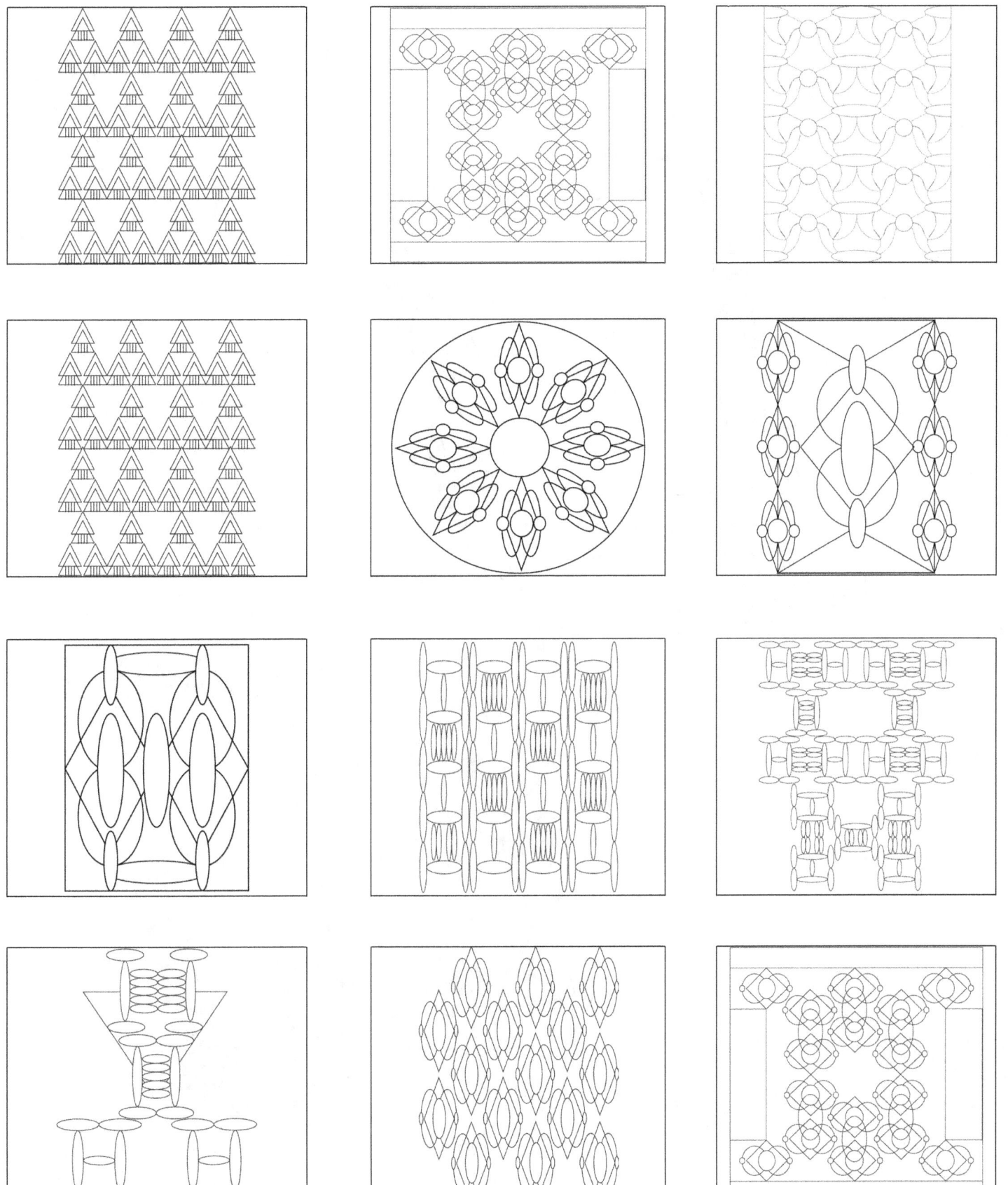

ART TO GO

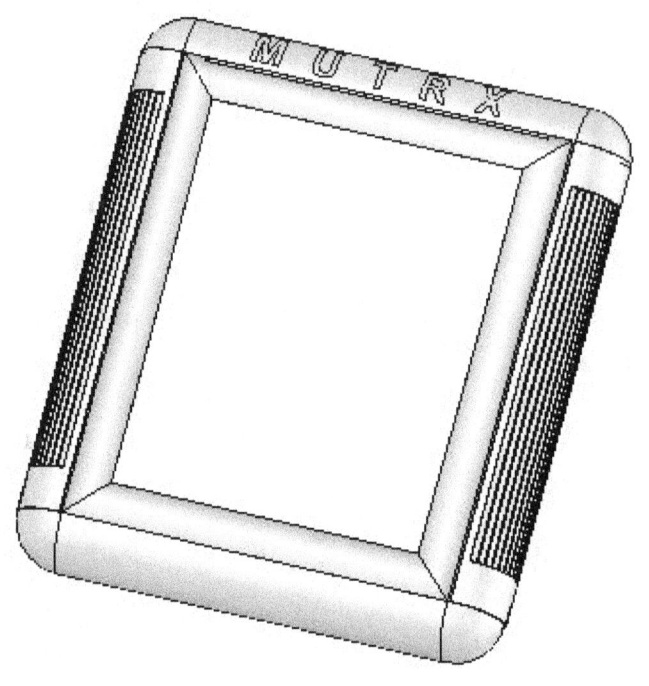

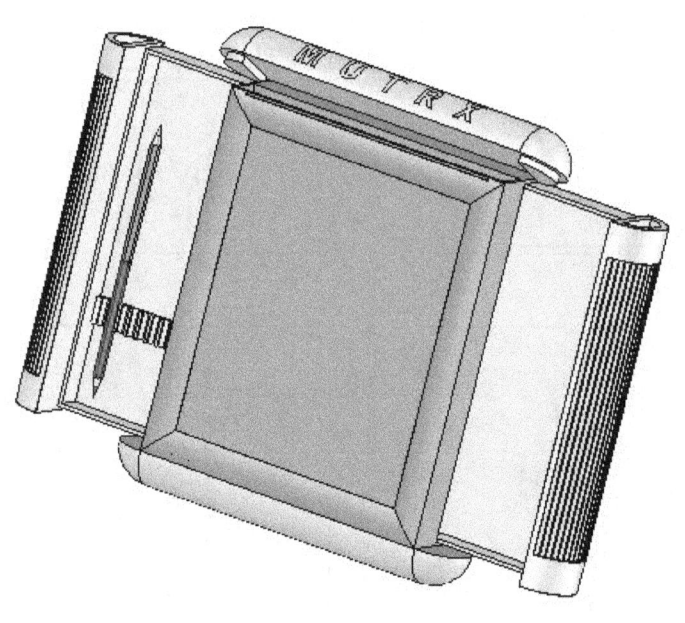

M7

JEWELRY BOXES

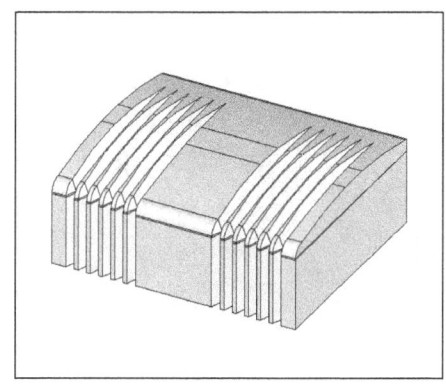 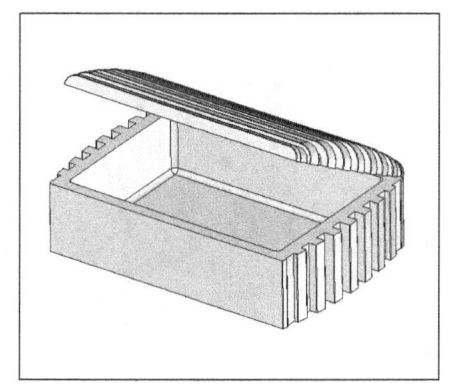 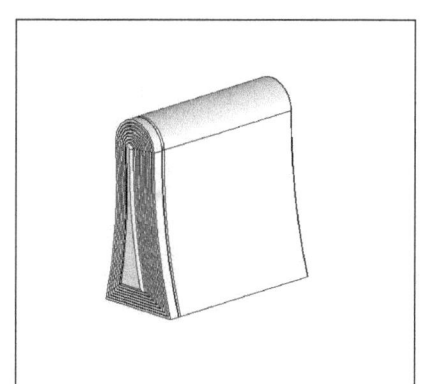

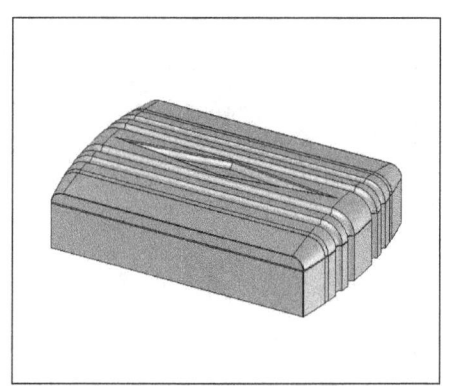 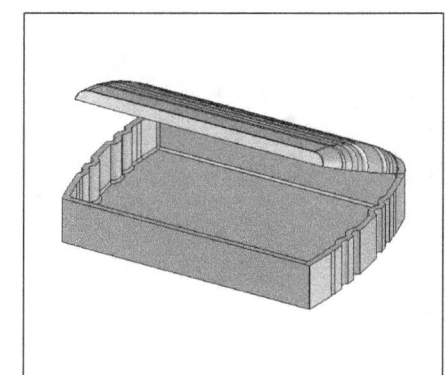 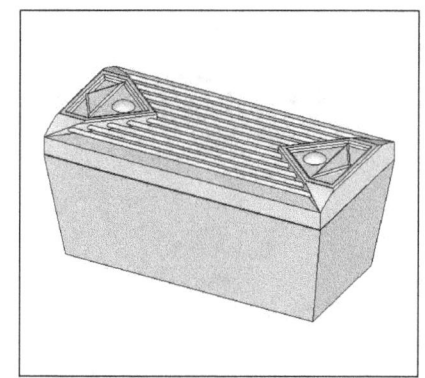

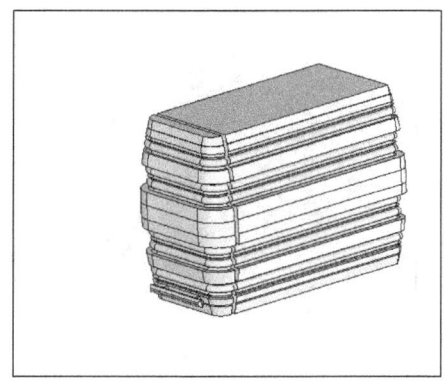 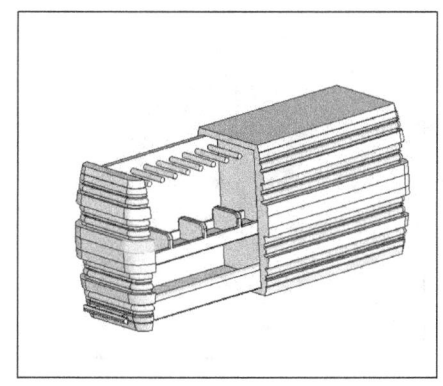 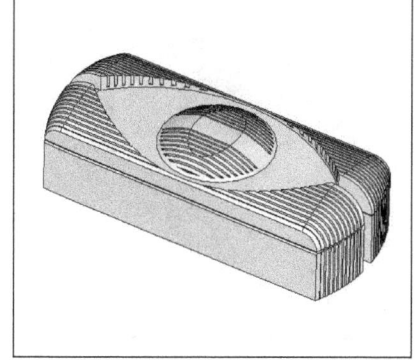

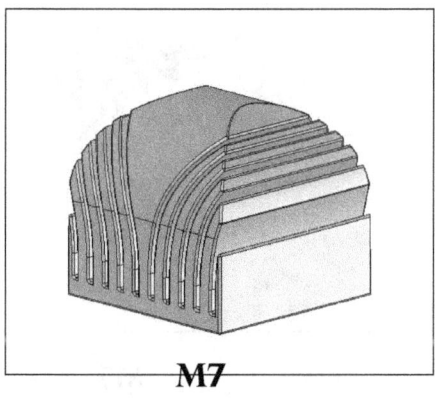

M7

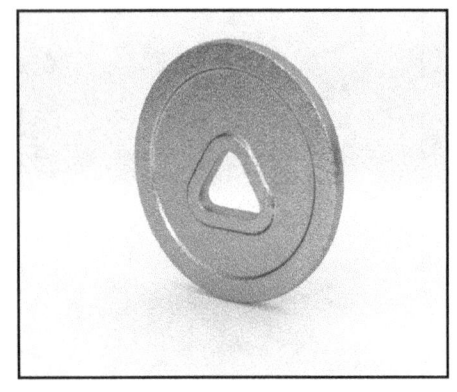
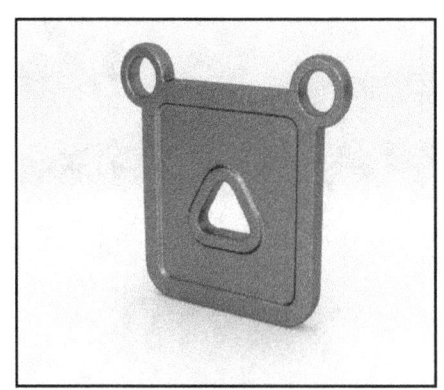
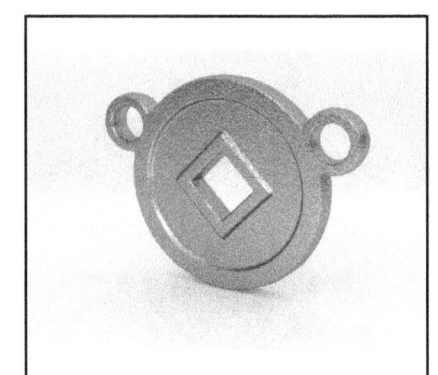

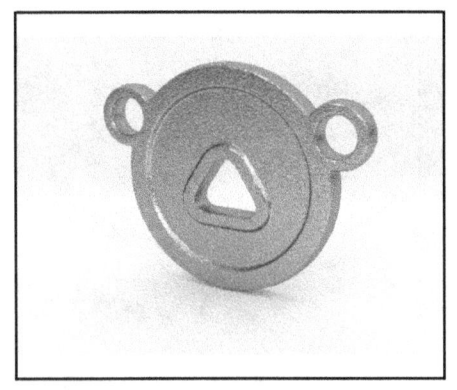
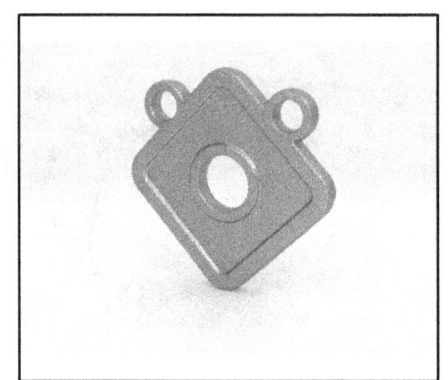
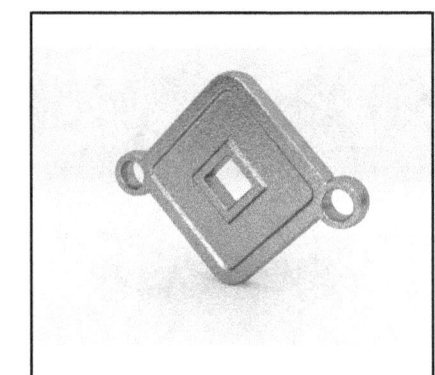

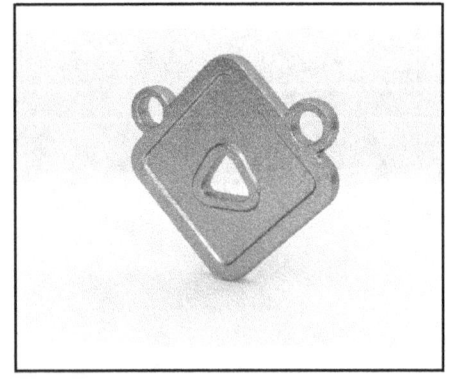
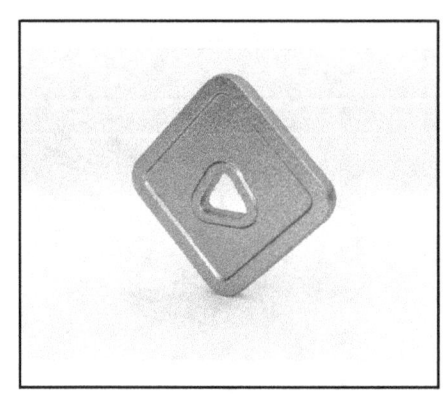
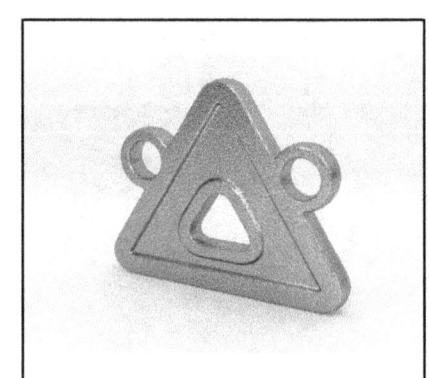

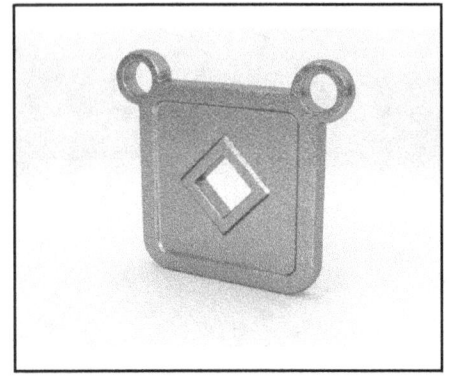
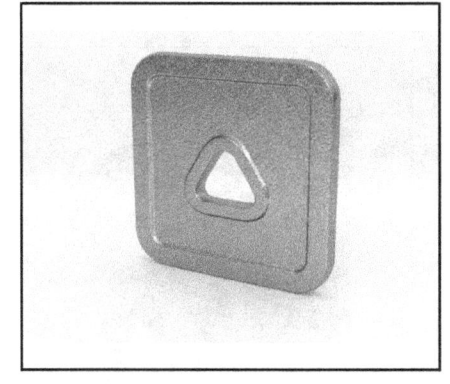
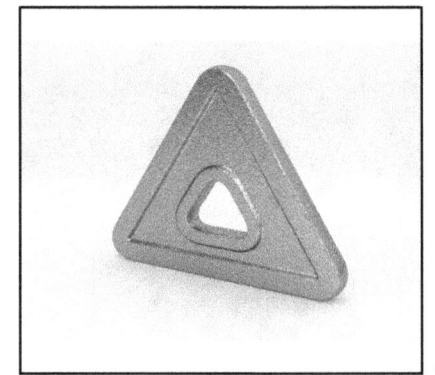

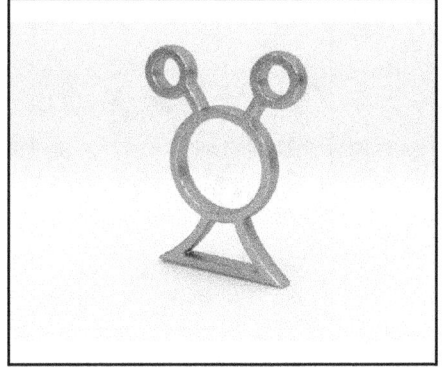
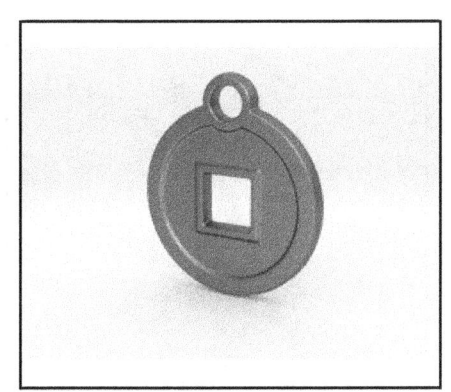
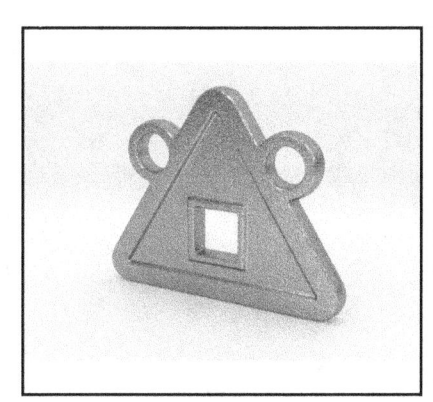
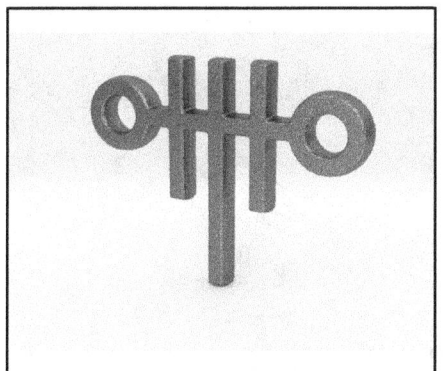
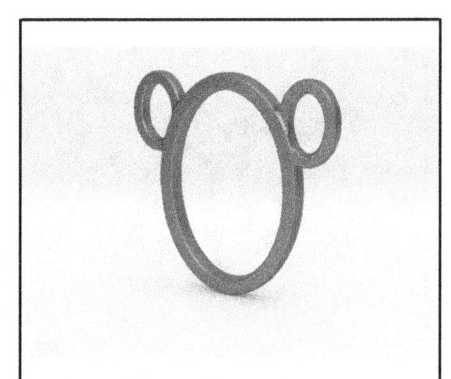
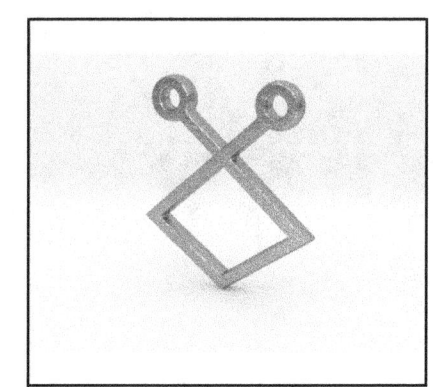
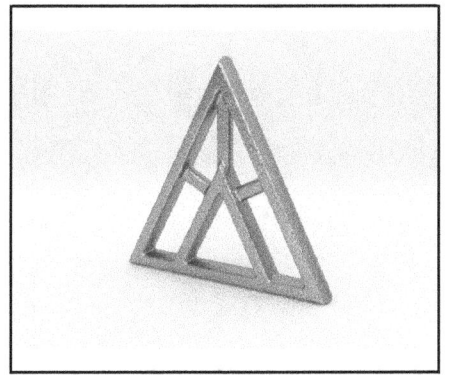
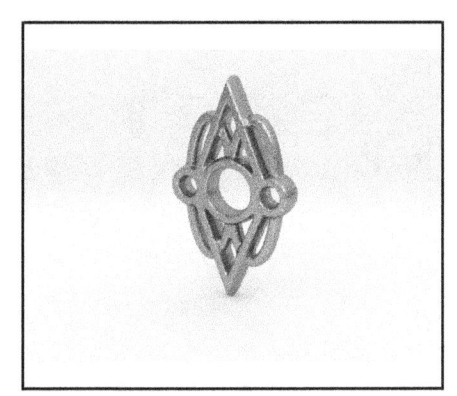
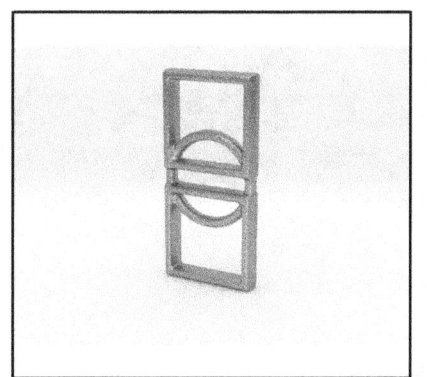
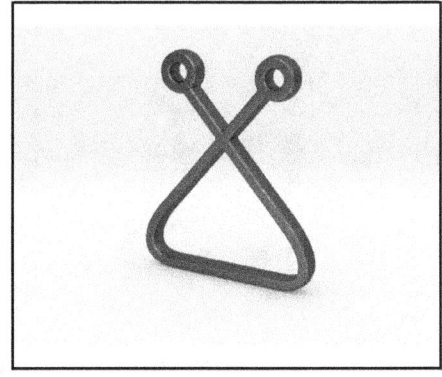
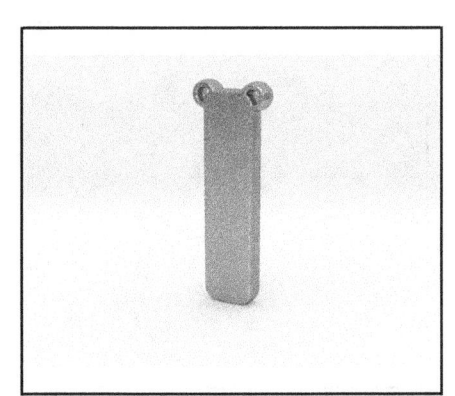
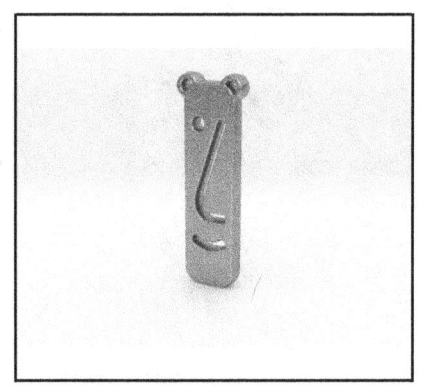

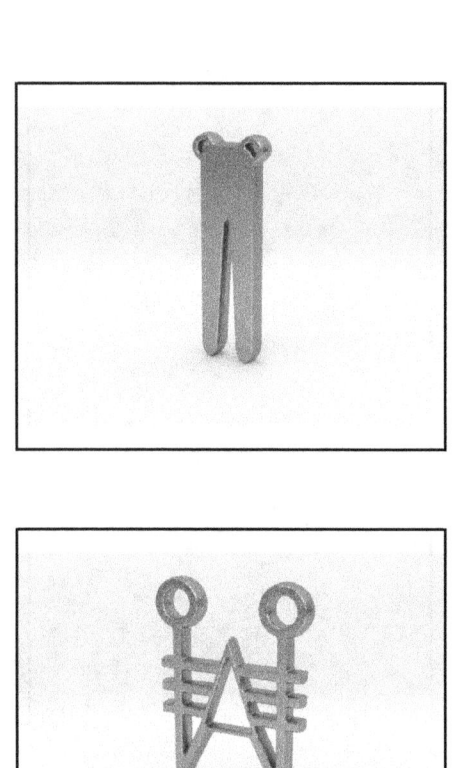 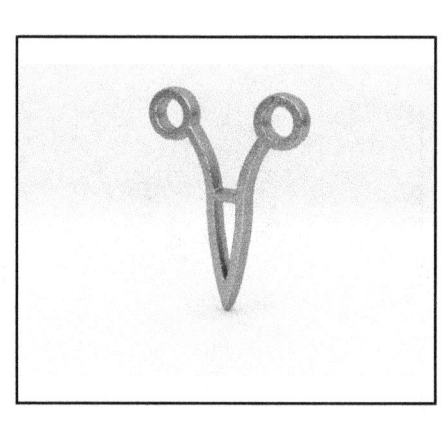 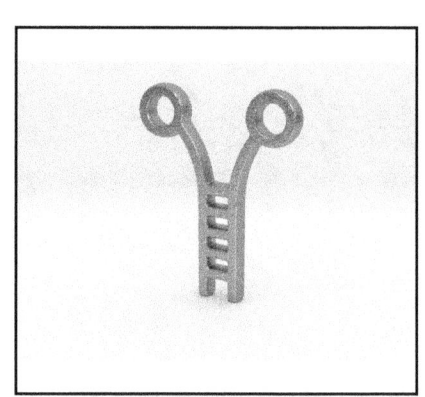

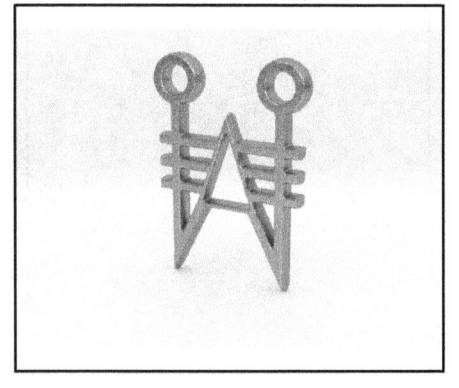 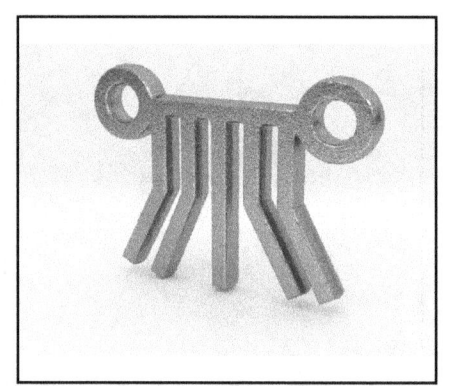 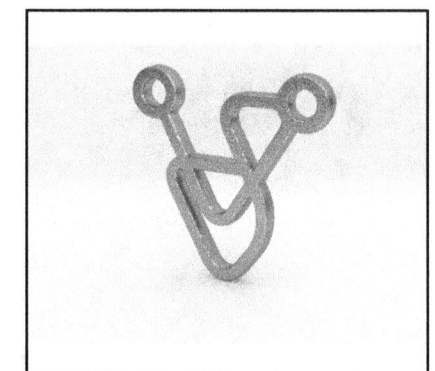

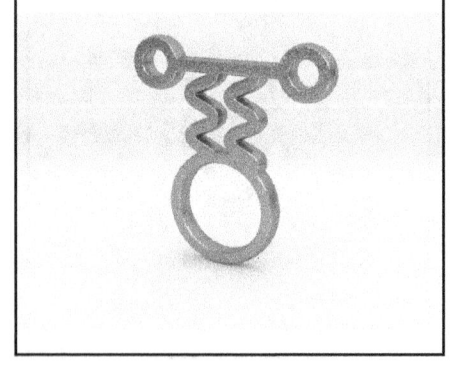 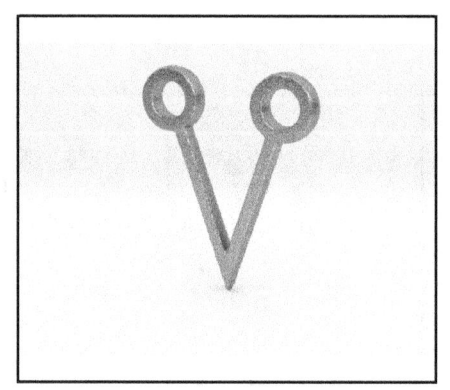 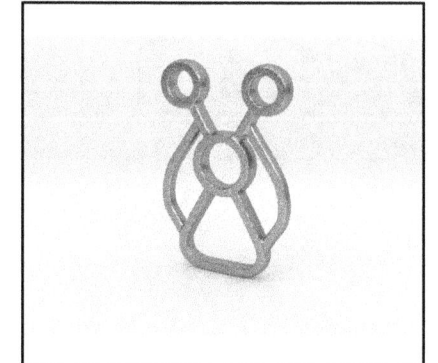

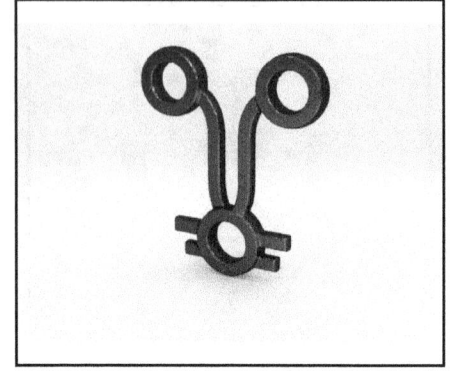 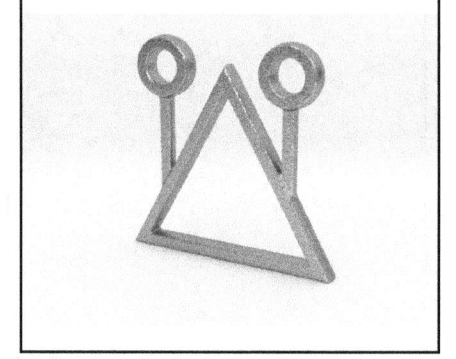 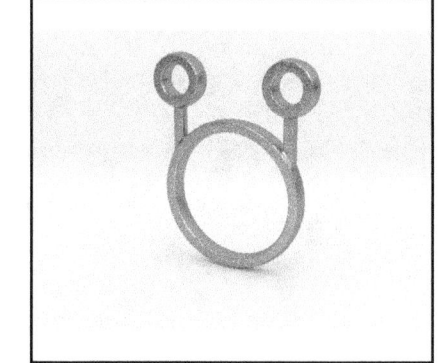

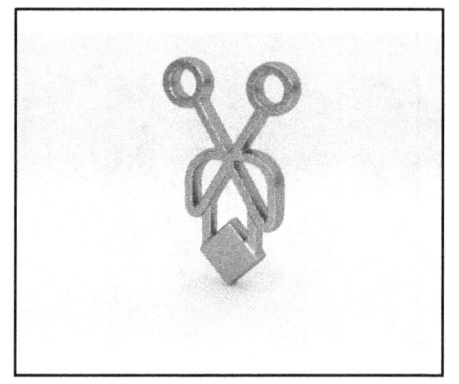
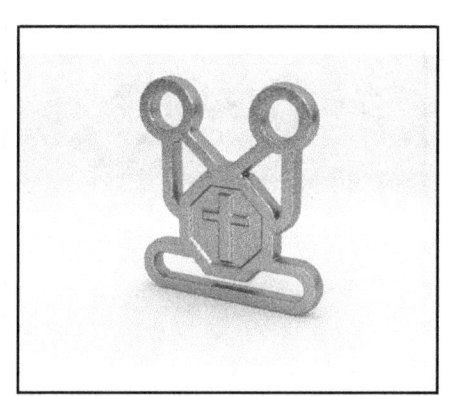
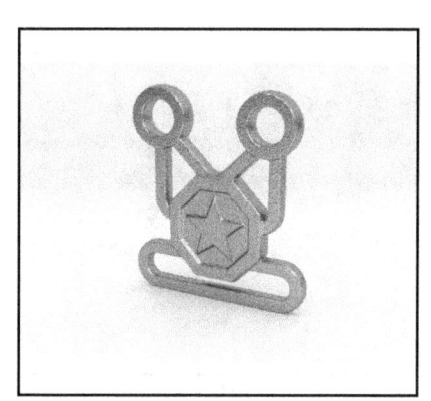

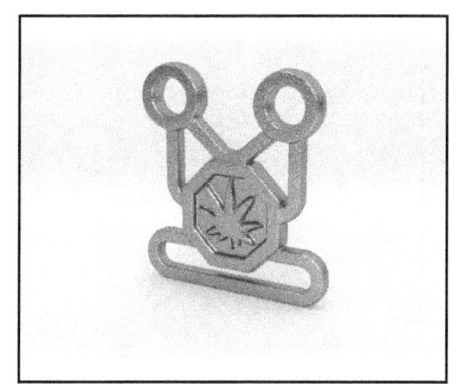
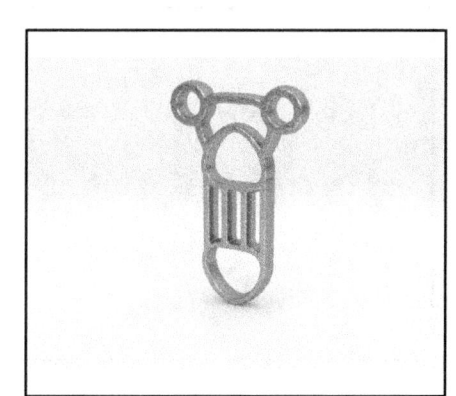
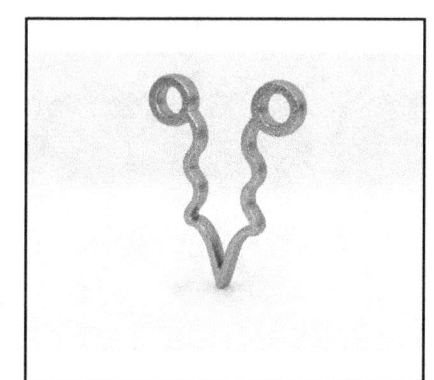

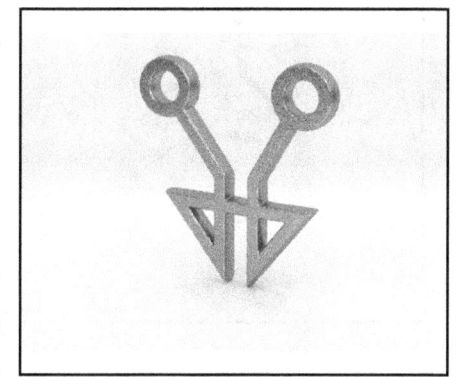
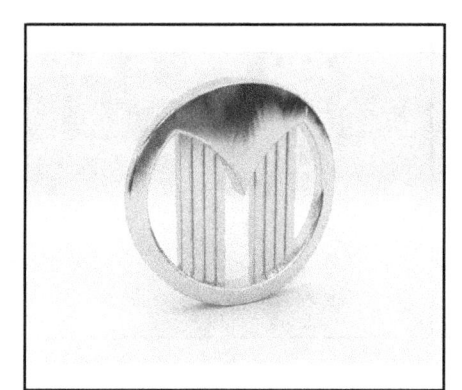
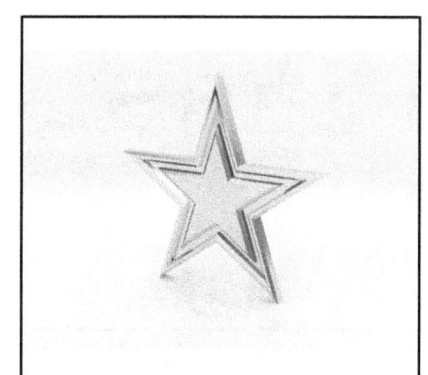

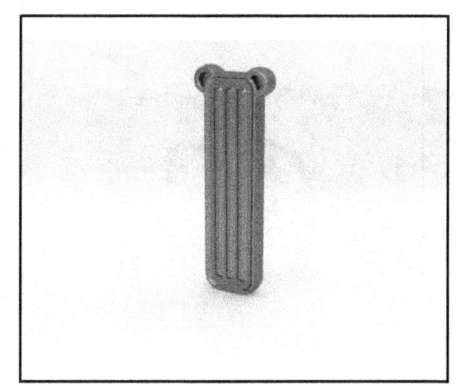
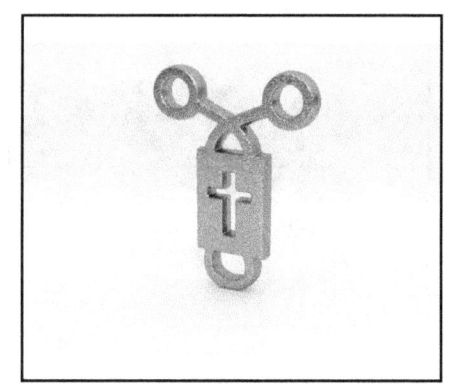
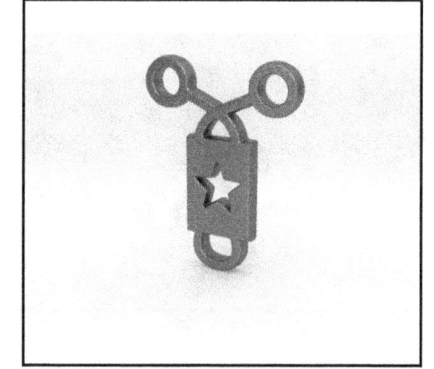

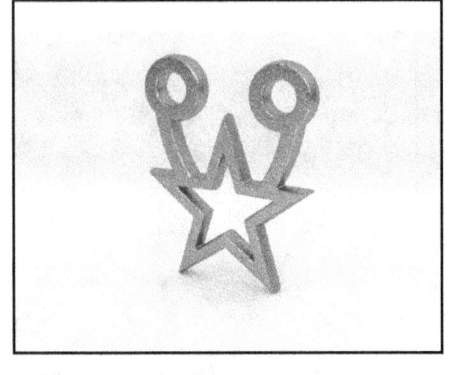
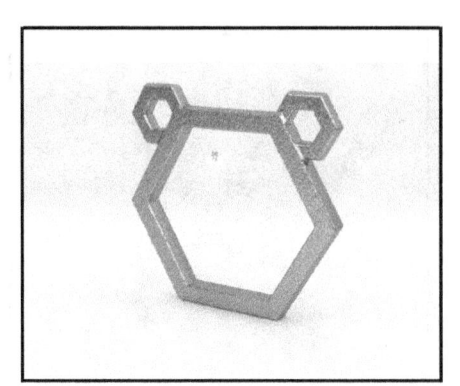
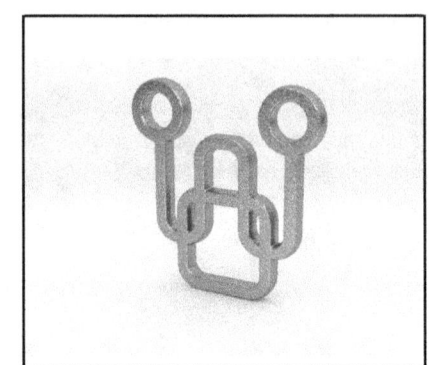
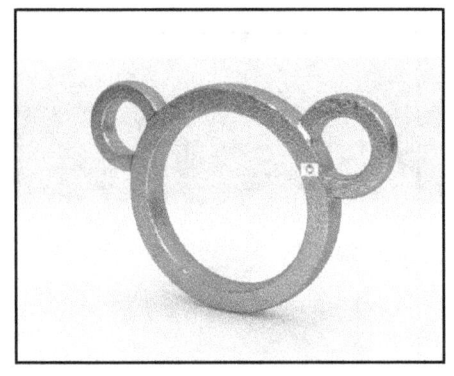
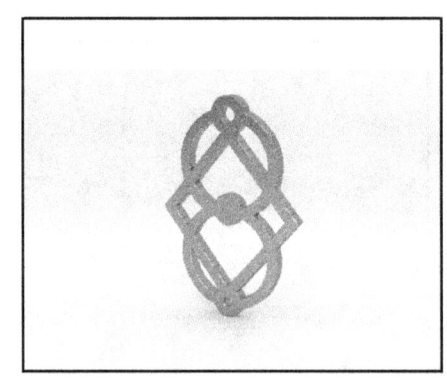
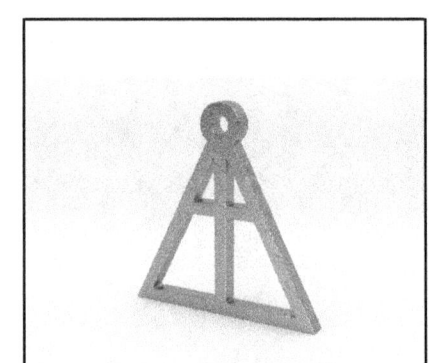
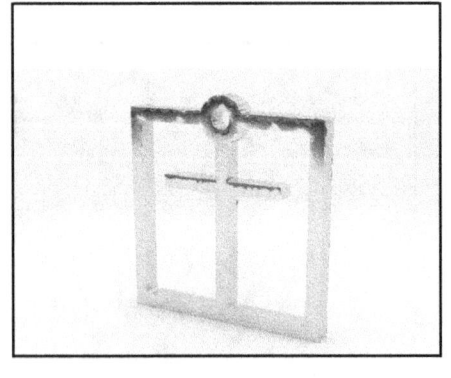
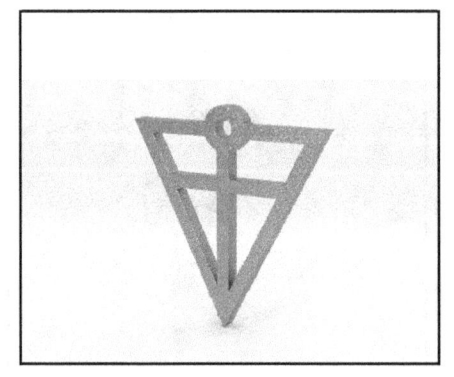
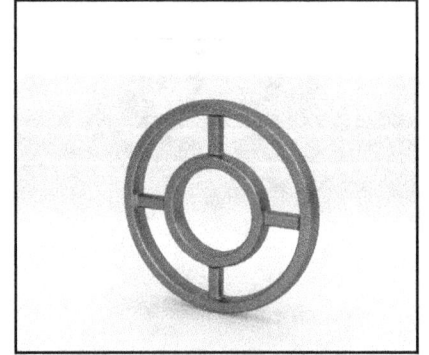
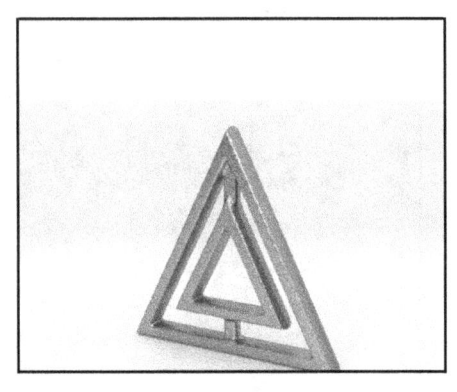
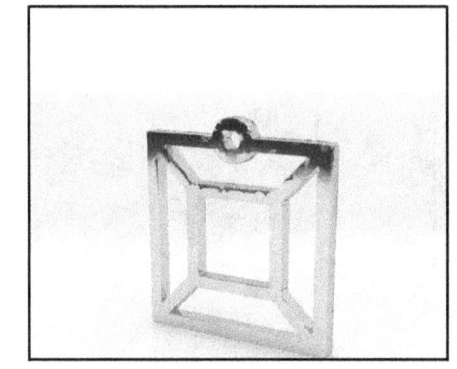
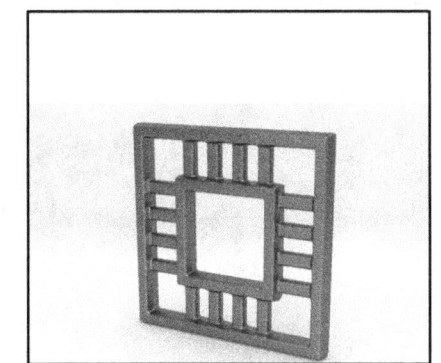

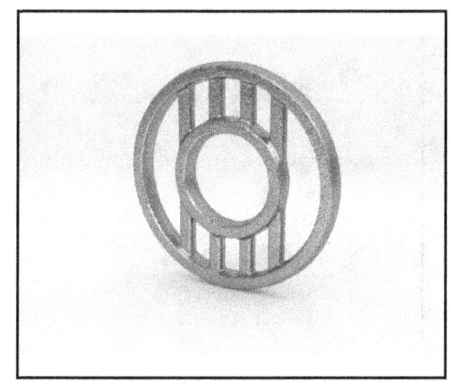 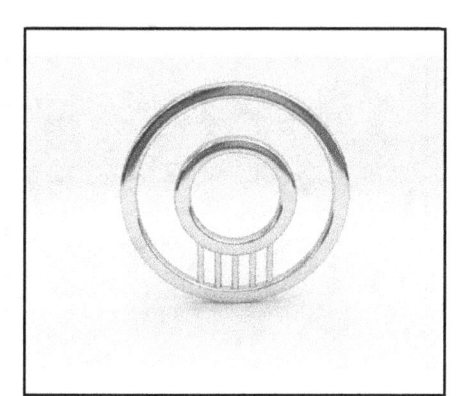 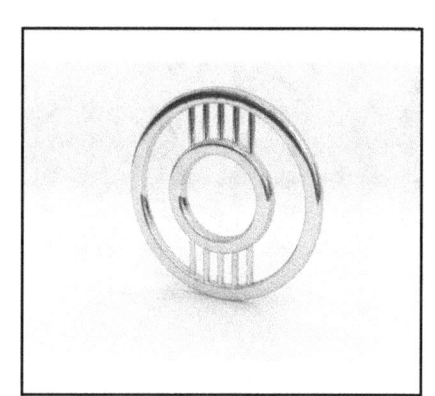

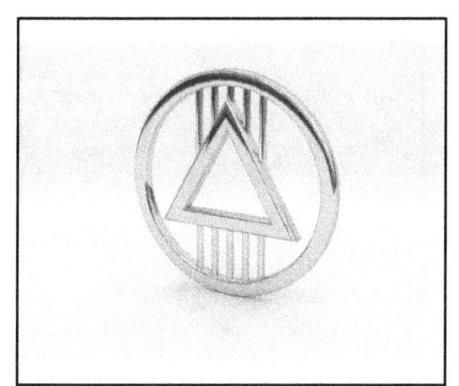 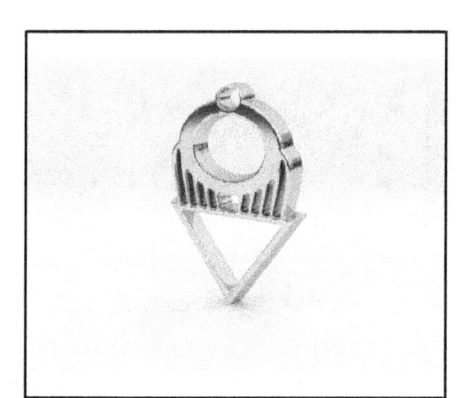 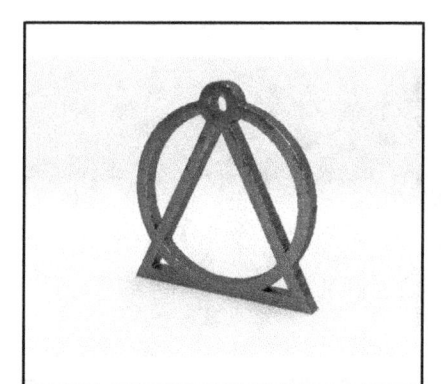

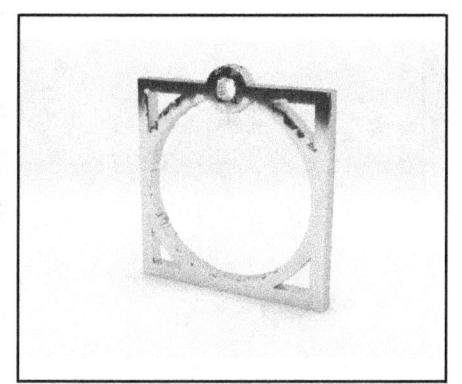 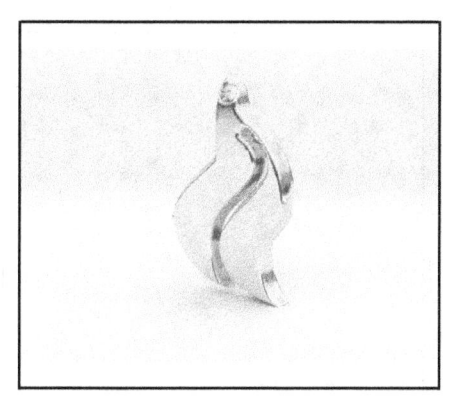 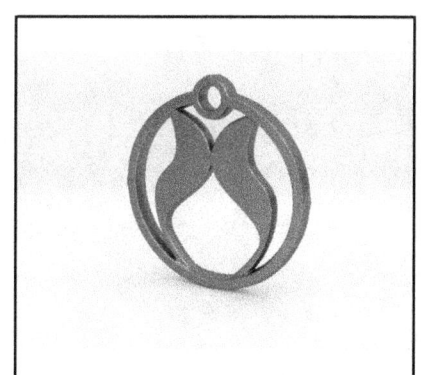

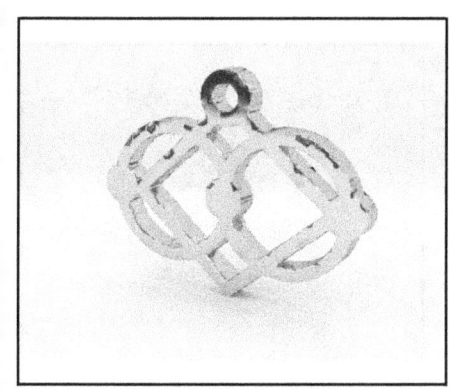 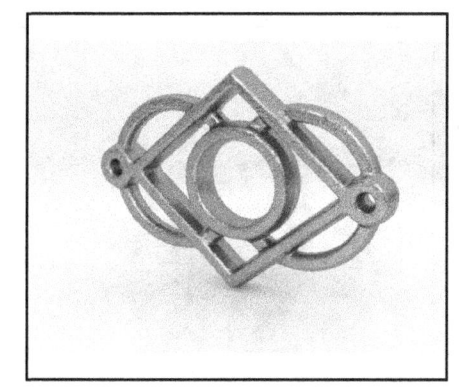 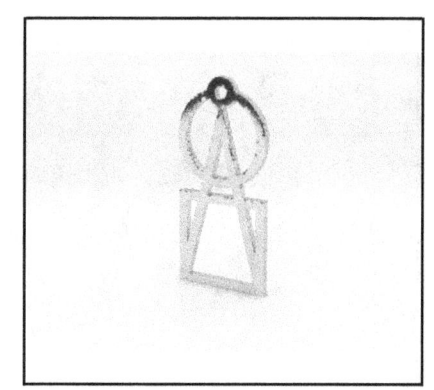

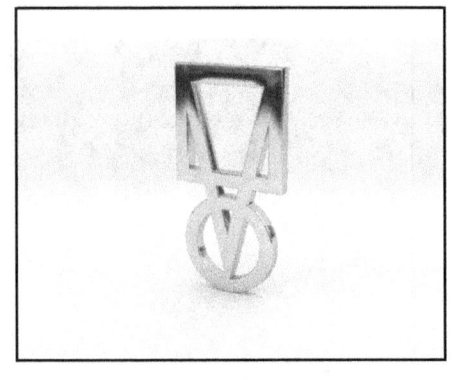 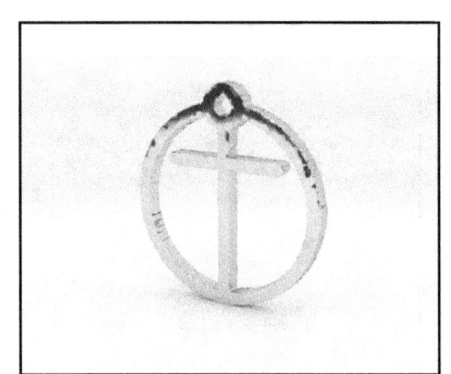 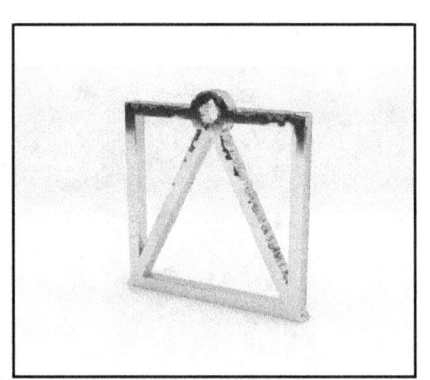

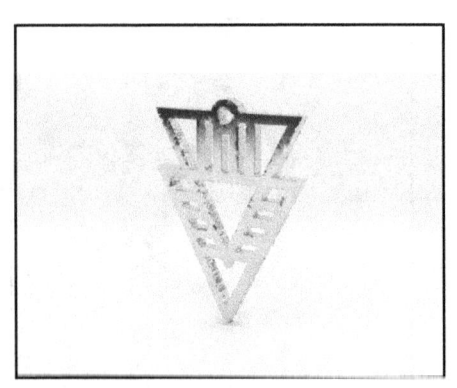 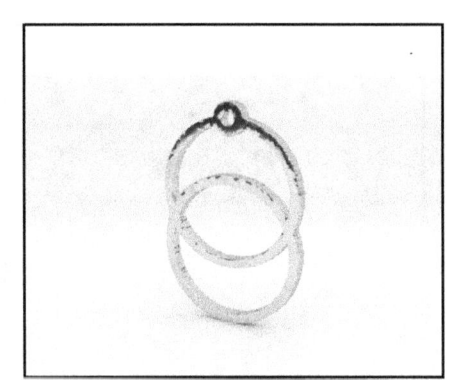 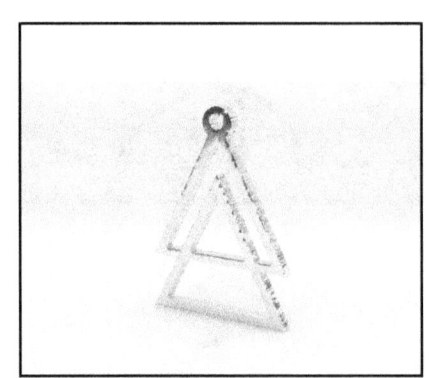

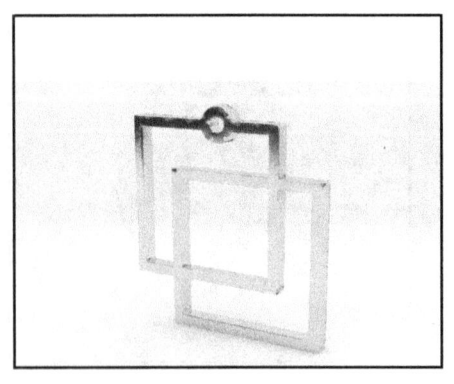 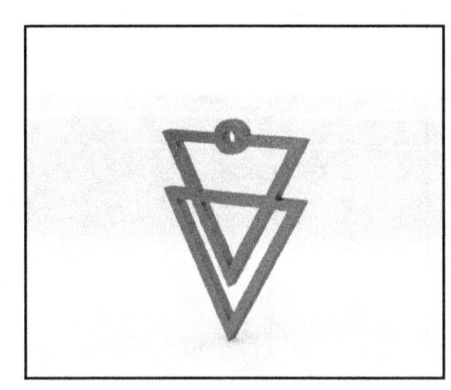 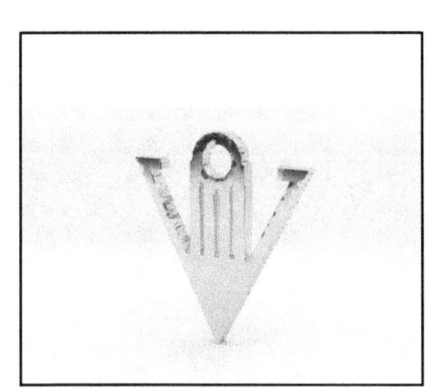

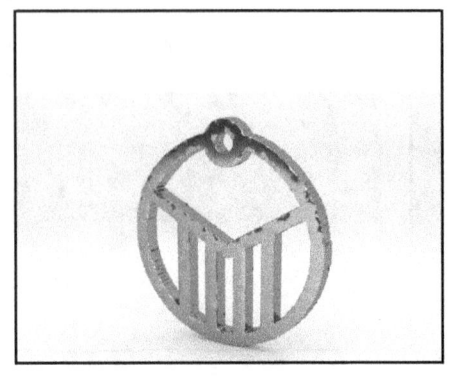 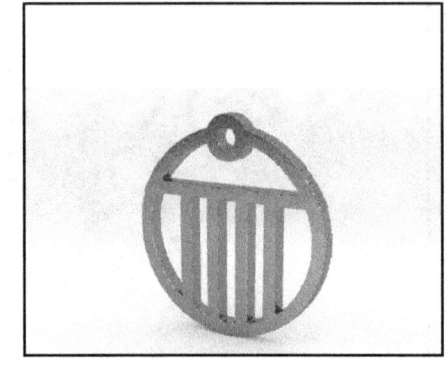 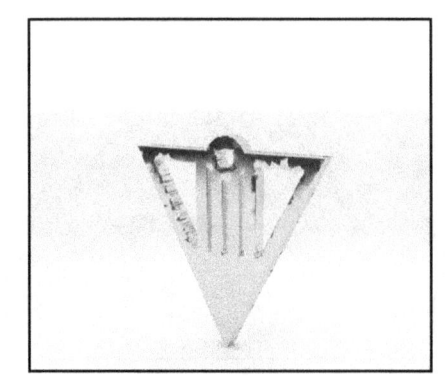

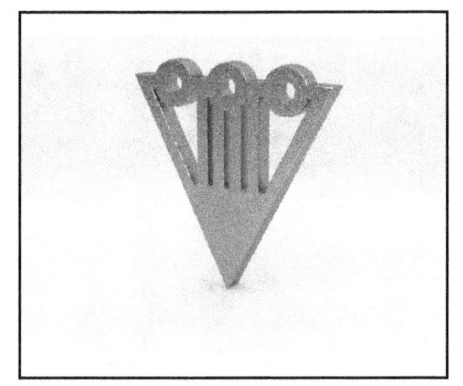

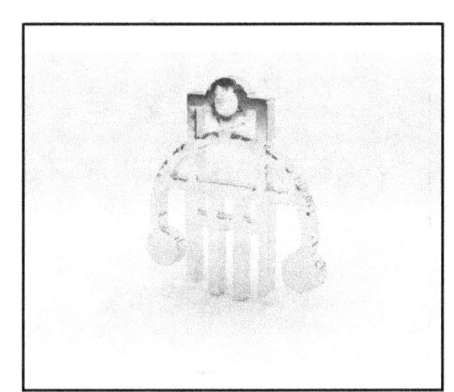

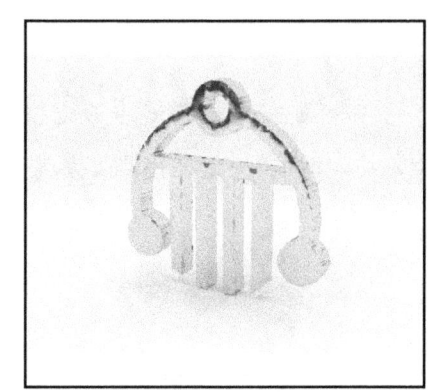

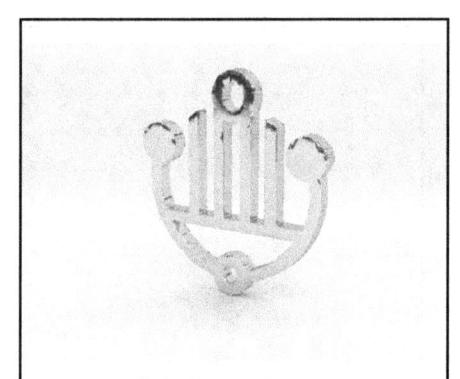

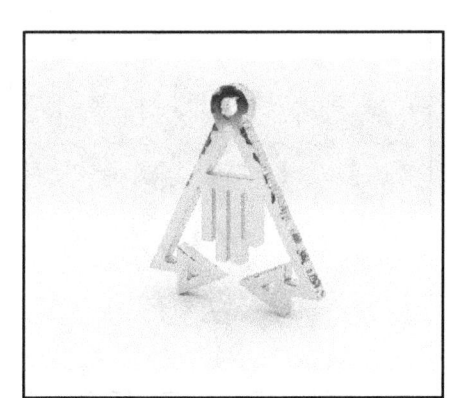

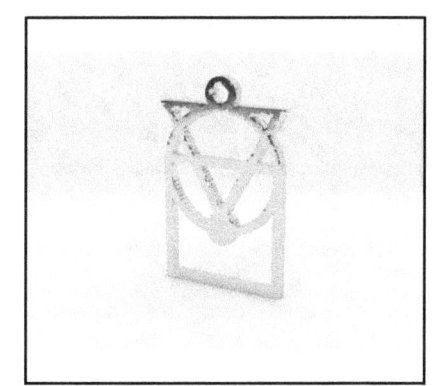

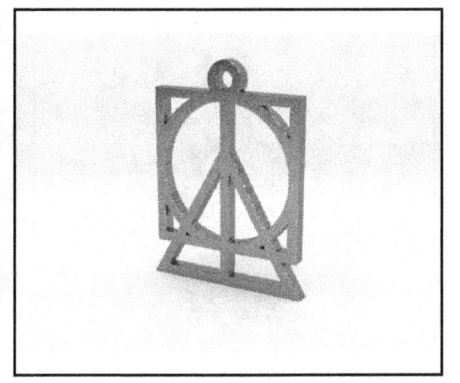

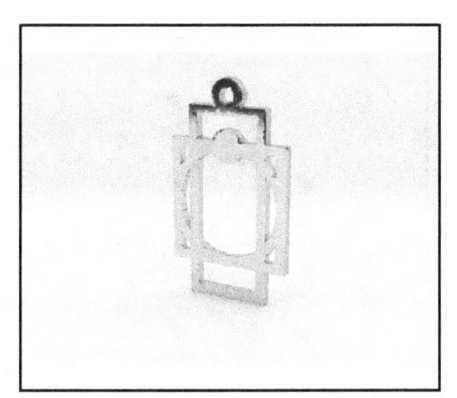

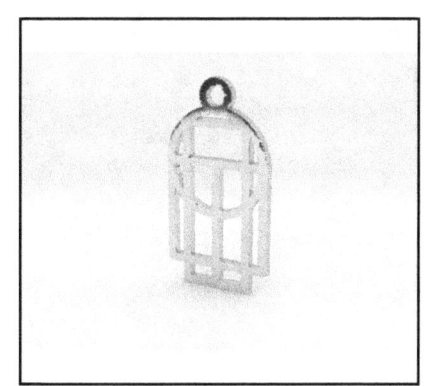

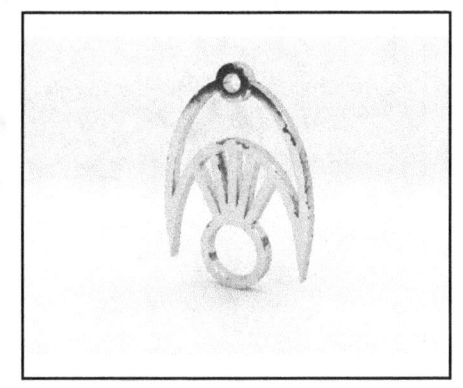

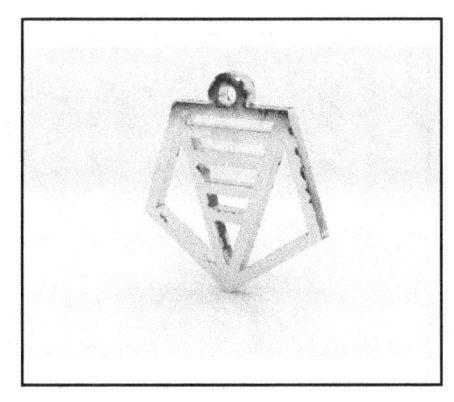

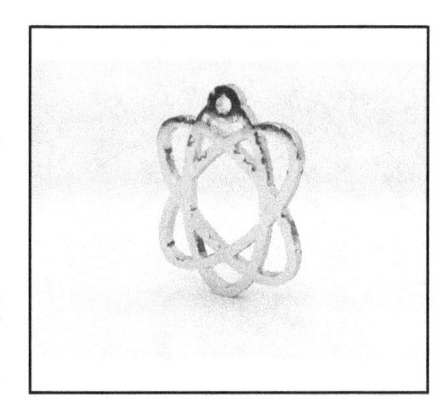

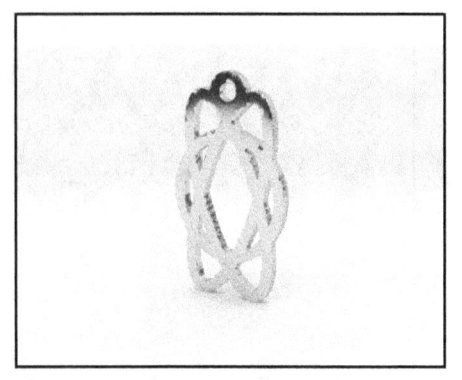
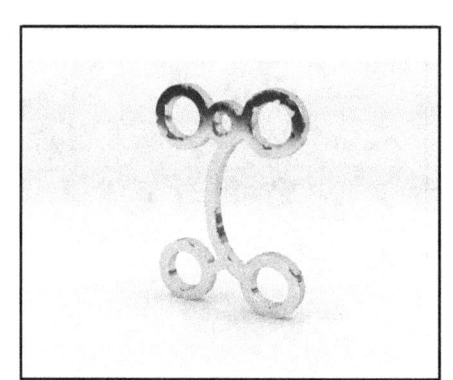
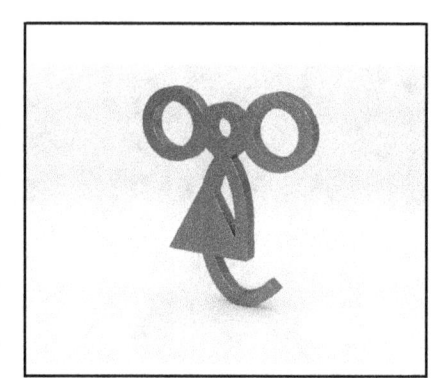
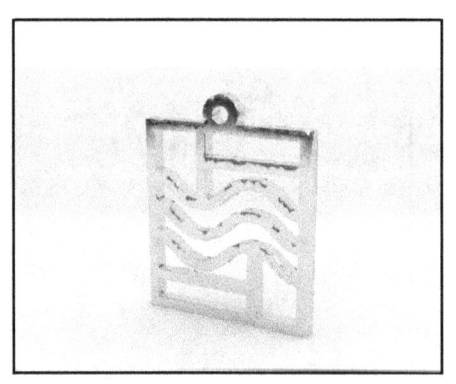
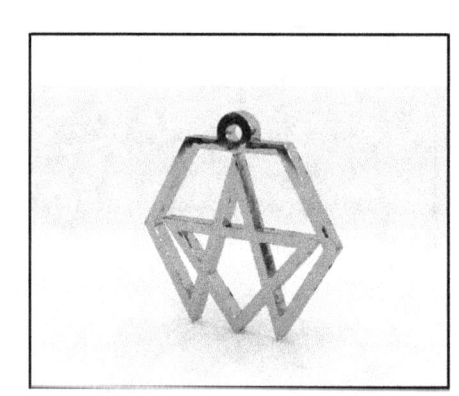
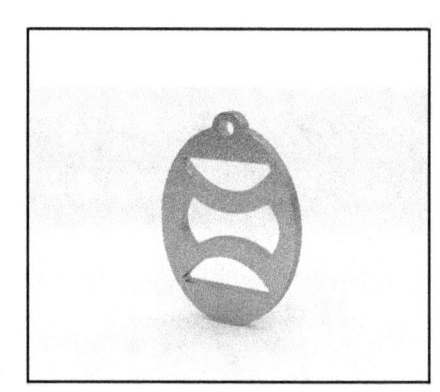
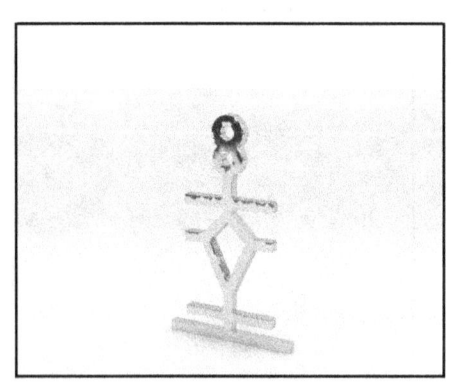
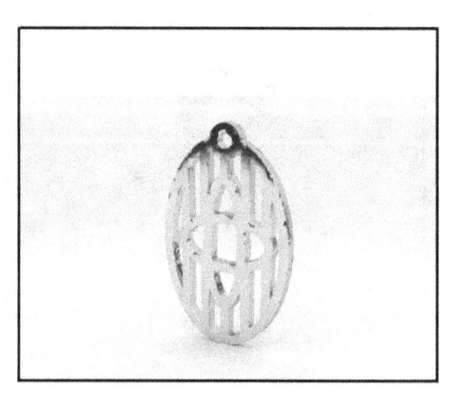
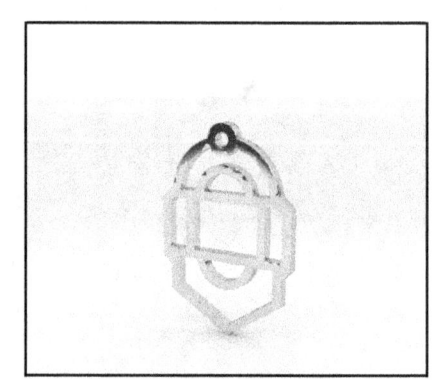
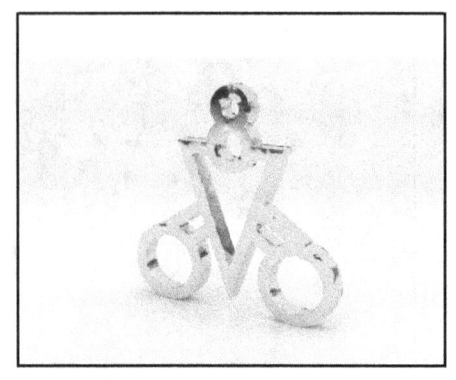
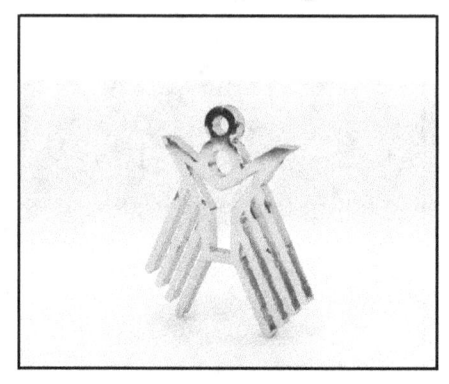
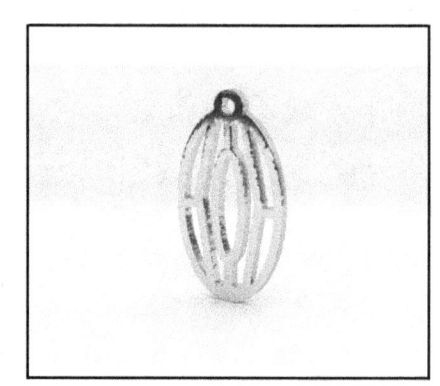

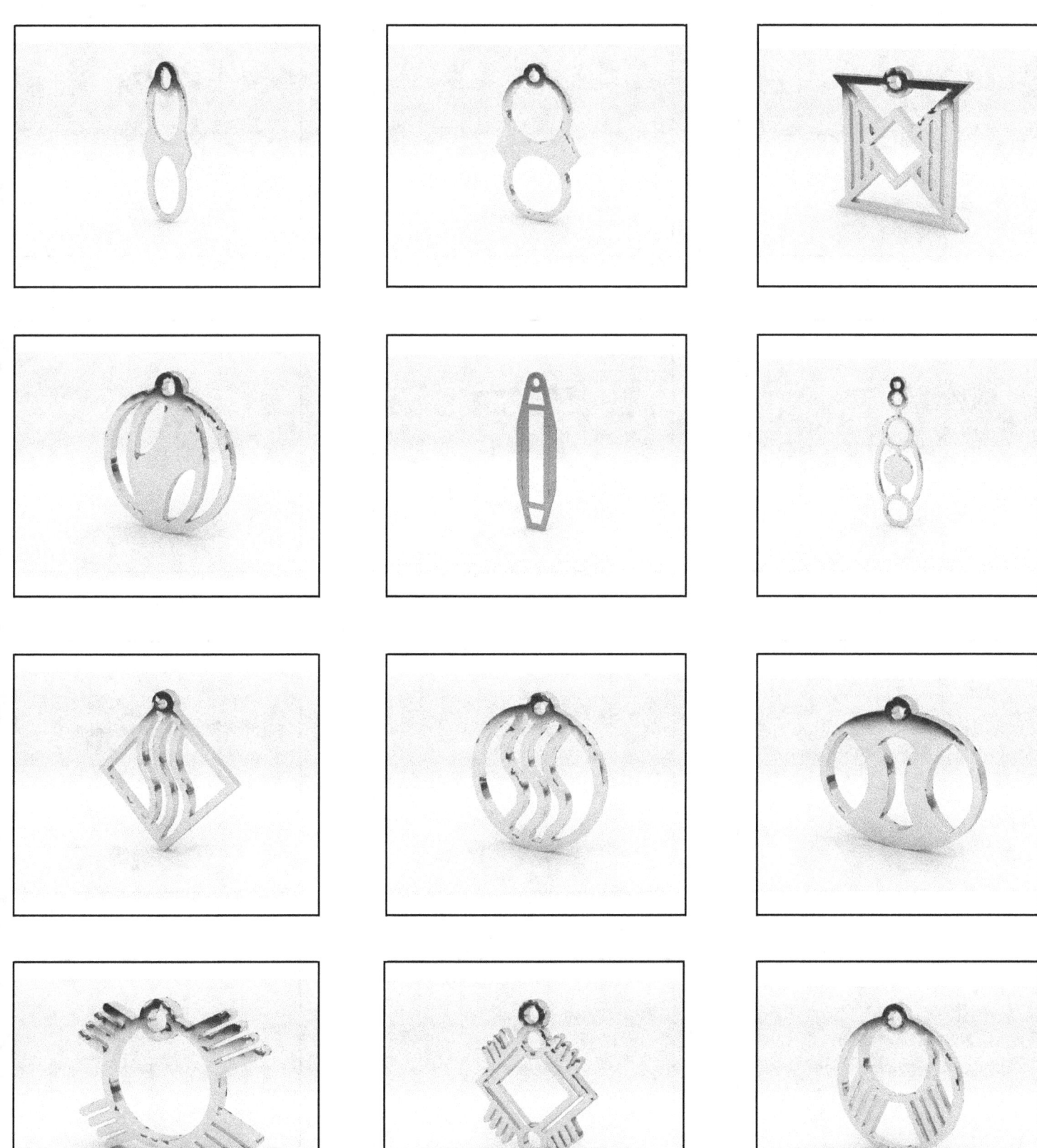

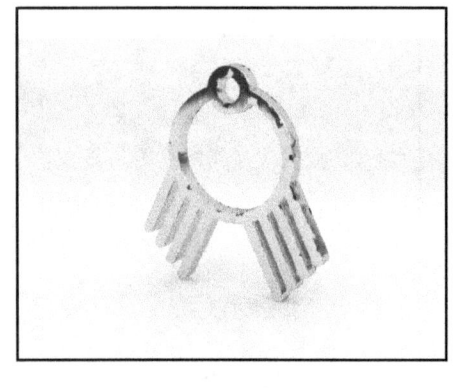 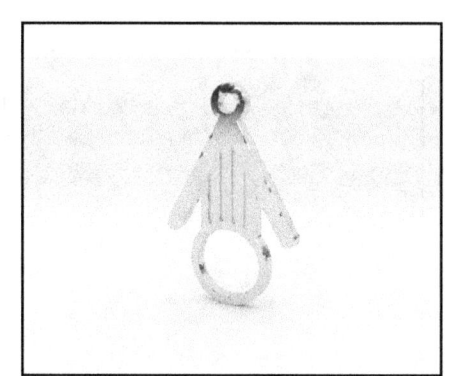 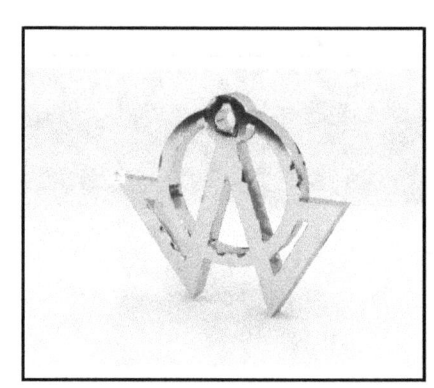

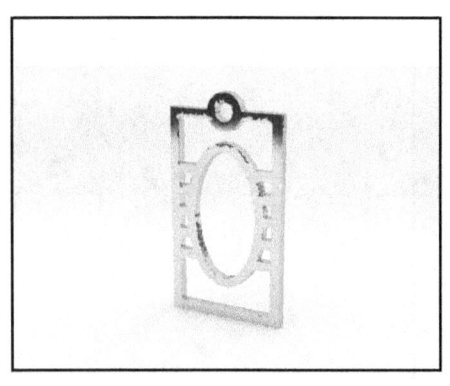 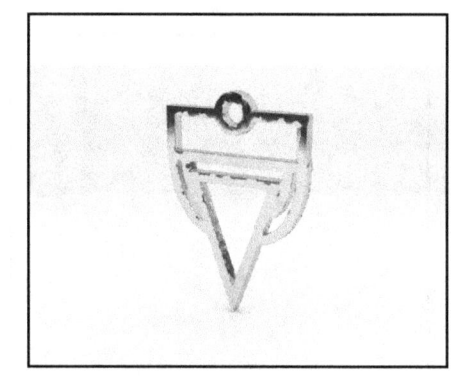 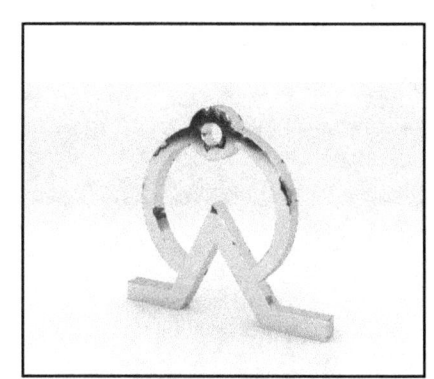

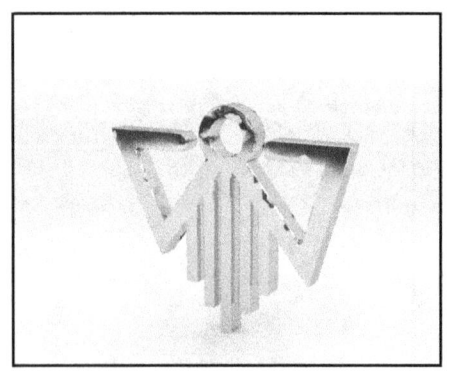 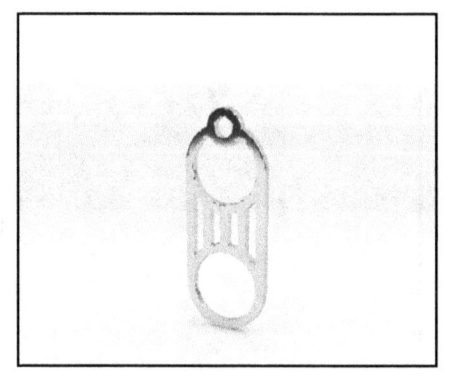 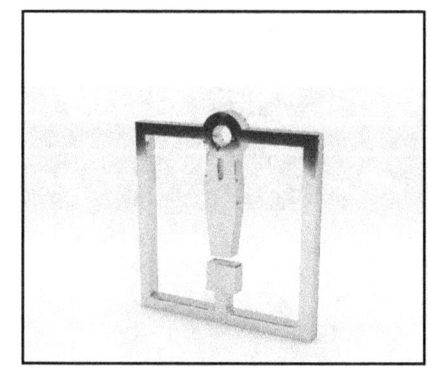

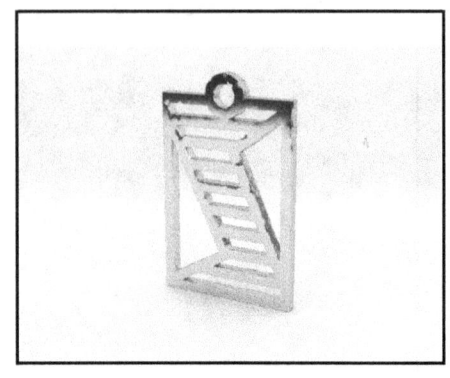 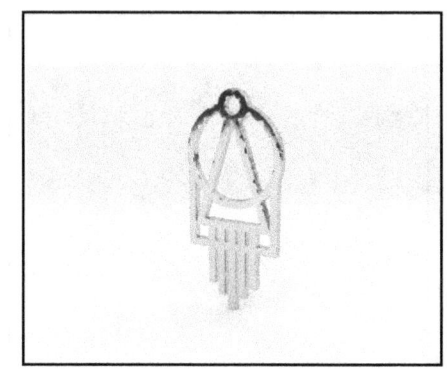 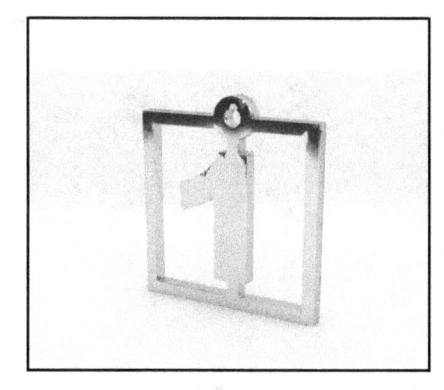

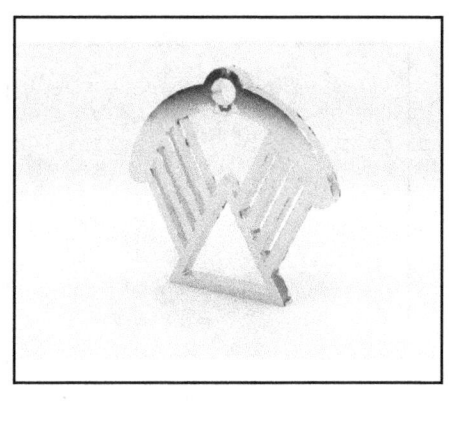
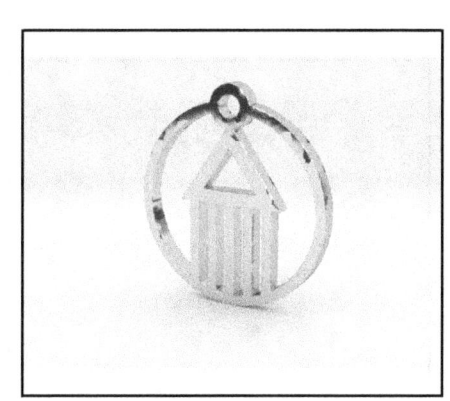
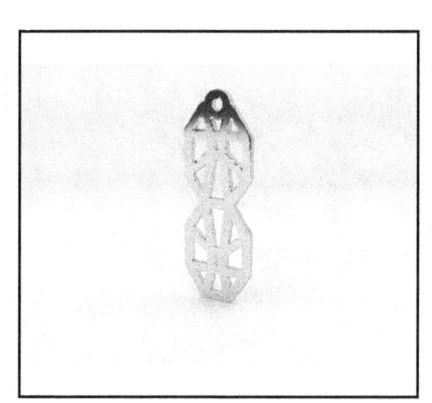
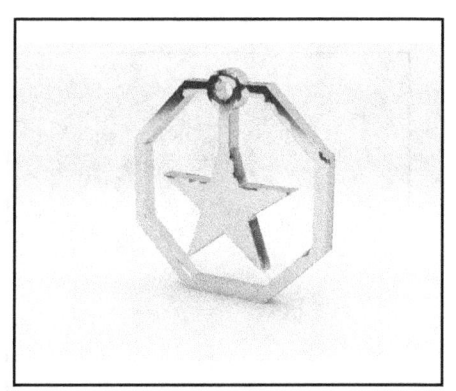
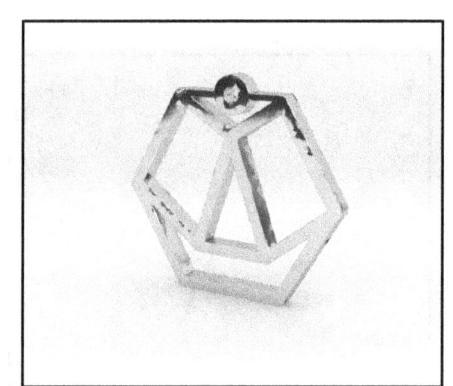
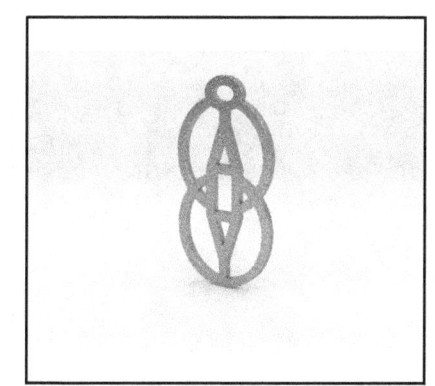
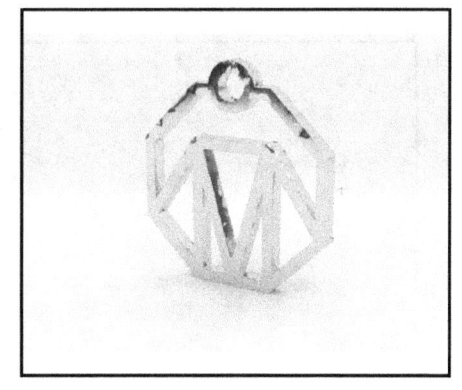
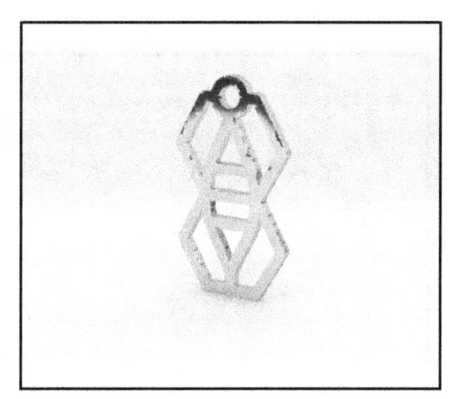
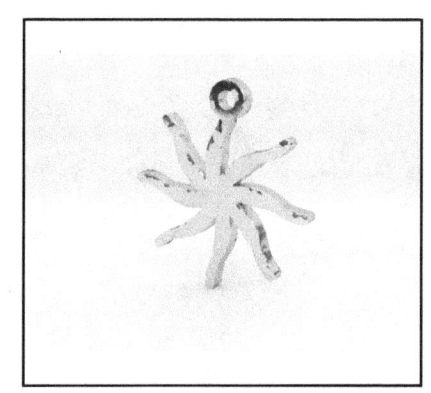
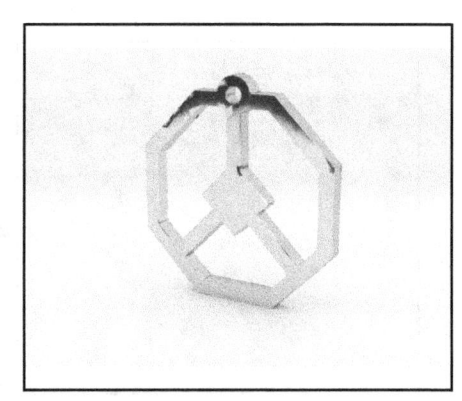
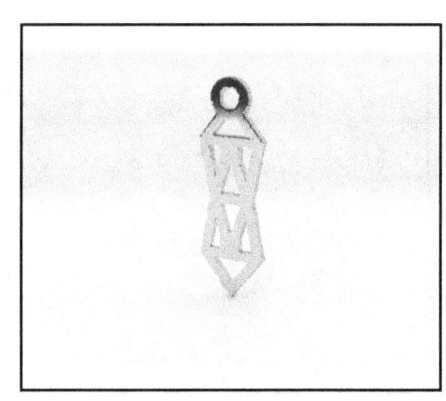
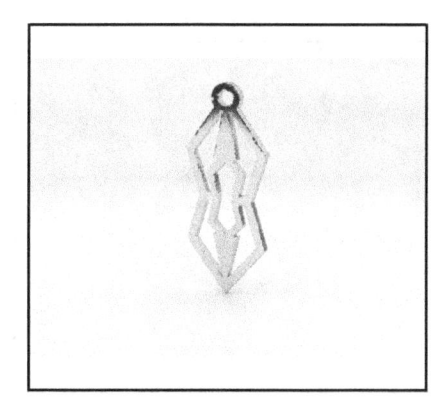

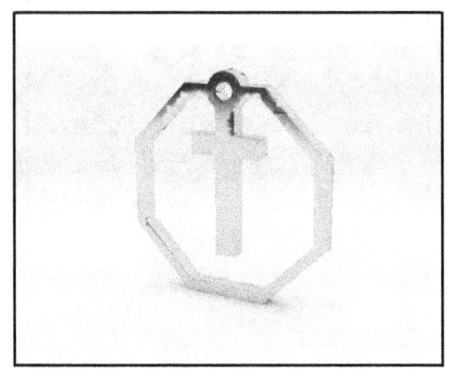 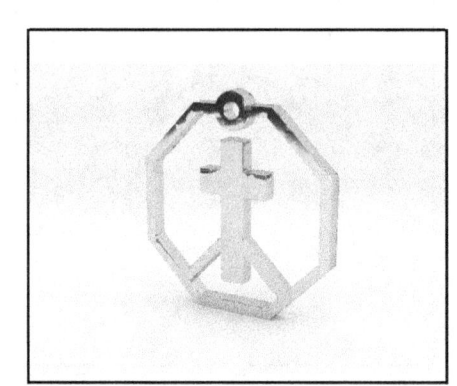 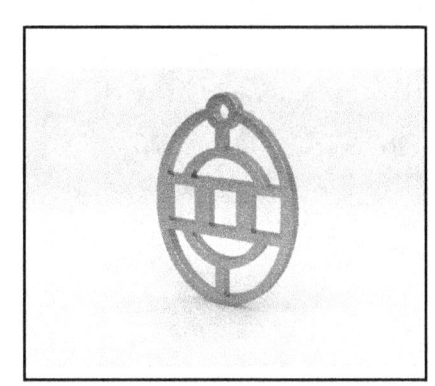

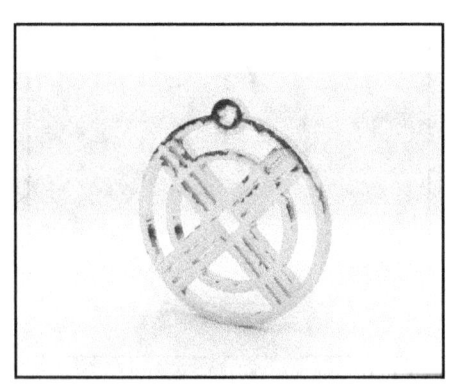 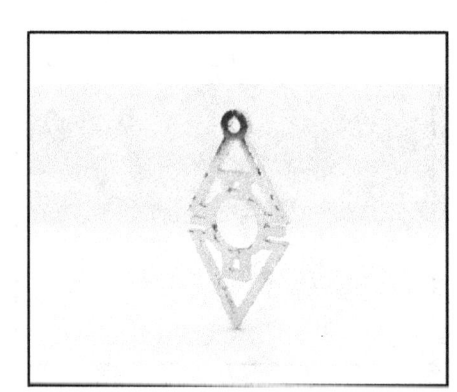 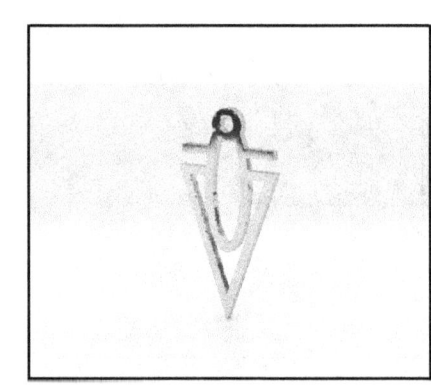

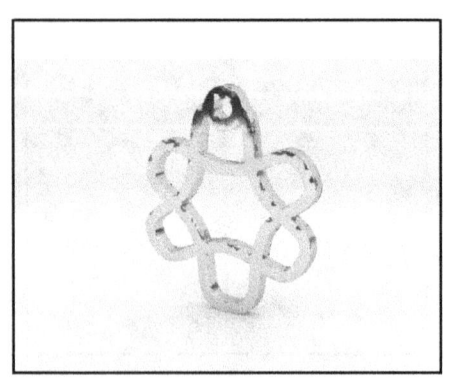 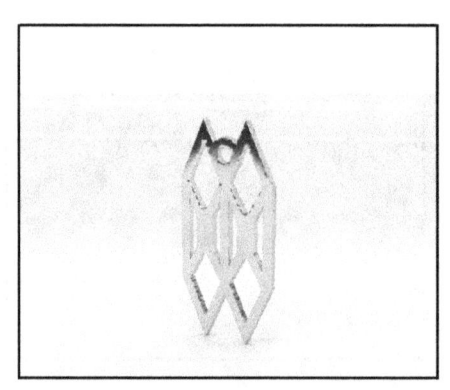 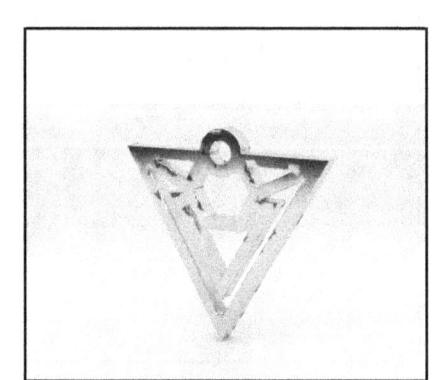

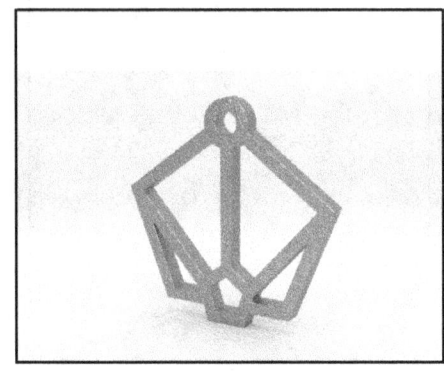 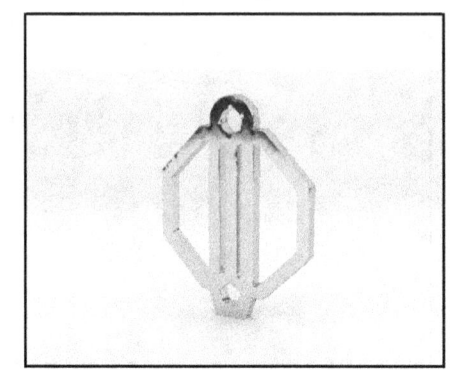 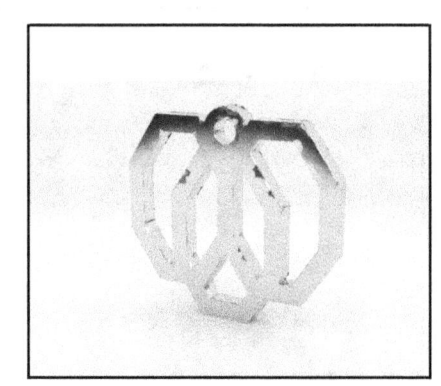

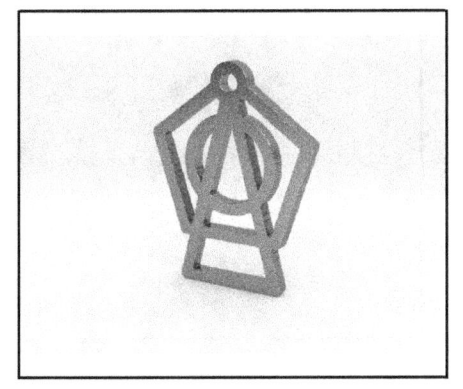
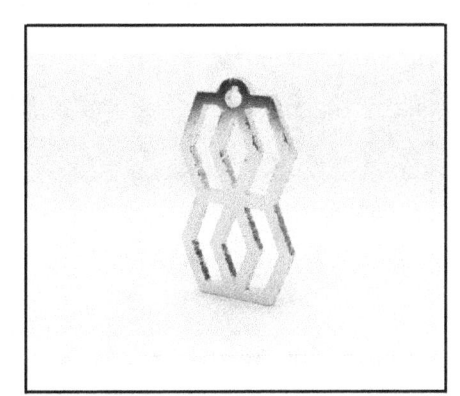
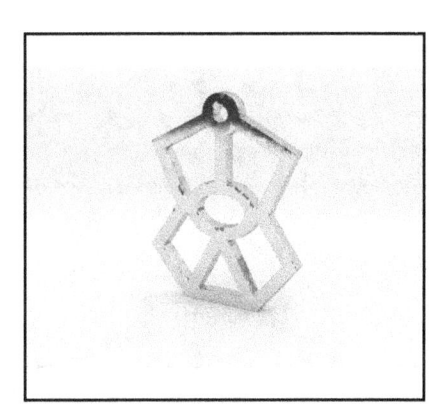
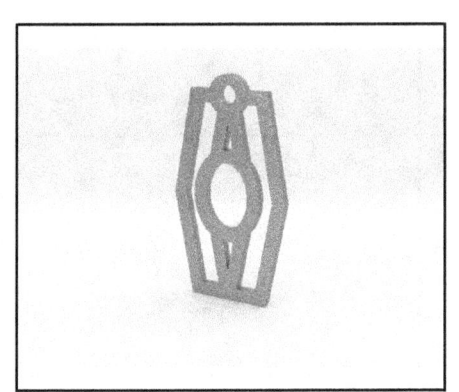
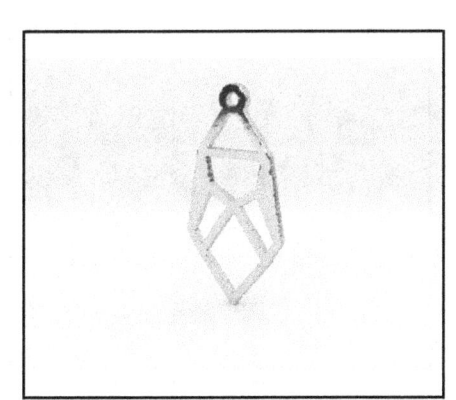
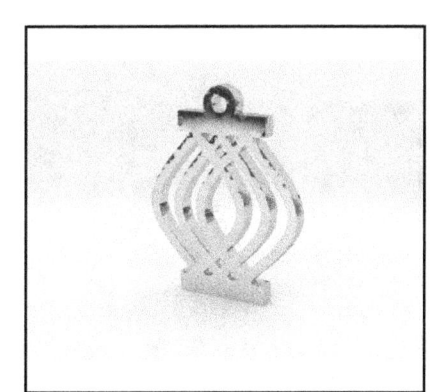
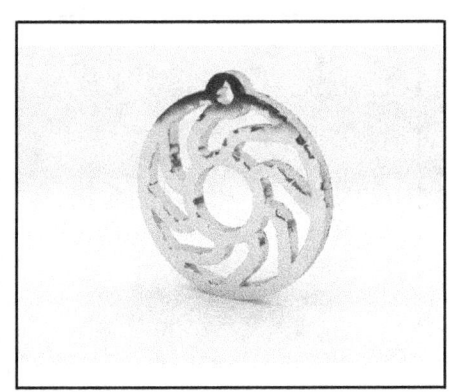
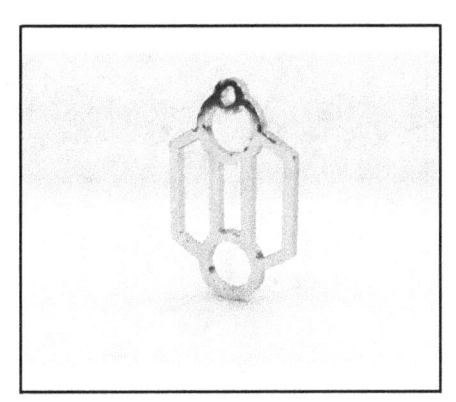
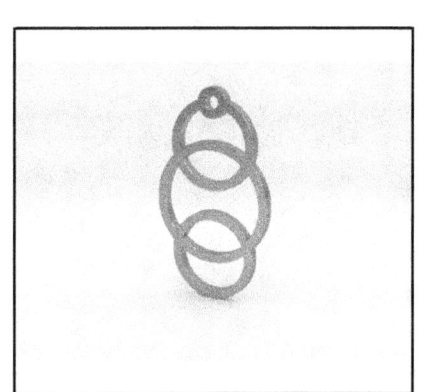
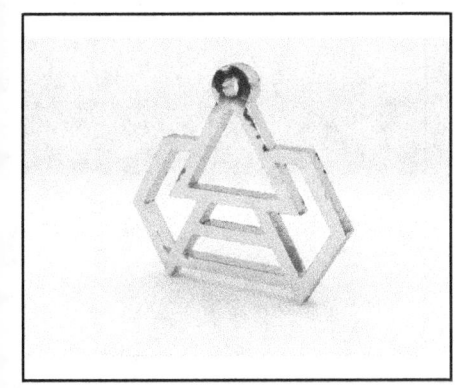
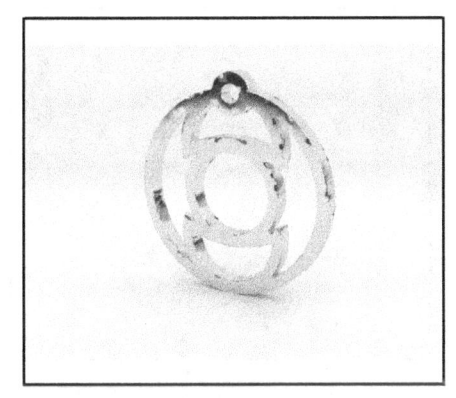
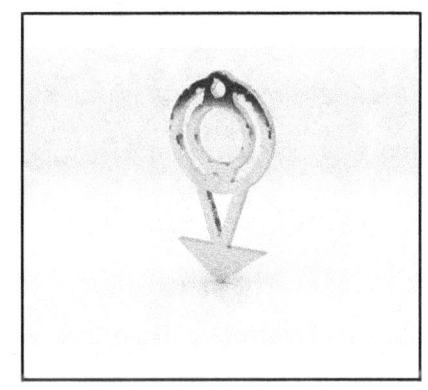

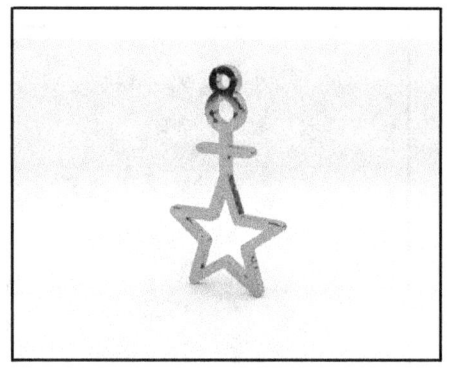
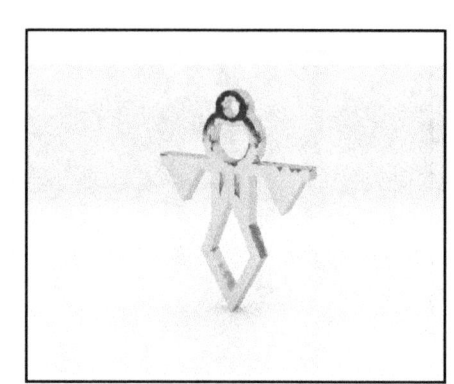
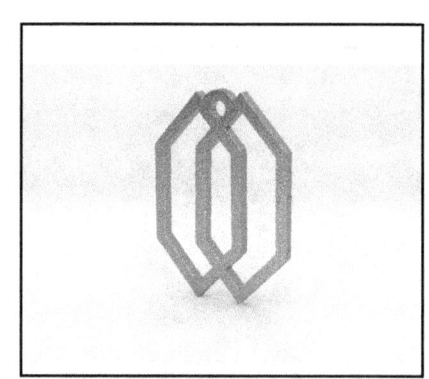
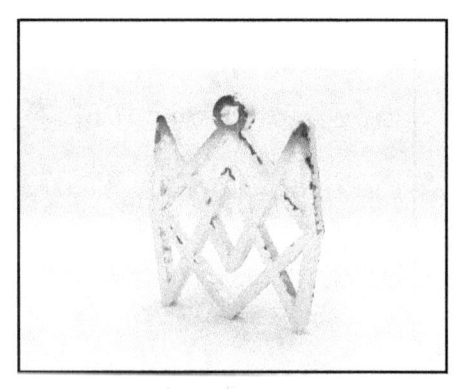
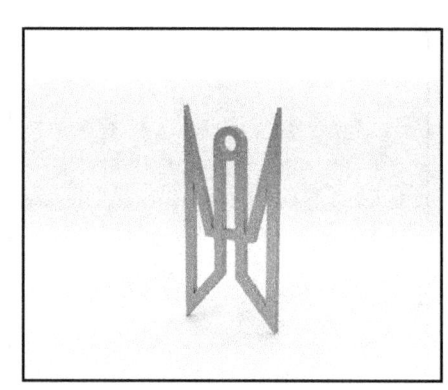
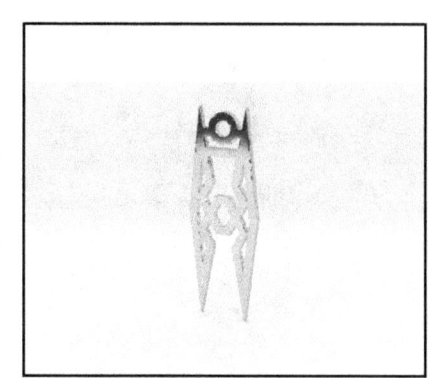
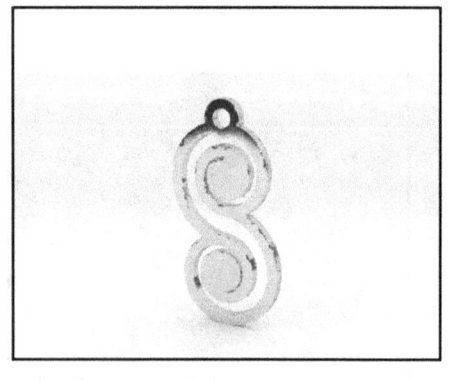
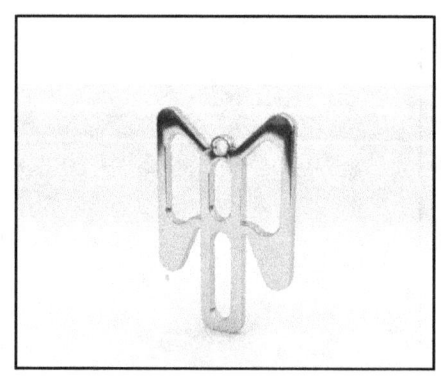
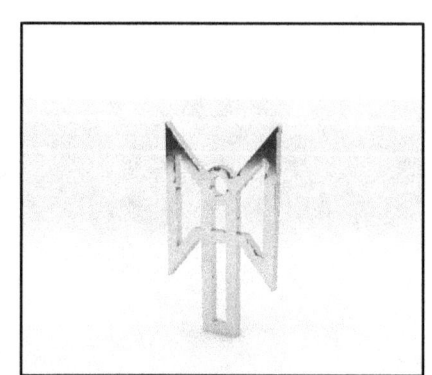
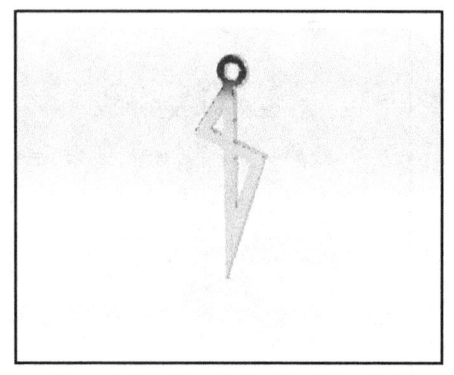
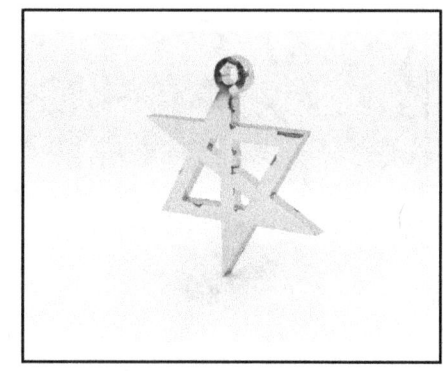
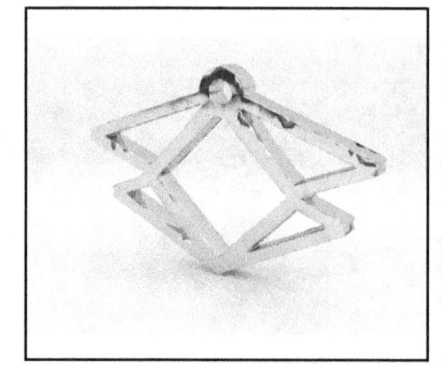

M7

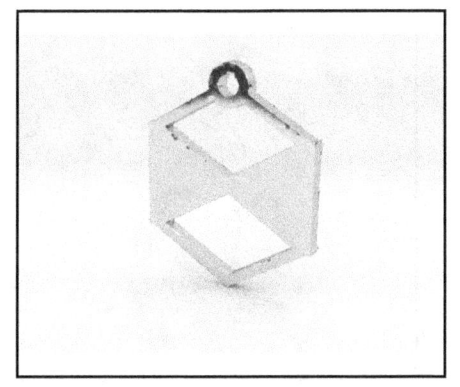
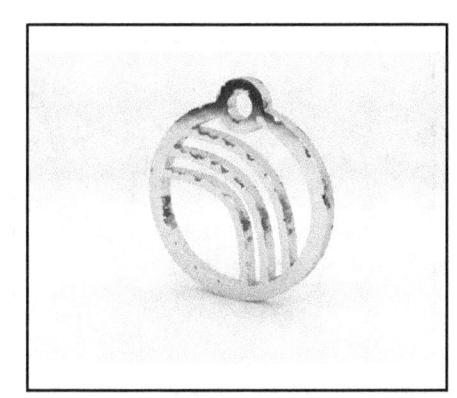
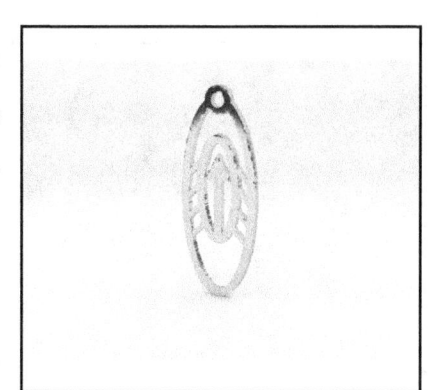
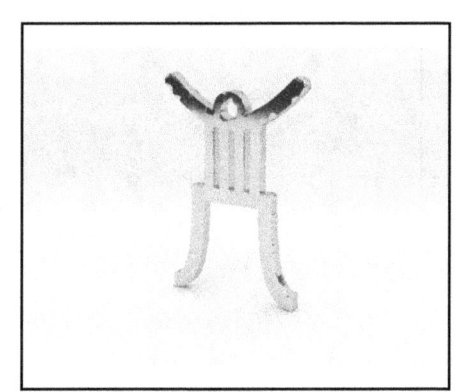
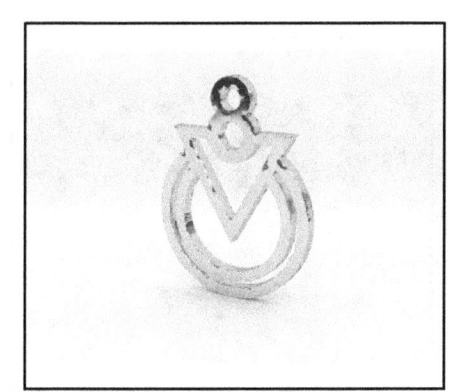
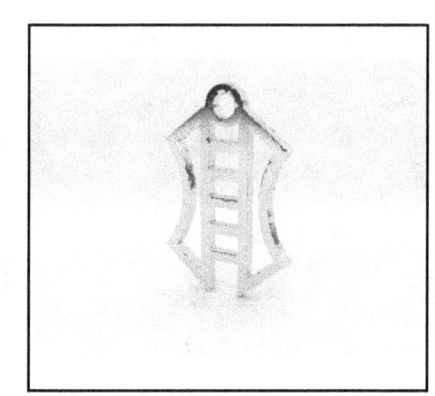
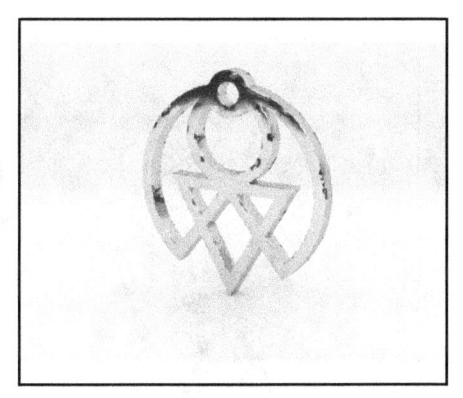
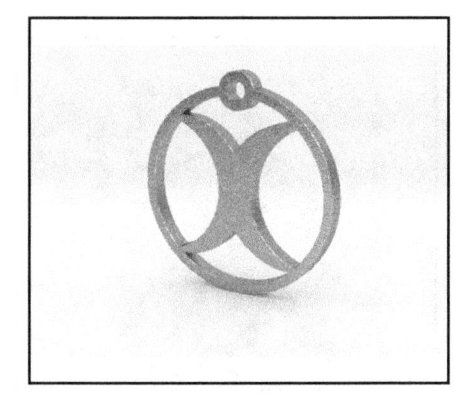
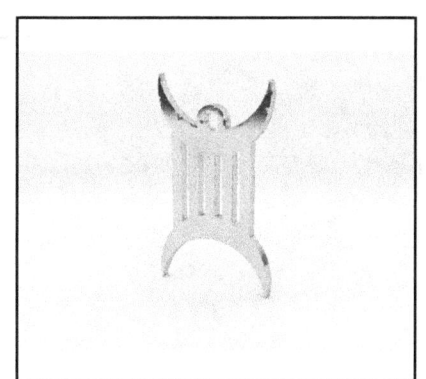
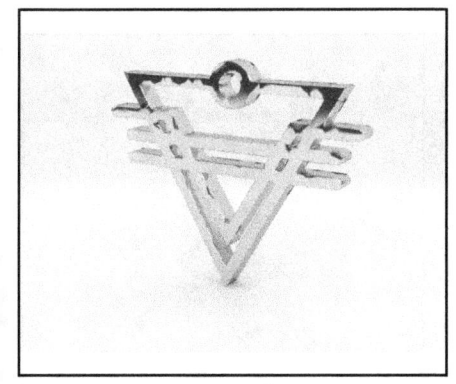
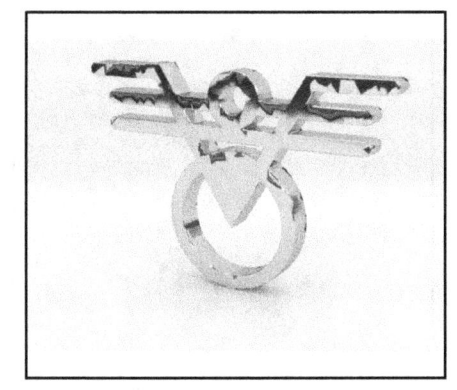
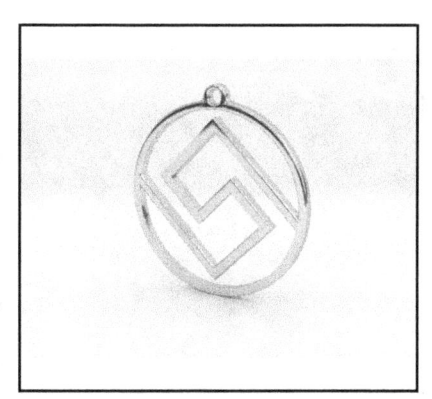

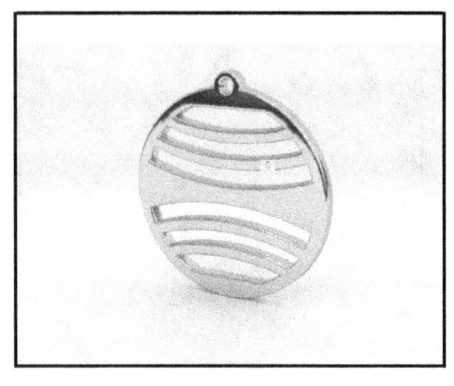 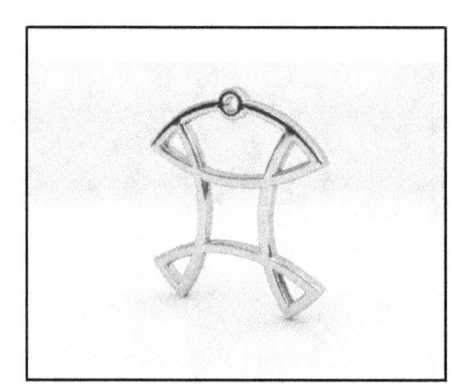 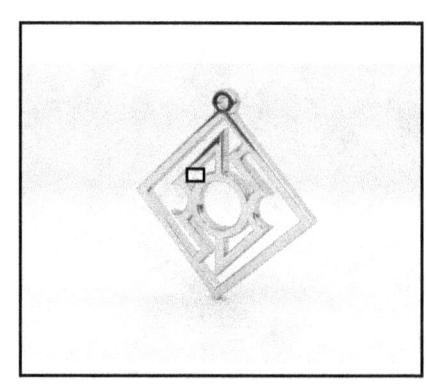

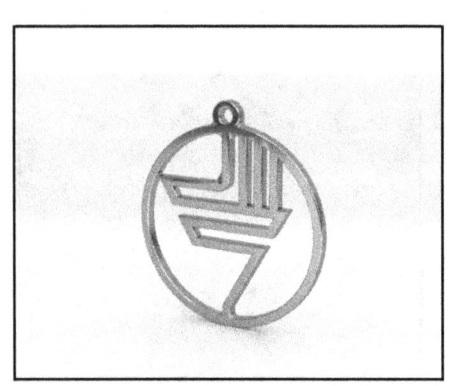 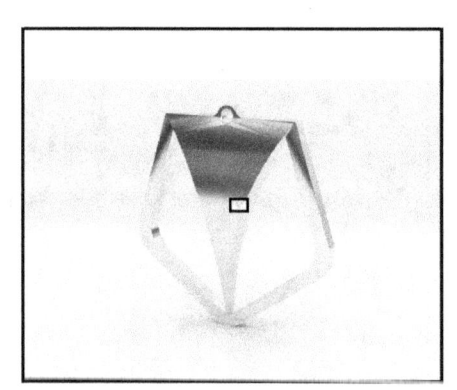 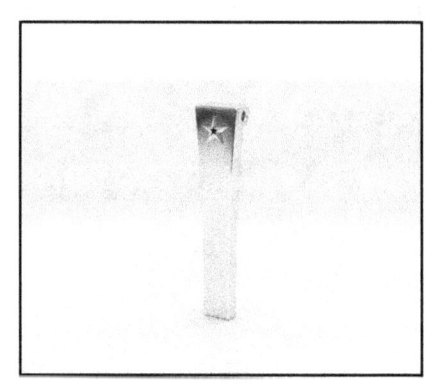

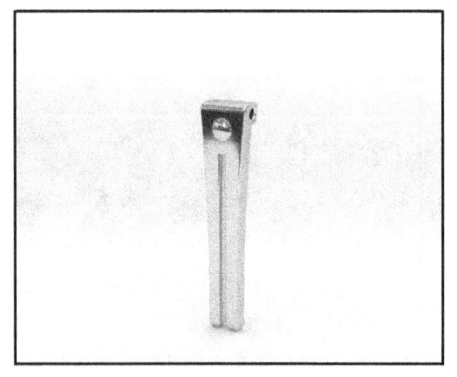 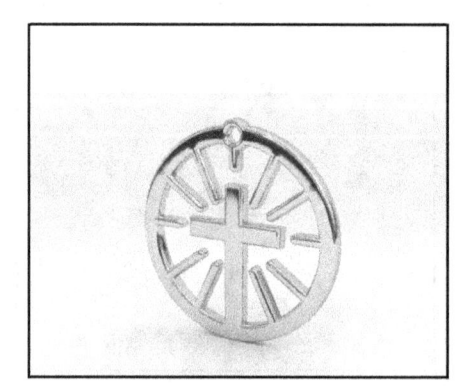 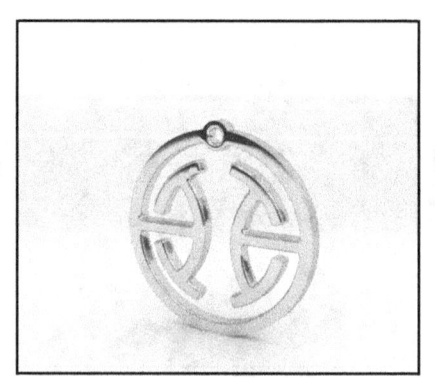

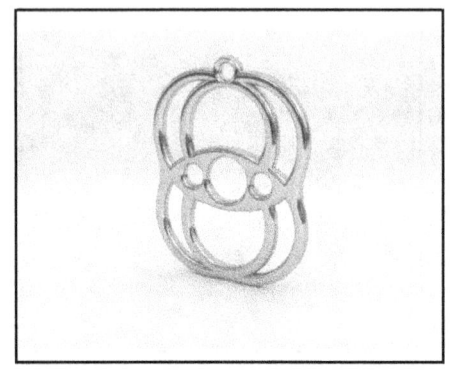 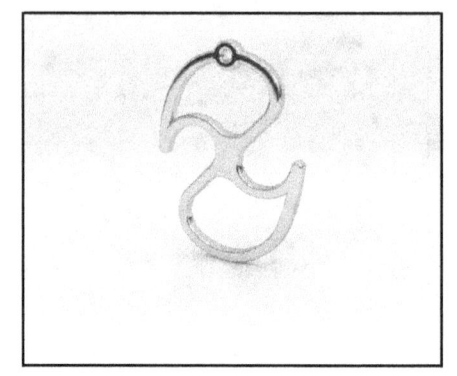 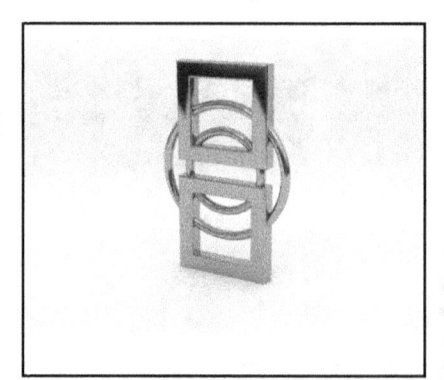

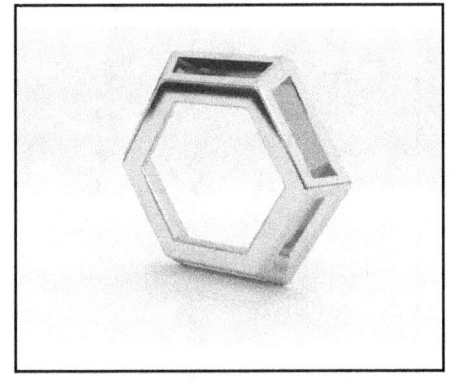
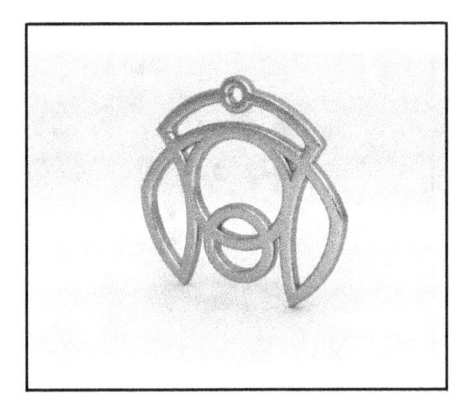
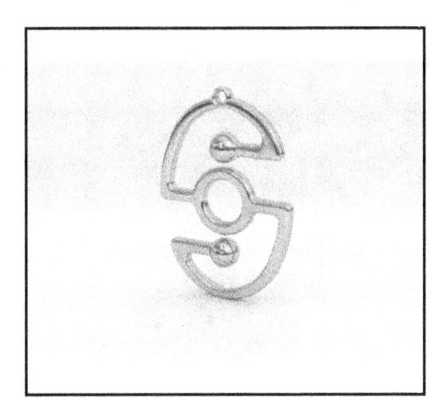
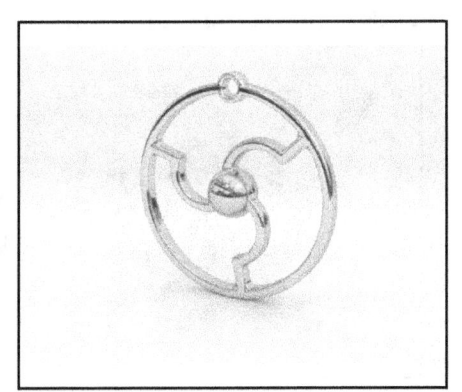
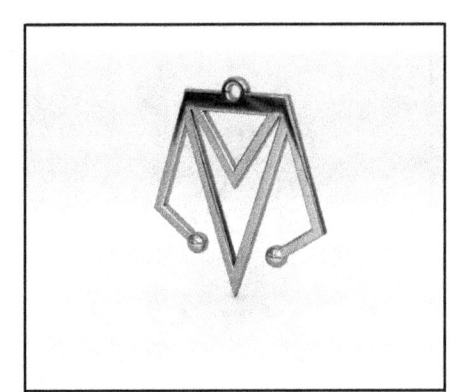
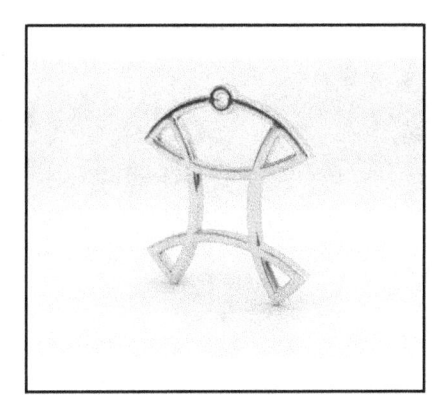
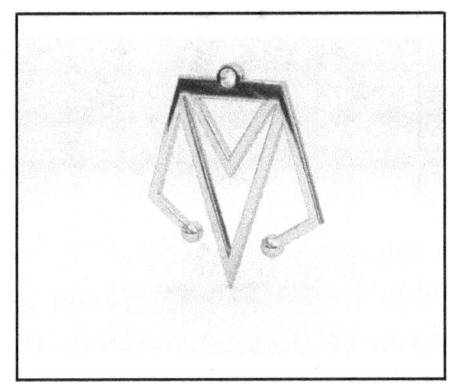
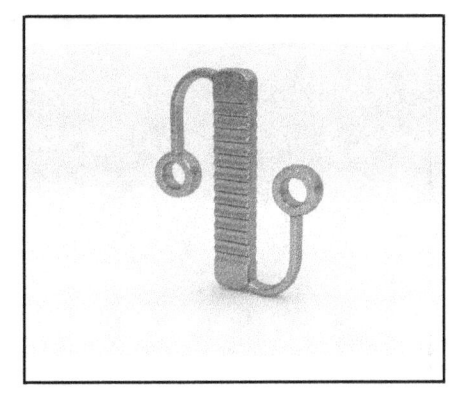
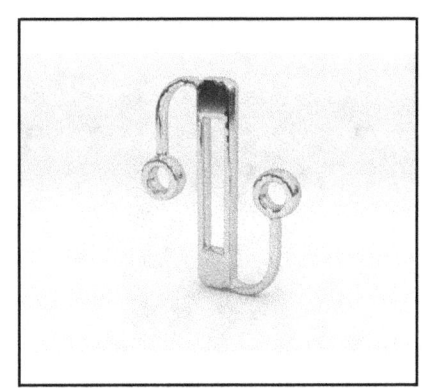
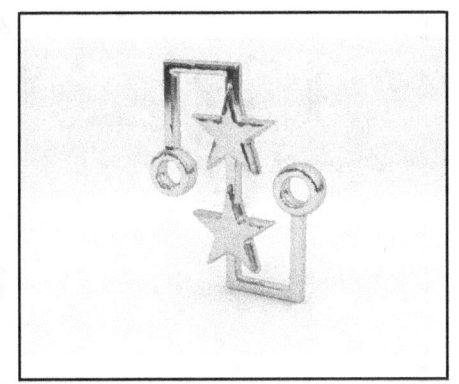
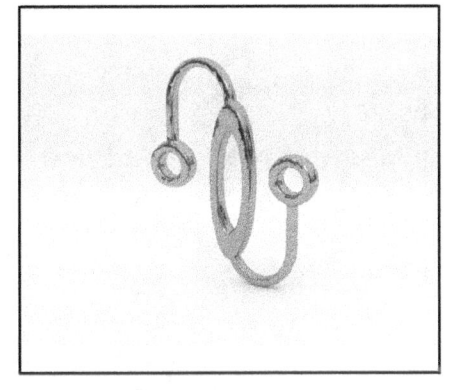
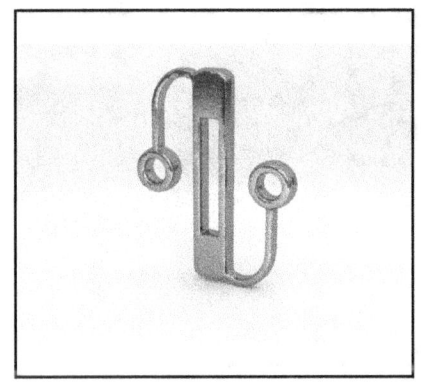

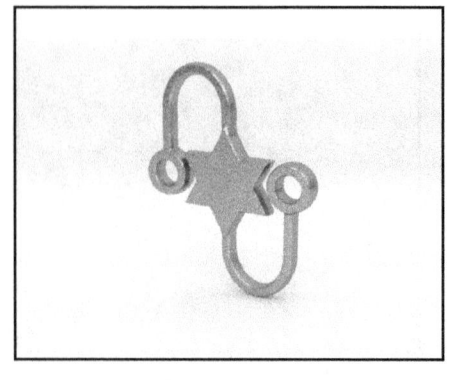
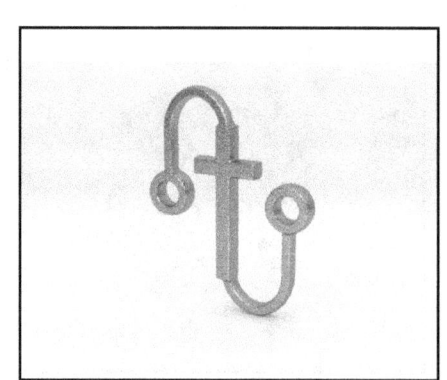
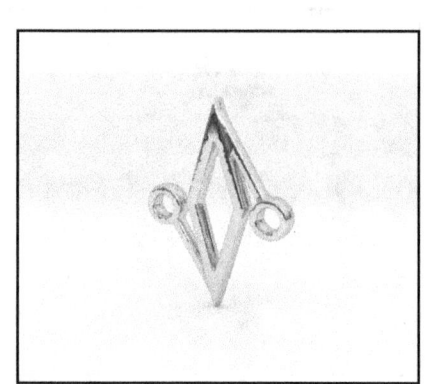
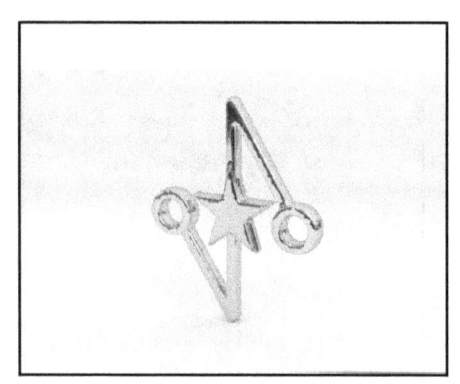
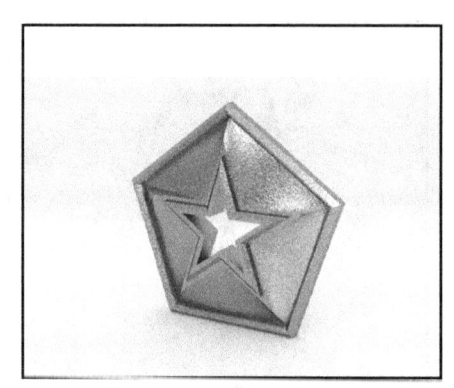
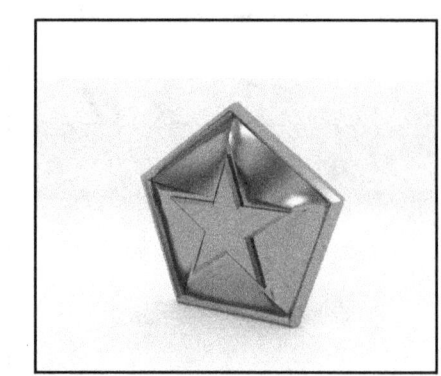
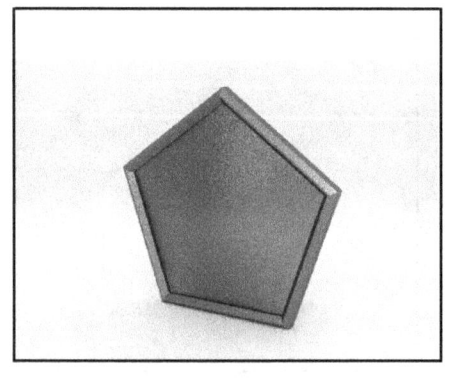
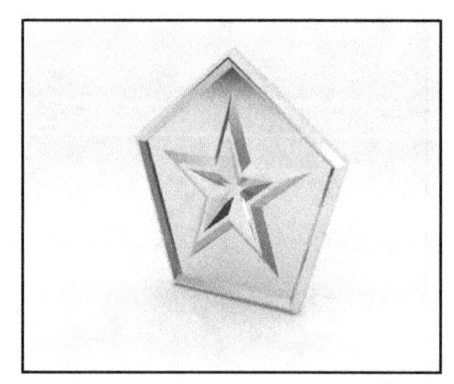
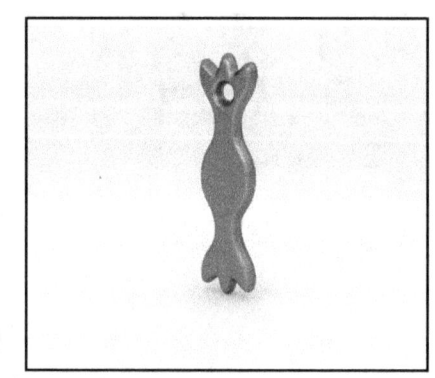
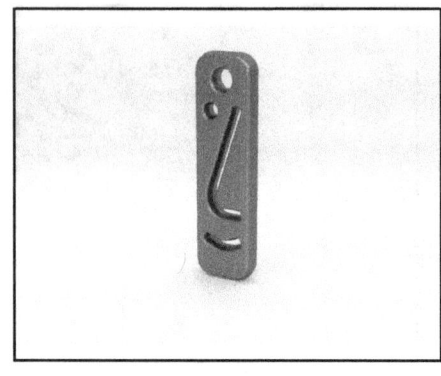
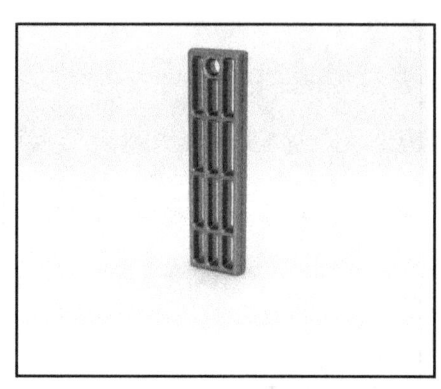
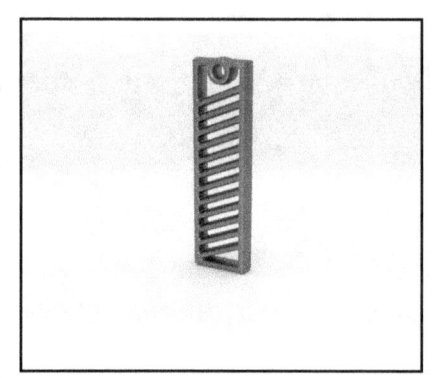

M7

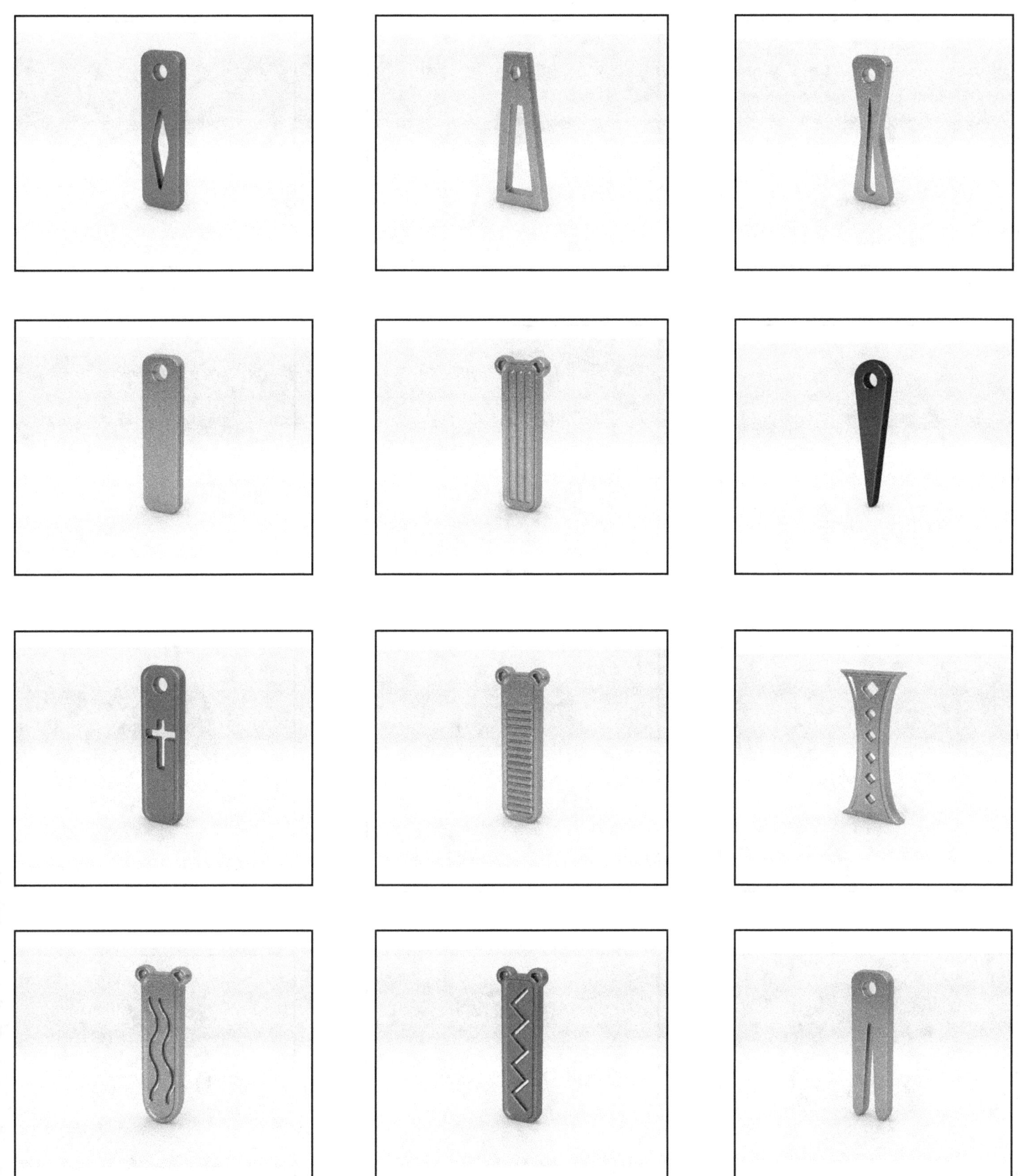

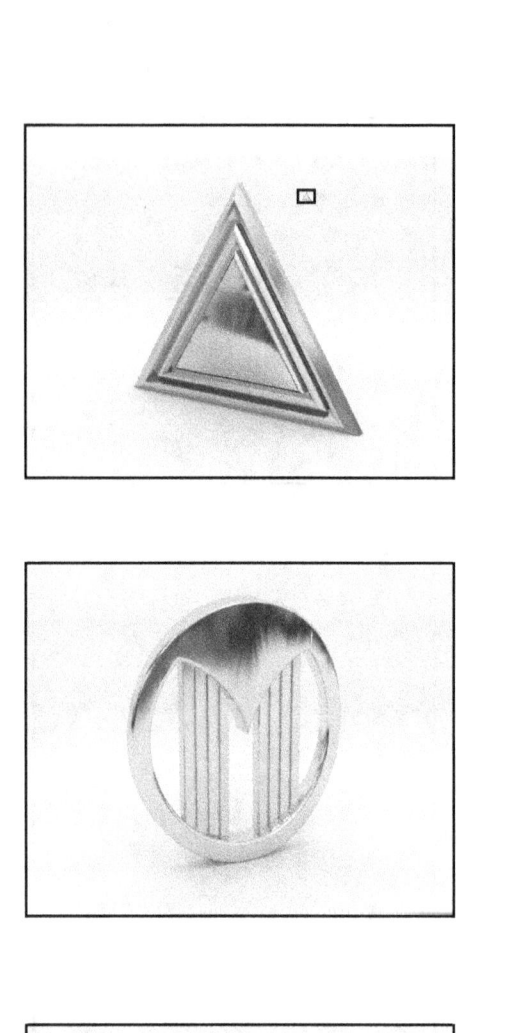
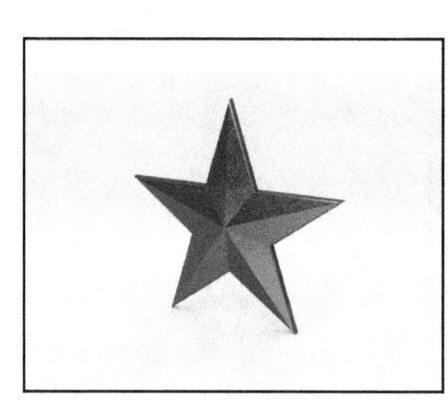
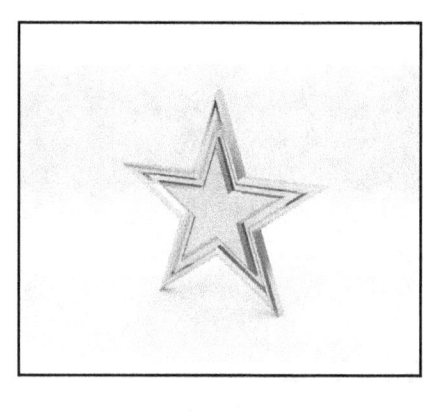
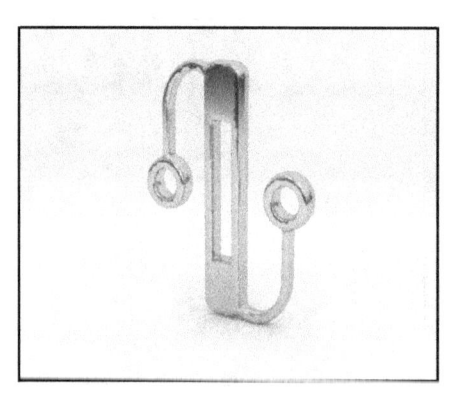
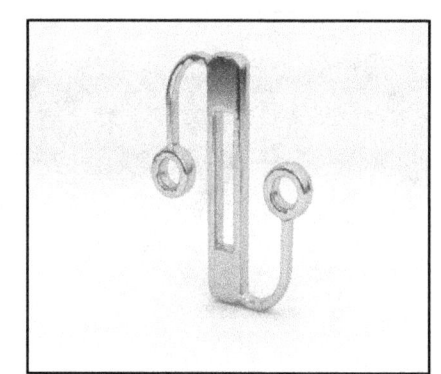
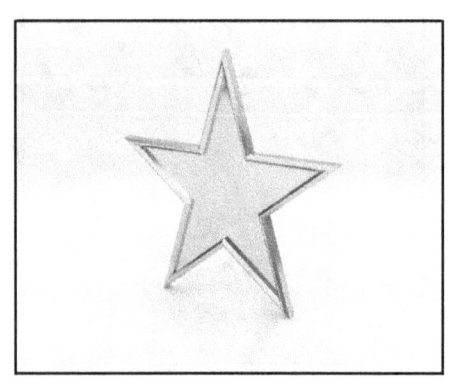
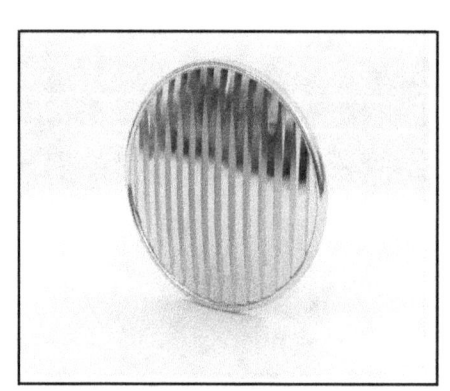
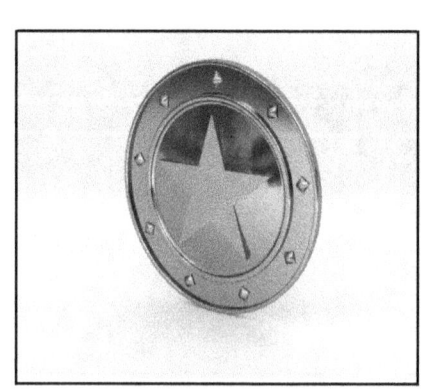
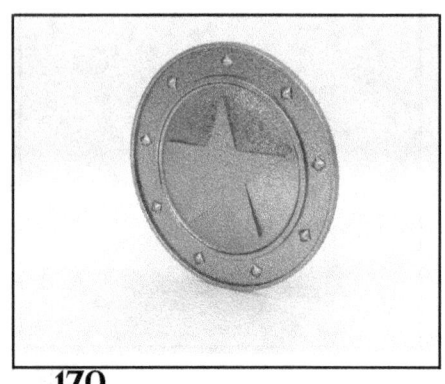
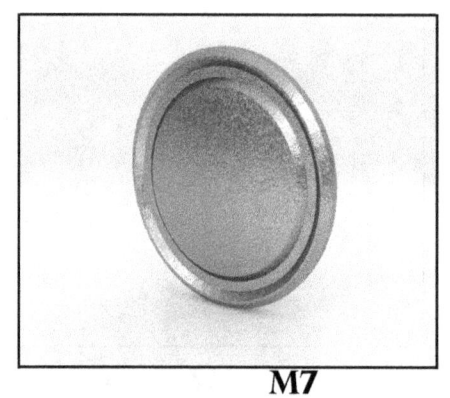
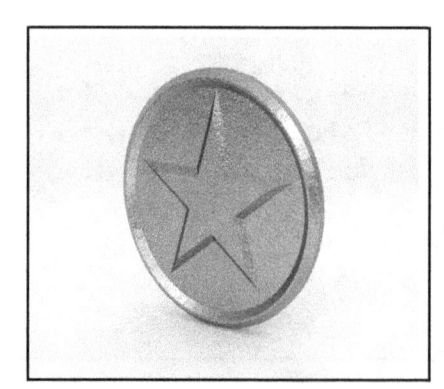

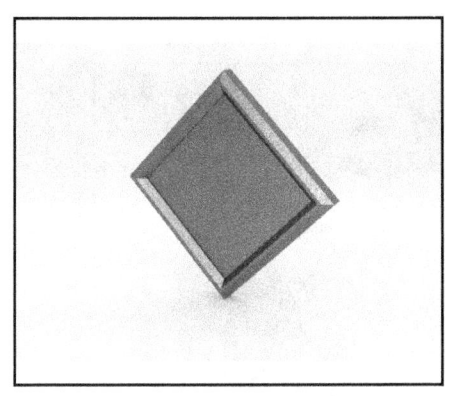
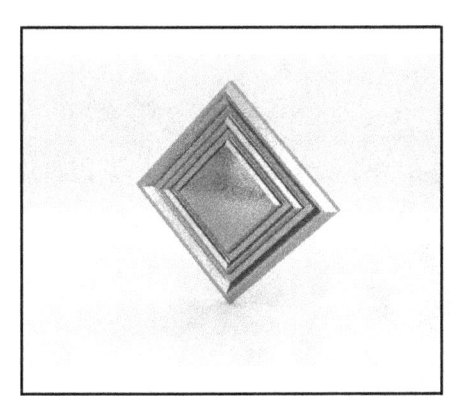
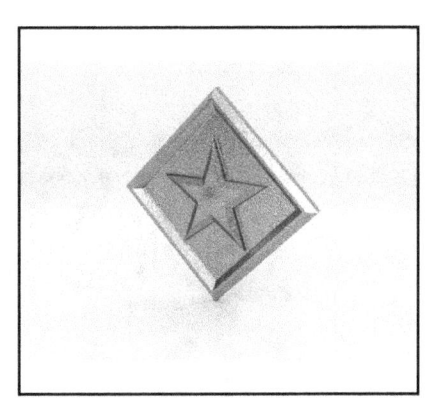
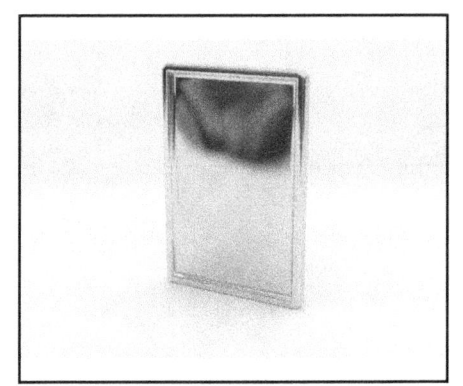
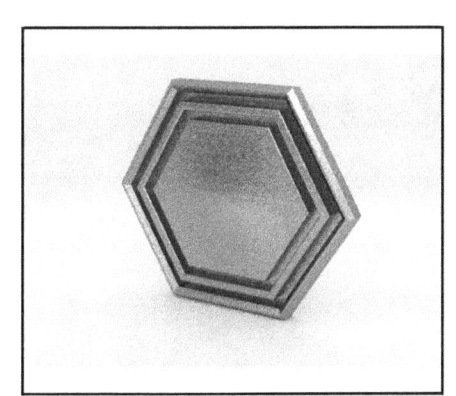
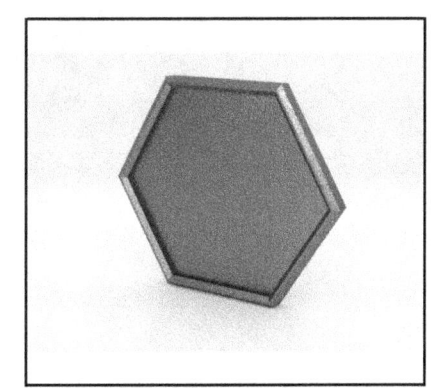
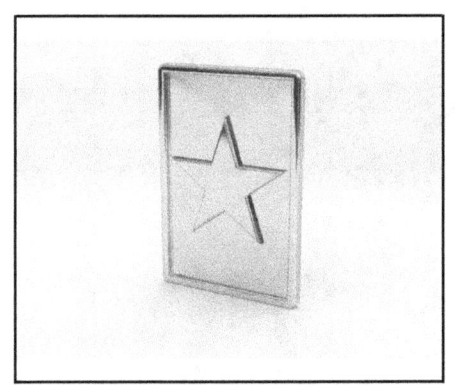
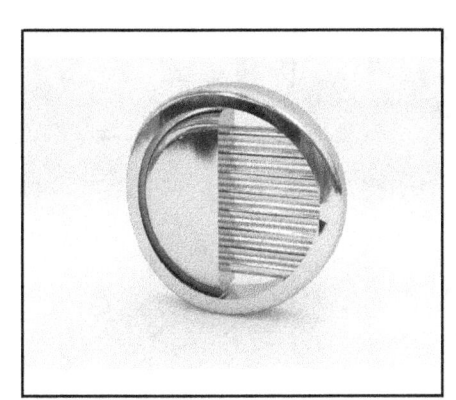
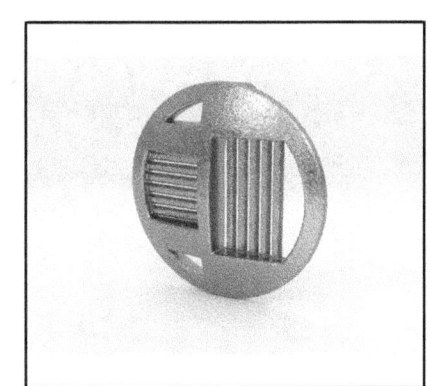
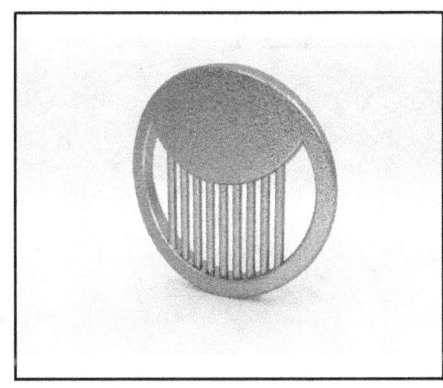
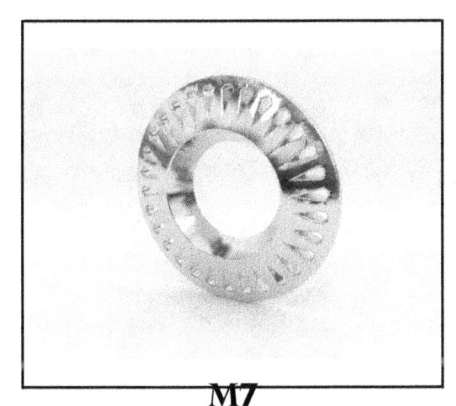
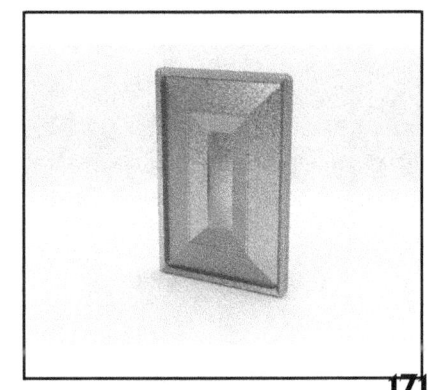

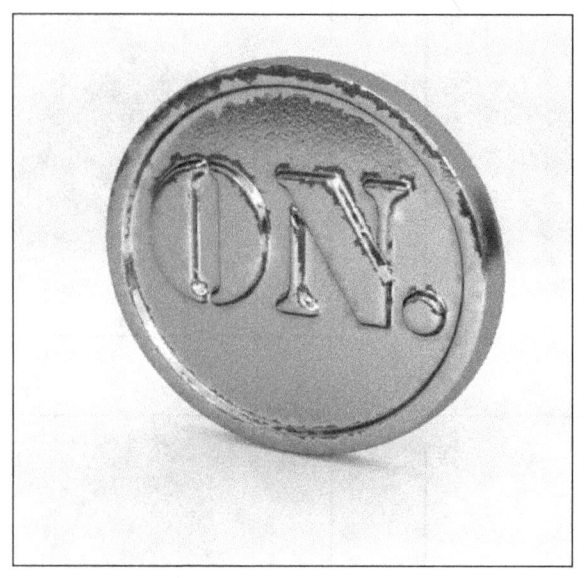

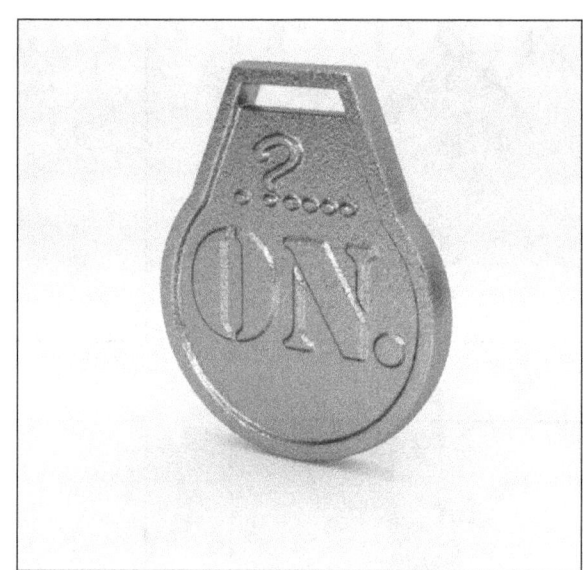

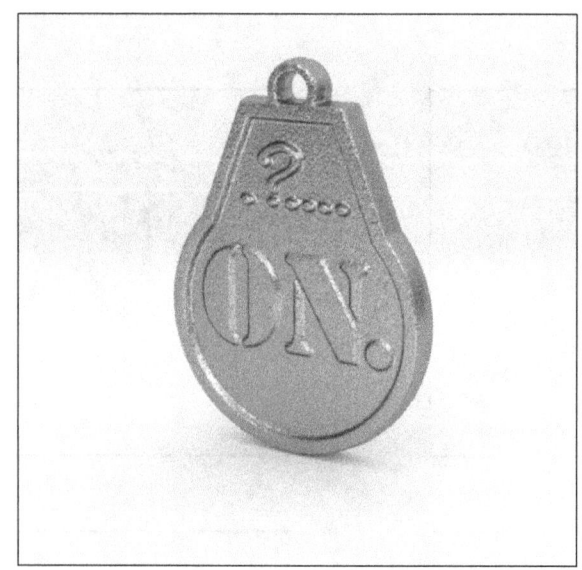

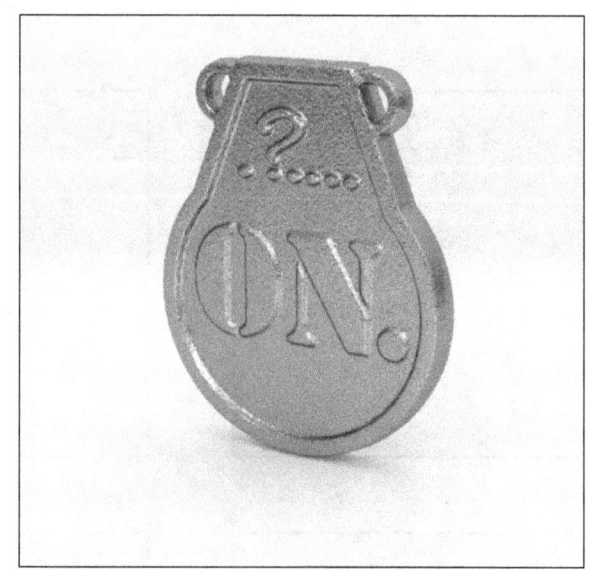

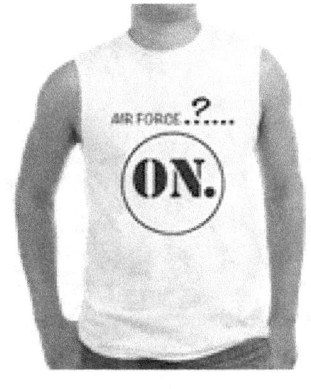
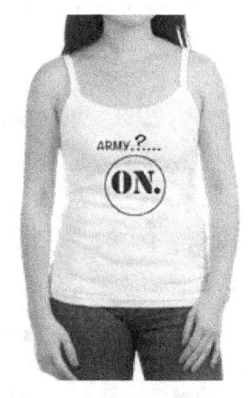
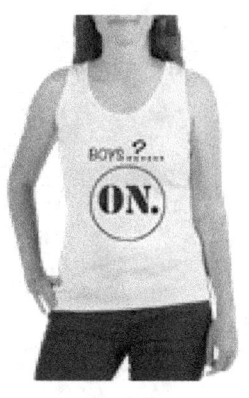
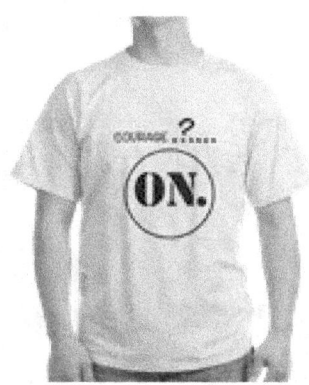
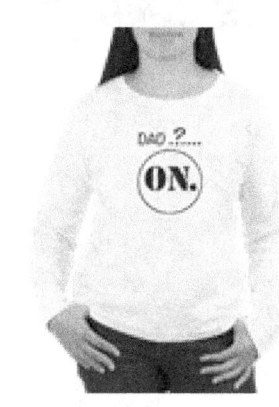
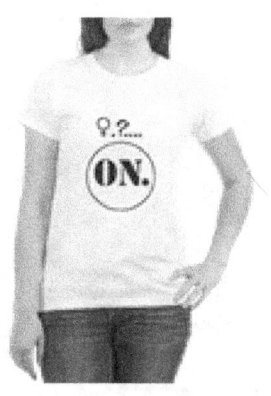

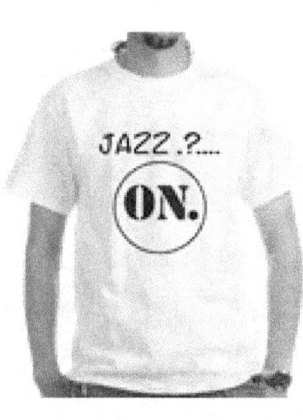
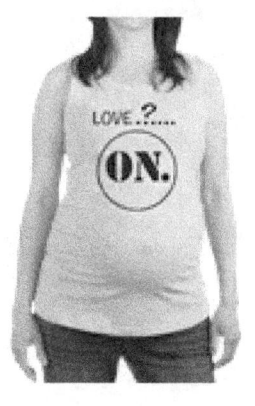
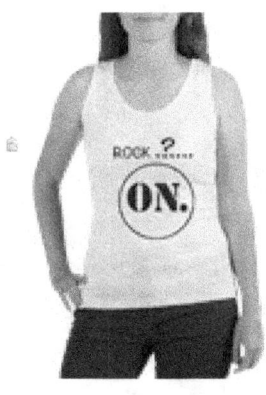
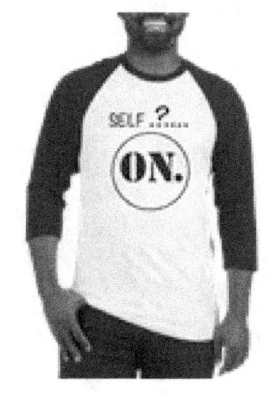
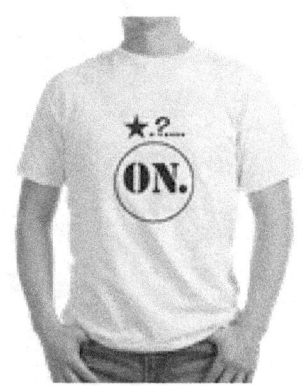

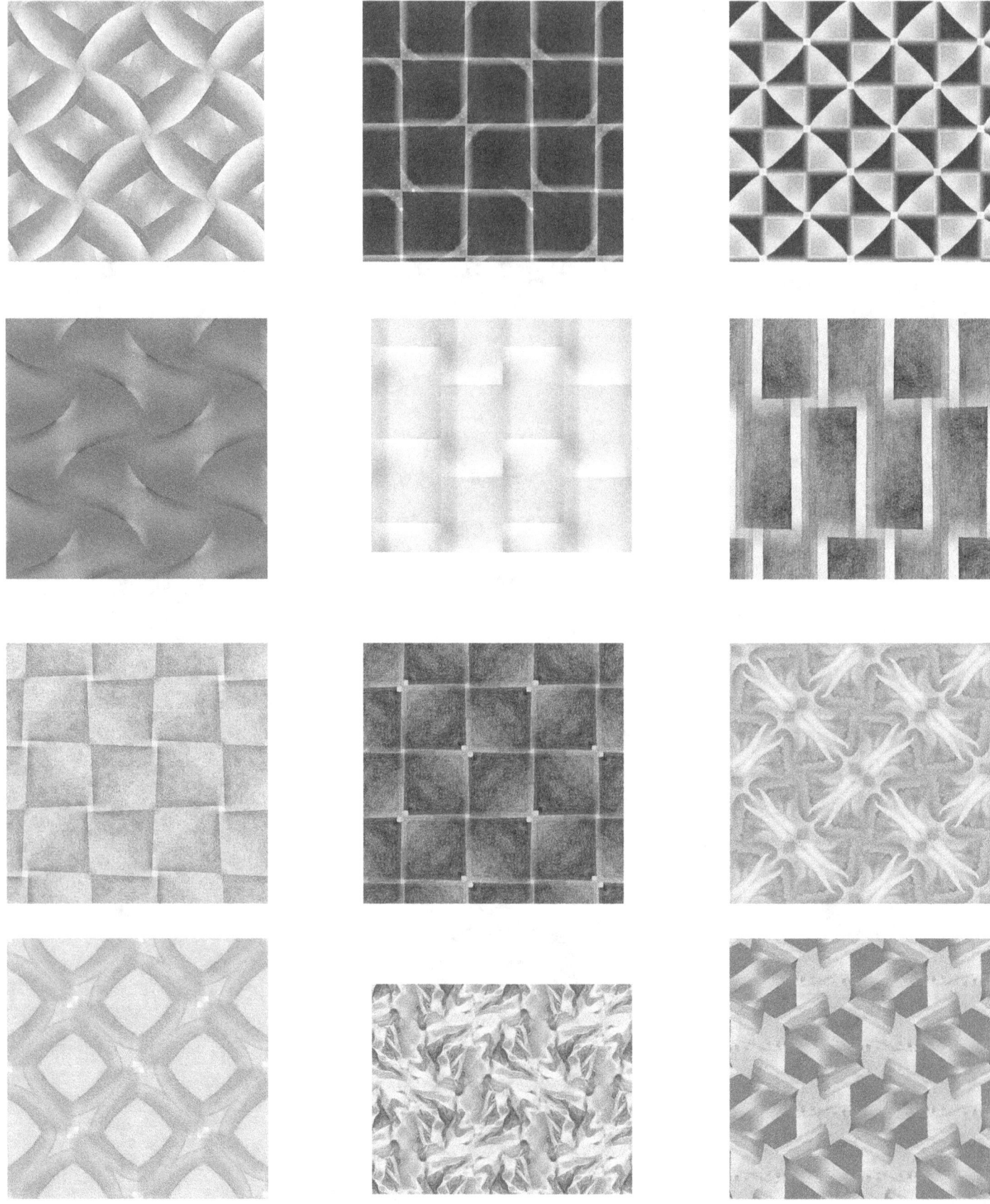

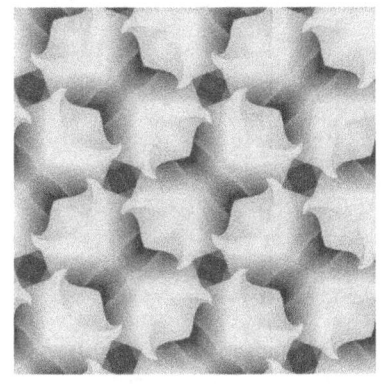
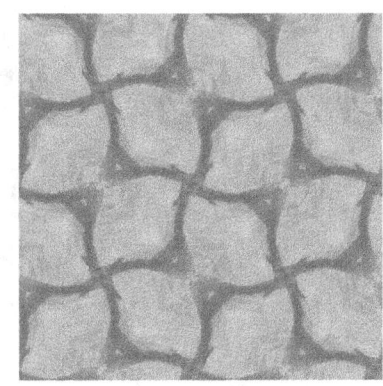
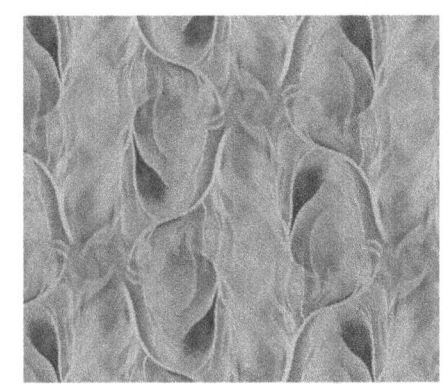

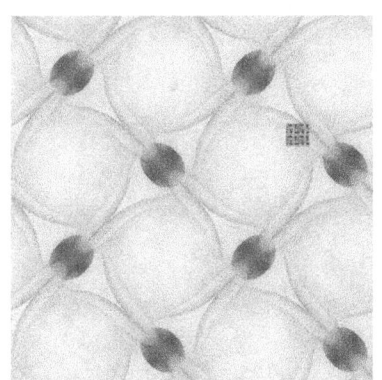
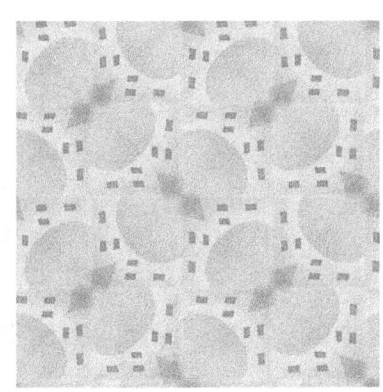
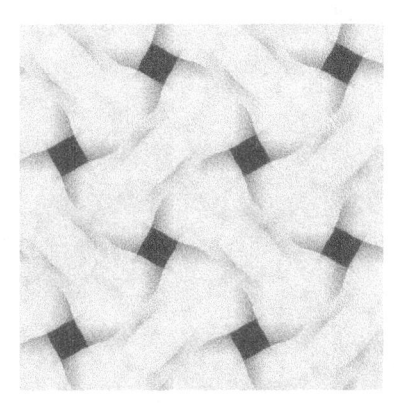

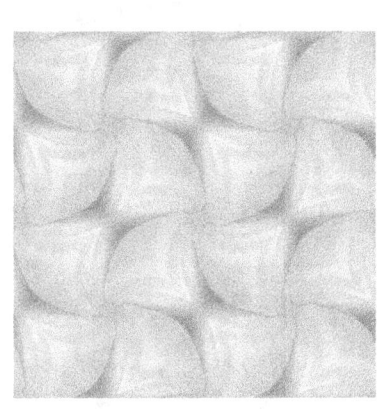

FABRIC

WALLCOVERINGS

WRAPPING PAPER

BEDDING

TOWELS

YOU NAME IT!!!!!

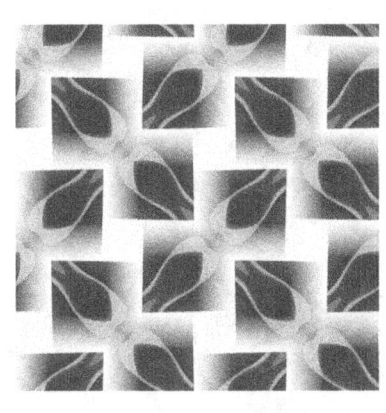

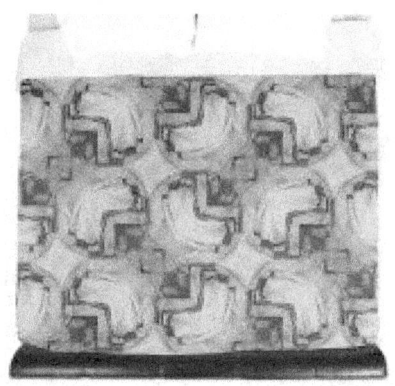

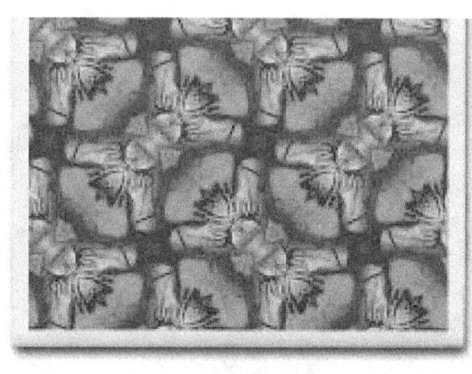

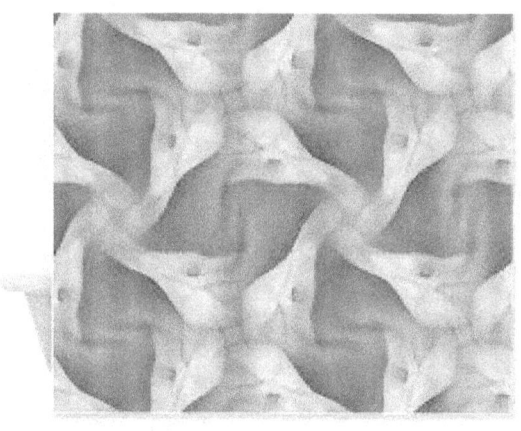

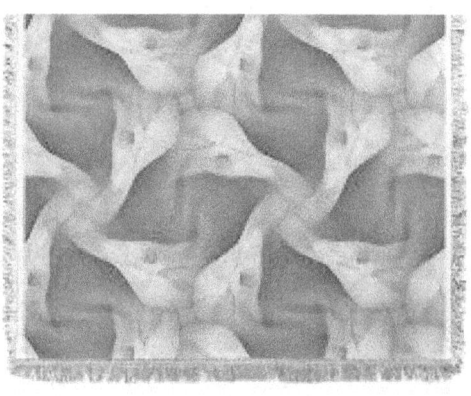

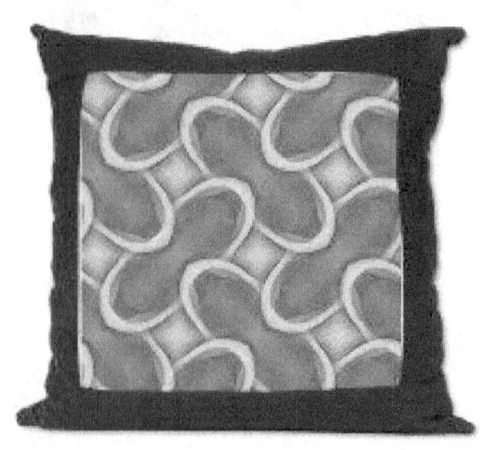

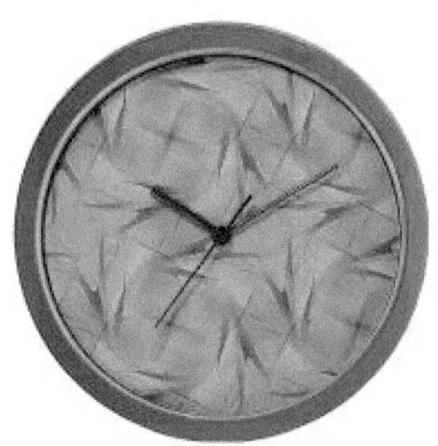

M7

PATTERNS - THE BOOKS

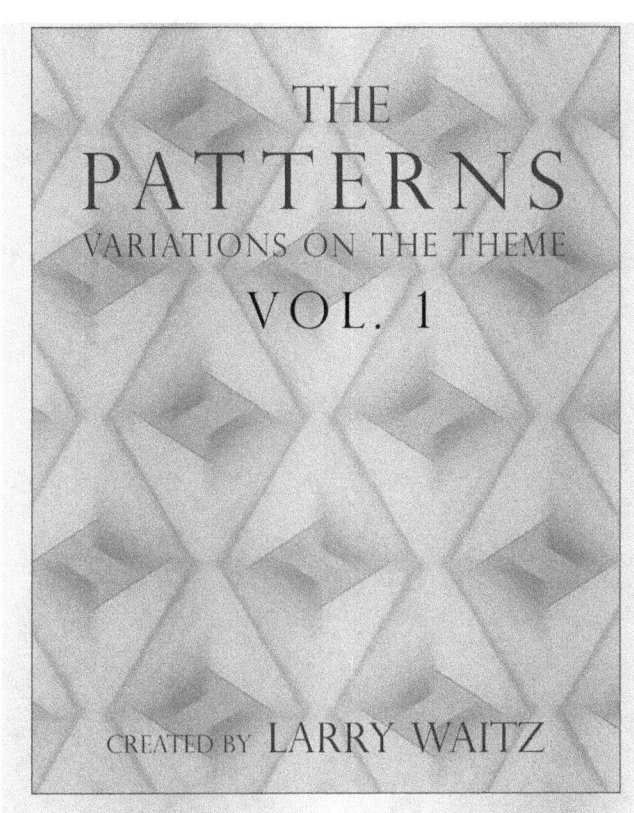

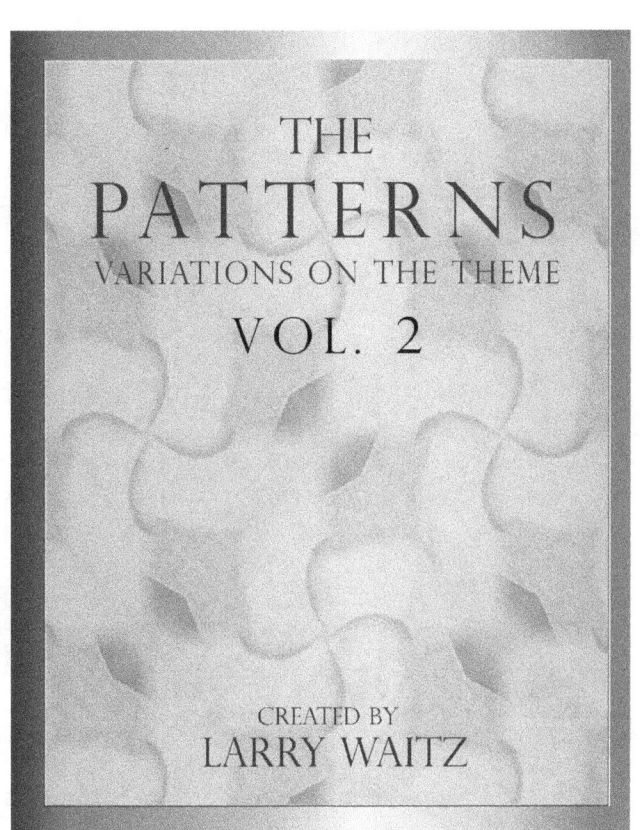

AVAILABLE ON AMAZON

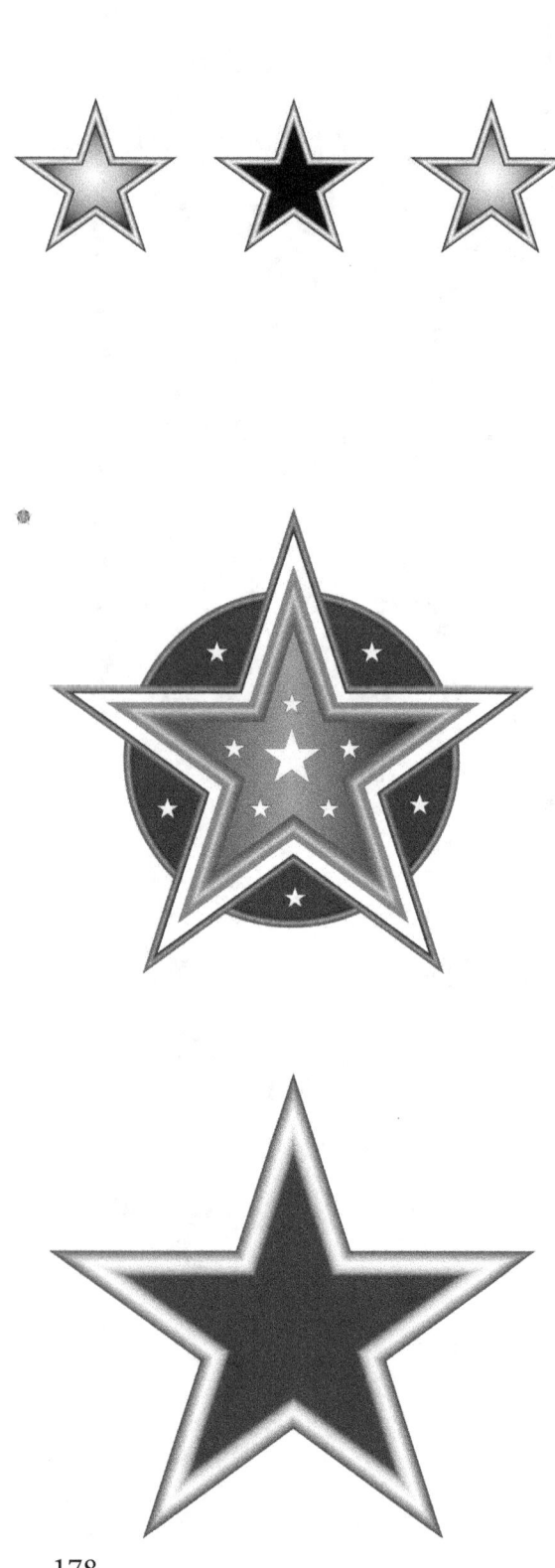

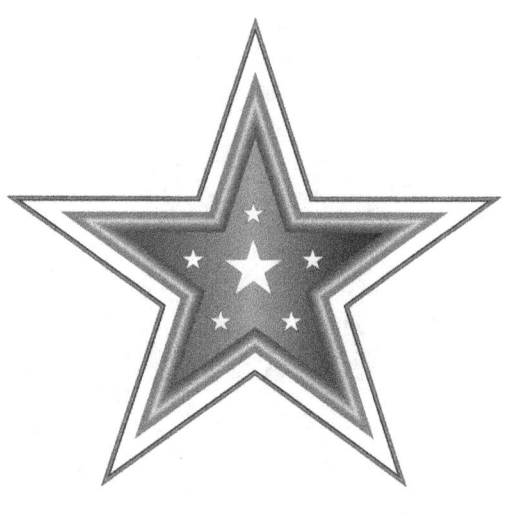

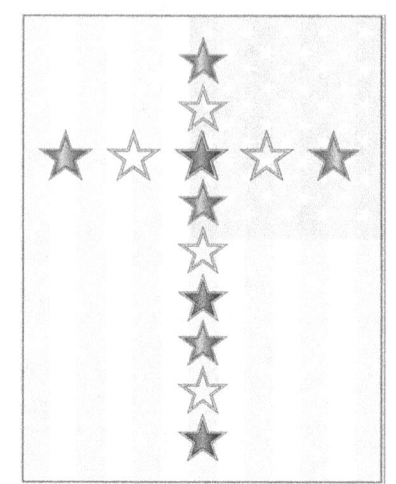

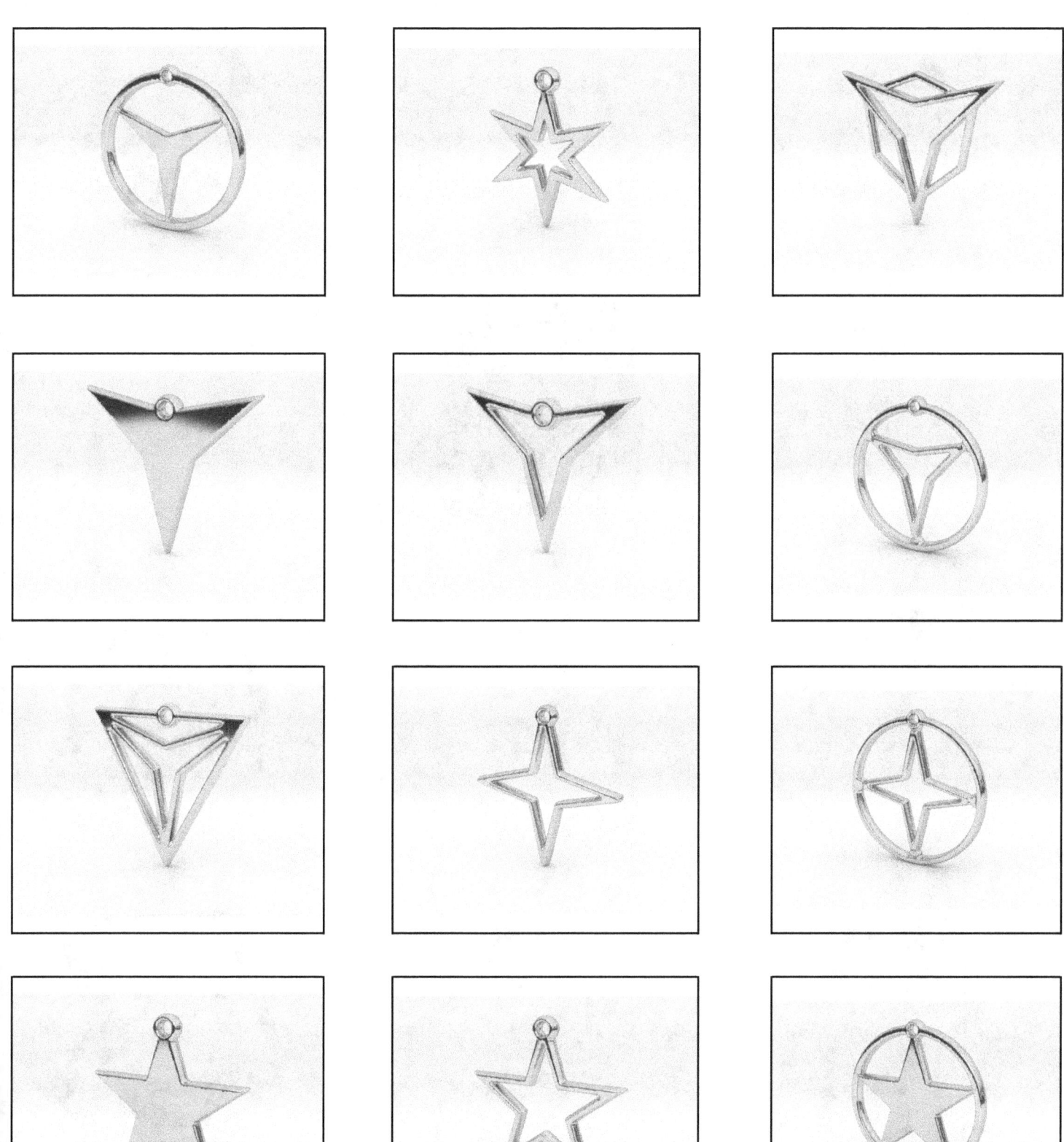

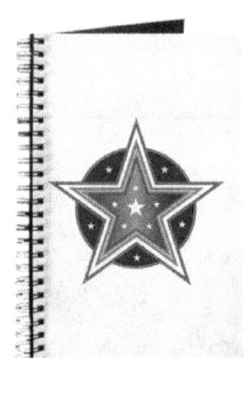

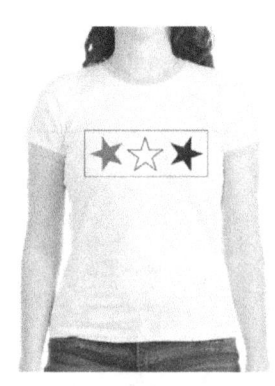

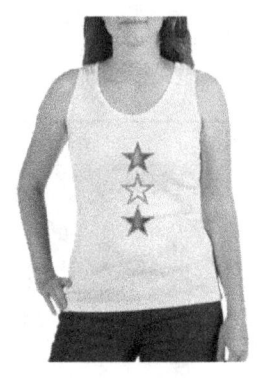

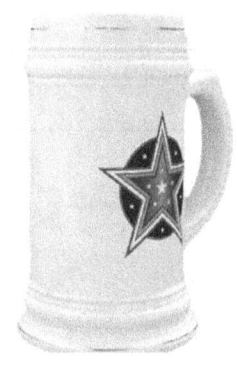

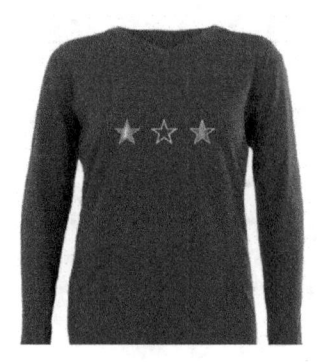

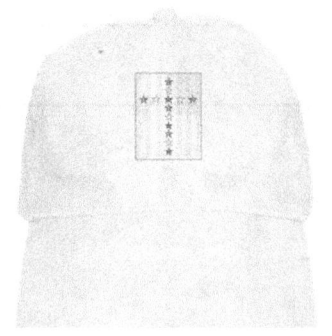

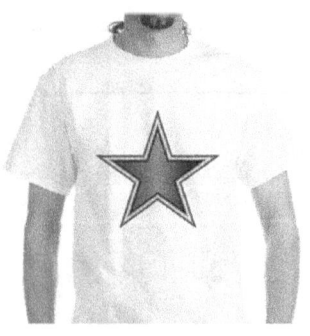

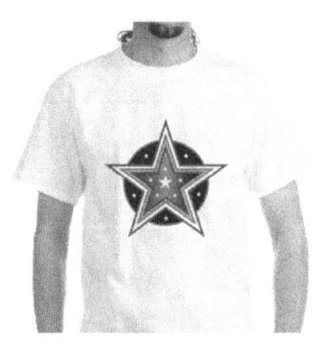

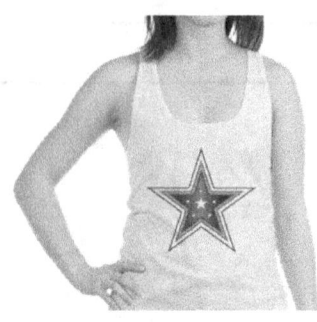

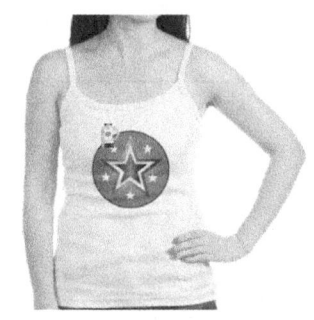

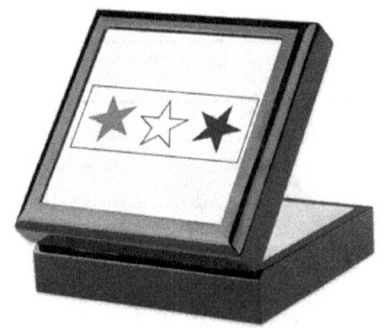

Think
9L7W

Think
AWESOME

Think
CHAMPION

Think
COOL

Think
DAD

Think
FREEDOM

Think
HEALTHY

Think
HUMOR

Think
JAZZ

Think
JAZZ

Think
M7

Think
OPTIMISM

Think
RESPECT

Think
ROCK & ROLL

Think
SELF

Think
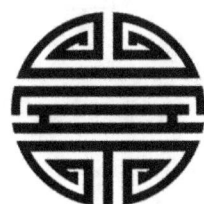

Think

Think
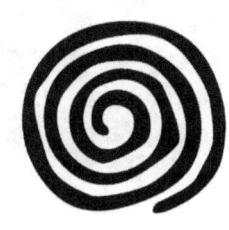

Think

Think
TERRIFIC

Think

Think
♂

Think
USA

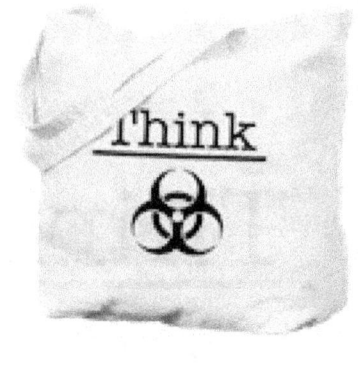
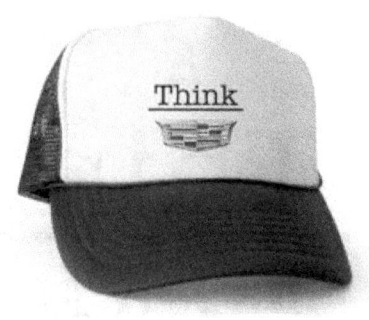
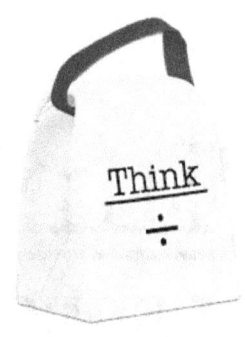
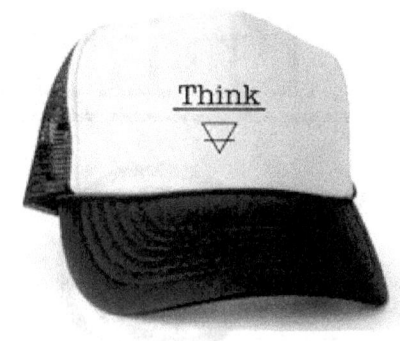
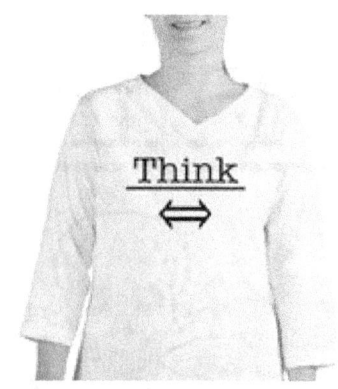
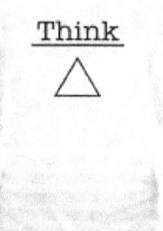
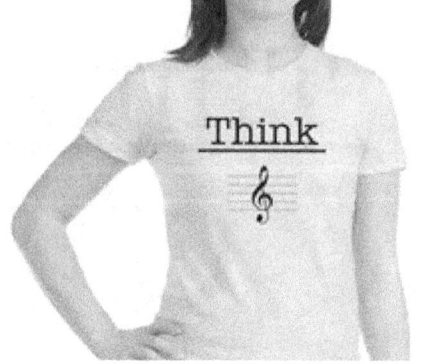
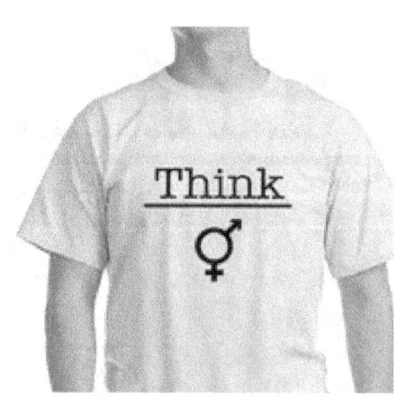
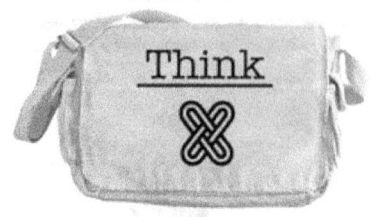
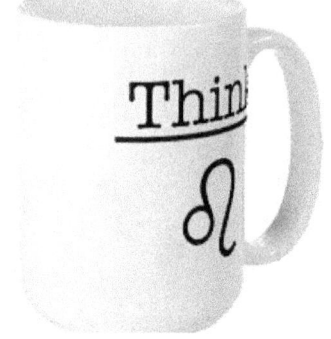
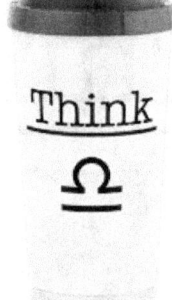
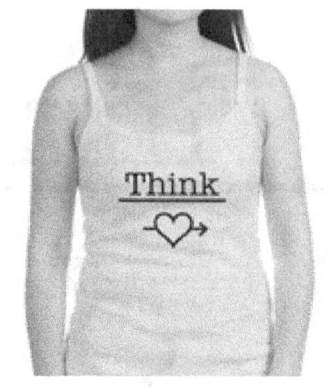

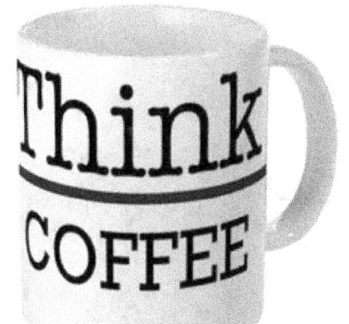

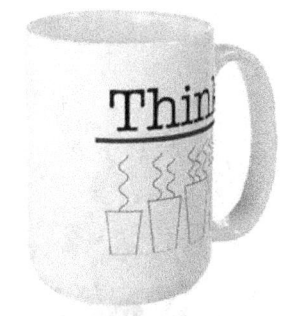

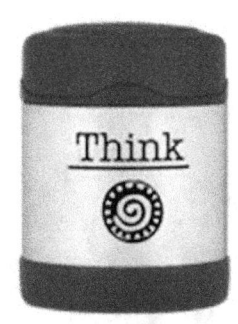

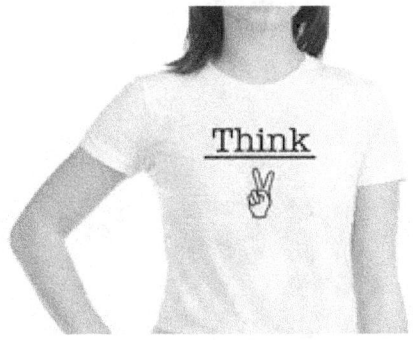

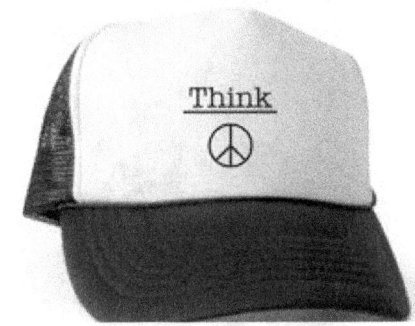

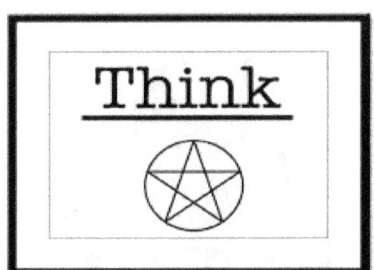

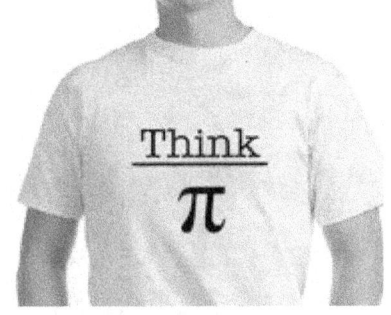

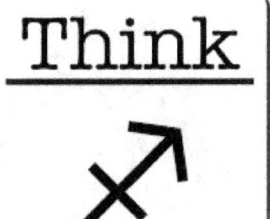

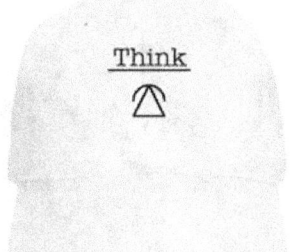

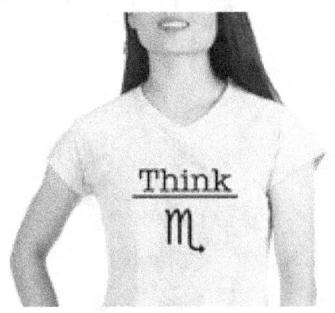

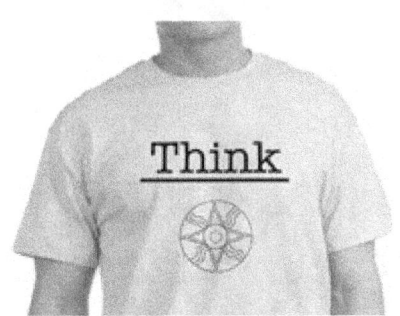

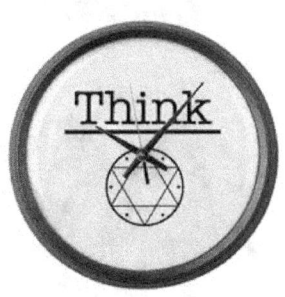

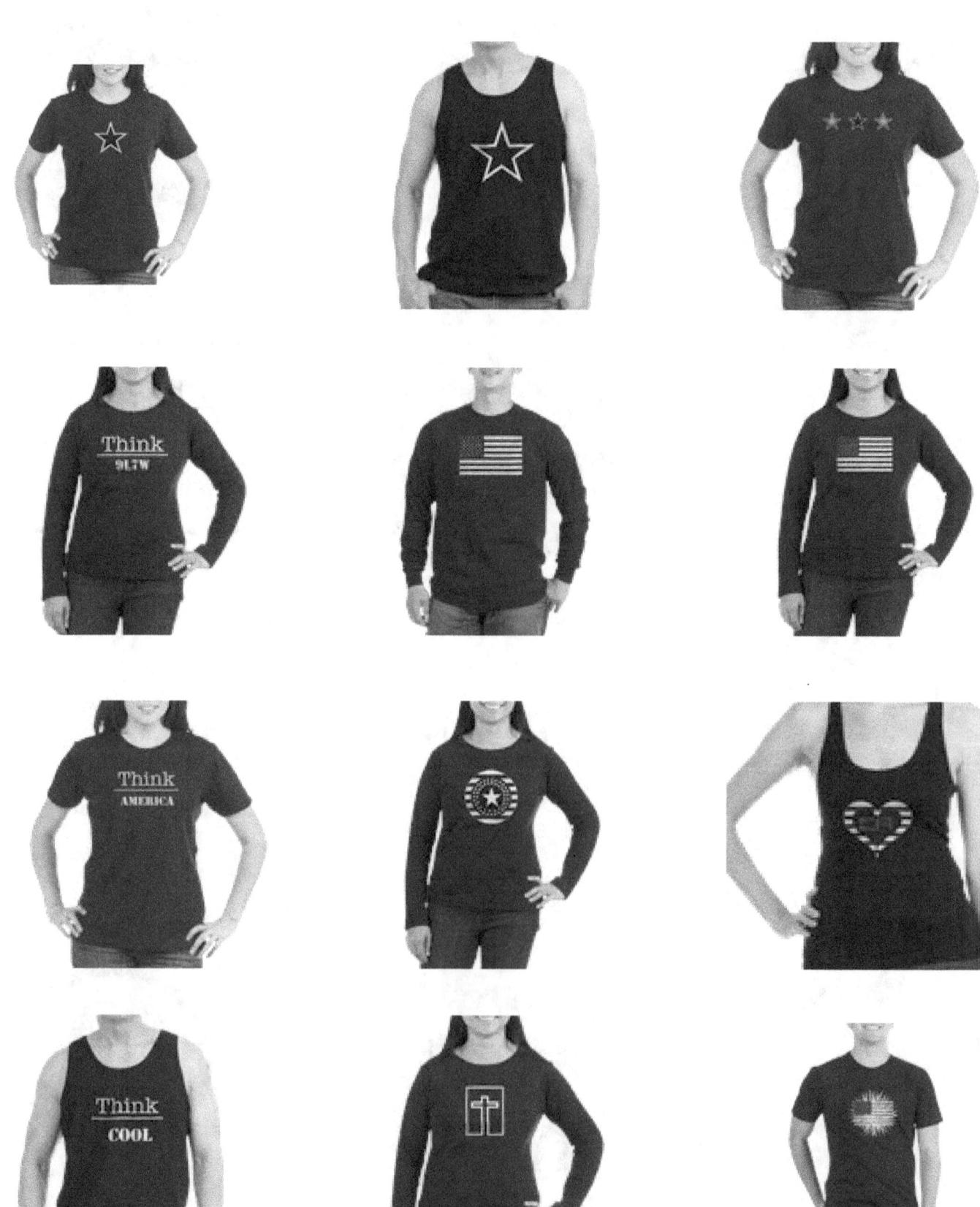

THE
END

www.ingramcontent.com/pod-product-compliance
Lightning Source LLC
Chambersburg PA
CBHW080959170526
45158CB00010B/2840